BASIC AND CLINICAL SCIENCE COURSE

Orbit, Eyelids, and Lacrimal System

Section 7

2010–2011

(Last major revision 2007–2008)

AMERICAN ACADEMY
OF OPHTHALMOLOGY
The Eye M.D. Association

LEO

LIFELONG
EDUCATION FOR THE
OPHTHALMOLOGIST®

The Basic and Clinical Science Course is one component of the Lifelong Education for the Ophthalmologist (LEO) framework, which assists members in planning their continuing medical education. LEO includes an array of clinical education products that members may select to form individualized, self-directed learning plans for updating their clinical knowledge. Active members or fellows who use LEO components may accumulate sufficient CME credits to earn the LEO Award. Contact the Academy's Clinical Education Division for further information on LEO.

The American Academy of Ophthalmology is accredited by the Accreditation Council for Continuing Medical Education to provide continuing medical education for physicians.

The American Academy of Ophthalmology designates this educational activity for a maximum of 10 *AMA PRA Category 1 Credits*™. Physicians should only claim credit commensurate with the extent of their participation in the activity.

The Academy provides this material for educational purposes only. It is not intended to represent the only or best method or procedure in every case, nor to replace a physician's own judgment or give specific advice for case management. Including all indications, contraindications, side effects, and alternative agents for each drug or treatment is beyond the scope of this material. All information and recommendations should be verified, prior to use, with current information included in the manufacturers' package inserts or other independent sources, and considered in light of the patient's condition and history. Reference to certain drugs, instruments, and other products in this course is made for illustrative purposes only and is not intended to constitute an endorsement of such. Some material may include information on applications that are not considered community standard, that reflect indications not included in approved FDA labeling, or that are approved for use only in restricted research settings. **The FDA has stated that it is the responsibility of the physician to determine the FDA status of each drug or device he or she wishes to use, and to use them with appropriate, informed patient consent in compliance with applicable law.** The Academy specifically disclaims any and all liability for injury or other damages of any kind, from negligence or otherwise, for any and all claims that may arise from the use of any recommendations or other information contained herein.

Cover image courtesy of Timothy J. McCulley, MD.

Basic and Clinical Science Course

Gregory L. Skuta, MD, Oklahoma City, Oklahoma, *Senior Secretary for Clinical Education*

Louis B. Cantor, MD, Indianapolis, Indiana, *Secretary for Ophthalmic Knowledge*

Jayne S. Weiss, MD, Detroit, Michigan, *BCSC Course Chair*

Section 7

Faculty Responsible for This Edition

John Bryan Holds, MD, *Chair,* St Louis, Missouri
Warren J. Chang, MD, Bloomington, Indiana
Roger A. Dailey, MD, Portland, Oregon
Jill Annette Foster, MD, Columbus, Ohio
Michael Kazim, MD, New York, New York
Timothy J. McCulley, MD, San Francisco, California
Ron W. Pelton, MD, PhD, Colorado Springs, Colorado
    Practicing Ophthalmologists Advisory Committee for Education
Martín H. Devoto, MD, *Consultant,* Buenos Aires, Argentina
Robert C. Kersten, MD, *Consultant,* Cincinnati, Ohio

Dr Dailey has received grant support from Allergan, Inc.
Dr Foster is a paid consultant for and has received speaking funds from Allergan, Inc.
Dr Holds is a paid consultant for Allergan, Inc.

The other authors state that they have no significant financial interest or other relationship with the manufacturer of any commercial product discussed in the chapters that they contributed to this course or with the manufacturer of any competing commercial product.

Recent Past Faculty

François Codère, MD
James A. Garrity, MD
Jeffrey A. Nerad, MD
Jerry K. Popham, MD

In addition, the Academy gratefully acknowledges the contributions of numerous past faculty and advisory committee members who have played an important role in the development of previous editions of the Basic and Clinical Science Course.

American Academy of Ophthalmology Staff

Richard A. Zorab, *Vice President, Ophthalmic Knowledge*

Hal Straus, *Director, Publications Department*

Carol L. Dondrea, *Publications Manager*

Christine Arturo, *Acquisitions Manager*

D. Jean Ray, *Production Manager*

Stephanie Tanaka, *Medical Editor*

Steven Huebner, *Administrative Coordinator*

**AMERICAN ACADEMY
OF OPHTHALMOLOGY**
The Eye M.D. Association

655 Beach Street
Box 7424
San Francisco, CA 94120-7424

Contents

General Introduction

The Basic and Clinical Science Course (BCSC) is designed to meet the needs of residents and practitioners for a comprehensive yet concise curriculum of the field of ophthalmology. The BCSC has developed from its original brief outline format, which relied heavily on outside readings, to a more convenient and educationally useful self-contained text. The Academy updates and revises the course annually, with the goals of integrating the basic science and clinical practice of ophthalmology and of keeping ophthalmologists current with new developments in the various subspecialties.

The BCSC incorporates the effort and expertise of more than 80 ophthalmologists, organized into 13 Section faculties, working with Academy editorial staff. In addition, the course continues to benefit from many lasting contributions made by the faculties of previous editions. Members of the Academy's Practicing Ophthalmologists Advisory Committee for Education serve on each faculty and, as a group, review every volume before and after major revisions.

Organization of the Course

The Basic and Clinical Science Course comprises 13 volumes, incorporating fundamental ophthalmic knowledge, subspecialty areas, and special topics:

1 Update on General Medicine
2 Fundamentals and Principles of Ophthalmology
3 Clinical Optics
4 Ophthalmic Pathology and Intraocular Tumors
5 Neuro-Ophthalmology
6 Pediatric Ophthalmology and Strabismus
7 Orbit, Eyelids, and Lacrimal System
8 External Disease and Cornea
9 Intraocular Inflammation and Uveitis
10 Glaucoma
11 Lens and Cataract
12 Retina and Vitreous
13 Refractive Surgery

In addition, a comprehensive Master Index allows the reader to easily locate subjects throughout the entire series.

References

Readers who wish to explore specific topics in greater detail may consult the references cited within each chapter and listed in the Basic Texts section at the back of the book.

These references are intended to be selective rather than exhaustive, chosen by the BCSC faculty as being important, current, and readily available to residents and practitioners.

Related Academy educational materials are also listed in the appropriate sections. They include books, online and audiovisual materials, self-assessment programs, clinical modules, and interactive programs.

Study Questions and CME Credit

Each volume of the BCSC is designed as an independent study activity for ophthalmology residents and practitioners. The learning objectives for this volume are given on page 1. The text, illustrations, and references provide the information necessary to achieve the objectives; the study questions allow readers to test their understanding of the material and their mastery of the objectives. Physicians who wish to claim CME credit for this educational activity may do so by mail, by fax, or online. The necessary forms and instructions are given at the end of the book.

Conclusion

The Basic and Clinical Science Course has expanded greatly over the years, with the addition of much new text and numerous illustrations. Recent editions have sought to place a greater emphasis on clinical applicability while maintaining a solid foundation in basic science. As with any educational program, it reflects the experience of its authors. As its faculties change and as medicine progresses, new viewpoints are always emerging on controversial subjects and techniques. Not all alternate approaches can be included in this series; as with any educational endeavor, the learner should seek additional sources, including such carefully balanced opinions as the Academy's Preferred Practice Patterns.

The BCSC faculty and staff are continuously striving to improve the educational usefulness of the course; you, the reader, can contribute to this ongoing process. If you have any suggestions or questions about the series, please do not hesitate to contact the faculty or the editors.

The authors, editors, and reviewers hope that your study of the BCSC will be of lasting value and that each Section will serve as a practical resource for quality patient care.

Objectives

Upon completion of BCSC Section 7, *Orbit, Eyelids, and Lacrimal System*, the reader should be able to

- describe the normal anatomy and function of orbital and periocular tissues

- identify general and specific pathophysiological processes (including congenital, infectious, inflammatory, traumatic, neoplastic, and involutional) that affect the structure and function of these tissues

- choose appropriate examination techniques and protocols for diagnosing disorders of the orbit, eyelids, and lacrimal system

- select from among the various imaging and ancillary studies available those that are most useful for the particular patient

- develop appropriate differential diagnoses for disorders of the orbital and periocular tissues

- compare the indications for enucleation, evisceration, and exenteration

- distinguish between functional and cosmetic indications in the surgical management of eyelids and periorbital conditions

- outline the principles of medical and surgical management of conditions affecting the orbit, eyelids, and lacrimal system

- recognize the major postoperative complications of orbital, eyelid, and lacrimal system surgery

PART I

Orbit

CHAPTER **1**

Orbital Anatomy

Dimensions

The orbits are the bony cavities that contain the globes, extraocular muscles, nerves, fat, and blood vessels. Each bony orbit is pear-shaped, tapering posteriorly to the apex and the optic canal. The medial orbital walls are approximately parallel and are separated by 25 mm in the average adult. The widest dimension of the orbit is approximately 1 cm behind the anterior orbital rim. Approximate measurements of the adult orbit are shown in Table 1-1. The orbital segment of the optic nerve is slightly curved and can move with the eye. This curve allows the eye to move forward with proptosis without damaging the nerve.

Topographic Relationships

The orbital septum arises from the orbital rims anteriorly. The paranasal sinuses are either rudimentary or very small at birth, and they increase in size through adolescence. They lie adjacent to the floor, medial wall, and anterior portion of the orbital roof. The orbital walls are composed of 7 bones: ethmoid, frontal, lacrimal, maxillary, palatine, sphenoid, and zygomatic. The composition of each of the 4 walls and the location in relation to adjacent extraorbital structures are shown in Figures 1-1, 1-2, and 1-3 and summarized in the following sections.

Roof of the Orbit
- composed of the frontal bone and the lesser wing of the sphenoid
- includes these important landmarks: the lacrimal gland fossa, which contains the orbital lobe of the lacrimal gland; fossa for the trochlea of the superior oblique tendon located 5 mm behind the superior nasal orbital rim; and supraorbital notch or foramen, which transmits the supraorbital vessels and branch of the frontal nerve
- located adjacent to anterior cranial fossa and frontal sinus

Lateral Wall of the Orbit
- composed of the zygomatic bone and the greater wing of the sphenoid; separated from the lesser wing portion of the orbital roof by the superior orbital fissure

Table 1-1 Adult Orbital Dimensions

Volume	30 cc
Entrance height	35 mm
Entrance width	40 mm
Medial wall length	45 mm
Distance from posterior globe to optic foramen	18 mm
Length of orbital segment of optic nerve	25–30 mm

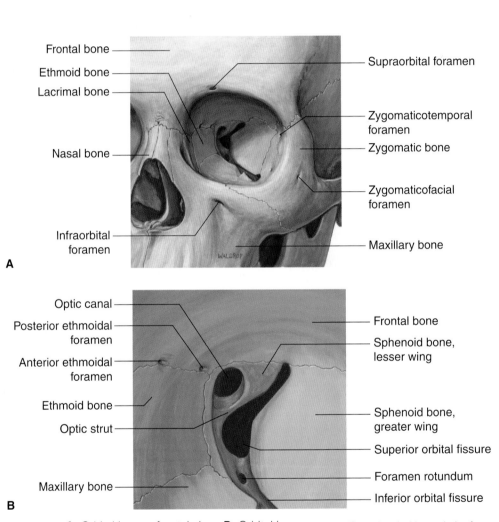

Figure 1-1 A, Orbital bones, frontal view. **B,** Orbital bones, apex. *(Reproduced with permission from Dutton JJ. Atlas of Clinical and Surgical Orbital Anatomy. Philadelphia: Saunders; 1994,1:8.)*

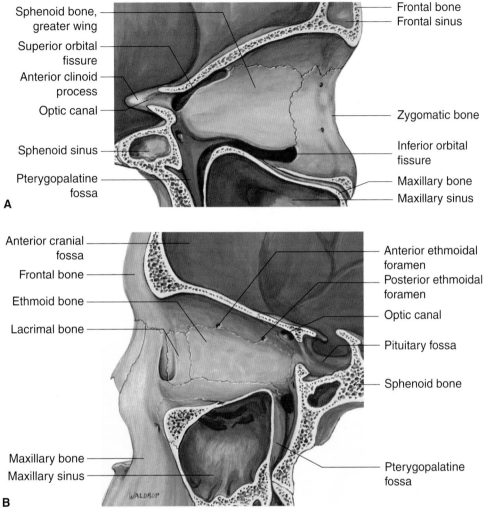

Sphenoid bone, greater wing
Superior orbital fissure
Anterior clinoid process
Optic canal
Sphenoid sinus
Pterygopalatine fossa
A

Frontal bone
Frontal sinus
Zygomatic bone
Inferior orbital fissure
Maxillary bone
Maxillary sinus

Anterior cranial fossa
Frontal bone
Ethmoid bone
Lacrimal bone
Maxillary bone
Maxillary sinus
B

Anterior ethmoidal foramen
Posterior ethmoidal foramen
Optic canal
Pituitary fossa
Sphenoid bone
Pterygopalatine fossa

WALDROP

Figure 1-2 **A,** Orbital bones, lateral wall, internal view. **B,** Orbital bones, medial wall, internal view. *(Reproduced with permission from Dutton JJ.* Atlas of Clinical and Surgical Orbital Anatomy. *Philadelphia: Saunders; 1994,1:9–10.)*

- includes these important landmarks: the *lateral orbital tubercle of Whitnall,* which has multiple attachments, such as the lateral canthal tendon, the lateral horn of the levator aponeurosis, the check ligament of the lateral rectus, Lockwood's ligament (the suspensory ligament of the globe), and Whitnall's ligament; and the *fronto-zygomatic suture,* located 1 cm above the tubercle
- located adjacent to the middle cranial fossa and the temporal fossa
- commonly extends anteriorly to the equator of the globe, helping protect the posterior half of the eye while still allowing wide peripheral vision
- is the thickest and strongest of the orbital walls

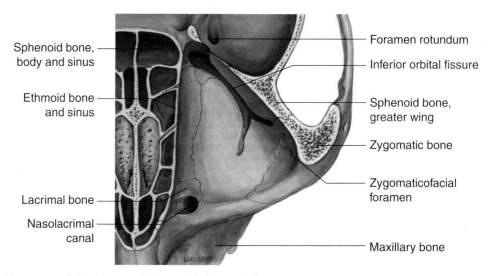

Figure 1-3 Orbital bones, inferior wall, internal view. *(Reproduced with permission from Dutton JJ.* Atlas of Clinical and Surgical Orbital Anatomy. *Philadelphia: Saunders; 1994,1:11.)*

Medial Wall of the Orbit

- composed of the ethmoid, lacrimal, maxillary, and sphenoid bones
- includes important landmarks such as the *frontoethmoidal suture,* which marks, approximately, the level of the cribriform plate, the roof of the ethmoids, and the floor of the anterior cranial fossa; the anterior and posterior ethmoidal arteries enter the orbit in the frontoethmoidal suture
- located adjacent to the ethmoid and sphenoid sinuses and nasal cavity
- (medial wall of the optic canal) forms the lateral wall of the sphenoid sinus

The thinnest walls of the orbit are the *lamina papyracea,* which covers the ethmoid sinuses along the medial wall, and the *maxillary bone,* particularly in its posteromedial portion. These are the bones most frequently fragmented as a result of indirect blowout fractures (see Chapter 6). Among children, infections of the ethmoid sinuses commonly extend through the lamina papyracea to cause orbital cellulitis and proptosis.

Floor of the Orbit

- composed of the maxillary, palatine, and zygomatic bones
- forms the roof of the maxillary sinus; does not extend to the orbital apex but instead ends at the pterygopalatine fossa; hence, it is the shortest of the orbital walls
- includes important landmarks such as the infraorbital groove and canal, which transmit the infraorbital artery and the maxillary division of the trigeminal nerve

Apertures

The orbital walls are perforated by several important apertures. (See Figs 1-1, 1-2, and 1-3.)

Ethmoidal Foramina

The anterior and posterior ethmoidal arteries pass through the corresponding ethmoidal foramina in the medial orbital wall along the frontoethmoidal suture. These foramina provide a potential route of entry into the orbit for infections and neoplasms from the sinuses.

Superior Orbital Fissure

The superior orbital fissure separates the greater and lesser wings of the sphenoid and transmits cranial nerves III, IV, and VI; the first (ophthalmic) division of cranial nerve (CN) V; and sympathetic nerve fibers. Most of the venous drainage from the orbit passes through this fissure by way of the superior ophthalmic vein to the cavernous sinus.

Inferior Orbital Fissure

The inferior orbital fissure is bounded by the sphenoid, maxillary, and palatine bones and lies between the lateral orbital wall and the orbital floor. It transmits the second (maxillary) division of CN V, including the zygomatic nerve, and branches of the inferior ophthalmic vein leading to the pterygoid plexus. The infraorbital nerve, which is a branch of the maxillary nerve, leaves the skull through the foramen rotundum and travels through the pterygopalatine fossa to enter the orbit at the infraorbital groove. The nerve travels anteriorly in the floor of the orbit through the infraorbital canal, emerging on the face of the maxilla 1 cm below the inferior orbital rim. The infraorbital nerve carries sensation from the lower eyelid, cheek, upper lip, upper teeth, and gingiva. Numbness in this distribution often accompanies blowout fractures of the orbital floor. The hypoesthesia typically improves with time.

Zygomaticofacial and Zygomaticotemporal Canals

The zygomaticofacial canal and zygomaticotemporal canal transmit vessels and branches of the zygomatic nerve through the lateral orbital wall to the cheek and the temporal fossa, respectively.

Nasolacrimal Canal

The nasolacrimal canal extends from the lacrimal sac fossa to the inferior meatus beneath the inferior turbinate in the nose. Through this canal passes the nasolacrimal duct, which is continuous from the lacrimal sac to the mucosa of the nose. (See Part III, Lacrimal System.)

Optic Canal

The optic canal is 8–10 mm long and is located within the lesser wing of the sphenoid. This canal is separated from the superior orbital fissure by the bony optic strut. The optic nerve, ophthalmic artery, and sympathetic nerves pass through this canal. The orbital end of the canal is the optic foramen, which normally measures less than 6.5 mm in diameter (adult). Optic canal enlargement accompanies the expansion of the nerve, as seen with optic nerve gliomas. Blunt trauma may cause an optic canal fracture, hematoma at the orbital apex, or shearing of the nerve at the foramen, resulting in optic nerve damage.

Soft Tissues

Periorbita

The periorbita is the periosteal covering of the orbital bones. At the orbital apex, it fuses with the dura mater covering the optic nerve. Anteriorly, the periorbita is continuous with the orbital septum and the periosteum of the facial bones. The line of fusion of these layers at the orbital rim is called the *arcus marginalis*. The periorbita is loosely adherent to the bone except at the orbital margin, sutures, fissures, foramina, and canals. In an exenteration, the periorbita can be easily separated except where these firm attachments are present. Subperiosteal fluid, such as pus or blood, is usually loculated within these boundaries. The periorbita is innervated by the sensory nerves of the orbit and is quite sensitive.

Intraorbital Optic Nerve

The intraorbital portion of the optic nerve is approximately 30 mm long. The nerve is somewhat longer than the orbit, making an S-shaped curve to allow for movement with the eye. The optic nerve is 4 mm in diameter and surrounded by pia mater, arachnoid, and dura mater, which are continuous with the same layers covering the brain. The dura mater covering the posterior portion of the intraorbital optic nerve fuses with the annulus of Zinn at the orbital apex and is continuous with the periosteum of the optic canal.

Extraocular Muscles and Orbital Fat

The extraocular muscles are responsible for the movement of the eye and for synchronous movements of the eyelids. All of the extraocular muscles, except the inferior oblique muscle, originate in the orbital apex and travel anteriorly to insert onto the eye or eyelid. The 4 rectus muscles (superior, medial, lateral, and inferior recti) originate in the annulus of Zinn. The levator muscle arises above the annulus on the lesser wing of the sphenoid. The superior oblique muscle originates slightly medial to the levator muscle and travels anteriorly through the trochlea on the superomedial orbital rim, where it turns posterolateral toward the eye. The inferior oblique muscle originates in the anterior orbital floor lateral to the lacrimal sac and travels posteriorly and laterally, within the lower eyelid retractors, to insert inferolateral to the macula.

In the anterior portion of the orbit, the rectus muscles are connected by a membrane known as the *intermuscular septum*. When viewed in the coronal plane, this membrane forms a ring that divides the orbital fat into the *intraconal fat (central surgical space)* and the *extraconal fat (peripheral surgical space)*. These anatomical designations on a magnetic resonance imaging scan or a computed tomographic scan are helpful for describing the location of a mass. Surgeons operating in the orbit find that a knowledge of these spaces helps direct the orbital dissection to the mass.

The orbit is further divided by many fine fibrous septa that unite and support the globe, optic nerve, and extraocular muscles (Fig 1-4). Accidental or surgical orbital trauma can

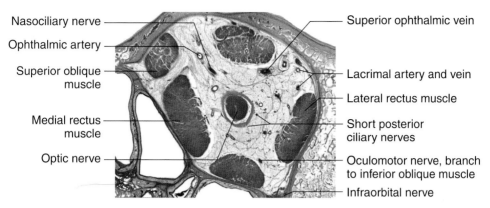

Nasociliary nerve

Ophthalmic artery

Superior oblique muscle

Medial rectus muscle

Optic nerve

Superior ophthalmic vein

Lacrimal artery and vein

Lateral rectus muscle

Short posterior ciliary nerves

Oculomotor nerve, branch to inferior oblique muscle

Infraorbital nerve

Figure 1-4 Mid-orbit at the widest extent of the extraocular muscles. *(Modified with permission from Dutton JJ. Atlas of Clinical and Surgical Orbital Anatomy. Philadelphia: Saunders; 1994,9:151.)*

disrupt this supporting system and contribute to globe displacement and restriction. In many cases of diplopia after fracture, restriction of eye movement is caused by the entrapment of the orbital connective tissue rather than by the muscles themselves.

The motor innervation of the extraocular muscles arises from cranial nerves III, IV, and VI. The superior rectus and levator muscles are supplied by the superior division of CN III (oculomotor). The inferior rectus, medial rectus, and inferior oblique muscles are supplied by the inferior division of CN III. The lateral rectus is supplied by CN VI (abducens). The cranial nerves to the rectus muscles enter the orbit posteriorly through the superior orbital fissure and travel through the intraconal fat to enter the muscles from the undersurface at the junction of the posterior third and anterior two thirds. Cranial nerve IV (trochlear) crosses over the levator muscle and innervates the superior oblique on the superior surface at its posterior third. The nerve to the inferior rectus travels anteriorly on the lateral aspect of the inferior rectus to enter the muscle on its posterior surface.

Annulus of Zinn

The annulus of Zinn is the fibrous ring formed by the common origin of the 4 rectus muscles (Fig 1-5). The ring encircles the optic foramen and the central portion of the superior orbital fissure. The superior origin of the lateral rectus muscle separates the superior orbital fissure into 2 compartments. The portion of the orbital apex enclosed by the annulus is called the *oculomotor foramen.* This opening transmits CN III (upper and lower divisions), CN VI, and the nasociliary branch of the ophthalmic division of CN V (trigeminal). The superior and lateral aspect of the superior orbital fissure external to the muscle cone transmits CN IV as well as 2 other branches of the ophthalmic division of CN V: the frontal and lacrimal nerves. Cranial nerve IV is the only nerve that innervates an extraocular muscle and does not pass directly into the muscle cone when entering the orbit. Cranial nerves III and VI pass directly into the muscle cone through the oculomotor foramen. The superior ophthalmic vein passes through the superior and lateral portion of the superior orbital fissure outside the oculomotor foramen.

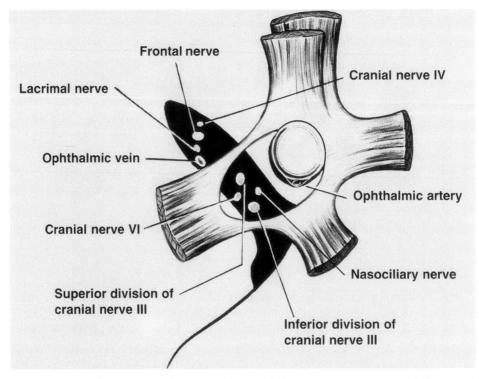

Figure 1-5 View of orbital apex, right orbit. The ophthalmic artery enters the orbit through the optic canal, whereas the superior and inferior divisions of cranial nerve III, cranial nerve VI, and the nasociliary nerve enter the muscle cone through the oculomotor foramen. Cranial nerve IV, the frontal and lacrimal nerves, and the ophthalmic vein enter through the superior orbital fissure and thus lie within the periorbita but outside of the muscle cone. Note that the presence of many nerves and arteries along the lateral side of the optic nerve mandates a superonasal surgical approach to the optic nerve in the orbital apex. *(Modified from Housepian EM. Intraorbital tumors. In: Schmidek HH, Sweet WH, eds.* Current Techniques in Operative Neurosurgery. *Orlando, FL: Grune & Stratton; 1976:148.)*

Vasculature of the Orbit

The blood supply to the orbit arises primarily from the ophthalmic artery, which is a branch of the internal carotid artery. Smaller contributions come from the external carotid artery via the internal maxillary artery and the facial artery. The ophthalmic artery travels underneath the intracranial optic nerve through the dura mater along the optic canal to enter the orbit. The major branches of the ophthalmic artery are the

- branches to the extraocular muscles
- central retinal artery (to the optic nerve and retina)
- posterior ciliary arteries (long to the anterior segment and short to the choroid)

Terminal branches of the ophthalmic artery travel anteriorly and form rich anastomoses with branches of the external carotid in the face and periorbital region.

The superior ophthalmic vein provides the main venous drainage of the orbit. This vein starts in the superonasal quadrant of the orbit and extends posteriorly through the

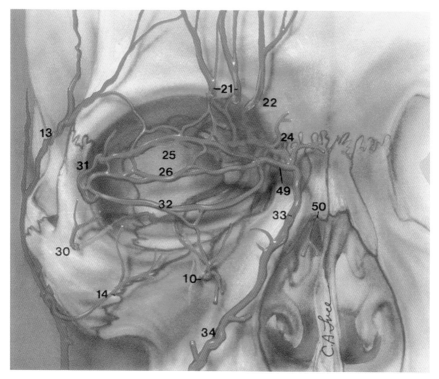

Figure 1-6 Anterior view of the arterial supply to the eyelids and orbit. The arteries shown are *10*, infraorbital; *13*, superficial temporal; *14*, transverse facial; *21*, supraorbital; *22*, supratrochlear; *24*, infratrochlear; *25*, superior peripheral arcade; *26*, superior marginal arcade; *30*, zygomaticofacial; *31*, lateral palpebral; *32*, inferior marginal arcade; *33*, angular; *34*, facial; *49*, medial palpebral; *50*, dorsal nasal. *(From Zide BM, Jelks GW, eds.* Surgical Anatomy of the Orbit. *New York: Raven; 1985:11.)*

superior orbital fissure into the cavernous sinus. Frequently, the superior ophthalmic vein appears on axial orbital computed tomographic scans as the only structure coursing diagonally through the superior orbit. Many anastomoses occur anteriorly with the veins of the face as well as posteriorly with the pterygoid plexus. See Figures 1-6 through 1-8.

Nerves

Sensory innervation to the periorbital area is provided by the ophthalmic and maxillary divisions of CN V (Fig 1-9). The ophthalmic division of CN V travels anteriorly from the ganglion in the lateral wall of the cavernous sinus, where it divides into 3 main branches: frontal, lacrimal, and nasociliary. The frontal and lacrimal nerves enter the orbit through the superior orbital fissure above the annulus of Zinn (see Fig 1-5) and travel anteriorly in the extraconal fat to innervate the medial canthus (supratrochlear branch), upper eyelid (lacrimal and supratrochlear branches), and forehead (supraorbital branch). The nasociliary branch enters the orbit through the superior orbital fissure within the annulus of Zinn, thus entering the intraconal space, where the nasociliary branch travels anteriorly to innervate the eye via the ciliary branches. The short ciliary nerves penetrate the sclera

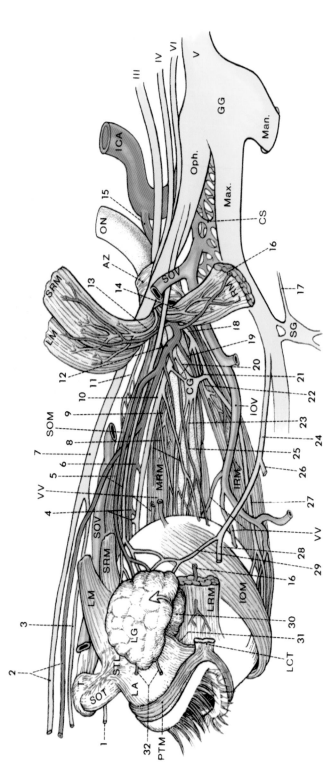

Figure 1-7 Side view of left orbit. *AZ*, annulus of Zinn; *CG*, ciliary ganglion; *CS*, cavernous sinus; *GG*, Gasserian ganglion; *ICA*, internal carotid artery; *IOM*, inferior oblique muscle; *IOV*, inferior ophthalmic vein; *IRM*, inferior rectus muscle; *LA*, levator aponeurosis; *LCT*, lateral canthal tendon; *LG*, lacrimal gland; *LM*, levator muscle; *LRM*, lateral rectus muscle; *Man.*, mandibular nerve; *Max.*, maxillary nerve; *MRM*, medial rectus muscle; *ON*, optic nerve; *Oph.,* ophthalmic nerve; *PTM*, pretarsal muscle; *SG*, sphenopalatine ganglion; *SOM*, superior oblique muscle; *SOT*, superior oblique tendon; *SOV*, superior ophthalmic vein; *SRM*, superior rectus muscle; *STL*, superior transverse ligament; *T*, trochlea; *VV*, vortex veins; *1*, infratrochlear nerve; *2*, supraorbital nerve and artery; *3*, supratrochlear nerve; *4*, anterior ethmoid nerve and artery; *5*, lacrimal nerve and artery; *6*, posterior ethmoid artery; *7*, frontal nerve; *8*, long ciliary nerves; *9*, branch of cranial nerve III to medial rectus muscle; *10*, nasociliary nerve; *11*, cranial nerve IV; *12*, ophthalmic (orbital) artery; *13*, superior ramus of cranial nerve III; *14*, cranial nerve VI; *15*, ophthalmic artery, origin; *16*, anterior ciliary artery; *17*, vidian nerve; *18*, inferior ramus of cranial nerve III; *19*, central retinal artery; *20*, sensory branches from ciliary ganglion to nasociliary nerve; *21*, motor (parasympathetic) nerve to ciliary ganglion from nerve to inferior oblique muscle; *22*, branch of cranial nerve III to inferior rectus muscle; *23*, short ciliary nerves; *24*, zygomatic nerve; *25*, posterior ciliary arteries; *26*, zygomaticofacial nerve; *27*, nerve to inferior oblique muscle; *28*, zygomaticotemporal nerve; *29*, lacrimal secretory nerve; *30*, lacrimal gland–palpebral lobe; *31*, lateral horn of levator aponeurosis; *32*, lacrimal artery and nerve terminal branches. *(From Stewart WB, ed. Ophthalmic Plastic and Reconstructive Surgery. 4th ed. San Francisco: American Academy of Ophthalmology Manuals Program; 1984.)*

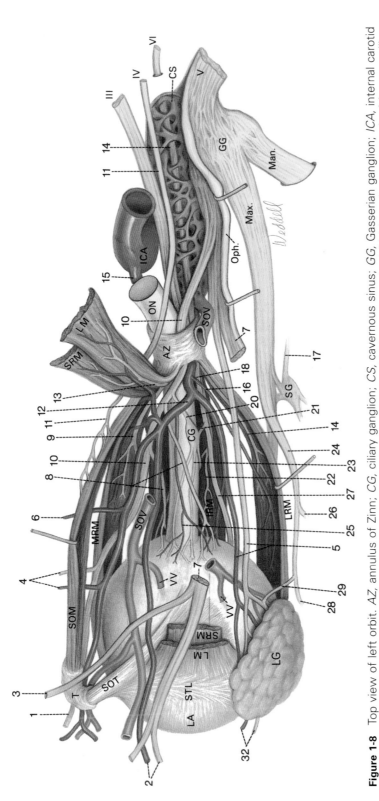

Figure 1-8 Top view of left orbit. *AZ,* annulus of Zinn; *CG,* ciliary ganglion; *CS,* cavernous sinus; *GG,* Gasserian ganglion; *ICA,* internal carotid artery; *IRM,* inferior rectus muscle; *LA,* levator aponeurosis; *LG,* lacrimal gland; *LM,* levator muscle; *LRM,* lateral rectus muscle; *Man.,* mandibular nerve; *Max.,* maxillary nerve; *MRM,* medial rectus muscle; *ON,* optic nerve; *Oph.,* ophthalmic nerve; *SG,* sphenopalatine ganglion; *SOM,* superior oblique muscle; *SOT,* superior oblique tendon; *SOV,* superior ophthalmic vein; *SRM,* superior rectus muscle; *STL,* superior transverse ligament; *T,* trochlea; *VV,* vortex veins; *1,* infratrochlear nerve; *2,* supraorbital nerve and artery; *3,* supratrochlear nerve; *4,* anterior ethmoid nerve and artery; *5,* lacrimal nerve and artery; *6,* posterior ethmoid artery; *7,* frontal nerve; *8,* long ciliary nerves; *9,* branch of cranial nerve III to medial rectus muscle; *10,* nasociliary nerve; *11,* cranial nerve IV; *12,* ophthalmic (orbital) artery; *13,* superior ramus of cranial nerve III; *14,* cranial nerve VI; *15,* ophthalmic artery, origin; *16,* anterior ciliary artery; *17,* vidian nerve; *18,* inferior ramus of cranial nerve III; *20,* sensory branches from ciliary ganglion to nasociliary nerve; *21,* motor (parasympathetic) nerve to ciliary ganglion from nerve to inferior oblique muscle; *22,* branch of cranial nerve III to inferior rectus muscle; *23,* short ciliary nerves; *24,* zygomatic nerve; *25,* posterior ciliary arteries; *26,* zygomaticofacial nerve; *27,* nerve to inferior oblique muscle; *28,* zygomaticotemporal nerve; *29,* lacrimal secretory nerve; *32,* lacrimal artery and nerve terminal branches. *(From Stewart WB, ed. Ophthalmic Plastic and Reconstructive Surgery. 4th ed. San Francisco: American Academy of Ophthalmology Manuals Program; 1984.)*

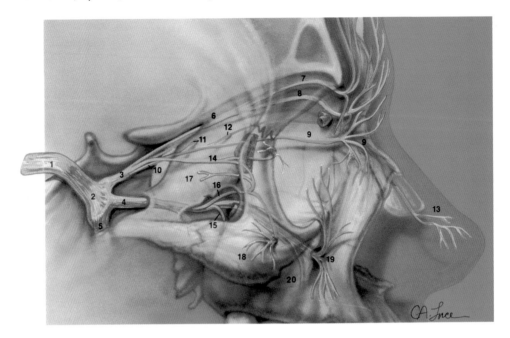

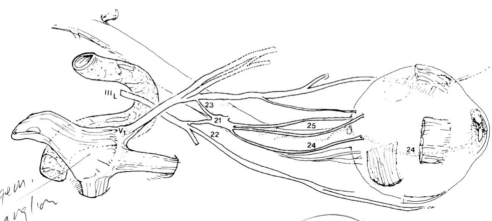

Figure 1-9 Sensory nerves. *1*, cranial nerve V; *2*, trigeminal ganglion; *3*, ophthalmic division of trigeminal nerve V₁; *4*, maxillary division of trigeminal nerve V₂; *5*, mandibular division of trigeminal nerve V₃; *6*, frontal nerve; *7*, supraorbital nerve; *8*, supratrochlear nerve (trochlea noted by *purple*); *9*, infratrochlear nerve; *10*, nasociliary nerve; *11*, posterior ethmoidal nerve; *12*, anterior ethmoidal nerve; *13*, external or dorsal nasal nerve; *14*, lacrimal nerve; *15*, posterior superior alveolar nerve; *16*, zygomatic nerve; *17*, zygomaticotemporal nerve; *18*, zygomaticofacial nerve; *19*, infraorbital nerve; *20*, anterior superior alveolar nerve; *21*, ciliary ganglion; *22*, nerve to inferior oblique; *23*, sensory root of ciliary ganglion; *24*, long ciliary nerves; *25*, short ciliary nerves. *(From Zide BM, Jelks GW, eds. Surgical Anatomy of the Orbit. New York: Raven; 1985:12.)*

after passing through the ciliary ganglion without synapse. The long ciliary nerves pass by the ciliary ganglion and enter the sclera, where they extend anteriorly to supply the iris, cornea, and ciliary muscle.

Motor innervation to the extraocular muscles has already been outlined. The muscles of facial expression, including the orbicularis oculi, procerus, corrugator superciliaris, and frontalis muscles, receive their motor supply via branches of CN VII (the facial nerve) that penetrate the undersurface of each muscle.

The parasympathetic innervation, which allows accommodation, pupillary constriction, and lacrimal gland stimulation, follows a complicated course. Parasympathetic innervation enters the eye as the short posterior ciliary nerves after synapsing with the ciliary ganglion. Parasympathetic innervation to the lacrimal gland originates in the lacrimal nucleus of the pons and eventually joins the lacrimal nerve to enter the lacrimal gland.

The sympathetic innervation to the orbit provides for pupillary dilation, vasoconstriction, smooth muscle function of the eyelids and orbit, and hidrosis. The nerve fibers follow the arterial supply to the pupil, eyelids, and orbit and travel anteriorly in association with the long ciliary nerves. Interruption of this innervation results in the familiar signs of Horner syndrome: ptosis of the upper eyelid, elevation of the lower lid, miosis, anhidrosis, and vasodilation.

Lacrimal Gland

The lacrimal gland is composed of a larger orbital lobe and a smaller palpebral lobe. The gland is located within a fossa of the frontal bone in the superior temporal orbit. Ducts from both lobes pass through the palpebral lobe and empty into the upper conjunctival fornix temporally. Frequently, a portion of the palpebral lobe is visible on slit-lamp examination with the upper eyelid everted. Biopsy is generally not performed on the palpebral lobe because it can interfere with drainage of the orbital lobe. Similarly, biopsy of the temporal fornix is avoided when possible. With age, the orbital lobe of the lacrimal gland may prolapse inferiorly out of the fossa and present as fullness or a mass in the lateral portion of the upper eyelid.

Periorbital Structures

Nose and Paranasal Sinuses

The bones forming the medial, inferior, and superior orbital walls are close to the nasal cavity and are pneumatized by the paranasal sinuses, which arise from and drain into the nasal cavity. The exact function of the sinuses is uncertain. They may serve to decrease the weight of the skull, or they may function as resonators of the voice. The sinuses may also support the nasal passages in trapping irritants and in warming and humidifying the air. Pathophysiologic processes in these spaces that secondarily affect the orbit include mucoceles, sinonasal carcinomas, phycomycoses, Wegener granulomatosis, and inverted papillomas, as well as sinusitis, which may cause orbital cellulitis or abscess.

The nasal cavity is divided into 2 nasal fossae by the nasal septum. The lateral wall of the nose has 3 bony projections: the superior, middle, and inferior conchae (turbinates). The conchae are covered by nasal mucosa, and they overhang the corresponding meatuses. Just cephalad to the superior concha is the sphenoethmoidal recess, into which the sphenoid sinus drains. The frontal sinus and the anterior and middle ethmoid air cells drain into the middle meatus. The nasolacrimal duct opens into the inferior meatus. The nasal cavity is lined by a pseudostratified, ciliated columnar epithelium with copious goblet cells. The mucous membrane overlying the lateral alar cartilage is hair-bearing and therefore less suitable for use as a composite graft in eyelid reconstruction than the mucoperichondrium over the nasal septum, which is devoid of hair.

The frontal sinuses develop from evaginations of the frontal recess and cannot be seen radiographically until the sixth year of life. Pneumatization of the frontal bone continues through childhood and is complete by early adulthood (Fig 1-10). The sinuses can develop asymmetrically and vary greatly in size and shape. The frontal sinuses are almost always separated by the midline intersinus septum. Each sinus drains through separate fronto-nasal ducts and empties into the anterior portion of the middle meatus.

The ethmoid air cells are thin-walled cavities that lie between the medial orbital wall and the lateral wall of the nose. They can extend into the frontal, lacrimal, and maxillary bones and may extend into the orbital roof. Ethmoid air cells in this area are called *supraorbital ethmoids*. The numerous small, thin-walled air cells of the ethmoid sinus are divided into 3 groups: anterior, middle, and posterior. The anterior and middle air cells drain into the middle meatus; the posterior air cells, into the superior meatus. The ethmoid air cells are present at birth and expand as the child grows. Orbital cellulitis is most

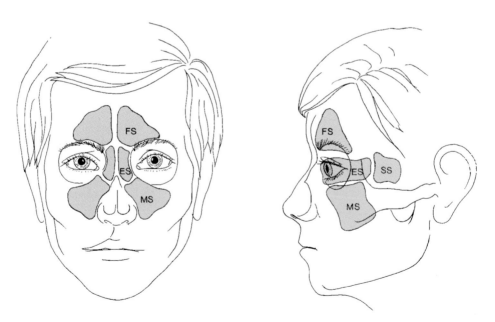

Figure 1-10 Relationship of the orbits to the paranasal sinuses: *FS,* frontal sinus; *ES,* ethmoid sinus; *MS,* maxillary sinus; *SS,* sphenoid sinus.

frequently secondary to ethmoid sinusitis spreading through the lamina papyracea into the orbit.

The sphenoid sinus evaginates from the posterior nasal roof to pneumatize the sphenoid bone. This sinus is divided into 2 cavities by a bony septum. Occasionally, pneumatization extends into the sphenoid, the pterygoid, and the occipital bone. The sphenoid sinus is rudimentary at birth and reaches full size after puberty. The sinus drains into the sphenoethmoid recess of each nasal fossa. The optic canal is located immediately superior and lateral to the sinus wall. Visual loss and visual field abnormalities can be direct sequelae of pathologic processes involving the sphenoid sinus.

The maxillary sinuses are the largest of the paranasal sinuses. Together, the roofs of each maxillary sinus form the floor of the orbit. The maxillary sinuses extend posteriorly in the maxillary bone to the inferior orbital fissure. The infraorbital nerve and artery travel along the roof of the sinus from posterior to anterior. The bony nasolacrimal canal lies within the medial wall. The sinus drains into the middle meatus of the nose by way of the maxillary ostium. Orbital blowout fractures commonly break the floor of the orbit, especially medial to the infraorbital canal. These fractures frequently damage the infraorbital nerve, causing hypoesthesia of the cheek.

Fossae and Fissures

The orbit communicates with several fossae surrounding it. These spaces include the middle cranial fossa, the pterygopalatine fossa, and the infratemporal fossa. The middle cranial fossa lies posterior to the orbit. With the exception of the optic nerve, most nerves and vessels passing between the orbit and brain travel through the superior orbital fissure. The optic nerve passes through the optic canal. Inferior and posterior to the orbit, and posterior to the maxillary sinus, lies the pterygopalatine fossa. This fossa extends laterally to become the infratemporal fossa. These 2 fossae communicate with the orbit via the inferior orbital fissure.

The superior orbital fissure extends upward and outward from the orbital apex between the orbital roof and the lateral wall of the orbit. The superior orbital fissure is formed by the lesser wing of the sphenoid bone medially and the greater wing of the sphenoid laterally. The superior orbital fissure transmits cranial nerves III, IV, and VI; the ophthalmic division of CN V; and the superior ophthalmic vein. The optic canal is medial to the superior orbital fissure within the lesser wing of the sphenoid bone. A narrow segment of bone, the optic strut, separates the optic canal from the superior orbital fissure.

The inferior orbital fissure extends anteriorly and laterally between the lateral and inferior orbital walls. The inferior orbital fissure connects the orbit to the pterygopalatine fossa posteriorly and the infratemporal fossa anteriorly. The maxillary division of CN V leaves the cranium through the foramen rotundum into the pterygopalatine fossa and then travels into the orbit through the inferior orbital fissure. The infraorbital vessels, the venous communications between the orbital veins and the pterygoid plexus, and the zygomatic branch of the maxillary nerve travel in through the inferior orbital fissure. The superior and inferior orbital fissures meet in the orbital apex.

For further discussion and illustrations of ocular anatomy, see BCSC Section 2, *Fundamentals and Principles of Ophthalmology.*

Dutton JJ. *Atlas of Clinical and Surgical Orbital Anatomy.* Philadelphia: Saunders; 1994.

Jordan DR, Anderson RA. *Surgical Anatomy of the Ocular Adnexa: A Clinical Approach.* Ophthalmology Monograph 9. San Francisco: American Academy of Ophthalmology; 1996.

Zide BM, Jelks GW, eds. *Surgical Anatomy of the Orbit.* New York: Raven; 1985.

CHAPTER 2

Evaluation of Orbital Disorders

The evaluation of an orbital disorder should distinguish orbital from periorbital and intraocular lesions. A detailed history is essential in establishing a probable diagnosis and in guiding the initial workup and therapy; such a history should include

- onset, course, and duration of symptoms (pain, diplopia, changes in vision) and signs (erythema, palpable mass, globe displacement)
- prior disease (such as thyroid-associated orbitopathy [TAO] or sinus disease) and therapy
- injury (especially head or facial trauma)
- systemic disease (especially cancer)
- family history

Old photographs are frequently helpful.

The 6 P's

In evaluating a patient, the clinician will find it helpful to remember the 6 P's: pain, proptosis, progression, palpation, pulsation, and periorbital changes.

Pain

Pain may be a symptom of inflammatory and infectious lesions, orbital hemorrhage, malignant lacrimal gland tumors, invasion from adjacent nasopharyngeal carcinoma, or metastatic lesions.

Proptosis

Proptosis often indicates the location of a mass because the globe is usually displaced away from the site of the mass. *Axial displacement* is caused by retrobulbar lesions such as cavernous hemangioma, glioma, meningioma, metastases, arteriovenous malformations, and any other mass lesion within the muscle cone. *Nonaxial displacement* is caused by lesions with a prominent component outside the muscle cone. *Superior displacement* is produced by maxillary sinus tumors invading the orbital floor and displacing the globe upward. *Inferomedial displacement* can result from dermoid cysts and lacrimal gland tumors. *Inferolateral displacement* can result from frontoethmoidal mucoceles, abscesses, osteomas, and sinus carcinomas. *Bilateral proptosis* in adults is caused most often by TAO; however, bilateral orbital involvement from lymphoma, vasculitis, idiopathic orbital inflammatory disease (pseudotumor), metastatic tumors, carotid cavernous fistulas, cavernous sinus thrombosis, or leukemia can also produce bilateral proptosis. *Unilateral proptosis* in adults is also most frequently caused by TAO. In children, bilateral proptosis may be caused by metastatic neuroblastoma, leukemia, or idiopathic orbital inflammatory disease.

Enophthalmos can occur secondary to sclerosing tumors such as metastatic breast carcinoma, in association with orbital varix, or from expansion of the bony orbit as a result of fracture and displacement of the orbital walls.

Progression

The rate of progression can be a helpful diagnostic indicator. Disorders with onset occurring over days to weeks are usually caused by idiopathic orbital inflammatory disease, cellulitis, hemorrhage, thrombophlebitis, rhabdomyosarcoma, TAO, neuroblastoma, metastatic tumors, or granulocytic sarcoma. Conditions with onset occurring over months to years are usually caused by dermoid cyst, benign mixed tumor, neurogenic tumor, cavernous hemangioma, lymphoma, fibrous histiocytoma, or osteoma.

Palpation

A mass that is palpable in the superonasal quadrant may be a mucocele, mucopyocele, encephalocele, neurofibroma, dermoid cyst, or lymphoma. A mass palpable in the superotemporal quadrant may be a prolapsed lacrimal gland, dermoid cyst, lacrimal gland tumor, lymphoma, or idiopathic orbital inflammatory disease. A lesion behind the equator of the globe is usually not palpable.

Pulsation

Pulsation without bruits may be produced by sphenoid wing defects that are associated with neurofibromatosis or meningoencephaloceles, or it may result from surgical removal of the orbital roof. Pulsation with or without bruits may result from high-flow carotid cavernous or dural cavernous fistulas or from orbital arteriovenous malformations.

Periorbital Changes

Periorbital changes may indicate underlying disorders. Table 2-1 lists various signs and their common causes.

Physical Examination and Laboratory Tests

Special attention to ocular motility, pupillary function, and ophthalmoscopy is necessary. Following the basic workup, radiologic studies are often required.

Table 2-1 **Periorbital Changes Associated With Orbital Disease**

Sign	Etiology
A salmon-colored mass in the cul-de-sac	Lymphoma (see Fig 5-16)
Eyelid retraction and eyelid lag	Thyroid-associated orbitopathy
Vascular congestion over the insertions of the rectus muscles (particularly the lateral rectus)	Thyroid-associated orbitopathy
Corkscrew conjunctival vessels	Arteriovenous fistula
Vascular anomaly of eyelid skin	Lymphangioma, varix, or capillary hemangioma
S-shaped eyelid	Plexiform neurofibroma or lacrimal gland mass
Anterior uveitis	Idiopathic orbital inflammatory syndrome or sarcoidosis
Eczematous lesions of the eyelids	Mycosis fungoides (T-cell lymphoma)
Ecchymoses of eyelid skin	Metastatic neuroblastoma, leukemia, or amyloidosis
Prominent temple	Sphenoid wing meningioma, metastatic neuroblastoma
Edematous swelling of lower eyelid	Meningioma, inflammatory tumor, metastases
Optociliary shunt vessels on disc	Meningioma
Frozen globe	Metastases or phycomycoses
Black-crusted lesions in nasopharynx	Phycomycoses
Facial asymmetry	Fibrous dysplasia or neurofibromatosis
Gaze-evoked amaurosis	Optic nerve sheath meningioma or other orbital apex tumors

Inspection

Globe displacement is the most common clinical manifestation of an orbital abnormality. It usually results from a tumor, a vascular abnormality, an inflammatory process, or a traumatic event.

Several terms are used to describe the position of the eye and orbit. *Proptosis* describes a forward displacement or bulging of a body part and is commonly used to refer to protrusion of the eye. *Exophthalmos* specifically describes proptosis of the eye and is sometimes used to describe the bulging of the eye associated with TAO. *Exorbitism* refers to an angle between the lateral orbital walls that is greater than 90°, which is usually associated with shallow orbital depth. This condition contrasts with *telorbitism (hypertelorism),* which refers to a wider-than-normal separation of the medial orbital walls. Generally, exorbitism and hypertelorism refer to congenital abnormalities. *Telecanthus* refers to a wide intercanthal distance in the presence of a normal interpupillary distance (ie, the medial walls are normally positioned). Telecanthus can imply either a bony or a soft tissue abnormality, and the term is used most commonly in describing acquired conditions. The eye may also be displaced vertically or horizontally by an orbital mass. Retrodisplacement of the eye into the orbit, *enophthalmos,* may occur because of volume expansion of the orbit (fracture) or secondary to sclerosing orbital tumors (eg, metastatic breast carcinoma).

Henderson JW, Campbell RJ, Farrow GM, et al. *Orbital Tumors*. 3rd ed. New York: Raven; 1994.

Rootman J, ed. *Diseases of the Orbit: A Multidisciplinary Approach*. 2nd ed. Philadelphia: Lippincott Williams & Wilkins; 2002.

Exophthalmometry is a measurement of the anterior–posterior position of the globe, generally from the lateral orbital rim to the anterior corneal surface (Hertel exophthalmometer). On average, the globes are more prominent in men than in women and more prominent in black patients than in white patients. An asymmetry of greater than 2 mm between the 2 eyes of a given patient suggests proptosis or enophthalmos. The accuracy of exophthalmometry with this instrument is enhanced when the examiner places his or her fifth finger in the patient's external auditory canal for stabilization. Proptosis may best be appreciated clinically when the examiner looks up from below with the patient's head tilted back ("worm's-eye view").

Pseudoproptosis is either the simulation of abnormal prominence of the eye or a true asymmetry that is not the result of increased orbital contents. Diagnosis should be postponed until a mass lesion has been ruled out. Causes of pseudoproptosis are

- enlarged globe
- extraocular muscle weakness or paralysis (allowing the eye to move forward)
- contralateral enophthalmos
- asymmetric orbital size
- asymmetric palpebral fissures (usually caused by ipsilateral eyelid retraction or facial nerve paralysis or contralateral ptosis)

Ocular movements may be limited in a specific direction of gaze by neoplasms or inflammations that involve a single extraocular muscle. TAO usually involves multiple muscles bilaterally, although the bilaterality is often markedly asymmetric. Most commonly, TAO involves the inferior rectus muscle with fibrosis, which restricts globe elevation and in extreme cases may cause hypotropia in primary gaze. When the patient attempts upgaze, intraocular pressure may rise. A large or rapidly enlarging orbital mass can also impair ocular movements, even in the absence of direct muscle invasion.

Eyelid abnormalities are common in TAO. Von Graefe sign refers to the temporal delay between the globe's and the upper lid's descent during downward discursion and is highly suggestive of a diagnosis of TAO. Retraction of the upper and lower lids and upper lid lag on downgaze are the most common physical signs of TAO. Capillary hemangiomas in the orbit often involve the skin of the eyelids, producing strawberry birthmarks that usually grow during the first year of life and then regress spontaneously. Plexiform neurofibromas often involve the lateral upper lids as well as the orbits and produce a "bag of worms" appearance and texture beneath the skin and conjunctiva. They may also cause an S-shaped curvature of the upper lids. Bilateral eyelid ecchymoses may occur in children with metastatic neuroblastoma.

Palpation

Palpation around the globe may disclose the presence of a mass in the anterior orbit, especially if the lacrimal gland is enlarged. Increased resistance to retrodisplacement of the globe is a nonspecific abnormality that may result either from a retrobulbar tumor or from diffuse inflammation such as TAO. The physician should also palpate regional lymph nodes.

Pulsations of the eye are caused by transmission of the vascular pulse through the orbit. This may result from either abnormal vascular flow or transmission of normal intracranial pulsations through a bony defect in the orbital walls. Abnormal vascular flow may be caused by arteriovenous communication, such as carotid cavernous sinus fistulas. Defects in the bony orbital walls may result from sinus mucoceles, surgical removal of bone, trauma, or developmental abnormalities, including encephalocele, meningocele, or sphenoid wing dysplasia occurring in patients with neurofibromatosis.

Auscultation

Auscultation with a stethoscope over the globe or on the mastoid bone may detect bruits in cases of carotid cavernous fistulas. The patient may also subjectively describe an audible bruit. Patients with such arteriovenous communications often have tortuous dilated epibulbar vessels that characteristically stop short of the limbus.

Workup Checklist

Thorough ophthalmic examination of a patient with proptosis is complex, and therefore, the clinician may find a checklist helpful to avoid omitting important observations and to record the findings of the examination in an organized format (Fig 2-1).

☐ Visual acuity
☐ Refraction
☐ Color vision
☐ Pupils
☐ Extraocular motility
☐ Anterior segment
☐ Posterior segment
☐ Intraocular pressure
☐ Anterior–posterior projection (exophthalmometry)
☐ Globe displacement
   – Horizontal
   – Vertical
☐ Eyelids
   Position
   Margin–reflex distance (MRD)
   Interpalpebral fissure
   Lagophthalmos
   Von Graefe sign

☐ Skin
☐ Oral and nasal examination
☐ Palpation
   Orbit
   Thyroid
   Regional lymph nodes
☐ Globe retropulsion
☐ Pulsation or thrill
☐ Bruit
☐ Valsalva
☐ Cranial nerves
   II   VI
   III   VII
   IV   VIII
   V
☐ Results of imaging
   Ultrasonography
   Computed tomography (CT) scan
   Magnetic resonance imaging (MRI)

Figure 2-1 Checklist for the evaluation of patients with proptosis.

Primary Studies

Historically, plain-film radiography and tomography were used in evaluating patients with orbital disease. However, these techniques have been rendered largely obsolete by the widespread use of more current techniques, including computed tomography (CT) and magnetic resonance imaging (MRI). Ultrasonography may be helpful in some cases.

Computed Tomography

Computed tomography has revolutionized the management of orbital disorders. The tissues in a tomographic plane are assigned a density value proportional to their coefficient of absorption of x-rays. A 2-dimensional image is electronically constructed from these density measurements. CT is the most valuable technique for delineating the shape, location, extent, and character of lesions in the orbit (Fig 2-2). CT helps refine the differential diagnosis; moreover, when orbitotomy is indicated, CT guides the selection of the surgical approach by relating the lesion to the surgical space or spaces of the orbit.

Orbital CT scans are usually obtained in 3-mm sections (as opposed to the thicker 5-mm sections usually utilized in head CT scans). Current CT scanners administer a dose of radiation of approximately 1–2 centi-Gray (cGy) per scanning plane. By comparison, a posteroanterior and lateral chest radiograph administers a dose of radiation of approximately 5 milli-Gray (mGy).

The visualization of tumors that are highly vascular (eg, meningioma) or those with altered vascular permeability is improved by the use of intravenous contrast-enhancing agents. CT has resolution and tissue-contrast capabilities allowing imaging of soft tissues, bones, contrast-containing blood vessels, and foreign bodies. Orbital images can be obtained in the axial plane, parallel to the course of the optic nerve, or in the coronal plane, showing the eye, optic nerve, and extraocular muscles in cross section. With older CT scanners, the patient's head has to be repositioned for direct imaging in each of the planes (coronal, sagittal, and axial) if highly detailed images are desired. Although these direct views provide the highest resolution, they require additional scanning time, increased radiation exposure, and sometimes difficult patient positioning. To avoid such difficulties, CT techniques can be used to reconstruct (reformat) any section in any direction (axial, coronal, or sagittal).

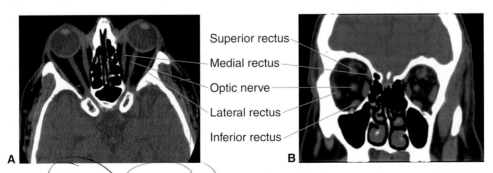

Superior rectus
Medial rectus
Optic nerve
Lateral rectus
Inferior rectus

A   B

Figure 2-2 Axial **(A)** and coronal **(B)** CT views of the orbit demonstrating normal anatomy. *(Courtesy of Thomas Y. Hwang, MD, PhD, and Timothy J. McCulley, MD.)*

This may reduce the need for direct coronal and sagittal scanning. However, the images obtained through direct scanning are sharper than those produced by reformatting.

In modern spiral (helical) CT scanners, there are multiple detector ports, and the scanner and the collecting tube move in a "spiral" fashion around the patient, generating a continuous data set. This results in rapid acquisition of a larger volume of data that, in combination with modern software, allows highly detailed reconstructions in all imaging planes. Because acquisition times are very short, there is a reduction in motion artifact and in the amount of radiation exposure, all of which make spiral CT an especially good modality for imaging children.

Three-Dimensional Computed Tomography

This technique allows reformatting of CT information into 3-dimensional projections of the bony orbital walls. Because this type of imaging requires thin sections and additional computer time, 3-dimensional CT is expensive. In some cases, 3-dimensional CT may aid in the conceptualization of orbital bone changes and facilitate preparation for craniofacial surgery or repairs of complex orbital fractures. Intraorbital contents cannot be visualized because of artifact.

Froula PD, Bartley GB, Garrity JA, Forbes G. The differential diagnosis of orbital calcification as detected on computed tomographic scans. *Mayo Clin Proc.* 1993;68:256–261.

Magnetic Resonance Imaging

Magnetic resonance imaging is a noninvasive imaging technique that does not employ ionizing radiation and has no known adverse biological effects (Figs 2-3, 2-4). MRI is based on the interaction of 3 physical components: atomic nuclei possessing an electrical charge, radiofrequency (RF) waves, and a powerful magnetic field.

Atoms with an unequal number of neutrons and protons possess an electrical charge and a nuclear spin, which generate a magnetic moment. These charged particles can be

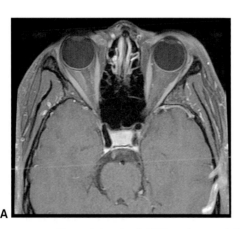
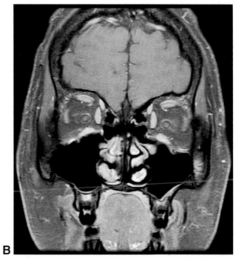

Figure 2-3 T1-weighted axial **(A)** and coronal **(B)** MR images of the orbit, with fat suppression. *(Courtesy of Thomas Y. Hwang, MD, PhD, and Timothy J. McCulley, MD.)*

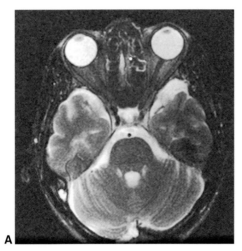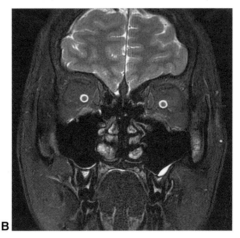

A   B

Figure 2-4 T2-weighted MR images of the orbit, axial without fat suppression **(A)** and coronal with fat suppression **(B)**. *(Courtesy of Thomas Y. Hwang, MD, PhD, and Timothy J. McCulley, MD.)*

manipulated to interact with a magnetic field and RF waves. Under normal conditions, the charged nuclei spin about axes that point in random directions. Although many elements are capable of generating magnetic resonance signals, the hydrogen atom was selected for use because it is the most abundant element in the body.

The magnetic field must be extremely powerful (2000–15,000 times greater than the earth's magnetic field) to affect the spinning hydrogen protons. The strength of the magnetic field is measured in tesla (T) or gauss (G) units (1 T = 10 kG). Current magnets in clinical use vary in strength from 0.1 to 1.5 T.

When a tissue containing hydrogen atoms is placed in the magnetic field, individual nuclei align themselves in the direction of the magnetic field. These aligned nuclei can be excited by an RF pulse emitted from a coil lying within the magnetic field. Excited nuclei align themselves against the static magnetic field; as the RF pulse is terminated, the nuclei flip back to their original magnetized position. As this occurs, the nuclei emit radiomagnetic energy that can be detected, processed, and imaged. The time it takes for this realignment to occur can be measured; it is called the *relaxation time.*

Each orbital tissue has specific magnetic resonance parameters that provide the information used to generate an image. These parameters include tissue proton density and relaxation times. *Proton density* is determined by the number of protons per unit volume of tissue. Fat has greater proton density per unit volume than bone and, therefore, has greater signal intensity. T1, or *longitudinal relaxation time,* is the time required for the net bulk magnetization to realign itself along the original axis. T2, or *transverse relaxation time,* is the mean relaxation time based on the interaction of hydrogen nuclei within a given tissue, an indirect measure of the effect the nuclei have on each other. Each tissue has different proton density and T1 and T2 characteristics, providing the image contrast necessary to differentiate tissues. Healthy tissues can have imaging characteristics different from those of diseased tissue, a good example being the bright signal associated with tissue edema seen on T2-weighted scans.

MRI is usually performed with images created from both T1 and T2 parameters. T1-weighted images generally offer the best anatomical detail of the orbit. They require a shorter acquisition time than the T2-weighted images and therefore reduce the potential for motion artifact. T2-weighted images have the advantage of showing methemoglobin brighter than melanin, whereas these 2 substances have the same signal intensity on T1-weighted images. The difference in brightness seen on T2 images can be helpful in differentiating melanotic lesions from hemorrhagic processes of the choroid. Gadolinium, a paramagnetic contrast agent given intravenously, allows enhancement of vascularized lesions so that they exhibit the same density as fat. It also demonstrates enhancement of lesions with abnormal vascular permeability. Special MR sequences have been developed to suppress the normal bright signal of fat on T1 images (fat suppression; see Fig 2-3) and the bright signal of cerebrospinal fluid on T2 images (fluid-attenuated inversion recovery, or FLAIR). Gradient echo sequences may reveal hemorrhage in vascular malformations that might be missed on T1- and T2-weighted images.

Comparison of CT and MRI

Although both CT and MRI are important modalities for the detection and characterization of orbital and ocular diseases, CT is currently the primary imaging technique. In general, CT provides better spatial resolution, allowing precise localization of a lesion; MRI provides better tissue contrast. Nevertheless, in most orbital conditions, the orbital fat provides sufficient natural tissue contrast to allow ready visualization of orbital tumors on CT. Further, suppression of the bright T1 signal of orbital fat on MRI may degrade image quality and cause signal artifact. MRI also remains significantly more expensive than CT. However, each of the techniques has advantages in specific situations, some of which are discussed next.

MRI resolution has been improved through the use of small-diameter surface coils and updated computer software (eg, fat suppression in the orbit). MRI offers advantages over CT in some situations. It allows the direct display of anatomical information in multiple planes (sagittal, axial, coronal, and any oblique plane) without requiring repositioning of the patient, although reformatting of spiral CT images has largely eliminated the need for direct imaging in coronal and sagittal planes. MRI provides better soft tissue definition than does CT, a capability that is especially helpful in the evaluation of demyelination and in vascular and hemorrhagic lesions. As with CT, contrast agents are available to improve MRI detail in selected cases.

Compared with CT, MRI also provides better tissue contrast of structures in the orbital apex, intracanalicular portion of the optic nerve, structures in periorbital spaces, and orbitocranial tumors, as there is no artifact from the skull base bones. Bone and calcification produce low signal on MRI. Bony structures may be evaluated by visualization of the signal void left by the bone. However, this is not possible when the bone is adjacent to structures that also create a signal void, such as air, rapidly flowing blood, calcification, and dura mater. Thus, CT is superior to MRI for the evaluation of fractures, bone destruction, and tissue calcification.

Motion artifact remains a problem in MRI, which requires more time to perform than does CT. Patient anxiety and claustrophobia may also be issues because of the tighter confines of the MRI equipment. To minimize claustrophobia, "open MRI" scanners, which have a markedly larger bore, are available. These scanners generally have lower resolution, however, and their use of MR surface coils may reintroduce the problem of claustrophobia.

MRI is contraindicated in patients who have ferromagnetic metallic foreign bodies in the orbit or periorbital soft tissue, ferromagnetic vascular clips from previous surgery, magnetic intravascular filters, or electronic devices in the body such as cardiac pacemakers. If necessary, such foreign material can be ruled out with plain films or CT. Certain types of eye makeup can produce artifacts and should be removed prior to MRI. Dental amalgam is not a ferromagnetic substance and is not a contraindication to MRI, but this material does produce artifacts and degrades the images to some degree. Medical monitoring of a patient with serious health problems is easier in the environment of the CT room than in the MRI chamber. Because patients with acute head trauma are usually being evaluated for bone fractures, acute hemorrhagic problems, and possible foreign bodies, CT is usually the best choice in such cases, especially because it can be performed more quickly. For subacute trauma, MRI may be preferable because it is better at differentiating between fresh and old hemorrhages (Fig 2-5).

Although CT and MRI yield different images, it is unusual for both techniques to be required in the evaluation of an orbital disorder. The choice between these modalities should be based on the specific patient's condition. In most cases, CT is the more effective

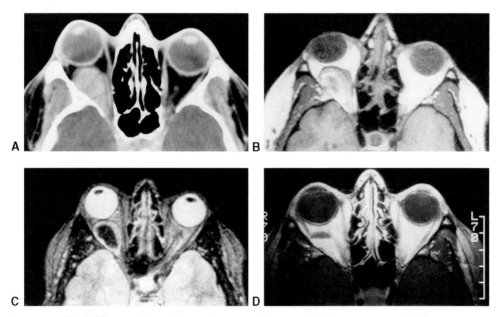

A   B

C   D

Figure 2-5 **A,** A CT scan of a patient with acute right exophthalmos as a result of a spontaneous orbital hemorrhage. The hematoma exhibits discrete margins, homogeneous consistency, and a radiodensity similar to that of blood vessels and muscle. **B,** A T1 MR scan obtained 4 days after the hemorrhage demonstrates the transient "bull's-eye" pattern characteristic of a hematoma beginning to undergo physical changes and biochemical hemoglobin degradation. **C,** A T2 MR scan obtained the same day as the T1 study shows a characteristic ring pattern. **D,** A T1 MR scan performed 3 months later shows that the hematoma has decreased in size. There is layering of the degraded blood components.

and economical choice (Table 2-2). When the orbitocranial junction or brain is involved, CT scanning and MRI may be complementary.

Ellis BD, Hogg JP. Neuroimaging for the general ophthalmologist. *Focal Points: Clinical Modules for Ophthalmologists.* San Francisco: American Academy of Ophthalmology; 1998, module 8.

Lee AG, Brazis PW, Garrity JA, White M. Imaging for neuro-ophthalmic and orbital disease. *Am J Ophthalmol.* 2004;138:852–862.

Mukherji SK, Tart RP, Fitzsimmons J, et al. Fat-suppressed MR of the orbit and cavernous sinus: comparison of fast spin-echo and conventional spin-echo. *Am J Neuroradiol.* 1994;15:1707–1714.

Newton TH, Bilaniuk LT, eds. *Radiology of the Eye and Orbit (Modern Neuroradiology.* Volume 4). New York: Raven; 1990.

Trobe JD, Gebarski SS. Looking behind the eyes. The proper use of modern imaging [editorial]. *Arch Ophthalmol.* 1993;111:1185–1186.

Wirtschafter JD, Berman EL, McDonald CS. *Magnetic Resonance Imaging and Computed Tomography.* Ophthalmology Monograph 6. San Francisco: American Academy of Ophthalmology; 1992.

Ultrasonography

Orbital ultrasonography is rarely used to examine patients with orbital disorders. The size, shape, and position of normal and abnormal orbital tissues can be determined by means of contemporary ultrasound techniques, but ultrasound is less helpful than CT or MRI. Two-dimensional images of these tissues can be obtained with B-scan ultrasonography. Standardized A-scan ultrasonography provides unidimensional images of the orbital soft tissues characterized by a series of spikes of varying height and width that demonstrate the particular echogenic characteristics of each tissue. Specific tissues, ultrasonographic

Table 2-2 Comparison of CT and MRI in Orbital Disease

CT	MRI
Good technique for most orbital conditions, especially fractures and thyroid-associated orbitopathy	Better technique for orbitocranial junction or intracranial imaging
Good view of bone and calcium	No view of bone or calcification
Poor definition of the orbital apex	Good view of orbital apex soft tissues unimpeded by bone
Better spatial resolution	More soft tissue detail
Reformatting or rescanning required to image in multiple planes	Simultaneous imaging of multiple planes
Improved imaging with contrast in many cases	Improved imaging with contrast in many cases
Less motion artifact because of shorter scanning time	More motion artifact because of longer scanning time
Less claustrophobic environment in scanner	Tighter confines in scanner
Good technique for patients with metallic foreign bodies	More contraindications (eg, patients with ferromagnetic metallic foreign bodies, aneurysm clips, and pacemakers)
Less expensive technique	More expensive technique

characteristics, and dynamic tissue manipulation techniques, such as compression, can be helpful in the diagnosis and localization of lesions. Areas of edema can sometimes be used to discern the degree of disease activity. Intraoperative localization of foreign bodies is possible with ultrasonography. *Doppler ultrasonography* can provide specific information regarding blood flow (eg, the velocity and direction of blood flow in patients with occlusive vascular disease or vascular abnormalities associated with increased blood flow).

However, analysis of orbital disease requires specialized equipment and experienced personnel, and office-based ultrasound equipment is generally not suitable for the evaluation of orbital tissues. Ultrasonography is of limited value in assessing lesions of the posterior orbit (because of sound attenuation) or the sinuses or intracranial space (because sound does not pass well through air or bone).

Aburn NS, Sergott RC. Orbital colour Doppler imaging. *Eye.* 1993;7:639–647.

Secondary Studies

Secondary studies that are performed for specific indications include venography and arteriography. These studies are rarely used but may be helpful in specific cases.

Venography

Before the age of CT and MRI, orbital venography was used in the diagnosis and management of orbital varices and in the study of the cavernous sinus. Contrast material is injected into the frontal or the angular vein to reveal a venous abnormality. Subtraction and magnification techniques have been used to increase the resolution of venography. Because moving blood generates a signal void during MR imaging, larger venous abnormalities and structures can be visualized well on MR venography.

Arteriography

Arteriography should be used only in patients with a high probability of an arterial lesion such as an aneurysm or arteriovenous malformation. Retrograde catheterization of the cerebral vessels is accomplished through the femoral artery. There is a small risk of serious neurological and vascular complications because the technique requires installation of the catheter and injection of radiopaque dye into the arterial system.

Visualization can be maximized by the use of selective injection of the internal and external carotid arteries, magnification to allow viewing of the smaller caliber vessels, and subtraction techniques to radiographically eliminate bone.

Conventional sequential filming techniques or newer digital systems can be used to obtain and store images. Although digital systems are more economical, they currently do not provide the same degree of resolution as conventional film techniques.

CT and MR Angiography

Because of the development of better hardware and software, precise CT and MR imaging of arteriovenous malformations, aneurysms, and arteriovenous fistulas is now possible without the expense and discomfort of intravascular catheterization and injection of contrast material, as well as the risks associated with these maneuvers. When determining which test to use, the ophthalmologist should consult with a radiologist to discuss the suspected lesion and to ensure selection of the imaging modality best suited for the patient.

Pathology

The diagnosis of an orbital lesion usually requires analysis of tissue obtained through an orbitotomy. Appropriate handling of the tissue specimen is necessary to ensure an accurate diagnosis. The majority of tissue samples are placed in formalin for permanent-section analysis. Frozen-section analysis is generally not used for definitive diagnosis of an orbital tumor. However, when the area of proposed biopsy is not obvious, frozen sections are helpful to confirm that appropriate tissue has been obtained for permanent-section analysis. Frozen-section analysis is also used intraoperatively to determine tumor margins, ensuring complete tumor removal. Tissue removed for frozen-section analysis should be placed in a dampened saline gauze and promptly sent to the frozen-section laboratory. If a lymphoproliferative lesion is suspected, some fresh tissue should be sent for analysis of flow cytometry.

Because of the vast array of possible unusual tumor types in the orbit, preoperative consultation with a pathologist familiar with orbital disease may be helpful to maximize the information gained from any orbital biopsy. In many cases, fresh tissue should be obtained and frozen for cell-surface marker studies. Cell-marker studies are required in the analysis of all orbital lymphoid lesions. These studies may permit differentiation of reactive lymphoid hyperplasia from lymphoma. Such studies may also indicate the presence of estrogen receptors in cases of metastatic prostate or breast carcinoma and thus provide useful information regarding sensitivity to hormonal therapy. Marker studies are also useful in the diagnosis of poorly differentiated tumors when light microscopy alone cannot yield a definitive diagnosis. Although cell-marker studies have largely replaced electron microscopy in the diagnosis of very undifferentiated tumors, it may nevertheless be worthwhile in these cases to preserve fresh tissue in glutaraldehyde for possible electron microscopy. In noncohesive tumors (hematologic or lymphoid), a touch prep may permit a diagnosis.

All biopsy specimens must be treated delicately so that crush artifact, which can confuse interpretation, is minimized. Permanent tissue biopsy specimens must be placed in fixatives immediately. If fine-needle aspiration biopsy is planned, a cytologist or trained technician must be available to handle the aspirate. In special cases, the biopsy can be performed under either ultrasonographic or CT control. Although a fine-bore needle occasionally yields a sufficient cell block, the specimen is usually limited to cytologic study. This technique may not permit as firm a diagnosis as is possible with larger biopsy specimens, in which light and electron microscopy can be used to evaluate the histologic pattern.

See BCSC Section 4, *Ophthalmic Pathology and Intraocular Tumors,* for more extensive discussion of pathology.

Laboratory Studies

Screening for abnormal thyroid function commonly includes T_3, T_4, and thyroid-stimulating hormone (TSH) tests. Results of these serum tests are abnormal in 90% of patients with TAO. However, if thyroid disease is strongly suspected and these results are normal, additional endocrine studies, including studies of thyroid-stimulating immuno-globulins or TSH-receptor antibodies, can be considered.

Wegener granulomatosis should be suspected in patients with sclerokeratitis or coexisting sinus disease and orbital mass lesions. Wegener granulomatosis may present as a chronic orbital inflammation. The disease affects the upper and lower respiratory tracts, the kidney, and the orbit, but limited forms may lack renal involvement. A useful test for this uncommon disease is the antineutrophil cytoplasmic antibody (ANCA) serum assay, which shows a cytoplasmic staining pattern (cANCA) in Wegener granulomatosis. The test results may be negative initially in localized disease. Biopsy of affected tissues classically shows vasculitis, granulomatous inflammation, and tissue necrosis, although necrotizing vasculitis is not always present in orbital biopsies. Early diagnosis and treatment of this disorder with cyclophosphamide and prednisone may be lifesaving.

Testing for serum angiotensin-converting enzyme and lysozyme may be helpful in the diagnosis of sarcoidosis. This multisystem granulomatous inflammatory condition may present with lacrimal gland enlargement, conjunctival granulomas, extraocular muscle or optic nerve infiltration, or solitary orbital granulomas. Diagnosis is confirmed through biopsy of 1 or more affected organs.

CHAPTER 3

Congenital Orbital Anomalies

Most congenital anomalies of the eye and orbit are apparent before birth. Developmental orbital defects can manifest at any time from conception until late in life. If an anomaly is caused by a slowing or cessation of a normal stage, the resulting deformity can be considered a pure arrest. An example is microphthalmia. However, a superimposed aberrant growth usually follows the original arrest, and the resulting deformity does not represent any previous normal stage of development. An example of this latter condition is formation of an orbital cyst following incomplete closure of the fetal fissure. As a rule, the more gross the abnormality, the earlier in development it occurred.

The examination of the child with an ocular or craniofacial malformation should focus on carefully defining the severity of the defect and ruling out associated changes. Syndromes may have specific associated ocular changes or secondary ocular complications such as exposure keratitis or strabismus related to orbital malposition. For further discussion, including illustrations, see also Embryology, in BCSC Section 2, *Fundamentals and Principles of Ophthalmology;* and BCSC Section 6, *Pediatric Ophthalmology and Strabismus.*

Anophthalmia

True anophthalmia is defined by Duke-Elder as a total absence of tissues of the eye. Three types of anophthalmia have been described. *Primary anophthalmia* is rare and usually bilateral. It occurs when the primary optic vesicle fails to grow out from the cerebral vesicle at the 2-mm stage of embryonic development. *Secondary anophthalmia* is rare and lethal and results from a gross abnormality in the anterior neural tube. *Consecutive anophthalmia* presumably results from a secondary degeneration of the optic vesicle.

As orbital growth is dependent on the size and growth of the globe, anophthalmic orbits are small, with hypoplastic eyelids and orbital adnexal structures.

Microphthalmia

Microphthalmia is much more common than anophthalmia and is defined as the presence of a small eye. Eyes vary in size depending on the severity of the defect. Most infants with a unilateral small orbit and no visible eye actually have a microphthalmic globe.

All microphthalmic children have hypoplastic orbits. Most microphthalmic eyes have no potential for vision, and treatment focuses on achieving a cosmetically acceptable appearance that is reasonably symmetric. Treatment begins shortly after birth and consists of socket expansion with progressively larger conformers, which are used until the patient can be fitted with a prosthesis at around age 3–4 months. In cases of severe bony asymmetry, intraorbital tissue expanders may be progressively inflated to enlarge the hypoplastic orbit.

Enucleation is usually not necessary for the fitting of a conformer or an ocular prosthesis and is ordinarily avoided because it may worsen the bony hypoplasia. The use of dermis-fat grafts as orbital implants following early enucleation has been reported as successful. These grafts appear to grow along with the patient, resulting in progressive socket expansion. For older microphthalmic children, craniofacial techniques have been utilized to reposition and resize the orbit. Such repairs are complex, as noted in the following discussion of craniofacial clefting.

Microphthalmos with orbital cyst results from the failure of the choroidal fissure to close in the embryo. This condition is usually unilateral but may be bilateral. The presence of an orbital cyst may be beneficial for stimulating normal growth of the involved orbital bone and eyelids. In some cases, the orbital cyst may have to be removed to allow for fitting of an ocular prosthesis.

Craniofacial Clefting

Craniofacial clefts occur because of a developmental arrest. Etiologic theories include a failure of neural crest cell migration and a failure of fusion of facial processes. Facial clefts in the skeletal structures are distributed around the orbit and maxilla; clefts in the soft tissues are most apparent around the lids and lips. Examples of clefting syndromes affecting the orbit and lids are mandibulofacial dysostosis (Treacher Collins–Franceschetti syndrome; Fig 3-1), oculoauricular dysplasia (Goldenhar syndrome), and some forms of midline clefts with hypertelorism.

The bones of the skull or orbit may also have congenital clefts through which the intracranial contents can herniate. These protruding contents can be the meninges

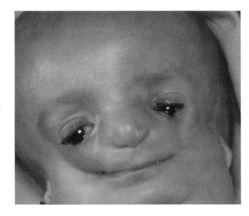

Figure 3-1 Treacher Collins–Franceschetti syndrome (mandibulofacial dysostosis). *(Courtesy of James Garrity, MD.)*

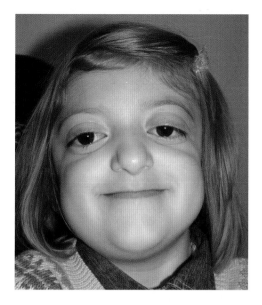

Figure 3-2 Crouzon syndrome (craniofacial dysostosis). *(Courtesy of Jill Foster, MD.)*

(meningocele), brain tissue *(encephalocele)*, or both meninges and brain tissue *(meningoencephalocele)*. When these herniations involve the orbit, they most commonly present anteriorly with a protrusion subcutaneously near the medial canthus or over the bridge of the nose. Straining or crying may produce an increase in the size of the mass, and the globe may be displaced temporally and downward. Such herniations less commonly move into the posterior orbit; these lesions may cause anterior displacement and pulsation of the globe. Treatment is surgical and should be carried out in collaboration with a neurosurgeon. Meningoceles and encephaloceles adjacent to the orbit are frequently associated with anomalies of the optic disc.

Craniosynostosis, the premature closure of 1 or more sutures in the bones of the skull, results in various skeletal deformities. Secondary intracranial hypertension can be a complication. Hypertelorism and proptosis are frequently observed in craniosynostosis syndromes such as Crouzon syndrome (craniofacial dysostosis; Fig 3-2) and Apert syndrome (acrocephalosyndactyly).

The severe orbital and facial defects associated with craniofacial deformities can sometimes be corrected with surgery. Bony and soft tissue reconstruction is generally needed. Such operations are often staged and usually require a team approach with multiple subspecialists.

Tumors

For a discussion of *dermoid cysts, lipodermoids, teratomas,* and *developmental vascular malformations and neoplasms,* see Chapter 5, Orbital Neoplasms.

CHAPTER **4**

Infectious and Inflammatory Disorders

Infections

Cellulitis

The most common cause of cellulitis is bacterial infection. However, in each clinical setting, the physician must define the etiology of the cellulitis in order to provide effective treatment. Failure to define the etiology may result in delayed identification of noninfectious (ie, autoimmune, malignant, foreign body) etiologies.

Bacterial infections of the orbit or periorbital soft tissues occur from 3 primary sources:

- direct spread from an adjacent sinusitis (most cases)
- direct inoculation following trauma or skin infection
- bacteremic spread from a distant focus (otitis media, pneumonia)

Although periorbital infections are typically classified as being either preseptal or orbital cellulitis, they often represent a continuum, with common underlying causes requiring similar treatment regimens. It must be emphasized that infectious cellulitis—whether preseptal or orbital—is most commonly caused by underlying sinusitis if no obvious source of inoculation is noted.

Preseptal cellulitis

Infectious preseptal cellulitis is defined as inflammation and infection confined to the eyelids and periorbital structures anterior to the orbital septum. The orbital structures posterior to the septum are not infected but may be secondarily inflamed. Eyelid edema, erythema, and inflammation may be severe. Usually, the globe is uninvolved. Pupillary reaction, visual acuity, and ocular motility are not disturbed. Pain on eye movement and chemosis are absent.

Designating the cellulitis as preseptal implies an infective process superficial to the orbital septum, one typically requiring less-intensive treatment than orbital cellulitis. Although preseptal cellulitis in adults is usually due to penetrating trauma or a cutaneous source of infection, in children the most common cause is underlying sinusitis. Historically, preseptal cellulitis in infants and children younger than 5 years was often associated with bacteremia, septicemia, and meningitis caused by *Haemophilus influenzae*. This cause of preseptal and orbital cellulitis has virtually been eliminated by the introduction of the *H influenzae* B (Hib) vaccine. Now, most cases of preseptal and orbital cellulitis in children are the result of gram-positive cocci infection. As some children fail to obtain appropriate immunization, the clinician should discuss the child's vaccinations with the parents, ensuring that all vaccinations are current. Workup should proceed quickly and include computed tomography (CT) of the orbit and sinuses if the eyelid swelling is profound enough to preclude examination of the globe and thereby exclude orbital cellulitis.

The patient should be treated in consultation with a primary care physician. Oral antibiotics and nasal decongestants, in cases of associated sinusitis, are typically effective therapy and are chosen if the examination of the child is reliable and follow-up examinations can be ensured. Hospitalization and intravenous (IV) antibiotics are indicated if the cellulitis progresses despite outpatient therapy, as cases of preseptal infection can progress to orbital cellulitis.

In teenagers and adults, preseptal cellulitis usually arises from a superficial source (eg, traumatic inoculation, infected chalazion, or epidermal inclusion cyst) and responds quickly to appropriate oral antibiotics and warm compresses. Initial antibiotic selection is based on the history, clinical findings, and initial laboratory studies. Prompt sensitivity studies are indicated so that the antibiotic selection can be revised, if necessary. *Staphylococcus aureus* is the most common pathogen in patients with preseptal cellulitis resulting from trauma. The infection usually responds rapidly to a penicillinase-resistant penicillin, such as methicillin or ampicillin-sulbactam. However, methicillin-resistant *S aureus* is increasingly encountered.

Imaging studies should be performed to rule out underlying sinusitis if no direct inoculation site is identified. If the patient does not respond quickly to oral antibiotics or if orbital involvement becomes evident, prompt hospital admission, CT, and IV antibiotics are usually indicated.

Surgical drainage may be necessary if preseptal cellulitis progresses to a localized abscess. Incision and drainage can usually be performed directly over the abscess, but care should be taken so that damage to the levator aponeurosis in the upper eyelid is avoided. To avoid contaminating the orbital soft tissues, the surgeon should not open the orbital septum.

Orbital cellulitis

In infectious orbital cellulitis, disease is present posterior to the orbital septum (Fig 4-1). In more than 90% of cases, orbital cellulitis occurs as a secondary extension of acute or chronic bacterial sinusitis (Table 4-1). Clinical findings of orbital cellulitis include fever, leukocytosis (75% of cases), proptosis, chemosis, ptosis, and restriction of and pain with ocular motility. Decreased visual acuity, color vision, and visual field as well as pupillary abnormalities suggest compressive optic neuropathy demanding immediate investigation and aggressive management. Delay in treatment may result in blindness, cavernous sinus thrombosis, cranial neuropathy, brain abscess, and death.

Evaluation of the orbit and paranasal sinuses, preferably by CT, is essential. Identification of sinusitis mandates otolaryngological consultation. Antibiotic therapy should provide broad-spectrum coverage because infections in adults usually include multiple organisms that may include gram-positive cocci, *H influenzae* and *Moraxella catarrhalis*,

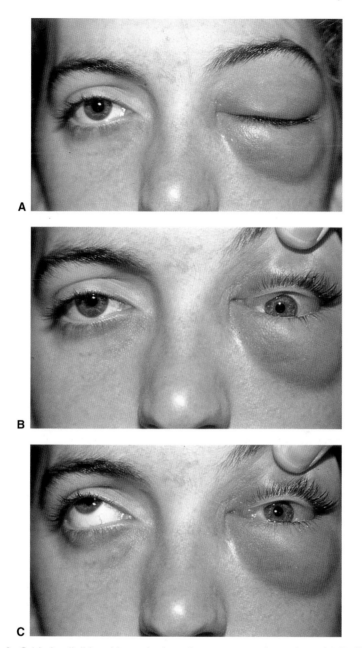

Figure 4-1 **A,** Orbital cellulitis with marked erythema, proptosis, and ptosis. **B,** Chemosis and hypo-ophthalmia are present. **C,** Vertical ductions are impaired OS. *(Courtesy of Jeffrey A. Nerad, MD.)*

and anaerobes. Although nasal decongestants may help spontaneous drainage of the infected sinus, early surgical intervention to drain the involved sinus is usually indicated, especially if orbital findings progress during IV antibiotic therapy. In contrast, orbital cellulitis in children is more often caused by a single gram-positive organism and is less likely to require surgical drainage of the infected sinus.

Table 4-1 Causes of Orbital Cellulitis

Extension from periorbital structures
Paranasal sinuses
Face and eyelids
Lacrimal sac (dacryocystitis)
Teeth (dental infection)
Exogenous causes
Trauma (rule out foreign bodies)
Surgery (after any orbital or periorbital surgery)
Endogenous causes
Bacteremia with septic embolization
Intraorbital causes
Endophthalmitis
Dacryoadenitis

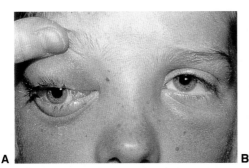 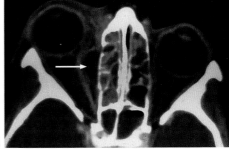

A   **B**

Figure 4-2   A, Right orbital cellulitis. Note proptosis and exotropia. **B,** CT scan of right orbital subperiosteal abscess *(arrow)*. Note medial rectus displaced by abscess. *(Courtesy of Robert C. Kersten, MD.)*

Orbital cellulitis following blowout fractures is generally limited to patients with underlying sinus disease. Prophylactic antibiotics are recommended if CT scans of orbital fractures suggest ongoing sinusitis. The risk of orbital cellulitis is increased if the medial wall is fractured.

A significant percentage of adult cases of orbital cellulitis proceed to abscess formation, which may present as progressive proptosis or globe displacement. Progression of infection and clinical deterioration can occur even in patients on appropriate antibiotics. Abscesses usually localize in the subperiosteal space (Fig 4-2), adjacent to the infected sinus, but may extend through the periosteum into the orbital soft tissues. Such abscesses should be suspected if patients on IV antibiotics do not show daily improvement. The clinician will find serial clinical examinations coupled with CT scans invaluable in detecting abscess localization and in planning the surgical approach for drainage.

Not all subperiosteal abscesses require surgical drainage. Isolated medial or inferior subperiosteal orbital abscesses in children younger than age 9 with underlying isolated ethmoid sinusitis, intact vision, and moderate proptosis typically respond to medical therapy. Expectant management can be offered, according to the guidelines set forth by Garcia and Harris, if *none* of the following criteria are present:

- patient 9 years or older
- presence of frontal sinusitis
- nonmedial location of SPA (subperiosteal abscess)
- large SPA
- suspicion of anerobic infection (presence of gas in abscess on CT)
- recurrence of SPA after prior drainage
- evidence of chronic sinusitis (eg, nasal polyps)
- acute optic nerve or retinal compromise
- infection of dental origin (anaerobic infection more likely)

Surgical drainage coupled with appropriate antibiotic therapy is recommended in older patients or more severe presentation and usually leads to dramatic clinical improvement within 24–48 hours. Concomitant sinus surgery is indicated if sinusitis is present. The refractory nature of orbital abscesses in adolescents and adults is thought to be due to the multiple drug-resistant pathogens, in particular, anaerobic organisms.

The majority of patients with orbital cellulitis and abscesses respond to appropriate medical or surgical treatment or to a combination of these. Orbital infections rarely spread posteriorly to the cavernous sinus. Cavernous sinus thrombosis is often heralded by the rapid progression of proptosis and by anesthesia in both the first and second divisions of the trigeminal nerve; in rare cases, by contralateral ophthalmoplegia as well. Meningitis and frank brain abscess may develop. A lumbar puncture may reveal acute inflammatory cells and the causative organism on stain and culture.

Garcia GH, Harris GJ. Criteria for nonsurgical management of subperiosteal abscess of the orbit. *Ophthalmology.* 2000;107:1454–1458.

Harris GJ. Subperiosteal abscess of the orbit: age as a factor in the bacteriology and response to treatment. *Ophthalmology.* 1994;101:585–595.

Necrotizing Fasciitis

Necrotizing fasciitis is an uncommon, severe bacterial infection involving the subcutaneous soft tissues, particularly the superficial and deep fasciae. Although a variety of organisms, including aerobic and anaerobic, gram-positive and gram-negative bacteria, may cause this disorder, recent attention has focused on group A *Streptococcus.*

This disorder develops quickly and is potentially fatal. It may occur in previously healthy persons, without a history of significant trauma, but many patients are immunocompromised by conditions such as diabetes mellitus and alcoholism. These infections may be accompanied by a shocklike syndrome. Typically, the initial clinical presentation is similar to that of orbital or preseptal cellulitis, with swelling, erythema, and pain. Because necrotizing fasciitis tends to track along avascular tissue planes, an early sign may be anesthesia over the affected area owing to involvement of deep cutaneous nerves. In addition, disproportionate complaints of pain may suggest the possibility of necrotizing fasciitis, as do typical changes in skin color progressing from rose to blue-gray with bullous formation and frank necrosis. Usually, the course is rapid and the patient requires ICU support.

Treatment includes early surgical debridement along with IV antibiotics. If the involved pathogen is unknown, then broad-spectrum coverage for gram-positive and gram-negative as well as anaerobic organisms is indicated. Clindamycin is of particular value as it is uniquely effective against the toxins produced by group A *Streptococcus*. To limit the inflammatory damage associated with the toxins, adjunctive corticosteroid therapy after the start of antibiotic therapy has been advocated. Some cases of necrotizing fasciitis limited to the eyelids can be cautiously followed with systemic antibiotic therapy and little or no debridement; this is considered only in cases that rapidly demarcate and show no signs of toxic shock.

Patients may experience rapid deterioration, culminating in hypotension, renal failure, and adult respiratory distress syndrome. Reported clinical series from all body sites show up to a 30% mortality rate, usually due to toxic-shock syndrome, but this appears uncommon in the periocular region.

Luksich JA, Holds JB, Hartstein ME. Conservative management of necrotizing fasciitis of the eyelids. *Ophthalmology.* 2002;109:2118–2122.

Marshall DH, Jordan DR, Gilberg SM, Harvey J, Arthurs BP, Nerad JA. Periocular necrotizing fasciitis: a review of five cases. *Ophthalmology.* 1997;104:1857–1862.

Shayegani A, MacFarlane D, Kazim M, Grossman ME. Streptococcal gangrene of the eyelids and orbit. *Am J Ophthalmol.* 1995;120(6):784–792.

Phycomycosis

Phycomycosis (also known as *mucormycosis*) is the most common and the most virulent fungal disease involving the orbit. The specific fungal genus that is involved is usually *Mucor* or *Rhizopus*. These fungi, belonging to the class Phycomycetes, almost always extend into the orbit from an adjacent sinus or the nasal cavity. The fungi invade blood vessel walls, producing thrombosing vasculitis. The resultant tissue necrosis promotes further fungal invasion.

Patients commonly present with proptosis and an orbital apex syndrome (internal and external ophthalmoplegia, ptosis, decreased corneal sensation, and decreased vision). Predisposing factors include systemic disease with associated metabolic acidosis, diabetes mellitus, malignancies, and treatment with antimetabolites or steroids. Diagnosis is confirmed by a biopsy of the necrotic-appearing tissues in the nasopharynx or the involved sinus or orbit. The histology shows nonseptate large branching hyphae that stain with hematoxylin-eosin, unlike most fungi (see the discussion of fungal infections in BCSC Section 5, *Neuro-Ophthalmology*).

Therapeutic measures consist of control of the underlying metabolic or immunologic abnormality, surgical excision of infected and necrotic tissues, and IV administration of amphotericin B or the newer liposomal amphotericin B or other lipid-encapsulated antifungal agents, which permits a higher cumulative dose with a reduced level of toxicity. Some authors have proposed adjunctive hyperbaric oxygen therapy. The role of primary exenteration has decreased, but it is unclear whether patient survival (typically poor) has been adversely affected by less-aggressive surgical excision.

Ferry AP, Abedi S. Diagnosis and management of rhino-orbitocerebral mucormycosis (phyco-mycosis). A report of 16 personally observed cases. *Ophthalmology.* 1983;90:1096–1104.

Kronish JW, Johnson TE, Gilberg SM, Corrent GF, McLeish WM, Scott KR. Orbital infections in patients with human immunodeficiency virus infection. *Ophthalmology.* 1996;103:1483–1492.

Aspergillosis

The fungus *Aspergillus* can affect the orbit in several distinct clinical entities. Acute aspergillosis is a fungal disease characterized by fulminant sinus infection with secondary orbital invasion. Patients present with severe periorbital pain, decreased vision, and proptosis. Diagnosis is confirmed by one or more biopsies. Gomori methenamine–silver nitrate stain shows septate branching hyphae of uniform width (see the discussion of fungal infections in BCSC Section 5, *Neuro-Ophthalmology*). Therapy consists of aggressive surgical excision of all infected tissues and administration of amphotericin B, flucytosine, or rifampin or a combination thereof.

Chronic aspergillosis is an indolent infection resulting in slow destruction of the sinuses and adjacent structures. Although the prognosis is much better than for acute fulminant disease, intraorbital and intracranial extension can occur in the chronic invasive form of fungal sinusitis as well and result in significant morbidity.

Chronic localized noninvasive aspergillosis also involves the sinuses and occurs in immunocompetent patients who may not have a history of atopic disease. Often, there is a history of chronic sinusitis, and proliferation of saprophytic organisms results in a tightly packed fungus ball. This type of aspergillosis is characterized by a lack of either inflammation or bone erosion.

Allergic aspergillosis sinusitis, a newer entity, occurs in immunocompetent patients with nasal polyposis and chronic sinusitis. Patients may have peripheral eosinophilia, an elevated total immunoglobulin E level, fungus-specific immunoglobulin E and immunoglobulin G levels, or positive skin test results for fungal antigens. CT reveals thick allergic mucin within the sinus as mottled areas of increased attenuation on nonenhanced images. Bone erosion and remodeling are frequently present but do not signify actual tissue invasion. Magnetic resonance imaging (MRI) may be more specific, showing signal void areas on T2-weighted scans. Sinus biopsy results reveal thick, peanut butter–like or green mucus, pathologic study of which reveals numerous eosinophils and eosinophil degradation products, as well as extramucosal fungal hyphae. Endoscopic debridement of the involved sinuses is indicated. Treatment with systemic and topical corticosteroids is also recommended. Orbital disease has been responsible for presentation in up to 17% of patients with allergic fungal sinusitis.

Como JA, Dismukes WE. Oral azole drugs as systemic antifungal therapy. *N Engl J Med.* 1994;330:263–272.

Klapper SR, Lee AG, Patrinely JR, Stewart M, Alford EL. Orbital involvement in allergic fungal sinusitis. *Ophthalmology.* 1997;104:2094–2100.

Levin LA, Avery R, Shore JW, Woog JJ, Baker AS. The spectrum of orbital aspergillosis: a clinicopathological review. *Surv Ophthalmol.* 1996;41:142–154.

Orbital Tuberculosis

Though not uncommon in endemic areas of the developing world, tuberculosis has reemerged in recent years as a public health threat in developed countries. It affects the orbit as a chronic inflammatory process, as a periostitis, or as a so-called cold abscess. The predominant route of spread to the orbit is hematogenous from a pulmonary focus, which is often subclinical. Less often, spread occurs from an adjacent tuberculous sinusitis. Proptosis, motility dysfunction, bone destruction, and chronic draining fistulas may be the presenting findings. In the developed world, this disease is most often associated with human immunodeficiency virus immunosuppression and inner-city poverty. The majority of recent orbital cases have been reported to occur in children, and the infection is often mistaken for an orbital malignancy. The disease is usually unilateral. Acid-fast bacilli may be difficult to detect in pathologic specimens, which usually show caseating necrosis, epithelioid cells, and Langhans giant cells. Skin testing and fine-needle aspiration biopsy with culture early in the course of the disease may help establish the diagnosis. Antituberculous therapy is usually curative.

Khalil M, Lindley S, Matouk E. Tuberculosis of the orbit. *Ophthalmology.* 1985;92:1624–1627.

Parasitic Diseases

Parasitic diseases of the orbit are generally limited to developing countries and include trichinosis and echinococcosis. *Trichinosis* is caused by ingestion of the nematode *Trichinella spiralis.* The eyelids and extraocular muscles may be inflamed by migration of the larvae. *Echinococcosis* is caused by the dog tapeworm *Echinococcus granulosus.* A hydatid cyst containing tapeworm larvae may form in the orbit. Rupture of such a cyst may cause progressive inflammation and a severe immune response. *Taenia solium,* the pork tapeworm, may also encyst and progressively enlarge in the orbital tissues, causing a condition known as *cysticercosis.*

Inflammations

Thyroid-Associated Orbitopathy

Thyroid-associated orbitopathy (TAO) (also known as *Graves ophthalmopathy, dysthyroid ophthalmopathy, thyroid eye disease, thyroid orbitopathy, thyrotoxic exophthalmos,* and other terms) is an autoimmune inflammatory disorder whose underlying cause continues to be elucidated. The clinical signs, however, are characteristic and include one or more of the following: eyelid retraction, lid lag, proptosis, restrictive extraocular myopathy, and compressive optic neuropathy (Figs 4-3 through 4-5). TAO was originally described as part of the triad comprising Graves disease, which includes the aforementioned orbital signs, hyperthyroidism, and pretibial myxedema. Though typically associated with Graves hyperthyroidism, TAO may also occur with Hashimoto thyroiditis (immune-induced hypothyroidism) or in the absence of thyroid dysfunction. The course of ophthalmopathy does not necessarily parallel the activity of the thyroid gland or the treatment of thyroid abnormalities.

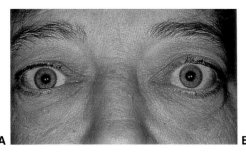 

Figure 4-3 **A,** Bilateral proptosis and upper eyelid retraction in a middle-aged woman with TAO. Note minimal signs of active inflammation. **B,** Marked inflammation 3 months later, with chemosis, eyelid swelling, and increased proptosis. *(Courtesy of Jeffrey A. Nerad, MD.)*

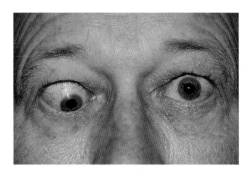

Figure 4-4 TAO, with proptosis, eyelid retraction, esotropia, and hypotropia resulting from fibrosis of the medial and inferior rectus muscles. *(Courtesy of George B. Bartley, MD.)*

Diagnosis

The diagnosis of TAO is made when 2 of the following 3 signs of the disease are present:

1. Concurrent or recently treated immune-related thyroid dysfunction (one or more of the following):

   a. Graves hyperthyroidism
   b. Hashimoto thyroiditis
   c. Presence of circulating thyroid antibodies without a coexisting dysthyroid state (partial consideration given): TSH-receptor (TSH-R) antibodies, thyroid-binding inhibitory immunoglobulins (TBII), thyroid-stimulating immunoglobulins (TSI), antimicrosomal antibody

2. Typical orbital signs (one or more of the following):

   a. Unilateral or bilateral eyelid retraction with typical temporal flare (with/or without lagophthalmos)
   b. Bilateral proptosis (as evidenced by comparison with patient's old photos)
   c. Restrictive strabismus in a typical pattern
   d. Compressive optic neuropathy
   e. Fluctuating eyelid edema/erythema
   f. Chemosis/caruncular edema

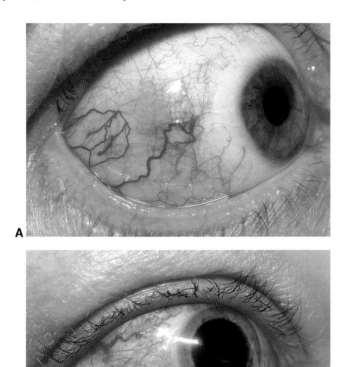

Figure 4-5 **A,** Conjunctival erythema over the insertions of the rectus muscles is a frequent sign of TAO. Typically, there is a clear zone between the anterior extent of the abnormally dilated blood vessels and the corneoscleral limbus. **B,** In contrast, the arterialization of blood vessels that occurs with a dural shunt is usually more diffuse and extends to the limbus. *(Courtesy of George B. Bartley, MD.)*

3. Radiographic evidence of TAO—unilateral/bilateral fusiform enlargement of one or more of the following (Figs 4-6 through 4-8):

   a. Medial rectus muscle
   b. Inferior rectus muscle
   c. Superior rectus/levator complex

If only orbital signs are present, the patient should continue to be observed for other orbital diseases and for the future development of a dysthyroid state.

Gerding MN, van der Meer JWC, Broenink M, Bakker O, Wiersinga WM, Prummel MF. Association of thyrotropin receptor antibodies with the clinical features of Graves' ophthalmopathy. *Clin Endocrinol.* 2000;52:267–271.

Mourits MP, Prummel MF, Wiersinga WM, Koornneef L. Clinical activity score as a guide in the management of patients with Graves' ophthalmopathy. *Clin Endocrinol.* 1997;47:9–14.

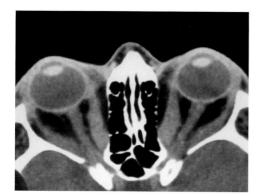

Figure 4-6 Extraocular muscle enlargement in TAO is characteristically fusiform and spares the tendons. *(Courtesy of Michael Kazim, MD.)*

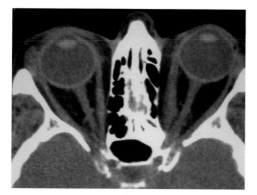

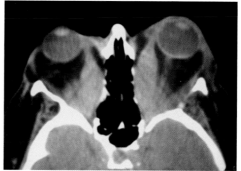

Figure 4-7 Some patients with TAO have relatively modest enlargement of the extraocular muscles but an increase in orbital fat, as shown in this CT scan. Note severe proptosis with straightening of the optic nerves. *(Courtesy of Michael Kazim, MD.)*

Figure 4-8 CT scan of a patient who has TAO and suffers from compressive optic neuropathy. Marked enlargement of the extraocular muscles with effacement of the perioptic fat is consistent with compressive optic neuropathy. *(Courtesy of Michael Kazim, MD.)*

Pathogenesis

During the last decade, the focus of in vitro research shifted attention away from the extraocular muscles/myocytes to the orbital fibroblasts as the primary target of the inflammatory process associated with TAO. Of particular importance is the recognition of the phenotypic difference of orbital fibroblasts that distinguishes them from fibroblasts derived from other sites in the body. Orbital fibroblasts—through the expression of characteristic surface receptors, gangliosides, and proinflammatory genes—play an active role in modulating the inflammatory process. Unlike fibroblasts from other parts of the body, orbital fibroblasts express CD40 receptors, generally found on B cells. When engaged by T cell–bound CD154, several fibroblast inflammatory genes are up-regulated, including interleukin-6 (Il-6), Il-8, and prostaglandin E_2 (PGE_2). In turn, synthesis of hyaluronan and glycosaminoglycan (GAG) is increased. The up-regulation of GAG synthesis is known to be elemental to the pathology of TAO, and it occurs at a rate that is 100-fold greater in orbital fibroblasts derived from patients with TAO than in abdominal fibroblasts in the same patients. This cascade of up-regulation is dampened by the addition of therapeutic levels of corticosteroids.

Orbital fibroblasts are embryologically derived from the neural crest and, as such, possess developmental plasticity. A subpopulation of orbital fibroblasts appears capable of undergoing adipocyte differentiation. It is believed that this response to the inflammatory matrix is responsible for the fatty hypertrophy that predominates in some patients, particularly those younger than 40 years.

The role of TSH-R has been investigated extensively. Though studies suggest the expression of TSH-R on all cells in the body, the role of TSH-R may be at the level of TSH-R–mRNA synthesis, which appears to be up-regulated in orbital fibroblasts. The effect of the up-regulation of the expression is not currently known. A circulating immunoglobulin (GD-IgG) is present in patients with active orbitopathy and acts through the IGF-1 receptor on orbital fibroblasts of patients with thyroid disease to stimulate hyaluronan synthesis. It is promising as a serologic marker of disease and as the potential target for therapeutically active blocking antibodies.

Bahn RS. Understanding the immunology of Graves' ophthalmopathy. Is it an autoimmune disease? *Endocrinol Metab Clin North Am.* 2000;29:287–296.

Kazim M, Goldberg RA, Smith TJ. Insights into the pathogenesis of thyroid-associated orbitopathy: evolving rationale for therapy. *Arch Ophthalmol.* 2002;120(3):380–386.

Wiersinga WM, Prummel MF. Pathogenesis of Graves' ophthalmopathy—current understanding [editorial]. *J Clin Endocrinol Metab.* 2001;86:501–503.

Epidemiology

A 1996 epidemiologic study of white American patients with TAO determined that the overall age-adjusted incidence rate for women was 16 cases per 100,000 population per year, whereas the rate for men was 3 cases per 100,000 population per year. TAO affects women approximately 6 times more frequently than men (86% versus 14% of cases, respectively). The peak incidence rates occurred in the age groups 40–44 years and 60–64 years in women and 45–49 years and 65–69 years in men. The median age at the time of diagnosis of TAO was 43 years (range, 8–88 years).

Clinical features

Among patients with TAO, approximately 90% have Graves hyperthyroidism, 1% have primary hypothyroidism, 3% have Hashimoto thyroiditis, and 6% are euthyroid. There is a close temporal relationship between the development of hyperthyroidism and TAO: in about 20% of patients, the diagnoses are made at the same time; in approximately 60% of patients, the eye disease occurs within 1 year of onset of the thyroid disease. Of those patients who have no history of abnormal thyroid function or regulation at the time of diagnosis of TAO, the risk of thyroid disease is approximately 25% within 1 year and 50% within 5 years. Although most patients with TAO have or will develop hyperthyroidism, only about 30% of patients with autoimmune hyperthyroidism have or will develop TAO.

Eyelid retraction is the most common ophthalmic feature of TAO, being present either unilaterally or bilaterally in more than 90% of patients at some point in their clinical course. Exophthalmos of 1 or both eyes affects approximately 60% of patients, restrictive extraocular myopathy is apparent in about 40% of patients, and optic nerve dysfunction occurs in 1 or both eyes in 6% of patients with TAO. Only 5% of patients have the complete constellation of classic findings: eyelid retraction, exophthalmos, optic nerve dysfunction, extraocular muscle involvement, and hyperthyroidism.

Upper eyelid retraction, either unilateral or bilateral, is documented in approximately 75% of patients at the time of diagnosis of TAO. Lid lag in downgaze also is a frequent early sign, being present either unilaterally or bilaterally in 50% of patients at the initial examination. The most frequent ocular symptom when TAO is first confirmed is dull, deep orbital pain or discomfort, which affects 30% of patients. Some degree of diplopia is noted by approximately 17% of patients, lacrimation or photophobia by 15%–20% of patients, and blurred vision by 7.5% of patients. Decreased vision attributable to optic neuropathy is present in less than 2% of eyes at the time of diagnosis of TAO.

Pretibial myxedema and acropachy accompany TAO in approximately 4% and 1% of patients, respectively, and are associated with a poor prognosis for the orbitopathy. Myasthenia gravis occurs in less than 1% of patients.

Bartley GB, Fatourechi V, Kadrmas EF, et al. Clinical features of Graves' ophthalmopathy in an incidence cohort. *Am J Ophthalmol.* 1996;121:284–290.

Treatment and prognosis

TAO is a self-limiting disease that on average lasts 1 year in nonsmokers and between 2 and 3 years in smokers, who are also up to 7 times more likely to develop the orbital manifestations of Graves disease. After the active disease plateaus, a quiescent burnt-out phase ensues. Reactivation of inflammation occurs in approximately 5%–10% of patients over their lifetime. Most patients with TAO require only supportive care, including use of topical ocular lubricants; in some cases, the use of topical cyclosporine has aided in reducing ocular surface irritation. Eating a reduced-salt diet limits water retention and orbital edema. Sleeping with the head of the bed elevated specifically reduces fluid retention within the orbit. Wearing wraparound sunglasses relieves symptoms of dry eye and photophobia. For those with diplopia, use of temporary prism lenses helps maintain binocular fusion during the active phase of the disease.

Poor prognostic features include smoking, rapidly progressive (typically congestive) orbitopathy, and the presence of dermopathy.

If orbital inflammation is severe, intervention may be necessary to prevent or ameliorate corneal exposure, globe subluxation, or optic neuropathy. Therapy usually is directed toward either decreasing orbital congestion and inflammation (by administration of systemic corticosteroids or by orbital radiotherapy) or expanding the orbital bony volume (by surgical orbital decompression).

Establishing a euthyroid state is an important part of the care of patients with TAO. Hyperthyroidism is most commonly treated with antithyroid drugs. If the patient does not tolerate the medications or if the medications fail to restore a persistent euthyroid state, the clinician usually uses radioactive iodine (RAI) as the next treatment modality. In some studies, TAO has been demonstrated to worsen after RAI treatment, presumably because of the release of TSH-R antigens, which incite an enhanced immune response. In addition, allowing a period of posttreatment hypothyroidism after RAI treatment may exacerbate ophthalmopathy via stimulation of TSH-R. Hyperthyroid patients with severe, active orbitopathy; those with elevated T_3 levels; and smokers appear to be at greatest risk for exacerbation of the orbitopathy after RAI treatment. Consequently, some patients are treated concurrently with prednisone. Although this may be a reasonable strategy for patients at high risk, the regular use of moderate-dose prednisone for 3 months, during which time the thyroid gland involutes, is not indicated for the average patient. Block-and-replace therapy with iodine 131 (^{131}I), methimazole, and thyroxine may prevent exacerbation of eye findings by limiting posttreatment TSH spikes. Patients with severe orbitopathy (rapidly progressive and congestive, with compressive optic neuropathy) may, as an alternative to RAI, benefit from thyroidectomy, which renders them euthyroid without extended antigen release.

Approximately 20% of patients with TAO undergo surgical treatment. In one review, 7% of patients underwent orbital decompression; 9%, strabismus surgery; and 13%, eyelid surgery. Only 2.5% required all 3 types of surgery. Men and older patients are more likely to have more severe orbitopathy requiring surgical intervention. Surgery should be delayed until the disease has stabilized, unless urgent intervention is required to reverse visual loss due to compressive optic neuropathy or corneal exposure unresponsive to maximal medical measures. Elective orbital decompression, strabismus surgery, and eyelid retraction repair are usually not considered until a euthyroid state has been maintained and the ophthalmic signs have been confirmed to be stable for 6–9 months.

Acute phase orbitopathy featuring compressive optic neuropathy is typically treated with oral corticosteroids. The usual starting dose is 1 mg/kg of prednisone. This dose is maintained for 2 to 4 weeks until a clinical response is appreciated. The dose is then reduced as rapidly as can be tolerated by the patient, based on the clinical response of optic nerve function. Though effective at reversing optic nerve compression, prednisone at these levels is poorly tolerated. There is an extensive list of potential systemic adverse effects, and these side effects limit the long-term use of prednisone. Thus, some authors have advocated the adjunctive use of orbital radiotherapy (2000 cGy). The mechanism for radiotherapy's effect on the orbit is not well understood, but beyond temporary lymphocyte sterilization, there is evidence that this dose induces terminal differentiation of fibroblasts and kills tissue-bound monocytes, which play an important role in antigen presentation.

A number of studies have demonstrated that the use of orbital radiotherapy reduces, by up to 90%, the need for acute phase surgical decompression to treat compressive optic neuropathy. A prospective clinical trial designed to assess the treatment results in patients with TAO followed 6 separate parameters (volume of muscle, volume of fat, proptosis, eyelid fissures, monocular range of motion, and diplopia fields). The treatment showed no statistically significant effect compared with the natural history of the disease. This trial excluded patients with optic neuropathy. Critics of the study have noted that the lack of apparent benefit can be ascribed to the inclusion of patients with inactive disease because the median time from onset of orbitopathy to radiation therapy was 1.3 years. Moreover, the sham-treated orbits in the study also failed to show any change in clinically measured parameters—further evidence of the stable phase of disease. Radiation therapy should be avoided in patients with diabetes or vasculitic disease, as the radiation may exacerbate retinopathy.

Orbital decompression, though historically indicated to treat optic neuropathy, severe orbital congestion, and advanced proptosis, has been used increasingly in recent years as an elective procedure to restore normal globe position in patients without sight-threatening ophthalmopathy. In the stable phase of disease, the surgical plan for decompression should be graded so that the greatest return to the premorbid state is provided and the risk of the procedure minimized. Preoperative review of the patients' old photos allows the surgeon to determine the amount of decompressive effect desired. The preoperative CT scan details the relative contributions of extraocular muscle enlargement and fat expansion to the proptosis (see Figs 4-6 through 4-8). Typically, there is a difference in the phenotype of the orbitopathy based on the patient's age. Patients younger than 40 years demonstrate enlargement of the orbital fat compartment, whereas those older than 40 typically show more significant extraocular muscle enlargement. This determines the effectiveness of bone vs fat decompression surgery. Orbital decompression may alter extraocular motility and, if indicated, should precede strabismus surgery.

If intractable diplopia in primary gaze or in the reading position persists, then strabismus surgery may be helpful in restoring single vision. Similarly, procedures to correct eyelid retraction may decrease corneal exposure and help improve appearance. Because extraocular muscle surgery may affect eyelid retraction, eyelid surgery should be undertaken last.

Gorman CA, Garrity JA, Fatourechi V, et al. A prospective, randomized, double-blind, placebo-controlled study of orbital radiotherapy for Graves' ophthalmopathy. *Ophthalmology.* 2001;108:1523–1534.

Kacker A, Kazim M, Murphy M, Trokel S, Close LG. "Balanced" orbital decompression for severe Graves' orbitopathy: technique with treatment algorithm. *Otolaryngol Head Neck Surg.* 2003;128(2):228–235.

Kazim M. Perspective—Part II: radiotherapy for Graves orbitopathy: the Columbia University experience. *Ophthal Plast Reconstr Surg.* 2002;18(3):173–174.

Kazim M, Trokel S, Moore S. Treatment of acute Graves orbitopathy. *Ophthalmology.* 1991;98(9):1443–1448.

Mourits MP, van Kempen-Harteveld ML, Garcia MB, Koppeschaar HP, Tick L, Terwee CB. Radiotherapy for Graves' orbitopathy: randomized placebo-controlled study. *Lancet.* 2000;355:1505–1509.

Trokel S, Kazim M, Moore S. Orbital fat removal. Decompression for Graves orbitopathy. *Ophthalmology.* 1993;100(5):674–682.

A long-term follow-up study of patients in an incidence cohort demonstrated that visual loss from optic neuropathy was uncommon and that persistent diplopia usually could be treated with prism spectacles. Subjectively, however, more than 50% of patients thought that their eyes looked abnormal, and 38% of patients were dissatisfied with the appearance of their eyes. Thus, although few patients experience long-term functional impairment from TAO, the psychological and aesthetic sequelae of the disease are considerable. Orbital decompression surgery is discussed in Chapter 7.

See Key Points 4-1.

Bartalena L, Marcocci C, Bogazzi F, et al. Relation between therapy for hyperthyroidism and the course of Graves' ophthalmopathy. *N Engl J Med.* 1998;338:73–78.

Bartley GB, Fatourechi V, Kadrmas EF, et al. Long-term follow-up of Graves ophthalmopathy in an incidence cohort. *Ophthalmology.* 1996;103:958–962.

KEY POINTS 4-1

Thyroid-associated orbitopathy (TAO) The following list highlights the essential points for the ophthalmologist to remember about TAO.

- Eyelid retraction is the most common clinical feature (and TAO is the most common cause of eyelid retraction).
- TAO is the most common cause of unilateral or bilateral proptosis.
- TAO is 6 times more common in women than in men.
- TAO is associated with hyperthyroidism in 90% of patients, but 6% are euthyroid.
- Severity of ophthalmopathy usually does not parallel serum levels of T_4 or T_3.
- Smoking is associated with increased risk and severity of TAO.
- Orbitopathy may be markedly asymmetric.
- Urgent care may be required for optic neuropathy or severe proptosis with corneal decompensation.
- If surgery is needed, the usual order is orbital decompression, followed by strabismus surgery, followed by eyelid retraction repair (see Chapter 7).
- Systemic corticosteroid treatment is usually reserved for patients with compressive optic neuropathy so that dysfunction is reduced while the patients await orbital radiotherapy or orbital decompression.

Nonspecific Orbital Inflammation

Orbital inflammation is typically an idiopathic process; less frequently, a specific local or systemic disease may be identified as the causative agent.

Both children and adults may be afflicted by idiopathic inflammations of the orbital tissues (Fig 4-9). *Nonspecific orbital inflammation (NSOI)* (also known as *orbital pseudotumor, idiopathic orbital inflammation,* and *orbital inflammatory syndrome*) is currently defined as an idiopathic tumorlike inflammation consisting of a pleomorphic cellular response and a fibrovascular tissue reaction. NSOI is usually confined to the orbit but may extend to the sinuses and the intracranial space. It has a variable but generally self-limited course.

The subclassification of NSOI is made on the basis of the anatomical target. The inflammation can primarily affect the lacrimal gland (dacryoadenitis), one or more extraocular muscles (myositis), the sclera and posterior tenons (scleritis), or the optic nerve sheath (inflammatory optic neuritis), or it can be restricted to the superior orbital fissure and cavernous sinus (Tolosa-Hunt syndrome). Alternatively, the process may diffusely involve the orbital fatty tissues.

Symptoms depend on the involved tissue; however, deep-rooted, boring pain is a typical feature of the process. Extraocular muscle restriction, proptosis, conjunctival inflammation, and chemosis are common, as are eyelid erythema and soft tissue swelling. Pain associated with ocular rotations suggests myositis. Visual acuity may be impaired if the optic nerve or posterior sclera is involved.

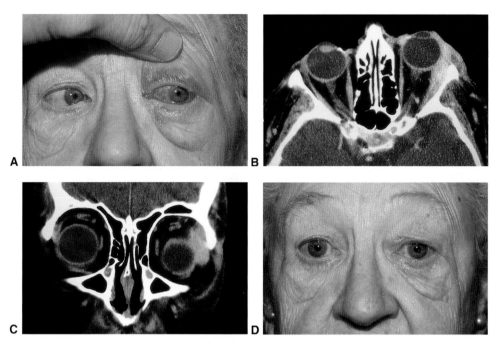

Figure 4-9 **A,** Acute onset of left eyelid inflammation, proptosis, pain, and left lateral rectus paresis. **B,** Axial CT scan demonstrating left eye proptosis and hazy inflammatory swelling of lateral rectus and lacrimal gland consistent with the diagnosis of orbital inflammatory disease. **C,** Coronal CT scan demonstrating inflammatory mass adjacent to the lateral rectus. **D,** Marked improvement of inflammatory changes following a 48-hour course of oral prednisone. *(Courtesy of Robert C. Kersten, MD.)*

A typical clinical presentation is often diagnostic and orbital imaging may confirm the diagnosis. Prompt response to systemic steroids helps confirm the diagnosis, although the physician must be aware that the inflammation associated with other orbital processes (eg, metastases, ruptured dermoid cysts, infections) may also improve with systemic steroid administration. A thorough systemic evaluation should be undertaken if there is any uncertainty regarding the diagnosis. Not all patients with NSOI present with the classic signs and symptoms. There may be atypical pain, limited inflammatory signs, or a fibrotic presentation termed *sclerosing NSOI*. Such lesions more commonly require biopsy for diagnosis. Otherwise, biopsies are reserved for cases that fail to respond rapidly to corticosteroids or for those with recurrence after treatment is discontinued. Simultaneous bilateral idiopathic inflammation in adults suggests the possibility of systemic vasculitis. In children, however, approximately one third of cases of NSOI are bilateral and are rarely associated with systemic disorders, even though half of the children have headache, fever, vomiting, abdominal pain, and lethargy.

Biopsy is not necessary in all cases because the findings on clinical, ultrasonographic, and radiologic (CT and MRI) examination may be sufficiently diagnostic to institute therapy. Peripheral blood eosinophilia, elevated erythrocyte sedimentation rate and antinuclear antibody levels, and mild cerebrospinal fluid pleocytosis can be found. In dacryoadenitis, CT reveals diffuse enlargement of the lacrimal gland (the most common anatomical target area to be affected). CT, MRI, and ultrasonography reveal thickening of the extraocular muscles if the inflammatory response has a myositic component. The extraocular muscle tendons of insertion may be thickened in up to 50% of patients with NSOI; in contrast, TAO typically spares the muscle insertions. An inflammatory infiltrate of the retrobulbar fat pad is commonly seen, and contrast enhancement of the sclera may be caused by tenonitis (producing the *ring sign*). B-scan ultrasonography often shows an acoustically hollow area corresponding to an edematous Tenon's capsule.

Histopathologically, NSOI is characterized by a pleomorphic cellular infiltrate consisting of lymphocytes, plasma cells, and eosinophils with variable degrees of reactive fibrosis. The fibrosis becomes more marked as the process becomes more chronic, and early or acute cases are usually more responsive to steroids than are the advanced stages associated with fibrosis. Although, historically, there was a tendency to group hypercellular lymphoid proliferations with the pseudotumors, hypercellular lymphoid proliferations are now recognized as different clinical and histopathologic entities. The sclerosing subtype demonstrates a predominance of fibrosis with sparse inflammation.

Treatment

Initial therapy consists of systemic corticosteroids. Beginning daily adult doses are typically 1 mg/kg of prednisone. Acute cases generally respond rapidly with an abrupt resolution of the associated pain. The use of steroids can be tapered as soon as the clinical response is complete, but this tapering should be done more slowly below about 40 mg/day and very slowly below 20 mg/day, based on the clinical response. Rapid reduction of systemic steroids may cause a recurrence of inflammatory symptoms and signs. Bilateral cases may require more prolonged courses of steroids than unilateral cases. Topical corticosteroid eyedrops may be helpful in decreasing the superficial inflammatory reaction and the anterior chamber reaction seen in some patients. Some investigators believe that the use of pulse-dosed IV dexamethasone followed by oral prednisone may produce clinical improvement when oral prednisone alone fails to control the inflammation. Because other pathologic orbital processes may be masked by steroids, an incomplete therapeutic response or recurrent disease suggests the need for orbital biopsy, which can provide histopathologic confirmation and exclude specific inflammatory diseases. After the diagnosis is confirmed, orbital irradiation (2000 cGy), antimetabolites or alkylating agents such as methotrexate or cyclophosphamide, and continued steroid therapy may be useful for controlling the disease. Rarely, orbital decompression is necessary if optic nerve compression is progressive.

The approach to pediatric cases differs, as orbital radiotherapy is typically reserved for patients older than 30 years. Most recently, new anti-inflammatory agents, including TNF-α blockers, have been used in recurrent cases or for those patients in whom corticosteroids are contraindicated. The risk profile of this class of drugs is still developing, but to date, anti-inflammatory drugs have proven effective in sparing steroid toxicity.

Sclerosing NSOI is a distinct subset of disease, with predominant fibrosis and minimal cellular inflammation. It responds poorly to steroids and to low-dose (2000 cGy) radiotherapy and typically requires more aggressive immunosuppression with cyclosporine, methotrexate, or cyclophosphamide.

Adams AB, Kazim M, Lehman TJ. Treatment of orbital myositis with adalimumab (Humira). *J Rheumatol.* 2005;32:1374–1375.

Mombaerts I, Goldschmeding R, Schlingemann RO, Koornneef L. What is orbital pseudotumor? *Surv Ophthalmol.* 1996;41:66–78.

Mombaerts I, Koornneef L. Current status in the treatment of orbital myositis. *Ophthalmology.* 1997;104:402–408.

Rootman J, McCarthy M, White V, Harris G, Kennerdell J. Idiopathic sclerosing inflammation of the orbit: a distinct clinicopathologic entity. *Ophthalmology.* 1994;101:570–584.

Cocaine-Induced Sclerosing Orbital Inflammation

A recently identified cause of progressive vasculopathic sclerosing sino-orbital disease is the use of inhaled cocaine. Though typically resulting in nasal septal perforation, in some cases the vascular compromise caused by cocaine use can incite progressive destruction of the sinus walls and induce sparse, chronic inflammatory infiltration of associated orbital soft tissue. Clinically, the patient suffers recurring bouts of orbital inflammation. The inflammation may initially be unilateral but most commonly is ultimately bilateral. There is associated pain that results from the induced ischemia. As the extraocular muscle fibrosis progresses, diplopia becomes evident. In the most severe cases, optic neuropathy may occur as a consequence of ischemia or traction. Radiographic evidence of the disease can be found on CT scans, which show the destruction of the nasal septum and the sinus walls. Orbital soft tissue changes are seen as a late radiographic sign.

The differential diagnosis includes prior infectious sinusitis with extensive obliterative sinus surgery, Wegener granulomatosis, lethal midline granuloma, and fungal sinusitis. Often, the history of cocaine use is difficult to elicit from the patient; consequently, the diagnostic and therapeutic course may be unnecessarily lengthened before the correct etiology is identified.

Treatment is limited to abstention from cocaine use. There are no measures to reverse the fibrosis; however, the resultant strabismus may be corrected when the orbital inflammation has resolved. Secondary infections can arise because of the nasal mucosal ischemia.

Tse DT, Goodwin WJ, Johnson T, Gilberg S, Meldrum M. Use of galeal or pericranial flaps for reconstruction or orbital and eyelid defects. *Arch Ophthalmol.* 1997;115(7):932–937.

Underdahl JP, Chiou AG. Preseptal cellulitis and orbital wall destruction secondary to nasal cocaine abuse. *Am J Ophthalmol.* 1998;125(2):266–268.

Sarcoidosis

Sarcoidosis is a multisystem disease of unknown origin. It occurs most commonly in persons of African or Scandinavian descent. The lungs are most commonly involved, but the orbit may be affected. Histopathologically, the lesions are composed of noncaseating collections of epithelioid histiocytes in a granulomatous pattern. A mononuclear inflammation often appears at the periphery of the granuloma. The lacrimal gland is the site most frequently affected within the orbit, and the inflammation is typically bilateral. Gallium scanning of the lacrimal glands is nonspecific but has been reported to demonstrate lacrimal gland involvement in 80% of patients with systemic sarcoidosis, although only 7% of patients have clinically detectable enlargement of the lacrimal glands. Other orbital soft tissues, including the extraocular muscles and optic nerve, may very rarely be involved. Infrequently, sinus involvement with adjacent lytic bone lesions spills over into the orbit.

A biopsy specimen of the affected lacrimal gland or of a suspicious conjunctival lesion may establish the diagnosis. Random conjunctival biopsies have a low yield. Chest radiography or CT to detect hilar adenopathy or pulmonary infiltrates, blood tests for angiotensin-converting enzyme, and measurement of serum lysozyme and serum calcium levels may be used to establish the diagnosis of sarcoidosis. As Gallium scanning is nonspecific, bronchoscopy with washings and biopsy may be needed to confirm the diagnosis.

Isolated orbital lesions demonstrating noncaseating granulomas can occur without associated systemic disease. This condition is termed *orbital sarcoid.*

See BCSC Section 5, *Neuro-Ophthalmology,* and Section 9, *Intraocular Inflammation and Uveitis,* for a more extensive discussion (including clinical photographs) of sarcoidosis.

Vasculitis

The vasculitides are inflammatory conditions in which the vessel walls are infiltrated by inflammatory cells. These lesions represent a type III hypersensitivity reaction to circulating immune complexes and usually lead to significant ocular or orbital morbidity. They are often associated with systemic vasculitis. The following discussion focuses mainly on the orbital manifestations of the vasculitides. See also BCSC Section 1, *Update on General Medicine,* and Section 5, *Neuro-Ophthalmology.*

Giant cell arteritis

Although the orbital vessels are inflamed in giant cell arteritis (GCA; also known as *temporal arteritis*), it is not typically thought of as an orbital disorder. The vasculitis affects the aorta and branches of the external and internal carotid arteries and vertebral arteries but usually spares the intracranial carotid branches, which lack an elastic lamina. Symptoms of visual loss are caused by central retinal artery occlusion or ischemic optic neuropathy, and diplopia may result from ischemic dysfunction of other cranial nerves. Symptoms of headache, scalp tenderness, jaw claudication, or malaise are often present. The erythrocyte sedimentation rate is markedly elevated in 90% of patients, and diagnostic confidence is increased if the C-reactive protein level and the platelet count are elevated. Temporal artery biopsy usually provides a definitive diagnosis, although bilateral biopsies are sometimes necessary due to intervals of normal tissue between pathologic segments. GCA should be managed as an ophthalmic emergency. Failure to diagnose and treat GCA immediately after loss of vision in 1 eye is particularly tragic because timely treatment with corticosteroids usually prevents an attack in the second eye. Generalized orbital ischemia resulting from temporal arteritis is a rare manifestation of the disease.

Goodwin JA. Temporal arteritis: diagnosis and management. *Focal Points: Clinical Modules for Ophthalmologists.* San Francisco: American Academy of Ophthalmology; 1992, module 2.

Polyarteritis nodosa

Like giant cell arteritis, polyarteritis nodosa is a vasculitis that may affect orbital vessels but does not usually cause orbital disease. Instead, the ophthalmic manifestations are the result of retinal and choroidal infarction. In this multisystem disease, small and medium-size arteries are affected by inflammation characterized by the presence of neutrophils and eosinophils, with necrosis of the muscularis layer.

Vasculitis associated with connective tissue disorders

A number of connective tissue disorders may be associated with systemic vasculitis, most commonly systemic lupus erythematosus, dermatomyositis, and rheumatoid arthritis. Vasculitis in these entities primarily affects retinal vessels and less often may affect conjunctival vessels. Symptomatic orbital vasculitis is rare.

Wegener granulomatosis

In Wegener granulomatosis, the disease process is characterized by necrotizing granulomatous vasculitis, lesions of the upper and lower respiratory tract, necrotizing glomerulonephritis, and a small-vessel vasculitis that may affect any organ system, including the orbit. Clinically, the full-blown syndrome includes sinus mucosal involvement with bone erosion, tracheobronchial necrotic lesions, cavitary lung lesions, and glomerulonephritis (Fig 4-10). The orbit and nasolacrimal drainage system may be involved by extension from the surrounding sinuses. Up to 25% of patients with Wegener granulomatosis have associated scleritis. Limited forms of the disease have been described in which the renal component is absent or in which there is solitary orbital involvement by a granulomatous and lymphocytic vasculitis. Such isolated orbital involvement may be unilateral or bilateral, may lack frank necrotizing vasculitis on histopathologic examination, and, in the absence of respiratory tract and renal findings, may be difficult to diagnose.

Characteristic pathologic findings consist of the triad of vasculitis, granulomatous inflammation (with or without giant cells), and tissue necrosis. Often, only 1 or 2 of these 3 are present on extrapulmonary biopsies. Antineutrophil cytoplasmic antibody (ANCA) titers measured by serum immunofluorescence have been shown to be associated with certain systemic vasculitides. The ANCA test distinguishes 2 types of immunofluorescence patterns. Diffuse granular fluorescence within the cytoplasm (c-ANCA) is highly specific for Wegener granulomatosis. This pattern is caused by autoantibodies directed against proteinase 3, which can also be detected by enzyme-linked immunosorbent assay (ELISA). Fluorescence surrounding the nucleus (p-ANCA) is an artifact of ethanol fixation and can be caused by autoantibodies against many different target antigens. This finding is therefore nonspecific and needs to be confirmed by ELISA for ANCA reacting with myeloperoxidase (MPO-ANCA). MPO-ANCA testing has a high specificity for small-vessel vasculitis. Absolute levels of ANCA do not imply disease severity or activity, but changing titers can give a general idea of disease activity or response to therapy. c-ANCA findings may be negative early in the course of the disease, especially in the absence of multisystem involvement.

Wegener granulomatosis may proceed to a fulminant, life-threatening course. Treatment relies on immunosuppression, usually cyclophosphamide, and should be coordinated with an

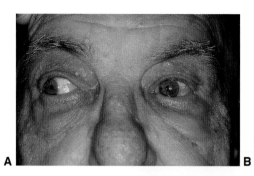
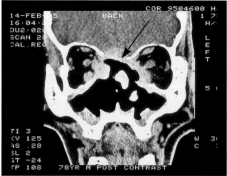

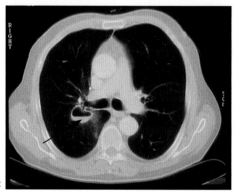

Figure 4-10 Wegener granulomatosis. **A,** Restrictive strabismus due to inflammatory tissue extending into medial aspects of orbit. **B,** Coronal CT scan showing extensive destruction of the nasal and sinus cavities with inflammatory tissue extending into orbits and brain *(arrow)*. **C,** CT of chest showing cavitary lung lesions *(arrow)*. *(Courtesy of Jeffrey Nerad, MD.)*

immunologist. Treatment with corticosteroids alone is associated with a significantly higher rate of mortality. Long-term treatment with trimethoprim-sulfamethoxazole (Bactrim) appears to suppress disease activity in some patients.

Thrombophlebitis

Thrombophlebitis of the orbital veins is an unusual condition characterized by conjunctival congestion, pain, and occasional varicosities of the eyelids. Motility disturbances and decreased vision may result from inflammation of the veins supplying the extraocular muscle and optic nerve. The condition may be idiopathic or associated with spread of a periorbital infection through the angular vein or from the cavernous sinus forward via the supraorbital veins.

CHAPTER 5

Orbital Neoplasms

Congenital Orbital Tumors

Hamartomas and Choristomas

Hamartomas are anomalous growths of tissue consisting only of mature cells normally found at the involved site. Classic examples are capillary hemangiomas and the characteristic lesions of neurofibromatosis. *Choristomas* are tissue anomalies characterized by types of cells not normally found at the involved site. Classic examples are dermoid cysts, epidermoid cysts, lipodermoids, and teratomas. These congenital and juvenile tumors are discussed further in BCSC Section 6, *Pediatric Ophthalmology and Strabismus*.

Dermoid cyst

Dermoid and epidermoid cysts are among the most common orbital tumors of childhood. These cysts are present congenitally and they enlarge progressively. The more superficial cysts usually become symptomatic in childhood, but deeper orbital dermoids may not become clinically evident until adulthood. Dermoid cysts are lined by keratinizing epidermis with dermal appendages, such as hair follicles and sebaceous glands. They contain an admixture of oil and keratin. In contrast, epidermoid cysts are lined by epidermis only and are usually filled with keratin; they do not contain dermal appendages.

Preseptal orbital dermoid cysts occur most commonly in the area of the lateral brow adjacent to the frontozygomatic suture; less often they may be found in the medial upper eyelid adjacent to the frontoethmoidal suture. Dermoid cysts commonly present as palpable smooth, painless, oval masses that enlarge slowly. They may be freely mobile or they may be fixed to periosteum at the underlying suture. If the dermoid occurs more posteriorly, in the temporal fossa, computed tomography (CT) is often indicated to rule out dumbbell expansion through the suture into the underlying orbit. Medial lesions in the infant should be distinguished from congenital encephaloceles and dacryoceles.

Dermoid cysts that do not present until adulthood often are not palpable because they are situated posteriorly in the orbit, usually in the superior and temporal portions adjacent to the bony sutures. The globe and adnexa may be displaced, causing progressive proptosis, and erosion or remodeling of bone can occur. Long-standing dermoids in the superior orbit may completely erode the orbital roof and become adherent to the dura mater. An uncommon variant is an intradiploic epidermoid cyst, which tends to present late, after it has broken through and expanded the bony perimeter. Less commonly, the clinical presentation may be orbital inflammation, which is incited by leakage of oil and keratin from the cyst. Expansion of the dermoid cyst and inflammatory response to leakage may result in an orbito-cutaneous fistula, which may also result following incomplete surgical removal.

Management Dermoid cysts are usually removed surgically. Because dermoids that present in childhood are often superficial, they can be excised through an incision placed in the upper eyelid crease or directly over the lesion (Fig 5-1). If possible, the cyst wall should be maintained during surgery. Rupture of the cyst can lead to an acute inflammatory process if part of the cyst wall or any of the contents remain within the eyelid or orbit. If the cyst wall is ruptured, the surgeon should remove the entire wall and then thoroughly irrigate the wound to remove all cyst contents. Surgical removal may be difficult if the cyst has leaked preoperatively and adhesions have developed.

Kersten RC. The eyelid crease approach to superficial lateral dermoid cysts. *J Pediatr Ophthalmol Strabismus.* 1988;25:48–51.

Shields JA, Kaden IH, Eagle RC Jr, Shields CL. Orbital dermoid cysts: clinicopathologic correlations, classification, and management. *Ophthal Plast Reconstr Surg.* 1997;13:265–276.

Lipodermoid

Lipodermoids are solid tumors usually located beneath the conjunctiva over the globe's lateral surface (Fig 5-2). These benign lesions may have deep extensions that can extend to the levator and extraocular muscles. Superficially, lipodermoids may have fine hairs that can be irritating to patients. These tumors typically require no treatment. If the lesion is large and cosmetically objectionable, only the anterior, visible portion should be excised; the overlying conjunctiva should be preserved, if possible. Care must be taken so that damage to the lacrimal gland ducts, extraocular muscles, and the levator aponeurosis is avoided. Lesions that may simulate lipodermoids are prolapsed orbital fat, prolapsed palpebral lobe of the lacrimal gland, and lymphomas (such processes are generally found only in adults).

Fry CL, Leone CR Jr. Safe management of dermolipomas. *Arch Ophthalmol.* 1994;112:1114–1116.

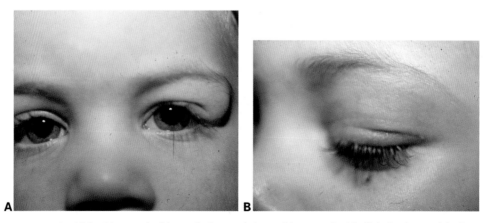

Figure 5-1 A child with a typical laterally located dermoid tumor (epithelial choristoma) before surgery **(A)** and after excision through a lateral lid crease incision **(B)**. *(Courtesy of Michael Kazim, MD.)*

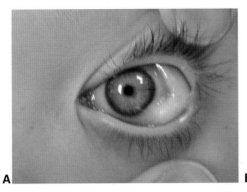
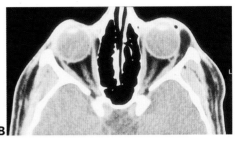

Figure 5-2 **A,** Lipodermoid of left lateral orbit. **B,** CT scan demonstrating lipodermoid, largely fat density in this case. *(Part A courtesy of Michael Kazim, MD. Part B courtesy of Jeffrey A. Nerad, MD.)*

Teratoma

Teratomas are rare tumors that arise from all 3 germinal layers (ectoderm, mesoderm, and endoderm). These tumors are usually cystic and can cause dramatic proptosis at birth. The globe and optic nerve may as a consequence be maldeveloped. Exenteration is sometimes performed because of the fear of malignancy. Some cystic teratomas can be removed and ocular function preserved.

Vascular Tumors

Capillary Hemangiomas

Capillary hemangiomas are common primary benign tumors of the orbit in children (Fig 5-3). They should be distinguished from cavernous hemangiomas (discussed next), which are the most common benign orbital tumors in adults. Capillary hemangiomas are seen primarily in children in the first year of life, often appearing in the first week or two after birth and enlarging dramatically over the first 6–12 months of life. They are more common in girls and in premature newborns. After the first year, these vascular tumors begin to involute; 75% of lesions resolve during the next 4 years of life.

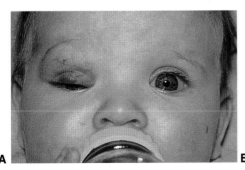
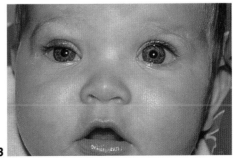

Figure 5-3 **A,** Capillary hemangioma of right upper eyelid. **B,** Marked regression of capillary hemangioma, 1 week after injection of steroid into lesion. *(Courtesy of Robert C. Kersten, MD.)*

The clinical appearance of a periorbital capillary hemangioma depends on the depth of the tumor under the skin. Most capillary hemangiomas are superficial and involve the skin, producing an elevated red discoloration with a dimpled texture. Hemangiomas located deeper within the orbit may cause a bluish discoloration or may present merely as a progressively enlarging mass without any overlying skin change. A rapidly growing mass may suggest a rhabdomyosarcoma. CT, though often helpful, cannot always distinguish between these 2 entities. Magnetic resonance imaging can be used to help distinguish among capillary hemangioma, venous malformation, and arteriovenous malformation, as it better demonstrates the characteristic fine intralesional vascular channels and also defines the speed of blood flowing within the lesion. Capillary hemangiomas usually have high blood flow derived from multiple fine feeder vessels.

Capillary hemangiomas have a propensity for the head and neck region and, in particular, the superonasal quadrant of the orbit and medial upper eyelid. Periocular hemangiomas are commonly associated with hemangiomas on other parts of the body. Capillary hemangiomas that involve the neck can compromise the airway and lead to respiratory obstruction. Multiple large visceral capillary hemangiomas can also produce thrombocytopenia (Kasabach-Merritt syndrome). Capillary hemangiomas of the eyelids and orbit may cause anisometropia, strabismus, or deprivation amblyopia. Cosmetic deformity is often significant.

Management

Patients with capillary hemangiomas should undergo close monitoring of visual acuity, with prompt amblyopia therapy as indicated. Ophthalmic indications for treatment of capillary hemangiomas are anisometropia, strabismus, and amblyopia. Severe disfigurement may necessitate therapy, but treatment should be deferred until it is clear that the natural course of the lesion will not lead to the desired result.

When therapy is indicated, initial treatment consists of local steroid injection, usually an equal mixture of 0.5 mL betamethasone (6 mg/mL) and 0.5 mL triamcinolone (40 mg/mL). This therapy is often dramatically successful. However, adverse effects include necrosis of the skin overlying the hemangioma, subcutaneous fat atrophy, systemic growth retardation, and embolic visual loss. Repeated injections may be necessary. Systemic steroids have also been used, especially in lesions that extend more deeply into the orbit. Injecting deep orbital lesions carries a higher risk of orbital hemorrhage and retinal emboli. The use of systemic steroids poses a slightly higher risk of systemic side effects. Whenever steroids are used as therapy for children, a pediatrician familiar with this therapy should be involved. Lesions that are smaller, those that are subcutaneous and nodular, and those that are refractory to steroids can be managed with surgical excision. Meticulous hemostasis must be maintained during the surgery. The use of systemic interferon-α has been reported; however, the systemic side effects have been significant and poorly tolerated in most cases. Radiation therapy has also been used, but it has the potential to cause cataract formation, bony hypoplasia, and future malignancy. Pulsed-dye laser therapy has not been shown to have any efficacy. High-potency topical corticosteroid (clobetasole) has shown efficacy in the treatment of superficial lesions. Sclerosing solutions are not recommended because of the severe scarring that results.

Cruz OA, Zarnegar SR, Myers SE. Treatment of periocular capillary hemangioma with topical clobetasol propionate. *Ophthalmology.* 1995;102(12):2012–2015.

Haik BG, Karcioglu ZA, Gordon RA, Pechous BP. Capillary hemangioma (infantile periocular hemangioma). *Surv Ophthalmol.* 1994;38:399–426.

Walker RS, Custer PL, Nerad JA. Surgical excision of periorbital capillary hemangiomas. *Ophthalmology.* 1994;101:1333–1340.

Cavernous Hemangioma

Cavernous hemangiomas are the most common benign neoplasms of the orbit in adults (Fig 5-4). Middle-aged women are most commonly affected. Proptosis is usually slowly progressive, although growth may accelerate if the patient is pregnant. Retinal striae, hyperopia, optic nerve compression, increased intraocular pressure, and strabismus may

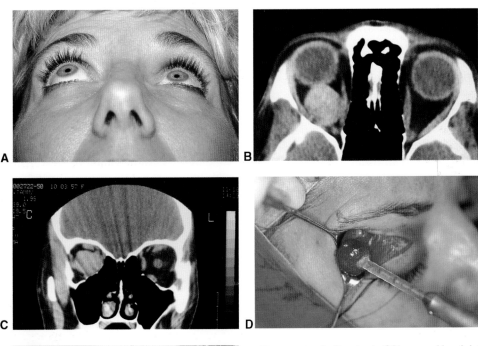

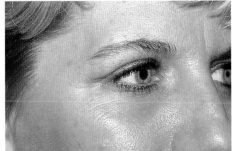

Figure 5-4 **A,** Proptosis OD caused by right orbital cavernous hemangioma. **B,** Axial CT scan showing large, well-circumscribed cavernous hemangioma within the muscle cone. **C,** Coronal CT scan demonstrates that the optic nerve is displaced supero-nasally by the mass. **D,** Lateral orbitotomy through an upper eyelid crease incision allows complete removal of the cavernous hemangioma (here affixed to a cryoprobe). **E,** Postoperative appearance with excellent camouflage of the healed incision within the eyelid crease. *(Courtesy of Robert C. Kersten, MD.)*

develop. The diagnosis can usually be established by CT, which shows a homogeneously enhanced, well-encapsulated mass. Old lesions may contain radiodense phleboliths. MRI demonstrates an enhancing lesion with small intralesional vascular channels containing slowly flowing blood. Arteriography and venography usually are not useful in diagnosis because the lesion has a very limited communication with the systemic circulation.

Histopathologically, the lesions are encapsulated and are composed of large cavernous spaces containing red blood cells. The walls of the spaces contain smooth muscle.

Management

Treatment consists of surgical excision if the lesion compromises ocular function. The surgical approach is dictated by the location of the lesion. Coronal imaging is important in determining the position of the cavernous hemangioma relative to the optic nerve. These tumors rarely undergo spontaneous involution.

Hemangiopericytoma

Hemangiopericytomas are uncommon encapsulated, hypervascular, hypercellular lesions that appear in middle age. Hemangiopericytomas resemble cavernous hemangiomas on contrast-enhanced CT and may look blue in surgery. MRI often also fails to distinguish the 2 lesions. Hemangiopericytomas are composed of plump pericytes that surround a rich capillary network. These lesions should be completely excised because they may recur, undergo malignant degeneration, and metastasize. Histopathologically, these lesions are unique in that microscopically "benign" lesions may recur and metastasize, whereas microscopically "malignant" lesions may remain localized. There is no correlation between the mitotic rate and the clinical behavior.

Lymphangioma

A lymphangioma is a relatively uncommon tumor that usually becomes apparent in the first decade of life. It may occur in the conjunctiva, eyelids, orbit, oropharynx, or sinuses. Lymphangiomas often enlarge during upper respiratory tract infections, probably because of the response of the lymphoid tissues within the lesion. They may present with sudden proptosis caused by spontaneous intralesional hemorrhage. The histogenesis of lymphangiomas remains unclear, but they are thought to represent combined vascular malformations with both venous and lymphatic components.

Histologically, these tumors are characterized by large, serum-filled spaces that are lined by flattened, delicate endothelial cells. The endothelial spaces have no pericytes or smooth muscle in their walls. Scattered follicles of lymphoid tissues are found in the interstitium. The tumors have an infiltrative pattern and are not encapsulated.

The natural history of lymphangiomas varies and is unpredictable. Some are localized and slowly progressive, whereas many of these lesions diffusely infiltrate orbital structures and may inexorably enlarge. A lymphangioma can present abruptly as a mass lesion if there is hemorrhage from interstitial capillaries. Blood may become loculated, leading to the formation of chocolate cysts containing old, dark blood. Ultrasonography, CT, or MRI may be useful for localizing these cysts. MRI may demonstrate pathognomonic features

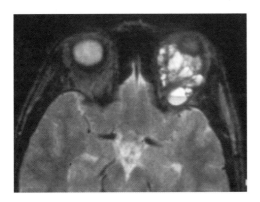

Figure 5-5 MR of a large multicystic lymphangioma of the left orbit. Note the fluid–fluid layering within some of the cysts—the result of intralesional hemorrhage. *(Courtesy of Michael Kazim, MD.)*

(multiple grapelike cystic lesions with fluid–fluid layering of the serum and red blood cells), confirming the diagnosis (Fig 5-5).

Management

In blood cysts associated with lymphangiomas, spontaneous regression is common. Thus, surgical intervention should be deferred unless vision is affected. If optic neuropathy or corneal ulceration threatens vision, aspiration of blood through a hollow-bore needle or by open surgical exploration can be attempted. Unfortunately, there is a high incidence of recurrent hemorrhage within lymphangiomas. Whenever possible, orbital hemorrhage from a lymphangioma is allowed to resorb spontaneously.

While lymphangiomas, especially those located anteriorly, often diffusely infiltrate the orbital structures, some posterior orbital lymphangiomas are more circumscribed and thus are amenable to total or subtotal surgical excision. Because of the infiltrating nature of lymphangioma, a subtotal resection is generally needed to avoid sacrificing important structures.

The carbon-dioxide and contact Nd:YAG lasers are useful adjuncts for surgery of the more solid and vascular lymphangiomas. Laser therapy improves hemostasis and it also can be used to cause shrinkage and scarring of some unresectable areas of tumor. Bipolar cautery can also be applied to shrink the tumor during surgical excision. The diaphanous cystic lesions can be more easily and completely removed if first injected with Tisseel, which helps stabilize and define the wall of the lesion.

In more extensive diffuse lesions of the orbit, a transcranial approach with removal of the orbital roof provides wide exposure and may better allow total or subtotal excision. In some patients, performing an orbital decompression to allow the globe to return to a more normal position may be preferable to attempting to excise an infiltrative vascular lesion.

It has been reported that noncontiguous intracranial vascular malformation may occur in up to 25% of patients with orbital lymphangiomas. These lesions have a low rate of spontaneous hemorrhage and are not treated prophylactically.

Boulos PR, Harissi-Dagher M, Kavalec C, Hardy I, Codère F. Intralesional injection of Tisseel fibrin glue for resection of lymphangiomas and other thin-walled orbital cysts. *Ophthal Plast Reconstr Surg.* 2005;21(3):171–176.

Harris GJ. Orbital vascular malformations: a consensus statement on terminology and its clinical implications. Orbital Society. *Am J Ophthalmol.* 1999;127:453–455.

Harris GJ, Sakol PJ, Bonavolonta G, De Conciliis C. An analysis of thirty cases of orbital lymphangioma: pathophysiologic considerations and management recommendations. *Ophthalmology.* 1990;97:1583–1592.

Kazim M, Kennerdell JS, Rothfus W, Marquardt M. Orbital lymphangioma: correlation of magnetic resonance images and intraoperative findings. *Ophthalmology.* 1992;99:1588–1594.

Rootman J, Hay E, Graeb D, Miller R. Orbital-adnexal lymphangiomas. A spectrum of hemodynamically isolated vascular hamartomas. *Ophthalmology.* 1986;93:1558–1570.

Arteriovenous Malformations

Arteriovenous malformations are developmental anomalies composed of abnormally formed anastomosing arteries and veins without an intervening capillary bed. Dilated corkscrew episcleral vessels may be prominent. Exsanguinating arterial hemorrhage may occur with surgical intervention. After these lesions are studied by arteriography, they may be treated by selective occlusion of the feeding vessels, followed by surgical excision of the malformations.

Arteriovenous fistula

As shown in Figures 5-6 and 5-7, arteriovenous fistulas are abnormal communications between previously normal arteries and veins. These acquired lesions may be caused by trauma or degeneration. There are 2 forms: the *carotid cavernous fistula* typically occurs after a basal skull fracture; the spontaneous *dural cavernous fistula* forms most often as a degenerative process in an older patient with systemic hypertension and atherosclerosis.

The high-flow carotid cavernous fistulas produce characteristic tortuous epibulbar vessels and a bruit that may be audible to the examiner and the patient. Pulsatile proptosis may also be present. Ischemic ocular damage results from diversion of arterialized blood into the venous system, which causes venous outflow obstruction. This in turn results in elevated intraocular pressure, choroidal effusions, blood in Schlemm's canal, and a nongranulomatous iritis. Increased pressure in the cavernous sinus can cause compression of cranial nerves III, IV, or, most commonly, VI, with associated muscle palsies.

Small meningeal arterial branches may communicate with the venous drainage producing a low-flow *dural cavernous fistula*. Because this type generally produces less blood flow than a carotid cavernous fistula, its onset can be insidious; and orbital congestion, proptosis, and pain may be mild. Arterialization of the conjunctival veins causes chronic red eye. Increased episcleral venous pressure results in asymmetric elevation of intraocular pressure on the ipsilateral side, and patients with chronic fistulas are at risk for glaucomatous optic disc damage. CT scans show diffuse enlargement of all the extraocular muscles resulting from venous engorgement and a characteristically enlarged superior ophthalmic vein. Small dural cavernous fistulas often close spontaneously. Recent data suggest that patients with dural cavernous fistulas are at higher risk of intracranial hemorrhage because of the arterialization of the venous system. As such, some have recommended more aggressive management of these lesions.

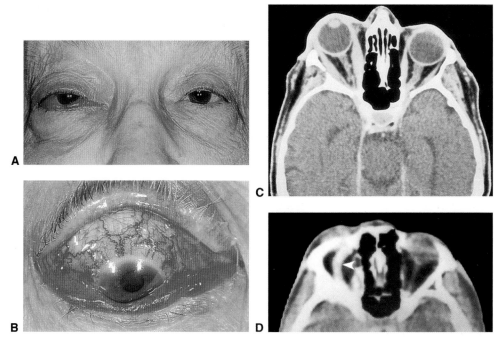

Figure 5-6 **A,** Carotid cavernous fistula, right eye, in elderly woman. **B,** Arterialization of epi-scleral and conjunctival vessels and chemosis of conjunctiva. **C,** CT scan demonstrating prop-tosis of right eye secondary to congested orbital tissues. Note enlarged medial rectus and lateral rectus muscles. **D,** Axial CT scan showing dilated superior ophthalmic vein *(arrowhead),* typical of carotid cavernous fistula. *(Parts A–C courtesy of Jeffrey A. Nerad, MD.)*

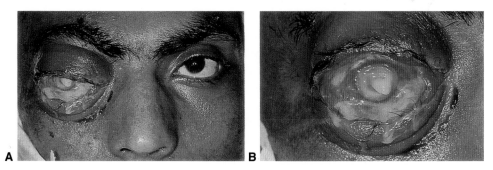

Figure 5-7 **A,** High-flow carotid cavernous fistula in a young man following head trauma. Note marked proptosis and exposure of eye. **B,** Corneal perforation resulting from exposure. *(Courtesy of Robert C. Kersten, MD.)*

Selective arteriography is used to evaluate arteriovenous fistulas of the orbit and cavern-ous sinus. Embolization using coils to obstruct the fistula is generally accomplished through an endovascular transarterial route. Occasionally, a transvenous approach is utilized to access the cavernous sinus. This too can be achieved endovascularly, through the jugular venous system; however, the cavernous sinus is more typically reached by transcutaneous canalization of the superior ophthalmic vein.

Meyers PM, Halbach VV, Dowd CF, et al. Dural carotid cavernous fistula: definitive endovascular management and long-term follow-up. *Am J Ophthalmol.* 2002;134:85–92.

Spinelli HM, Falcone S, Lee G. Orbital venous approach to the cavernous sinus: an analysis of the facial and orbital venous system. *Ann Plast Surg.* 1994;33(4):377–383.

Orbital varix

An orbital varix can occur primarily as dilations of preexisting venous channels (Fig 5-8). Proptosis that increases when the patient's head is dependent or after a Valsalva maneuver suggests the presence of an orbital varix. The diagnosis can be confirmed via contrast-enhanced spiral CT. Rapid spiral CT during the Valsalva maneuver or other means of decreasing venous return shows characteristic enlargement of the engorged varix. Phleboliths can sometimes be seen on plain-film radiographs. Patients may exhibit enophthalmos at rest, when the varix is not engorged. If the diagnosis is suspected, biopsy should be avoided because significant bleeding can be anticipated. Treatment is usually conservative. Surgery is reserved for relief of significant pain or for cases in which the varix threatens vision because of compressive optic neuropathy. Complete surgical excision is difficult as the varix is intertwined with normal orbital structures and directly communicates with the abundant venous reservoir in the cavernous sinus. Intraoperative embolization of the lesion aids surgical removal; excision follows. Embolization with coils inserted through a distal venous cutdown has also been reported to diminish symptoms.

Orbital hemorrhage

An orbital hemorrhage may result from trauma or spontaneous bleeding from vascular malformations. Rarely, a spontaneous hemorrhage may be caused by a sudden increase in venous pressure (eg, a Valsalva maneuver). An orbital hemorrhage almost always occurs in the superior subperiosteal space. It should be allowed to spontaneously resorb unless there is associated visual compromise, in which case urgent drainage is indicated.

Atalla ML, McNab AA, Sullivan TJ, Sloan B. Nontraumatic subperiosteal orbital hemorrhage. *Ophthalmology.* 2001;108:183–189.

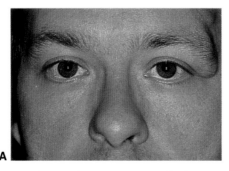 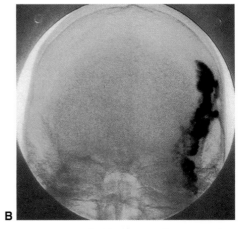

A   B

Figure 5-8 **A,** Congenital varix of left upper eyelid and temple. **B,** Venogram demonstrating large venous channels in periorbital area. *(Courtesy of Jeffrey A. Nerad, MD.)*

Neural Tumors

Neural tumors include optic nerve gliomas, neurofibromas, meningiomas, and schwannomas.

Optic Nerve Glioma

Optic nerve gliomas are uncommon, usually benign tumors that occur predominantly in children in the first decade of life (Fig 5-9). *Malignant* optic nerve gliomas (glioblastomas) are very rare and tend to affect adult males. Initial signs and symptoms of malignant gliomas include massive swelling and hemorrhage of the optic nerve head and severe retroorbital pain. Despite treatment, including high-dose radiotherapy, these tumors result in death.

Approximately 25%–50% of optic nerve gliomas are associated with neurofibromatosis. The chief clinical feature is gradual, painless, unilateral, axial proptosis associated with loss of vision and an afferent pupillary defect. Other ocular findings may include optic atrophy, optic disc swelling, and strabismus. The chiasm is involved in roughly half of cases of optic nerve glioma. Intracranial involvement may be associated with decreased function of the hypothalamus and pituitary gland.

In most cases, optic nerve gliomas are self-limited and show minimal growth. These characteristics have led some authors to consider them benign hamartomas. However, cystic enlargement of the lesions associated with sudden visual loss can occur even without true cellular growth. Long-term follow-up of gliomas has shown that some tumors progress, especially when they present with midbrain involvement. Such cases of intracranial growth may prove fatal.

Gross pathology of resected tumors usually reveals a smooth, fusiform intradural lesion. Microscopically, the benign tumors in children are considered to be juvenile pilocytic (hairlike) astrocytomas. Other histopathologic findings include arachnoid hyperplasia, mucosubstance, and Rosenthal fibers. Optic gliomas arising in patients with neurofibromatosis often proliferate in the subarachnoid space. Those occurring in patients without neurofibromatosis usually expand within the optic nerve without invasion of the dura mater.

Optic nerve gliomas can usually be diagnosed by means of orbital imaging. CT and MRI usually show fusiform enlargement of the optic nerve. MRI also shows cystic degeneration, if it is present, and may be more accurate in defining the extent of an optic canal lesion and intracranial disease.

It is usually unnecessary to perform a biopsy of a suspected optic nerve glioma. If a biopsy sample is obtained from the peripheral portion of the nerve, the presence of reactive meningeal hyperplasia occurring adjacent to the optic nerve glioma may cause the lesion to be misinterpreted as a fibrous meningioma.

Management

The treatment of optic nerve gliomas is controversial. Although most cases remain stable or progress very slowly, the occasional case behaves aggressively. There are rare reports of spontaneous regression of optic nerve and visual pathway gliomas. A treatment plan must be carefully individualized for each patient. The following options may be considered.

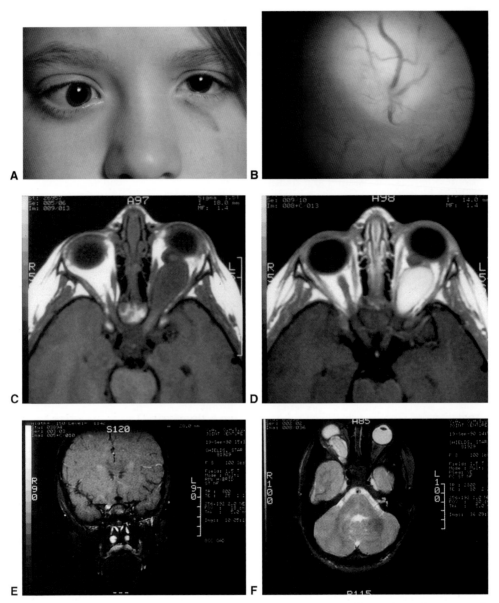

Figure 5-9 **A,** Clinical photograph of a child with right optic nerve glioma displaying proptosis with esotropia. **B,** Funduscopic view of same patient. Note swollen disc with obscured disc margins. **C,** T1-weighted axial MRI of optic nerve glioma demonstrating kinking of the optic nerve. **D,** T1-weighted image with contrast of the same patient. **E,** Coronal MRI demonstrates involvement of the optic nerve near the chiasm. **F,** T2-weighted axial MRI demonstrating enlargement of the right optic nerve with apparent kink. Note that the central enlarged optic nerve is surrounded by tumor in the perineural space. *(Courtesy of Roger A. Dailey, MD.)*

Observation only Presumed optic nerve glioma, particularly with good vision on the involved side, may be carefully followed if the radiographic evidence is characteristic of this type of tumor and if the glioma is confined to the orbit. Follow-up examinations and appropriate radiographic studies, preferably MRI, must be performed at regular intervals. Many patients maintain good vision and never require surgery.

Surgical excision When the tumor grows rapidly, the goal is to isolate the tumor from the optic chiasm so that chiasmal invasion is prevented. The surgeon should use an intracranial approach to obtain a free surgical margin. Even if the tumor enlarges slowly and remains confined to the orbit, corneal exposure and cosmesis may also become indications for surgical excision. Removal through an intracranial approach may also be indicated at the time of initial diagnosis or after a short period of observation if the tumor involves the prechiasmatic, intracranial portion of the optic nerve. Complete excision is possible if the tumor ends 2–3 mm anterior to the chiasm. Excision may also be required if the glioma causes an increase in intracranial pressure.

Radiation therapy Radiation therapy as sole treatment is considered if the tumor cannot be resected (usually chiasmal or tract lesions) and if symptoms (particularly neurological) progress. Postoperative radiation of the chiasm and optic tract may also be considered if good radiographic studies document subsequent growth of the tumor within the chiasm or if chiasmal and optic tract involvement is extensive. Radiation is generally held as a last resort for children with incomplete development.

Chemotherapy Combination chemotherapy using actinomycin D and vincristine has also been reported to be effective in patients with progressive chiasmatic/hypothalamic gliomas. Chemotherapy may delay the need for radiation therapy and thus enhance long-term intellectual development and preservation of endocrinologic function in children.

In summary, any treatment plan must be carefully individualized. Therapeutic decisions must be based on the tumor growth characteristics, the extent of optic nerve and chiasmal involvement as determined by clinical and radiographic evaluation, the visual acuity of the involved and uninvolved eye, the presence or absence of concomitant neurological or systemic disease, and the history of previous treatment.

Dutton JJ. Gliomas of the anterior visual pathway. *Surv Ophthalmol.* 1994;38:427–452.

Jenkin D, Angyalfi S, Becker L, et al. Optic glioma in children: surveillance, resection, or irradiation? *Int J Radiat Oncol Biol Phys.* 1993;25:215–225.

Listernick R, Charrow J, Greenwald M, Mets M. Natural history of optic pathway tumors in children with neurofibromatosis type 1: a longitudinal study. *J Pediatr.* 1994;125:63–66.

Massry GG, Morgan CF, Chung SM. Evidence of optic pathway gliomas after previously negative neuroimaging. *Ophthalmology.* 1997;104:930–935.

Neurofibroma

Neurofibromas are tumors composed chiefly of proliferating Schwann cells within the nerve sheaths (Figs 5-10, 5-11). Axons, endoneural fibroblasts, and mucin are also noted

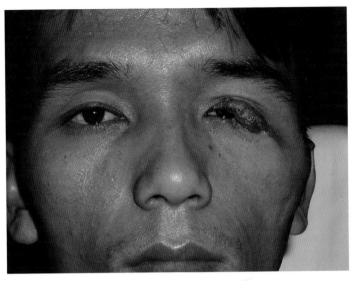

Figure 5-10 Ptosis of left upper eyelid, especially laterally, characteristic of plexiform neurofibroma infiltration. *(Courtesy of Jerry Popham, MD.)*

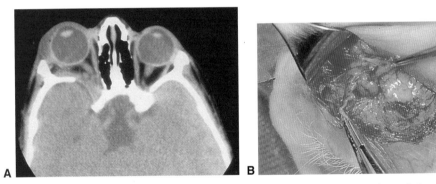

A   **B**

Figure 5-11 **A,** CT scan of patient with neurofibromatosis demonstrating slight proptosis, plexiform neurofibromas, and sphenoid wing dysplasia. **B,** Plexiform neurofibroma excision during ptosis surgery. Percutaneous palpation of the subcutaneous fibrous neoplastic cords visible here produces a "bag-of-worms" consistency. *(Courtesy of Jeffrey A. Nerad, MD.)*

histologically. *Plexiform neurofibromas* are infiltrative tumors that usually occur in neurofibromatosis 1 (NF1). They are well vascularized and can seldom be completely removed by surgical excision. *Discrete neurofibromas* are less common than the plexiform type. They can usually be excised surgically without recurrence. Surgery in either instance is limited to tumors that compromise vision or produce disfigurement.

Neurofibromatosis 1

Also known as *von Recklinghausen disease,* NF1 is inherited through an autosomal dominant gene with irregular penetrance. Because NF1 is characterized by the presence of hamartomas involving the skin, eye, central nervous system, and viscera, it is classified as a phakomatosis. Neurofibromatosis 1 is the most common phakomatous disorder. Among the disorders associated with this syndrome are

- café-au-lait spots, which are areas of increased epidermal melanin caused by distinctive giant melanosomes (the number of café-au-lait spots generally increases in late childhood)
- axillary freckling
- fibroma molluscum (pedunculated skin nodules composed of connective tissue and other elements)
- plexiform neurofibromas (diffuse proliferations of Schwann cells within nerve sheaths), which frequently involve the lateral area of the upper eyelid and cause an S-shaped contour of the eyelid margin (on dissection, these tumors appear as tortuous, fibrous cords that infiltrate normal tissues)
- dysplasia of orbital walls (pulsating proptosis may be produced by sphenoid bone dysplasia)
- congenital glaucoma and pigmented iris (Lisch) nodules
- optic nerve gliomas (approximately 25%–50% of all patients with optic nerve gliomas have neurofibromatosis)

See BCSC Section 6, *Pediatric Ophthalmology and Strabismus*, for further discussion of neurofibromatosis and other phakomatoses.

Farris SR, Grove AS Jr. Orbital and eyelid manifestations of neurofibromatosis: a clinical study and literature review. *Ophthal Plast Reconstr Surg.* 1996;12:245–259.

Meningioma

Meningiomas are invasive tumors that arise from arachnoid villi and usually originate intracranially along the sphenoid wing with secondary extension into the orbit through the bone, the superior orbital fissure, or the optic canal (Figs 5-12, 5-13). Ophthalmic manifestations are related to the location of the primary tumor. Meningiomas arising near the sella and optic nerves cause early visual defects and papilledema or optic atrophy. Tumors arising near the pterion (posterior end of the parietosphenoid fissure, at the lateral portion of the sphenoid bone) often produce a temporal fossa mass and proptosis. Eyelid edema (especially of the lower eyelid) and chemosis are common. Primary optic nerve meningiomas can produce axial proptosis with preserved vision. In contrast, small *en plaque* meningiomas can produce early profound vision loss without any proptosis.

Sphenoid wing meningiomas produce hyperostosis of the involved bone and hyperplasia of associated soft tissues. Bone absorption and destruction are rare. When contrast enhancement is used, MRI helps define the extent of meningiomas along the dura. The presence of a dural tail helps distinguish a meningioma from fibrous dysplasia.

Primary orbital meningiomas are much less common than those that arise intracranially and secondarily invade the orbit. Primary orbital meningiomas usually originate in the arachnoid of the optic nerve sheath. These optic nerve sheath meningiomas occur most commonly in women in their third and fourth decades of life. Symptoms usually include a gradual, painless, unilateral loss of vision. Examination typically shows decreased visual acuity and a relative afferent pupillary defect. Proptosis and ophthalmoplegia may also be

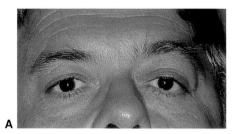

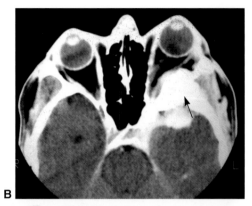

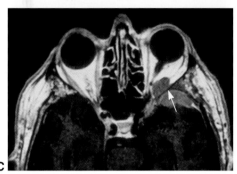

Figure 5-12 **A,** Left proptosis and fullness of left temple secondary to sphenoid wing meningioma. **B,** CT scan showing orbital and intracranial meningioma arising from sphenoid wing. Note hyperostosis of the sphenoid bone *(arrow)*. **C,** MRI showing enhancement of both the intraorbital and intracranial components of another sphenoid wing meningioma. Note the absence of hyperostosis *(arrow)*, which is less typical. *(Part A courtesy of Jeffrey A. Nerad, MD. Parts B and C courtesy of Michael Kazim, MD.)*

present. At presentation, the optic nerve head may appear normal, atrophic, or swollen, and optociliary shunt vessels may be visible. Occasionally, optic nerve sheath meningiomas occur bilaterally and are associated with neurofibromatosis.

Imaging characteristics are usually sufficient to allow diagnosis of optic nerve sheath meningiomas. Both CT and MRI show diffuse tubular enlargement of the optic nerve with contrast enhancement. In some cases, CT can show calcification within the meningioma, a sign that on plain x-ray is termed *tram-tracking*. MRI reveals a fine pattern of enhancing striations emanating from the lesion in a longitudinal fashion. These striations represent the infiltrative nature of what otherwise appears to be an encapsulated lesion. As with the sphenoid wing variant, MRI can show dural extension into the chiasm and the intracranial space. The en plaque variant appears as a focal knobby excrescence of the optic nerve that enhances with both CT and MRI.

Malignant meningioma is rare and results in rapid tumor growth that is not responsive to surgical resection, radiotherapy, or chemotherapy. Histologically, malignant meningiomas are indistinguishable from the more common benign group.

Management

Sphenoid wing meningiomas are typically observed until they produce functional consequences, such as profound proptosis, compressive optic neuropathy, motility impairment, or cerebral edema. Treatment includes subtotal resection of the tumor through a combined approach to the intracranial and orbital component. Complete surgical resection is not a practical goal because the dural tail of the tumor extends far beyond the

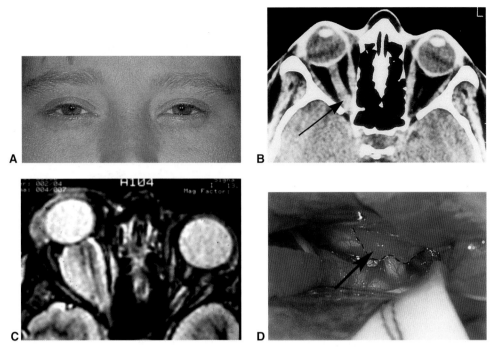

Figure 5-13 **A,** Primary optic nerve meningioma of right optic nerve, with minimal proptosis. **B,** CT scan showing thickened right optic nerve with calcification *(arrow).* **C,** MRI showing a fusiform enlargement of the right optic nerve sheath with preservation of the centrally located optic nerve. **D,** The meningioma is exposed through a craniotomy and superior orbitotomy. Intraoperative view shows intracranial prechiasmal optic nerve. Note cuff *(arrow, dashes)* of meningioma wrapping around optic nerve extending out from optic canal. *(Parts A, B, and D courtesy of Jeffrey A. Nerad, MD. Part C courtesy of Michael Kazim, MD.)*

surgical field. The goal of surgery is to reverse the volume-induced compressive effects of the lesion. Postoperative radiotherapy is advocated to reduce the risk of recurrence of the residual tumor.

Treatment of optic nerve sheath meningiomas must be individualized. Both the extent of visual loss and the presence of intracranial extension are important factors in treatment planning. Observation is indicated if vision is minimally affected and no intracranial extension is present. If the tumor is confined to the orbit and visual loss is significant or progressive, radiation therapy should be considered. Fractionated stereotactic radiotherapy often results in stabilization or improvement of visual function. If the patient is observed or treated with radiation, periodic MRI is necessary to identify possible intracranial extension. With rare exceptions, attempts to surgically excise optic nerve sheath meningiomas result in visual loss. Thus, surgery is reserved for patients with severe visual loss and profound proptosis. In such cases, the optic nerve is excised with the tumor, from the back of the globe to the chiasm, if the preoperative MRI scan suggests the opportunity for complete resection.

Andrews DW, Faroozan R, Yang BP, et al. Fractionated stereotactic radiotherapy for the treatment of optic nerve sheath meningiomas: preliminary observations of 33 optic nerves in

30 patients with historical comparison to observation with or without prior surgery. *Neurosurgery.* 2002;51:890–904.

Dutton JJ. Optic nerve sheath meningiomas. *Surv Ophthalmol.* 1992;37:167–183.

Turbin RE, Thompson CR, Kennerdell JS, Cockerham KP, Kupersmith MJ. A long-term visual outcome comparison in patients with optic nerve sheath meningioma managed with observation, surgery, radiotherapy, or surgery and radiotherapy. *Ophthalmology.* 2002;109(5): 890–899.

Wright JE, McNab AA, McDonald WI. Primary optic nerve sheath meningioma. *Br J Ophthalmol.* 1989;73:960–9606.

Schwannoma

Schwannomas, sometimes known as *neurilemomas,* are proliferations of Schwann cells that are encapsulated by perineurium. These tumors have a characteristic biphasic pattern of solid areas with nuclear palisading *(Antoni A pattern)* and myxoid areas *(Antoni B pattern).* Hypercellular schwannomas sometimes recur even after what is thought to be complete removal, but they seldom undergo malignant transformation. These tumors are usually well encapsulated and can be excised with relative ease.

Mesenchymal Tumors

Rhabdomyosarcoma

Rhabdomyosarcoma is the most common primary orbital malignancy of childhood (Fig 5-14). The average age of onset is 8–10 years. Although the classic clinical picture is one of a child with sudden onset and rapid evolution of unilateral proptosis, the rhabdomyosarcoma that is more typical among children in their early teens has a less dramatic course: gradually progressive proptosis lasting from weeks to more than a month. There is often a marked adnexal response with edema and discoloration of the eyelids. Ptosis and strabismus may also be present. A mass may be palpable, particularly in the superonasal

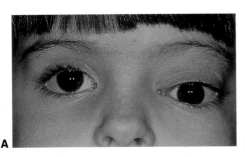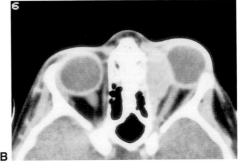

Figure 5-14 **A,** Six-year-old girl with rapid onset of axial proptosis, lateral and downward displacement of left eye. **B,** CT scan demonstrating a medial orbital mass proven by biopsy to be rhabdomyosarcoma. *(Courtesy of Jeffrey A. Nerad, MD.)*

quadrant of the eyelid. However, the tumor may be retrobulbar, involve any quadrant of the orbit, and may rarely arise from the conjunctiva. The patient sometimes has an unrelated history of trauma to the orbital area that can lead to a delay in diagnosis and treatment.

If a rhabdomyosarcoma is suspected, the workup should proceed on an urgent basis. CT and MRI can be used to define the location and extent of the tumor. CT is particularly helpful if the tumor has caused bony destruction, although the orbital walls remain intact in most cases.

A biopsy should be undertaken, usually through an anterior orbitotomy. It is often possible to completely remove a rhabdomyosarcoma if it has a pseudocapsule. If this is not practical, there is some indication that the smaller the volume of residual tumor, the more effective is the combination of radiation and chemotherapy in achieving cure. In diffusely infiltrating tumors, a large biopsy should be obtained so that adequate material is available for frozen sections, permanent light-microscopy sections, electron microscopy, and immunohistochemistry. Cross-striations are often not visible on light microscopy and may be more readily apparent on electron microscopy.

The physician should palpate the cervical and preauricular lymph nodes of the patient with orbital rhabdomyosarcoma to rule out regional metastases. A chest radiograph, bone marrow aspirate and biopsy, and lumbar puncture should be obtained to search for more distant metastases. Sampling of the bone marrow and the cerebrospinal fluid is best performed, if possible, with the patient under anesthesia at the time of the initial orbital biopsy.

Rhabdomyosarcomas arise from undifferentiated pluripotential mesenchymal elements in the orbital soft tissues and not from the extraocular muscles. They may be grouped into 4 categories:

1. *Embryonal.* This is by far the most common type found in the orbits of infants and children, accounting for more than 80% of cases. The embryonal form has a predilection for the superonasal quadrant of the orbit. The tumor is composed of loose fascicles of undifferentiated spindle cells, only a minority of which show cross-striations in immature rhabdomyosarcomas on trichrome staining. Embryonal rhabdomyosarcomas are associated with a good (94%) survival rate.

2. *Alveolar.* This form has a predilection for the inferior orbit and accounts for 9% of orbital rhabdomyosarcomas. The tumor displays regular compartments composed of fibrovascular strands in which rounded rhabdomyoblasts either line up along the connective tissue strands or float freely in the alveolar spaces. This is the most malignant form of rhabdomyosarcoma, with a 10-year survival rate of 10%.

3. *Pleomorphic.* Pleomorphic rhabdomyosarcoma is the least common and the most differentiated form. In this type, many of the cells are straplike or rounded, and cross-striations are easily discovered with trichrome stain. The pleomorphic variety has the best prognosis (97% survival rate).

4. *Botryoid.* This rare variant of embryonal rhabdomyosarcoma appears grapelike. It is not found in the orbit as a primary tumor; rather, the botryoid variant occurs as a secondary invader from the paranasal sinuses or from the conjunctiva.

Management

Before 1965, the standard treatment of orbital rhabdomyosarcoma was orbital exenteration and the survival rate was poor. Since 1965, radiation therapy and systemic chemotherapy have become the mainstays of primary treatment, based on the guidelines set forth by the Intergroup Rhabdomyosarcoma Studies I–IV. Exenteration is reserved for recurrent cases. The total dose of local radiation varies from 4500 to 6000 cGy, given over a period of 6 weeks. The goal of systemic chemotherapy is to eliminate microscopic cellular metastases. Survival rates with radiation and chemotherapy are better than 90% if the orbital tumor has not invaded or extended beyond the bony orbital walls. Adverse effects of radiation in a child are common and include cataract, radiation dermatitis, and bony hypoplasia if the child has not completed orbital development.

Kodet R, Newton WA Jr, Hamoudi AB, Asmar L, Wharam MD, Maurer HM. Orbital rhabdomyosarcomas and related tumors in childhood: relationship of morphology to prognosis—an Intergroup Rhabdomyosarcoma Study. *Med Pediatr Oncol.* 1997;29:51–60.

Mannor GE, Rose GE, Plowman PN, Kingston J, Wright JE, Vardy SJ. Multidisciplinary management of refractory orbital rhabdomyosarcoma. *Ophthalmology.* 1997;104:1198–1201.

Shields CL, Shields JA, Honavar SG, Demirci H. Clinical spectrum of primary ophthalmic rhabdomyosarcoma. *Ophthalmology.* 2001;108:2284–2292.

Miscellaneous Mesenchymal Tumors

Tumors of fibrous connective tissue, cartilage, and bone are uncommon lesions that may involve the orbit. A number of these mesenchymal tumors were likely incorrectly classified before the availability of immunohistochemical staining, which distinguished them and enabled their accurate classification.

Fibrous histiocytoma is the most common orbital neoplasm. It is characteristically very firm and displaces normal structures. Both fibroblastic and histiocytic cells in a storiform (matlike) pattern are found in these locally aggressive tumors. Fewer than 10% have metastatic potential. This tumor is sometimes difficult to distinguish clinically and histologically from hemangiopericytoma.

A newly described entity, *solitary fibrous tumor* is composed of spindle-shaped cells that are strongly CD34-positive on immunohistochemical studies. It can occur anywhere in the orbit. It may recur, undergo malignant degeneration, and metastasize if incompletely excised.

Fibrous dysplasia (Fig 5-15) is a benign developmental disorder of bone that may involve a single region or be polyostotic. CT scans show hyperostotic bone and MR images show the lack of dural enhancement that distinguishes this condition from meningioma. When associated with cutaneous pigmentation and endocrine disorders, the condition is known as *Albright syndrome*. Resection or debulking is performed when the lesion results in disfigurement or vision loss due to stricture of the optic canal.

Katz BJ, Nerad JA. Ophthalmic manifestations of fibrous dysplasia—a disease of children and adults. *Ophthalmology.* 1998;105:2207–2215.

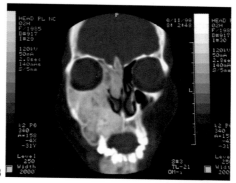

A **B**

Figure 5-15 Fibrous dysplasia. **A,** This young woman manifests facial asymmetry due to fibrous dysplasia. **B,** CT scan shows characteristic hyperostosis of involved facial bones. *(Courtesy of Jerry Popham, MD.)*

Osteomas are benign tumors that can involve any of the paraorbital sinuses. CT scans show dense hyperostosis with well-defined margins. The lesions can produce proptosis, compressive optic neuropathy, and orbital cellulitis secondary to obstructive sinusitis. Most are incidental lesions that require no treatment because they are slow growing. Complete excision is advised when the tumor is symptomatic.

Malignant mesenchymal tumors such as *liposarcoma, fibrosarcoma, chondrosarcoma,* and *osteosarcoma* rarely appear in the orbit. When chondrosarcomas and osteosarcomas are present, they usually destroy normal bone and have characteristic calcifications visible in radiographs and CT scans. Children with a history of bilateral retinoblastoma are at higher risk for osteosarcoma, chondrosarcoma, or fibrosarcoma, even if they have not been treated with therapeutic radiation.

Lymphoproliferative Disorders

Lymphoid Hyperplasia and Lymphoma

Lymphoproliferative lesions of the ocular adnexa constitute a heterogeneous group of neoplasms that are defined by clinical, histologic, immunologic, molecular, and genetic characteristics. Lymphoproliferative neoplasms account for more than 20% of all orbital tumors.

Most orbital lymphoproliferative lesions are non–Hodgkin lymphomas. The incidence of non–Hodgkin lymphoma of all anatomical sites has been increasing at a rate of 3%–4% per year (representing a 50% increase over the last 15 years), and non–Hodgkin lymphoma is now the fourth most common malignancy among men and women. The incidence of orbital lymphomas has been increasing at an even greater rate. Workers with long-term exposure to bioactive solvents and reagents are at increased risk for non–Hodgkin lymphoma, as are older persons and patients with chronic autoimmune diseases.

Identification and classification of lymphoproliferative disorders

Classification of non–Hodgkin lymphomas is evolving and largely based on nodal architecture. Extranodal sites, including the orbit, have been included in the Revised European American Lymphoma (REAL) classification. However, orbital extranodal disease appears to represent a biological continuum and to behave unpredictably. Often, patients with orbital lymphoid infiltrates that appear benign histologically eventually develop extraorbital lymphoma, whereas others with malignant lymphoma of the ocular adnexa may respond satisfactorily to local therapy without subsequent systemic involvement (Figs 5-16, 5-17). Currently, 70%–80% of orbital lymphoproliferative lesions are designated as malignant lymphomas on the basis of monoclonal cell-surface markers, whereas 90% are found to be malignant on the basis of molecular genetic studies. The significance of this discrepancy is not yet clear, as

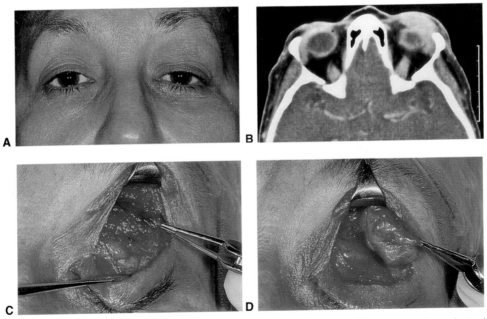

Figure 5-16 **A,** Left upper eyelid ptosis and fullness. An upper eyelid mass can be palpated under orbital rim. **B,** CT scan demonstrating left lacrimal gland enlargement with infiltration of anterior orbital tissues consistent with orbital lymphoma. **C,** Anterior orbitotomy is performed for biopsy of the mass. Note large mass *(grasped in forceps)* positioned between preaponeurotic fat and superior orbital rim. **D,** Incisional biopsy of mass is performed, confirming diagnosis of lymphoma. *(Courtesy of Jeffrey A. Nerad, MD.)*

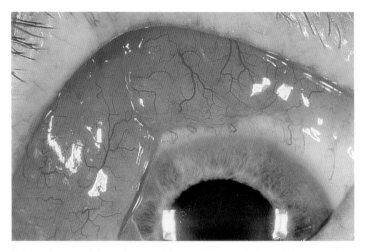

Figure 5-17 Subconjunctival lymphoma. Note characteristic salmon-patch appearance of lesion. *(Courtesy of Jeffrey A. Nerad, MD.)*

polymerase chain reaction studies have shown that, over time, some conjunctival lymphoid lesions fluctuate between being monoclonal and polyclonal.

The vast majority of orbital lymphomas are B cell–derived. T-cell lymphoma is rare and more lethal. B-cell lymphoma is divided into Hodgkin and non-Hodgkin tumors, with the former rarely metastasizing to the orbit. Malignant non-Hodgkin B-cell lymphoma accounts for more than 90% of orbital lymphoproliferative disease.

Based on the REAL classification, the following represent the 4 most common orbital lymphomas:

1. *Mucosa-associated lymphoid tissue (MALT) lymphomas* account for 40%–60% of orbital lymphomas. MALT lesions were originally described as occurring in the gastrointestinal tract, where approximately 50% of MALT lymphomas arise. Studies have suggested that proliferation of early MALT tumors may be antigen-driven. Therapy directed at the antigen (eg, against *Helicobacter pylori* in gastric lymphomas) may result in regression of early lesions. There is evidence to suggest that some conjunctival MALT lymphomas are associated with chronic Chlamydia infection. In contrast with MALT lymphomas of other areas of the body, those of the ocular adnexa do not appear to be preferentially associated with mucosal tissue (ie, conjunctiva or lacrimal gland).

   Although MALT lymphomas have a low grade of malignancy, long-term follow-up has demonstrated that at least 50% of patients will develop systemic disease at 10 years. MALT lymphomas may undergo spontaneous remission in 5%–15% of cases. They may undergo histologic transformation to a higher-grade lesion, usually of a large cell type, in 15%–20% of cases. Such transformation usually occurs after several years and is not related to therapy.

2. *Chronic lymphocytic lymphoma (CLL)* also represents a low-grade lesion of small mature-appearing lymphocytes.

3. *Follicullar center lymphoma* represents a low-grade lesion with follicular centers.
4. *High-grade lymphomas* include large cell lymphoma, lymphoblastic lymphoma, and Burkitt lymphoma.

See also BCSC Section 4, *Ophthalmic Pathology and Intraocular Tumors.*

Clinical presentation

The typical lymphoproliferative lesion presents as a gradually progressive, painless mass. These tumors are often located anteriorly in the orbit or beneath the conjunctiva, where they may feature the typical salmon-patch appearance. Lymphoproliferative lesions, whether benign or malignant, usually mold to surrounding orbital structures rather than invade them; consequently, disturbances of extraocular motility or visual function are unusual. Reactive lymphoid hyperplasias and low-grade lymphomas often have a history of slow expansion over a period of months to years. Orbital imaging reveals a characteristic puttylike molding of the tumor to normal structures. Bone erosion or infiltration is usually not seen except with high-grade malignant lymphomas. Up to 50% of orbital lymphoproliferative lesions arise in the lacrimal fossa. Lymphomas in the retrobulbar fat may appear more infiltrative. Approximately 17% of orbital lymphoid lesions occur bilaterally, but this does not necessarily indicate the presence of extraorbital disease.

Diagnosis

For all lymphoproliferative lesions, an open biopsy is preferred to obtain an adequate tissue specimen, which is used to establish a diagnosis and to characterize the lesion as to its morphologic, immunologic, cytogenetic, and molecular properties under the REAL classification. A portion of the tissue should be placed in a suitable fixative for light-microscopic studies. The majority of the specimen should be sent fresh to a molecular diagnostics laboratory for possible flow cytometry and polymerase chain reaction analysis. Alternatively, fine-needle aspiration biopsy can provide adequate sample volume to establish all but the morphologic characteristics of the lesion.

Both reactive hyperplasia and malignant lymphoma are hypercellular proliferations with sparse or absent stromal components. Histopathologically, light microscopy may reveal a continuum from reactive hyperplasia, to low-grade lymphoma, to a higher-grade malignancy. Within this spectrum, it may be difficult to characterize a given lesion by light microscopy alone. In such cases, immunopathology and molecular diagnostic studies have been proposed as aids to further categorization.

Malignant lymphomas are thought to represent clonal expansions of abnormal precursor cells. Immunologic identification of cell-surface markers on lymphocytes can be used to classify tumors as containing B cells or T cells and as being either monoclonal or polyclonal in origin. Specific monoclonal antibodies directed against surface light-chain (κ or λ) immunoglobulins are used to study cells in smears, histologic sections, or cell suspensions to determine whether the cells represent monoclonal (ie, malignant) proliferations.

Newer techniques of molecular analysis allow more precise identification of tumor clonality by extracting, amplifying, and hybridizing tumor DNA with radioactively labeled nucleotide probes. DNA hybridization is more sensitive than cell-surface marker typing in detecting clonality, but this technique is also more time-consuming and expensive. DNA genetic studies have demonstrated that most lymphoproliferative lesions that appear to be immunologically polyclonal actually harbor small mono-clonal proliferations of B lymphocytes. The finding of monoclonality, established by either immunophenotype or molecular genetics, does not predict which tumors will ultimately result in systemic disease.

Approximately 90% of orbital lymphoproliferations prove monoclonal and 10% poly-clonal by molecular genetic studies, but both types of lesions may have prior, concur-rent, or future systemic spread. This occurs in greater than half of periocular lymphomas, with 20%–30% of periocular lymphoproliferative lesions having a history of previous or concomitant systemic disease and an additional 30% developing it over 5 years. The ana-tomical site of origin offers some prediction of the risk of having or developing systemic non–Hodgkin lymphoma. The risk is lowest for conjunctival lesions, greater for orbital lesions, and highest for lesions arising in the eyelid. Lymphoid lesions developing in the lacrimal fossa may carry a greater risk of systemic disease than those occurring elsewhere in the orbit. Bilateral periocular involvement markedly increases the risk of systemic dis-ease, but such involvement is not definitive evidence of systemic disease. It is also clear that the risk of systemic disease increases for decades after the original lesion is diagnosed, regardless of the initial lesion's location in the orbit or its clonality.

Management

Because the various lymphoproliferative lesions show great overlap in terms of clinical behavior, all patients with hypercellular lymphoid lesions (whether monoclonal or poly-clonal) should be examined by an oncologist. Depending on the histologic type of the lesion, the examination may include a general physical examination, a complete blood count, a bone marrow biopsy, a liver and spleen scan, a chest radiograph, and serum immunoprotein electrophoresis. The oncologist may also recommend CT of the thorax and abdomen to check for mediastinal and retroperitoneal lymph node involvement. The patient should be reexamined periodically because systemic lymphoma may occur many years after the presentation of an isolated orbital lymphoid neoplasm.

Although systemic corticosteroids are useful in idiopathic orbital inflammation (pseu-dotumor), they are not recommended in the treatment of lymphoproliferative lesions. Radiotherapy is the treatment of choice for patients with localized ocular adnexal lym-phoproliferative disease. A dose of 2000–3000 cGy is administered. This regimen achieves local control in virtually all cases and, if the lesion is isolated, may prevent systemic spread. A surgical cure usually cannot be achieved because of the infiltrative nature of lymphoid tumors.

The treatment of low-grade lymphoid lesions that have already undergone systemic dissemination is somewhat controversial because indolent lymphomas are generally refractory to chemotherapy and are associated with long-term survival, even if untreated. Many oncologists take a watchful waiting approach and treat only symptomatic disease. Lymphomas that are more aggressive require radiation, aggressive chemotherapy, or both; up to one third of these lesions can be cured.

Coupland SE, Krause L, Delecluse H-J, et al. Lymphoproliferative lesions of the ocular adnexa: analysis of 112 cases. *Ophthalmology.* 1998;105:1430–1441.

Jenkins C, Rose GE, Bunce C, et al. Histological features of ocular adnexal lymphoma (REAL classification) and their association with patient morbidity and survival. *Br J Ophthalmol.* 2000;84:907–913.

Johnson TE, Tse DT, Byrne GE Jr, et al. Ocular-adnexal lymphoid tumors: a clinicopatho-logic and molecular genetic study of 77 patients. *Ophthal Plast Reconstr Surg.* 1999;15: 171–179.

Kennerdell JS, Flores NE, Hartsock RJ. Low-dose radiotherapy for lymphoid lesions of the orbit and ocular adnexa. *Ophthal Plast Reconstr Surg.* 1999;15:129–133.

Margo CE, Mulla ZD. Malignant tumors of the orbit: analysis of the Florida Cancer Registry. *Ophthalmology.* 1998;105:185–190.

Sullivan TJK, Whitehead, et al. Lymphoproliferative disease of the ocular adnexa: a clinical and pathologic study with statistical analysis of 69 patients. *Ophthal Plast Reconstr Surg.* 2005;21(3):177–188.

White WL, Ferry JA, Harris NL, Grove AS Jr. Ocular adnexal lymphoma: a clinicopathologic study with identification of lymphomas of mucosa-associated lymphoid tissue type. *Ophthalmology.* 1995;102:1994–2006.

Plasma Cell Tumors

Lesions composed predominantly of mature plasma cells may be plasmacytomas or localized plasma cell–rich pseudotumors. Multiple myeloma should be ruled out, particularly if there is bone destruction or any immaturity or mitotic activity among the plasmacytic elements. Some lesions are composed of lymphocytes and lymphoplasmacytoid cells that combine properties of both lymphocytes and plasma cells. Plasma cell tumors display the same spectrum of clinical involvement as do lymphoproliferative lesions but are much less common.

Histiocytic Disorders

Langerhans cell histiocytosis, formerly known as *histiocytosis X,* is a collection of rare disorders of the mononuclear phagocytic system. These disorders are now thought to result from abnormal immune regulation. All subtypes are characterized by an accumulation of proliferating dendritic histiocytes. The disease occurs most commonly in children, with a peak incidence between 5 and 10 years of age, and varies in severity from benign lesions with spontaneous resolution to chronic dissemination resulting in death. Older names representing the various manifestations of histiocytic disorders (*eosinophilic granuloma of bone, Hand-Schüller-Christian syndrome,* and *Letterer-Siwe disease*) are being displaced by the terms *unifocal* and *multifocal eosinophilic granuloma of bone,* and *diffuse soft tissue histiocytosis.*

The most frequent presentation in the orbit is a lytic defect usually affecting the superotemporal orbit or sphenoid wing and causing relapsing episodes of orbital inflammation often misinterpreted initially as infectious orbital cellulitis. Ultimately, the mass may cause proptosis. Younger children more often present with significant overlying soft tissue inflammation; they are also more likely to have evidence of multifocal or systemic involvement. Even if the initial workup shows no evidence of systemic dissemination, younger patients require regular observation for detection of subsequent multiorgan involvement.

Histiocytic disorders have a reported survival rate of only 50% in patients presenting under 2 years of age; if the disease develops after age 2, the survival rate rises to 87%. Treatment of localized orbital disease consists of confirmatory biopsy with debulking, which may be followed by intralesional steroid injection or low-dose radiation therapy. Spontaneous remission has also been reported. Although destruction of the orbital bone may be extensive at the time of presentation, the bone usually reossifies completely. Children with systemic disease are treated aggressively with chemotherapy.

Kramer TR, Noecker RJ, Miller JM, Clark LC. Langerhans cell histiocytosis with orbital involvement. *Am J Ophthalmol.* 1997;124:814–824.

Trocme SD, Baker RH, Bartley GB, Henderson JW, Leiferman KM. Extracellular deposition of eosinophil major basic protein in orbital histiocytosis X. *Ophthalmology.* 1991;98:353–356.

Woo KI, Harris GJ. Eosinophilic granuloma of the orbit: understanding the paradox of aggressive destruction responsive to minimal intervention. *Ophthal Plast Reconstr Surg.* 2003;19:429–439.

Xanthogranuloma

Adult xanthogranuloma of the adnexa and orbit is often associated with systemic manifestations. These manifestations are the basis for classification into the following 4 syndromes:

1. Adult onset xanthogranuloma (AOX)
2. Adult onset asthma with periocular xanthogranuloma (AAPOX)
3. Necrobiotic xanthogranuloma (NBX)
4. Erdheim-Chester disease (ECD)

NBX is the most frequently reported, followed by ECD, AAPOX, and AOX.

AOX is an isolated xanthogranulomatous lesion without systemic involvement. Juvenile xanthogranuloma is a separate non-Langerhans histiocytic disorder that occurs as a self-limited, corticosteroid-sensitive, and usually focal subcutaneous disease of childhood. See BCSC Section 6, *Pediatric Ophthalmology and Strabismus,* for a more detailed discussion of juvenile xanthogranuloma.

AAPOX is a syndrome that includes periocular xanthogranuloma, asthma, lymphadenopathy, and, often, increased IgG levels.

NBX is characterized by the presence of subcutaneous lesions in the eyelids and anterior orbit; the lesions may also occur throughout the body. Although skin lesions are seen in all of these syndromes, the lesions in NBX have a propensity to ulcerate and fibrose. Frequent systemic findings include paraproteinemia and multiple myeloma.

ECD, the most devastating of the adult xanthogranulomas, is characterized by dense, progressive, recalcitrant fibrosclerosis of the orbit and internal organs, including the mediastinum and pericardium and the pleural, perinephric, and retroperitoneal spaces. Whereas xanthogranuloma of the orbit and adnexa tends to be anterior in AOX, AAPOX, and NBX, it is often diffuse in ECD and leads to visual loss. Bone involvement is common and death frequent, despite aggressive therapies.

Sivak-Callcott JA, Rootman J, Rasmussen SL, et al. Adult xanthogranulomatous disease of the orbit and ocular adnexal: new immunohistochemical findings and clinical review. *Br J Ophthalmol.* 2006;90:602–608.

Lacrimal Gland Tumors

Most lacrimal gland masses represent idiopathic inflammation (dacryoadenitis variant of orbital pseudotumor). They present with acute inflammatory signs and usually respond to anti-inflammatory medication and thus do not require surgical intervention and biopsy (see Chapter 4 under the heading Nonspecific Orbital Inflammation). Of those lacrimal gland tumefactions not presenting with inflammatory signs and symptoms, the majority represent lymphoproliferative disorders (discussed previously): up to 50% of orbital lymphomas develop in the lacrimal fossa. Only a minority of lacrimal fossa lesions are epithelial neoplasms of the lacrimal gland.

CT is helpful in evaluating lesions in the lacrimal gland region. CT contour analysis can be used to differentiate inflammatory conditions and lymphoid proliferations from frank lacrimal gland neoplasms. Inflammatory and lymphoid proliferations within the lacrimal gland tend to cause it to expand diffusely and appear elongated, whereas epithelial neoplasms appear as isolated globular masses. Inflammatory and lymphoproliferative lesions usually contour around the globe, whereas epithelial neoplasms tend to displace and indent it. The bone of the lacrimal fossa is remodeled in response to a slowly growing benign epithelial lesion of the lacrimal gland, whereas there is typically no change in the bone due to a lymphoproliferative lesion.

Epithelial Tumors of the Lacrimal Gland

Approximately 50% of epithelial tumors are benign mixed tumors (pleomorphic adenomas) and about 50% are carcinomas. Approximately half of the carcinomas are adenoid cystic, and the remainder are malignant mixed tumor primary adenocarcinoma, mucoepidermoid carcinoma, or squamous carcinoma.

Pleomorphic adenoma

Shown in Figure 5-18, pleomorphic adenoma (benign mixed tumor) is the most common epithelial tumor of the lacrimal gland. This tumor usually occurs in adults during the fourth and fifth decades of life and affects slightly more males than females. Patients present with a progressive, painless downward and inward displacement of the globe with axial proptosis. Symptoms are usually present for more than 12 months.

A firm lobular mass may be palpated near the superior lateral orbital rim, and orbital imaging often reveals enlargement or expansion of the lacrimal fossa. On CT scans, the lesion appears well circumscribed but may have a slightly nodular configuration.

Microscopically, benign mixed tumors have a varied cellular structure consisting primarily of a proliferation of benign epithelial cells and a stroma composed of spindle-shaped

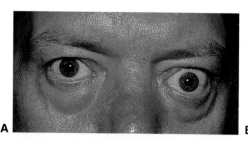

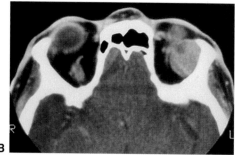

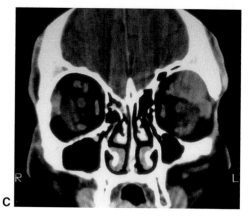

Figure 5-18 **A,** Proptosis and downward displacement of left eye in a man with benign mixed tumor of lacrimal gland. **B,** Axial CT scan showing tumor in lacrimal fossa. No bony remodeling is present in this case. **C,** Coronal CT scan showing rounded mass in lacrimal gland consistent with benign mixed tumor. *(Courtesy of Robert C. Kersten, MD.)*

cells with occasional cartilaginous, mucinous, or even osteoid degeneration or metaplasia. This variability accounts for the designation *mixed tumor.* The lesion is circumscribed by a pseudocapsule.

Management   Treatment is complete removal of the tumor with its pseudocapsule and a surrounding margin of orbital tissue. Surgery should be performed without a preliminary biopsy: in an early study, the recurrence rate was 32% when the capsule of the pleomorphic adenoma was incised for direct biopsy. Although the validity of the study has been questioned, a total resection is recommended. In recurrences, the risk of malignant degeneration is 10% per decade.

> Rose GE, Wright JE. Pleomorphic adenoma of the lacrimal gland. *Br J Ophthalmol.* 1992;76: 395–400.

Adenoid cystic carcinoma

Also known as *cylindroma,* adenoid cystic carcinoma is the most common malignant tumor of the lacrimal gland. This highly malignant tumor may cause pain because of perineural invasion and bone destruction. The relatively rapid course, with a history of generally less than 1 year, and early onset of pain help differentiate this malignant tumor from benign mixed tumor, which tends to show progressive proptosis for more than a year and is painless. The tumor usually extends into the posterior orbit because of its capacity to infiltrate and its lack of true encapsulation.

Microscopically, this tumor is made of disarmingly benign-appearing cells that grow in tubules, solid nests, or a cribriform Swiss-cheese pattern. The basaloid morphology is associated with worse survival than the cribriform variant. Infiltration of the orbital tissues, including perineural invasion, is often seen in microscopic sections.

Malignant mixed tumor

These lesions are histologically similar to benign mixed tumors, but they have areas of malignant change, usually poorly differentiated adenocarcinomas. They typically arise from long-standing primary benign mixed tumors or from a benign mixed tumor that has recurred following initial incomplete excision or violation of the pseudocapsule (see under the heading "Pleomorphic adenoma"). Radical orbitectomy with bone removal and exenteration has been performed, but long-term survival is poor.

Management of malignant lacrimal gland tumors

Suspicion of a malignant lacrimal gland tumor warrants percutaneous biopsy with permanent histopathologic confirmation. Exenteration and radical orbitectomy with removal of the roof, lateral wall, and floor along with the overlying soft tissues and anterior portion of the temporalis muscle have failed to produce improvement in long-term survival rates. High-dose radiation therapy (conventional electrons, photons, and neutrons have all been used), in conjunction with surgical debulking, may be offered as an alternative. Intracarotid chemotherapy followed by exenteration has also been advocated; however, the duration of follow-up is not adequate to prove the efficacy of this treatment. Despite these measures, perineural extension into the cavernous sinus often occurs, and the typical clinical course is that of multiple painful recurrences with ultimate mortality from intracranial extension or, less commonly, from systemic metastases (which are managed by local resection), usually occurring a decade or more after the initial presentation.

Bartley GB, Harris GJ. Adenoid cystic carcinoma of the lacrimal gland: is there a cure . . . yet? *Ophthal Plast Reconstr Surg.* 2002;18:315–318.

Font RF, Smith SL, Bryan RG. Malignant epithelial tumors of the lacrimal gland. A clinicopathologic study of 21 cases. *Arch Ophthalmol.* 1998;116:613–616.

Tellado MV, McLean IW, Specht CS, Varga J. Adenoid cystic carcinomas of the lacrimal gland in childhood and adolescence. *Ophthalmology.* 1997;104:1622–1625.

Tse DT, Benedetto P, Dubovy S, Schiffman JC, Feuer WJ. Clinical analysis of the effect of intraarterial cytoreductive chemotherapy in the treatment of lacrimal gland adenoid cystic carcinoma. *Am J Ophthalmol.* 2006;141:44–53.

Wright JE, Rose GE, Garner A. Primary malignant neoplasms of the lacrimal gland. *Br J Ophthalmol.* 1992;76:401–407.

Nonepithelial Tumors of the Lacrimal Gland

Most of the nonepithelial lesions of the lacrimal gland represent lymphoid proliferation or inflammations. Up to 50% of orbital lymphoproliferative lesions occur in the lacrimal gland. Inflammatory conditions such as idiopathic orbital inflammatory syndrome and sarcoidosis are covered in Chapter 4. Lymphoepithelial lesions may also occur either in Sjögren syndrome or as a localized lacrimal gland and salivary gland lesion (the so-called *Mikulicz syndrome*).

Benign lymphocytic infiltrates may be seen in middle-aged patients, particularly females, who develop bilateral swellings of the lacrimal gland, producing a dry eye syndrome. This condition can occur insidiously or following a symptomatic episode of lacrimal gland inflammation. The enlargement of the lacrimal glands may not be clinically apparent. Biopsy specimens of the affected glands show a spectrum of lymphocytic infiltration, from scattered patches of lymphocytes to lymphocytic replacement of the lacrimal gland parenchyma, with preservation of the inner duct cells, which are surrounded by proliferating myoepithelial cells (*epimyoepithelial islands*). This latter combination of lymphocytes and epimyoepithelial islands has led some authors to designate this manifestation as a lymphoepithelial lesion. Some patients with lymphocytic infiltrates may also have systemic rheumatoid arthritis and, therefore, have classic Sjögren syndrome. These lesions may develop into low-grade B-cell lymphoma (see earlier discussion of lymphoproliferative disorders). Associated dry eye symptoms may improve with the use of topical cyclosporine.

Secondary Orbital Tumors

Secondary orbital tumors are those that extend into the orbit from contiguous structures, such as the globe, the eyelids, the sinuses, or the brain.

Globe and Eyelid Origin

Tumors and inflammations can invade the orbit from within the eye (especially from choroidal melanomas and retinoblastomas) or from the eyelid (eg, sebaceous gland carcinoma, squamous cell carcinoma, and basal cell carcinoma). Primary eyelid tumors are discussed in Chapter 11. Retinoblastoma, choroidal melanoma, and other ocular neoplasms are covered in BCSC Section 4, *Ophthalmic Pathology and Intraocular Tumors*; and Section 6, *Pediatric Ophthalmology and Strabismus*.

Sinus Origin

Most tumors that secondarily involve the orbit arise from the nose or the paranasal sinuses. Proptosis and globe displacement are common, and the diagnosis is usually readily apparent on orbital CT or MRI. Imaging must be carried to the base of the sinuses for the proper evaluation of these lesions.

Mucoceles and *mucopyoceles* of the sinuses (Fig 5-19) are cystic structures with pseudostratified ciliated columnar (respiratory) epithelium. Resulting from obstruction of the sinus excretory ducts, mucoceles and mucopyoceles frequently invade the orbit by expansion and erosion of the bones of the orbital walls. The cysts are usually filled with thick mucoid secretions. If infected and filled with pus, the lesion is called a *pyocele*. Most mucoceles arise from the frontal or ethmoidal sinuses. Preoperative diagnosis can usually be established by characteristic findings on orbital imaging. Surgical treatment includes evacuation of the mucocele and reestablishment of drainage of the affected sinus or obliteration of the sinus by mucosal stripping and packing with bone or fat.

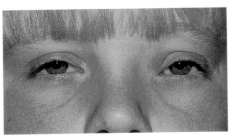
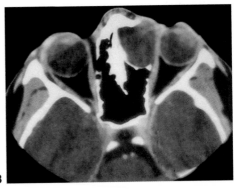

Figure 5-19 **A,** Fullness of superonasal left upper eyelid and lateral displacement of left medial canthal tendon in a boy with ethmoidal mucocele. **B,** CT scan demonstrating anterior ethmoidal mucocele pushing eye and medial canthal tendon laterally. *(Courtesy of Robert C. Kersten, MD.)*

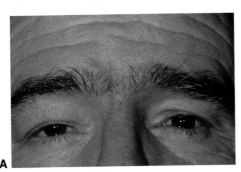
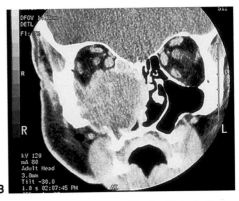

Figure 5-20 Squamous cell carcinoma of the sinus extending into the orbit. **A,** Clinical photo; note minimal proptosis despite large tumor of the sinus extending into the orbit. **B,** CT scan; sinus cancers typically do not show early clinical signs, usually presenting after the tumor has grown to a large size. *(Courtesy of Jeffrey Nerad, MD.)*

Another result of sinus outflow pathology is the silent sinus syndrome. Chronic subclinical sinusitis presumably causes thinning of the bone of the involved sinus, leading to enophthalmos due to collapse of the orbital floor. This collapse may occur in association with a recent significant change in atmospheric pressure as occurs, for example, during airplane travel or scuba diving. The upper eyelid may appear relatively retracted and there may be transient diplopia. Treatment includes restoration of normal sinus drainage and reconstruction of the orbital floor.

Squamous cell carcinoma is the most common epithelial tumor secondarily invading the orbit (Fig 5-20). Malignancies usually arise within the maxillary sinuses, followed by the nasopharynx or the oropharynx. Nasal obstruction, epistaxis, or epiphora may be associated with the growth of such tumors. Treatment is usually a combination of surgical excision and radiation therapy and often includes exenteration if the periorbita is traversed by tumor.

Nonepithelial tumors that can invade the orbit from the sinuses, nose, and facial bones include a wide variety of benign and malignant lesions. Among the most common of these are *osteomas, fibrous dysplasia,* and miscellaneous *sarcomas.*

Johnson LN, Krohel GB, Yeon EB, Parnes SM. Sinus tumors invading the orbit. *Ophthalmology.* 1984;91:209–217.

Soparkar CN, Patrinely JR, Cuaycong MJ, et al. The silent sinus syndrome. A cause of spontaneous enophthalmos. *Ophthalmology.* 1994;101:772–778.

Metastatic Tumors

Metastatic Tumors in Children

In children, distant tumors metastasize to the orbit more frequently than to the globe (in contrast to adults, who more frequently have metastases to the choroid).

Neuroblastoma

Metastatic orbital neuroblastoma typically produces an abrupt ecchymotic proptosis that may be bilateral. A deposition of blood in the eyelids may lead to the mistaken impression of injury. Horner syndrome may also be apparent in some cases. Commonly, bone destruction is apparent, particularly in the lateral orbital wall/sphenoid marrow. Metastases typically occur late in the course of the disease, when the primary tumor can be detected readily in the abdomen, mediastinum, or neck (Fig 5-21). Treatment is primarily chemotherapy. Radiotherapy is reserved for cases of impending vision loss due to compressive optic neuropathy. The survival rate is related to the patient's age at diagnosis. Patients diagnosed before 1 year of age have a 90% survival rate. Only 10% of those diagnosed at an older age survive. Congenital neuroblastoma of the cervical ganglia may produce an ipsilateral Horner syndrome with heterochromia.

Miller NR, ed. *Walsh and Hoyt's Neuro-Ophthalmology.* 4th ed. Baltimore: Williams & Wilkins; 1988;3:1296–1300.

Leukemia

In advanced stages, leukemia may produce unilateral or bilateral proptosis. *Acute lymphoblastic leukemia* is the type of leukemia most likely to metastasize to the orbit. A primary leukemic orbital mass, called *granulocytic sarcoma,* or *chloroma,* is a rare variant of myelogenous leukemia. Least common are metastases to the subarachnoid space of the optic nerve. These cases present with sudden vision loss and swelling of the optic nerve. They constitute an emergency and are treated with orbital radiotherapy. Typically, orbital lesions present in advance of blood or bone marrow signs of leukemia, which almost invariably follow within several months. Special stains for cytoplasmic esterase in the cells (Leder stain) indicate that these are granulocytic precursor cells. Chances for survival are enhanced if chemotherapy is instituted before the discovery of leukemic involvement in bone marrow or peripheral blood.

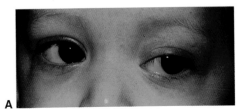
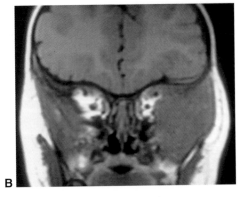

A **B**

Figure 5-21 **A,** A child with a metastatic left orbital neuroblastoma. **B,** MRI demonstrates a large infiltrating lesion of the left sphenoid wing extending into the orbital soft tissues and the temporalis fossa. *(Courtesy of Michael Kazim, MD.)*

Stockl FA, Dolmetsch AM, Saornil MA, Font RL, Burnier MN Jr. Orbital granulocytic sarcoma. *Br J Ophthalmol.* 1997;81:1084–1088.

Metastatic Tumors in Adults

Although virtually any carcinoma of the internal organs and cutaneous malignant melanoma can metastasize to the orbit (Figs 5-22, 5-23), breast and lung tumors account for the majority of orbital metastases. The occurrence of pain, proptosis, inflammation, bone destruction, and early ophthalmoplegia suggests the possibility of metastatic carcinoma.

Some 75% of patients have a history of a known primary tumor, but in 25% the orbital metastasis may be the presenting sign. The extraocular muscles are frequently involved because of their abundant blood supply. The second most common site is the bone marrow space of the sphenoid bone because of the relatively high volume of low-flow blood in this site (Fig 5-24). Lytic destruction of this part of the lateral orbital wall is highly suggestive of metastatic disease. Elevation of serum carcinoembryonic antigen levels also may suggest a metastatic process. Fine-needle aspiration biopsy can be performed in the office and may obviate the need for orbitotomy and open biopsy.

Breast carcinoma

The most common primary source of orbital metastases in women is breast cancer. Metastases may occur many years after the breast has been removed; thus, a history should always include inquiries about previous cancer surgery. Breast metastasis to the orbit may elicit a fibrous response that causes enophthalmos and possibly restriction of ocular motility (see Fig 5-23).

Some patients with breast cancer respond favorably to hormonal therapy. This response usually correlates with the presence of estrogen and other hormone receptors found in

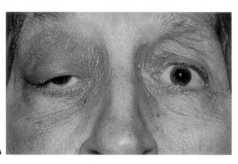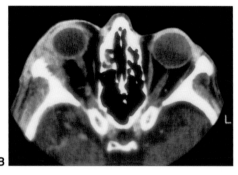

A B

Figure 5-22 **A,** Right upper eyelid ptosis, superior orbital mass, and eyelid inflammation in an elderly man with prostate carcinoma. **B,** CT scan showing superotemporal orbital mass with adjacent bony changes proven by biopsy to be metastatic prostate cancer. *(Courtesy of Robert C. Kersten, MD.)*

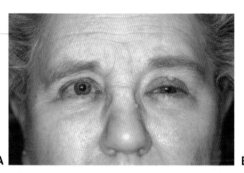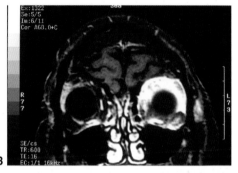

A B

Figure 5-23 **A,** Woman with enophthalmos and motility restriction secondary to metastatic breast carcinoma to the orbit. **B,** MRI showing diffuse inferior infiltration of orbit. *(Courtesy of John B. Holds, MD.)*

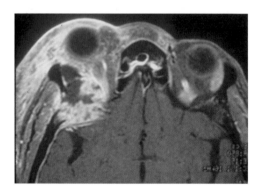

Figure 5-24 MRI of a metastatic adenocarcinoma infiltrating the marrow space of the sphenoid wing, which is a common site for hematogenous spread to the orbit, because of the low-flow venous channels in the bone marrow. *(Courtesy of Michael Kazim, MD.)*

the tumor tissue. If metastatic breast cancer is found at the time of orbital exploration, fresh tissue should be submitted for estrogen-receptor assay even if this test was previously performed because estrogen-receptor content may vary between the primary and the metastatic lesion. Hormone therapy is most likely to help patients whose tumors are receptor-positive.

Bronchogenic carcinoma

The most frequent source of orbital metastasis in men is bronchogenic carcinoma. The primary lesion may be quite small, and CT of suspicious lung lesions may be performed in patients suspected of having orbital metastases.

Prostatic carcinoma

Metastatic prostatic carcinoma can produce a clinical picture resembling that of acute pseudotumor. Typically, a lytic bone lesion is identified on a CT scan.

Management of Orbital Metastases

The treatment of metastatic tumors of the orbit is usually palliative, consisting of local radiation therapy. Some metastatic tumors, such as carcinoids and renal cell carcinomas, may be candidates for wide excision of the orbital lesion because some patients may survive for many years following resection of isolated metastases from these primary tumors. Consultation with the patient's oncologist should identify candidates who might benefit from wide excision.

Char DH, Miller T, Kroll S. Orbital metastases: diagnosis and course. *Br J Ophthalmol.* 1997;81:386–390.

Henderson JW, Campbell RJ, Farrow GM, et al. *Orbital Tumors.* 3rd ed. New York: Raven; 1994.

Rootman J, ed. *Diseases of the Orbit: A Multidisciplinary Approach.* Philadelphia: Lippincott; 1988.

CHAPTER 6

Orbital Trauma

Orbital trauma can damage the facial bones and adjacent soft tissues. Fractures may be associated with injuries to orbital contents, intracranial structures, and paranasal sinuses. Orbital hemorrhage and embedded foreign bodies may also be present and have secondary effects on the orbital soft tissues. Decreased visual acuity, intraocular injuries, strabismus, eyelid malpositions, and ptosis may occur.

Because of the high incidence of concomitant intraocular injury, an ocular examination must always be performed on patients who have sustained orbital trauma. Ocular damage accompanying orbital trauma may include hyphema, angle recession, corneoscleral laceration, retinal tear, retinal dialysis, and vitreous hemorrhage.

Midfacial (Le Fort) Fractures

Le Fort fractures involve the maxilla and are often complex and asymmetric (Figs 6-1, 6-2). By definition, Le Fort fractures must extend posteriorly through the pterygoid plates. Treatment may include dental stabilization with arch bars and open reduction of the fracture with rigid fixation using miniplating and microplating systems. These fractures may be divided into 3 categories, *although clinically they often do not conform precisely to these groupings.*

- *Le Fort I* is a low transverse maxillary fracture above the teeth with no orbital involvement.
- *Le Fort II* fractures generally have a pyramidal configuration and involve the nasal, lacrimal, and maxillary bones as well as the medial orbital floor.
- *Le Fort III* fractures cause craniofacial disjunction in which the entire facial skeleton may be completely detached from the base of the skull and suspended only by soft tissues. The orbital floor and medial and lateral orbital walls are involved.

Orbital Fractures

Zygomatic Fractures

Zygomaticomaxillary complex (ZMC) fractures are called *tripod fractures* (Fig 6-3), although the zygoma is usually fractured at 4 of its articulations with the adjacent bones

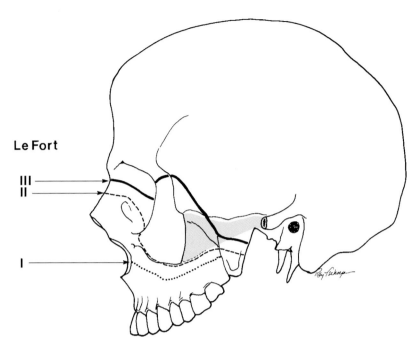

Le Fort

III
II

I

Figure 6-1 Le Fort fractures (lateral view). Note that all the fractures extend posteriorly through the pterygoid plates. *(Modified from Converse JM, ed.* Reconstructive Plastic Surgery: Principles and Procedures in Correction, Reconstruction, and Transplantation. *2nd ed. Philadelphia: Saunders; 1977:2.)*

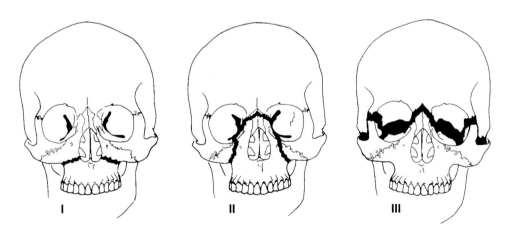

I   II   III

Figure 6-2 Le Fort's classification of midfacial fractures. Le Fort I, horizontal fracture of the maxilla, also known as Guérin fracture. Le Fort II, pyramidal fracture of the maxilla. Le Fort III, craniofacial disjunction. *(Modified from Converse JM, ed.* Reconstructive Plastic Surgery: Principles and Procedures in Correction, Reconstruction, and Transplantation. *2nd ed. Philadelphia: Saunders; 1977:2.)*

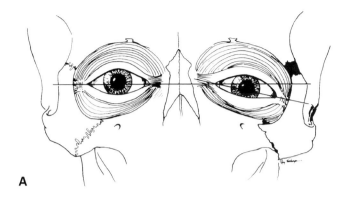

A

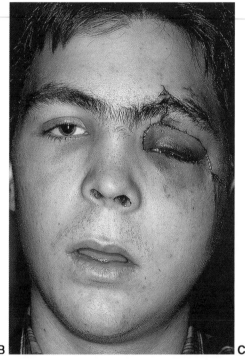

B

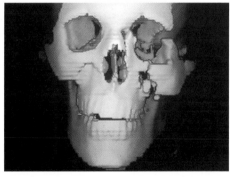

C

Figure 6-3 **A,** Zygomatic fracture (anterior view). Downward displacement of the globe and lateral canthus as a result of frontozygomatic separation and downward displacement of the zygoma and the floor of the orbit. **B,** Globe ptosis and lateral canthal dystopia due to widely displaced zygomaticomaxillary complex (ZMC) fracture. **C,** Three-dimensional CT scan of a ZMC fracture. Note the displaced zygoma and an additional fracture of the medial buttress. *(Part A modified from Converse JM, ed. Reconstructive Plastic Surgery: Principles and Procedures in Correction, Reconstruction, and Transplantation. 2nd ed. Philadelphia: Saunders; 1977:2. Parts B and C reproduced with permission from Nerad JA. The Requisites in Ophthalmology: Oculoplastic Surgery. Philadelphia: Mosby; 2001:340.)*

(lateral orbital rim, inferior orbital rim, zygomatic arch, and lateral wall of the maxillary sinus). The zygomaticomaxillary complex fracture involves the orbital floor to varying degrees. If the zygoma is not significantly displaced, no treatment is necessary. Zygomaticomaxillary complex fractures can cause globe displacement, cosmetic deformity, diplopia, and trismus due to fracture impingement on the coronoid process of the mandible.

When treatment is indicated, the best results are obtained with open reduction of the fracture and fixation with miniature metal plates that are attached with bone screws. Exact realignment and stabilization of the maxillary buttress and the lateral orbital wall are essential for accurate fracture reduction and can be achieved through a sublabial or buccal sulcus incision. It is not necessary to routinely explore the orbital floor in all patients unless there is concern that orbital contents may have been entrapped in fracture reduction.

Shumrick KA, Kersten RC, Kulwin DR, Sinha PK, Smith TL. Extended access/internal approaches for the management of facial trauma. *Arch Otolaryngol Head Neck Surg.* 1992;118:1105–1112.

Shumrick KA, Kersten RC, Kulwin DR, Smith CP. Criteria for selective management of the orbital rim and floor in zygomatic complex and midface fractures. *Arch Otolaryngol Head Neck Surg.* 1997;123:378–384.

Orbital Apex Fractures

Orbital apex fractures usually occur in association with other fractures of the face, orbit, or skull and may involve the optic canal, superior orbital fissure, and structures that pass through them. Possible associated complications include damage to the optic nerves, with decreased visual acuity; cerebrospinal fluid leaks; and carotid cavernous sinus fistulas. Indirect traumatic optic neuropathy usually results from stretching, tearing, twisting, or bruising of the fixed canalicular portion of the nerve as the cranial skeleton suffers sudden deceleration. In most patients, thin-section computed tomography (CT) through the orbital apex and anterior clinoid processes demonstrates fractures at or adjacent to the optic canal. The management of neurogenic visual loss after blunt head trauma is discussed at the end of this chapter.

Orbital Roof Fractures

Orbital roof fractures are usually caused by blunt trauma or missile injuries and are more common in young children who have not yet pneumatized the frontal sinus. The brain and cribriform plate may be involved. Frontal trauma in older patients tends to be absorbed by the frontal sinus, which acts as a crumple zone, preventing extension along the orbital roof. Complications include intracranial injuries, cerebrospinal fluid rhinorrhea, pneumocephalus, subperiosteal hematoma, ptosis, and extraocular muscle imbalance. The entrapment of extraocular muscles is rare, with most early diplopia being due to hematoma, edema, or contusion of the orbital structures. In severely comminuted fractures, pulsating exophthalmos may occur as a delayed complication. Young children may develop nondisplaced linear roof fractures after fairly minor trauma, which may present with delayed ecchymosis of the upper eyelid. Most roof fractures do not require repair.

Indications for surgery are generally neurosurgical, and treatment involves a team approach with a neurosurgeon and an orbital surgeon.

Greenwald MJ, Boston D, Pensler JM, Radkowski MA. Orbital roof fractures in childhood. *Ophthalmology.* 1989;96:491–496.

Medial Orbital Fractures

Direct (naso-orbital-ethmoidal) fractures (Fig 6-4) usually result from the face striking solid surfaces. These fractures commonly involve the frontal process of the maxilla, the lacrimal bone, and the ethmoid bones along the medial wall of the orbit. Patients characteristically have a depressed bridge of the nose and traumatic telecanthus. Complications include cerebral and ocular damage, severe epistaxis due to avulsion of the anterior ethmoidal artery, orbital hematoma, cerebrospinal fluid rhinorrhea, damage to the lacrimal drainage system, lateral displacement of the medial canthus, and associated fractures of the medial orbital wall and floor. Treatment includes repair of the nasal fracture and miniplate stabilization. Transnasal wiring of the medial canthus is used less frequently, as miniplate fixation often allows precise bony reduction.

Indirect (blowout) fractures are frequently extensions of blowout fractures of the orbital floor. Isolated blowout fractures of the medial orbital wall also may occur. Surgical intervention is seldom necessary unless the medial rectus muscle or its associated tissues are

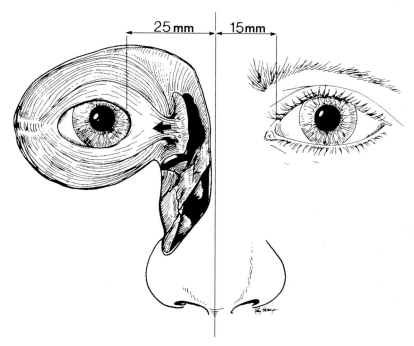

Figure 6-4 Lateral displacement of the medial orbital wall results in traumatic telecanthus and rounding of the medial canthus. *(Modified from Beyer CK, Fabian FL, Smith B. Naso-orbital fractures, complications, and treatment. Ophthalmology. 1982;89:458.)*

entrapped. Significant enophthalmos is uncommon after isolated medial wall blowouts. Emphysema of the eyelids and orbit is commonly associated with fractures of the medial orbital wall. (Fractures of the sinuses may allow air to enter the subcutaneous tissues, and this air may be seen on radiographs.)

Large, isolated medial wall fractures may result in cosmetically noticeable enophthalmos; however, the risk of enophthalmos is greatest when both the floor and the medial wall are fractured. If surgery is required, the medial orbital wall may be approached by continuing the exploration of the floor up along the medial wall via the eyelid or trans-conjunctival approach. An alternative approach is a medial orbitotomy through the skin or caruncle.

Nolasco FP, Mathog RH. Medial orbital wall fractures: classification and clinical profile. *Otolaryngol Head Neck Surg.* 1995;112:549–556.

Orbital Floor Fractures

Direct fractures of the orbital floor can extend from fractures of the inferior orbital rim. Indications for repair of the orbital floor in these cases are the same as those for indirect (blowout) fractures. Indirect fractures of the orbital floor are not associated with fracture of the inferior orbital rim.

Past theory held that blowout fractures were caused by a sudden increase in intraorbital pressure resulting from the application of force by a nonpenetrating object, usually smaller in diameter than the orbital entrance. According to this theory, the contents of the orbit are compressed posteriorly toward the apex of the orbit, and the orbital bones break at their weakest point, usually the posterior medial part of the floor in the maxillary bone. The orbital contents may be entrapped or may prolapse through the fracture into the maxillary sinus. More recently, it has been suggested that the striking object may cause a compressive force at the inferior rim, and this force leads directly to buckling of the orbital floor. In this case, the degree of increased orbital pressure determines whether orbital tissues are pushed down through the fracture into the maxillary antrum.

Kersten RC. Blowout fracture of the orbital floor with entrapment caused by isolated trauma to the orbital rim. *Am J Ophthalmol.* 1987;103:215–220.
Whitehouse RW, Batterbury M, Jackson A, Noble JL. Prediction of enophthalmos by computed tomography after 'blow out' orbital fracture. *Br J Ophthalmol.* 1994;78:618–620.

Blowout fractures of the orbital floor are suggested by the patient's history, physical examination, and radiographs (Fig 6-5). There is a history of the orbital entrance being struck by an object, usually one larger than the diameter of the orbital opening (eg, a ball, an automobile dashboard, or a fist). An orbital blowout fracture should be suspected in any patient who has received a periorbital blow forceful enough to cause ecchymosis. Physical examination typically reveals the following:

- *Eyelid signs.* Ecchymosis and edema of the eyelids may be seen, but external signs of injury can be absent.
- *Diplopia with limitation of upgaze, downgaze, or both.* Limited vertical movement of the globe, vertical diplopia, and pain in the inferior orbit on attempted vertical movement of the globe are consistent with entrapment of the inferior rectus muscle

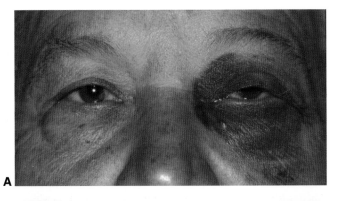

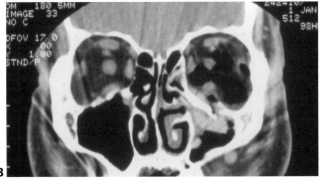

Figure 6-5 **A,** Periocular ecchymosis associated with an orbital fracture. **B,** Coronal CT scan demonstrating orbital emphysema, a floor fracture, and prolapse of intraorbital contents into the maxillary sinus. *(Courtesy of Warren J. Chang, MD.)*

or its adjacent septa in the fracture. Orbital edema and hemorrhage or damage to the extraocular muscles or their innervation can also limit movement of the globe. A significant limitation of both horizontal and vertical eye movements should alert the examiner to the likelihood of nerve damage or of generalized soft tissue injury. Limitations of globe movements caused by hemorrhage or edema generally improve during the first 1–2 weeks after injury. If entrapment is present, a traction test should show restriction of passive movement of the eye; however, restriction can also result from edema and hemorrhage. A vertical traction test, sometimes called a *forced duction test,* is performed most easily with the instillation of anesthetic eyedrops followed by a cotton pledget containing 4% cocaine solution applied in the inferior cul-de-sac for several minutes. Using a toothed forceps, the examiner grasps the insertion of the inferior rectus muscle through the conjunctiva and attempts to rotate the globe gently up and down. Comparing the intraocular pressure (IOP) as measured in primary position and in upgaze usually shows a significant increase in upgaze if the inferior rectus is entrapped. Comparing ductions and versions also helps differentiate paretic from entrapped extraocular muscles.

- *Enophthalmos and ptosis of the globe.* These findings occur with large fractures in which the orbital soft tissues prolapse into the maxillary sinus. A medial wall fracture, if associated with the orbital floor fracture, may significantly contribute to enophthalmos because of prolapse of the orbital tissues into both the ethmoid and the maxillary sinuses. Enophthalmos may be masked by orbital edema immediately following the injury, but enophthalmos becomes more apparent as the orbital edema subsides and contracture pulls the soft tissues farther into the sinus.

- *Hypoesthesia in the distribution of the infraorbital nerve.*
- *Emphysema of the orbit and eyelids.* Any fracture that extends into a sinus may allow air to escape into the subcutaneous tissues, but this occurs most commonly with medial wall fractures.

In patients with orbital floor fractures, vision loss can result from injury to the optic nerve or increased orbital pressure causing a *compartment syndrome* (discussed under Traumatic Visual Loss With Clear Media). An orbital hemorrhage should be suspected if loss of vision is associated with proptosis and increased IOP. Injuries to the globe and ocular adnexa may also be present.

Computed tomographic scans with coronal or sagittal views are usually indicated to help guide treatment. They allow evaluation of fracture size and extraocular muscle relationships, providing information that can be used to help predict enophthalmos and muscle entrapment.

The majority of blowout or other orbital floor fractures do not require surgical intervention. Orbital blowout fractures are usually observed for 7–10 days so that swelling and orbital hemorrhage can subside. Oral steroids (1 mg/kg per day for the first 7 days) decrease edema and may also limit the risk of long-term diplopia from inferior rectus contracture and fibrosis.

An exception to initial observation occurs in pediatric patients, in whom the inferior rectus muscle may become tightly trapped beneath a trapdoor fracture. In these patients, vertical globe excursion is significantly limited, and CT reveals the inferior rectus muscle within the maxillary sinus. Attempted ocular excursions may stimulate the oculocardiac reflex, causing pain, nausea, and bradycardia. Urgent repair should be undertaken in these cases. Release of the entrapped muscle without delay may limit ultimate restriction and fibrosis.

Egbert JE, May K, Kersten RC, Kulwin DR. Pediatric orbital floor fracture: direct extraocular muscle involvement. *Ophthalmology.* 2000;107:1875–1879.
Jordan DR, Allen LH, White J, et al. Intervention within days for some orbital floor fractures: the white-eyed blowout. *Ophthal Plast Reconstr Surg.* 1998;14:379–390.

Although the indications for surgery are controversial, certain guidelines are helpful in determining when surgery is advisable:

- *Diplopia with limitation of upgaze and/or downgaze within 30° of the primary position with a positive traction test result 7–10 days after injury and with radiologic confirmation of a fracture of the orbital floor.* These findings indicate functional entrapment of tissues affecting the inferior rectus muscle. Diplopia may improve significantly over the course of the first 2 weeks as orbital edema, hemorrhage, or both resolve and as some of the entrapped tissues stretch. However, if the findings are still present after 2 weeks and if the entrapped tissues are not freed, vertical diplopia is likely to persist. As mentioned previously, tight entrapment of the inferior rectus muscle with a frozen globe is an indication for immediate repair.

- *Enophthalmos that exceeds 2 mm and that is cosmetically unacceptable to the patient.* Enophthalmos is usually masked by orbital edema immediately after the trauma, and several weeks may pass before the extent of this problem is fully appreciated. Appropriate measurements must be taken at the initial evaluation and at subsequent visits. If significant enophthalmos is present within the first 2 weeks and associated with a large orbital floor fracture, even greater enophthalmos can be anticipated in the future.
- *Large fractures involving at least half of the orbital floor, particularly when associated with large medial wall fractures (determined by CT).* Orbital fractures of this size have a high incidence of subsequent significant enophthalmos.

Gilbard SM, Mafee MF, Lagouros PA, Langer BG. Orbital blowout fractures: the prognostic significance of computed tomography. *Ophthalmology.* 1985;92:1523–1528.

Harris GJ, Garcia GH, Logani SC, Murphy ML. Correlation of preoperative computed tomography and postoperative ocular motility in orbital blowout fractures. *Ophthal Plast Reconstr Surg.* 2000;16:179–187.

Hawes MJ, Dortzbach RK. Surgery on orbital floor fractures: influence of time of repair and fracture size. *Ophthalmology.* 1983;90:1066–1070.

Rubin PAD, Bilyk JR, Shore JW. Management of orbital trauma: fractures, hemorrhage, and traumatic optic neuropathy. *Focal Points: Clinical Modules for Ophthalmologists.* San Francisco: American Academy of Ophthalmology; 1994, module 7.

Management

When surgery is indicated for blowout fractures of the orbital floor, it generally is preferable to proceed with the repair within 2 weeks of the initial trauma. Formation of scar tissue and contracture of the prolapsed tissue make later correction of entrapment and diplopia difficult. Patients with extraocular muscle entrapment on CT have profoundly limited vertical excursions. Larger fractures in which eventual enophthalmos is anticipated are also easier to fix within the first 2 weeks of the trauma; however, satisfactory correction of enophthalmos can usually be obtained even if surgery is delayed.

The surgical approach to blowout fractures of the orbital floor can be made through an infraciliary incision or a conjunctival (inferior fornix) incision combined with a lateral cantholysis. The approaches through the lower eyelid have the following steps in common: elevation of the periorbita from the orbital floor, release of the prolapsed tissues from the fracture, and usually the placement of an implant over the fracture to prevent recurrent adhesions and prolapse of the orbital tissues.

The development of miniplating and microplating systems and their various metallic orbital implants has significantly improved the management of large unstable orbital floor fractures. Orbital implants can be alloplastic (porous polyethylene, Supramid, GORE-TEX, Teflon, silicone sheet, or titanium mesh) or autogenous (split cranial bone, iliac crest bone, or fascia). The harvesting of autogenous grafts requires an additional operative site, and bone grafts are rarely indicated.

Delayed treatment of blowout fractures to correct debilitating strabismus and diplopia or cosmetically unacceptable enophthalmos may include exploration of the orbital floor in an attempt to free the scarred tissues entrapped or prolapsed through the fracture and to replace them in the orbit. Other measures are strabismus surgery and procedures to camouflage the enophthalmos with its associated narrowed palpebral fissure and deep superior sulcus.

Complications of blowout fracture surgery include decreased visual acuity or blindness, diplopia, undercorrection or overcorrection of enophthalmos, lower eyelid retraction, infraorbital nerve hypoesthesia, infection, extrusion of the implant, lymphedema, and damage to the lacrimal pump.

Intraorbital Foreign Bodies

If foreign bodies within the orbit are radiopaque, they can be localized by plain-film radiographs or by CT or magnetic resonance imaging (MRI). (Some wooden foreign bodies may be missed on CT and are seen better on MRI. However, MRI should be avoided if there is a possibility that the foreign object is ferromagnetic.) If an embedded foreign body causes an orbital infection that drains to the skin surface, it is sometimes possible to locate the object by surgically following the fistulous tract posteriorly. Treatment of orbital foreign bodies initially involves culturing the wound (or the foreign body if it is removed) and administering antibiotics. Foreign bodies should be removed if they are composed of vegetable matter or if they are easily accessible in the anterior orbit. In many cases, objects can be safely observed without surgery if they are inert and have smooth edges or are located in the posterior orbit. Specifically, BBs are common intraorbital foreign bodies and are usually best left in situ. Magnetic resonance imaging can be safely performed with a BB in the orbit.

Finkelstein M, Legmann A, Rubin PAD. Projectile metallic foreign bodies in the orbit: a retrospective study of epidemiologic factors, management, and outcomes. *Ophthalmology.* 1997;104:96–103.

McGuckin JF Jr, Akhtar N, Ho VT, Smergel EM, Kubacki EJ, Villafana T. CT and MR evaluation of a wooden foreign body in an in vitro model of the orbit. *Am J Neuroradiol.* 1996;17:129–133.

Orbital Hemorrhage

Hemorrhage into the orbit can arise after trauma or surgery or occur spontaneously in association with an underlying orbital lymphangioma or varix (Fig 6-6). Lateral canthotomy and cantholysis, orbital decompression, or surgical drainage is seldom necessary unless visual function is compromised by (1) compression of the optic nerve or (2) increased orbital pressure that impedes arterial perfusion. Occasionally, a blood (hematic) cyst may form following accidental trauma, usually beneath the periosteum.

Kersten RC, Kersten JL, Bloom HR, Kulwin DR. Chronic hematic cysts of the orbit. Role of magnetic resonance imaging in diagnosis. *Ophthalmology.* 1988;95:1549–1553.

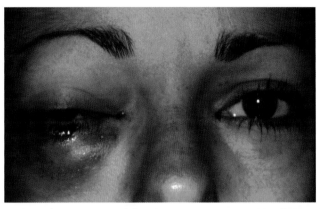

Figure 6-6 Proptosis and ecchymosis following spontaneous orbital hemorrhage associated with an orbital varix. Because of severe visual loss, the patient had lateral canthotomy and inferior cantholysis. *(Courtesy of Warren J. Chang, MD.)*

Traumatic Visual Loss With Clear Media

Many patients complain of decreased vision following periocular trauma. The decrease may be due to injuries of the cornea, lens, vitreous, or retina as previously discussed. Patients without globe damage may also complain of decreased vision because of serosanguinous drainage obscuring incident light. In addition, swelling of the eyelids may cause difficulty in opening the eyes sufficiently to clear the visual axis. However, a small percentage of patients have true visual loss without any evidence of globe injury. Visual loss in this setting suggests traumatic dysfunction of the optic nerve. Such visual loss usually results from 1 of 3 mechanisms:

- direct injury to the optic nerve from a penetrating wound
- disruption of the blood supply to the optic nerve due to a compartment syndrome, in which posttraumatic orbital edema or hemorrhage causes orbital pressure to increase above arterial perfusion pressure
- indirect injury caused by force from a frontal blow transmitted to the optic nerve in the orbital apex and optic canal

All patients with decreased visual acuity following periorbital trauma should be immediately examined for evidence of direct globe injury. Two key diagnostic questions should be answered when the patient has reduced vision with an apparently normal globe:

- Is an afferent pupillary defect present?
- Is there a "tight" orbit?

Detection of an afferent defect in the presence of an intact globe strongly suggests traumatic optic neuropathy. However, the examiner must remember that detection of an afferent defect may be difficult if the patient has received narcotics that can cause bilateral pupillary constriction. The second key diagnostic determination is that of intraorbital pressure. Periorbital trauma may cause significant retrobulbar hemorrhage or edema, which can lead to proptosis, ptosis, and limitation of extraocular motility. A Schiøtz tonometer or Tono-Pen may be used in the emergency room to measure IOP, which is increased in the tight orbit in response to the underlying increased orbital pressure. Although fundus examination may reveal a central retinal artery occlusion, visual loss is more often caused by occlusion of the posterior ciliary arteries, which have a lower perfusion pressure than the central retinal artery.

Patients with a tight orbit, increased IOP, and decreased visual acuity with afferent pupillary defect should undergo emergent decompression of the orbit. This is most easily achieved by disinsertion of the lids from the lateral canthus, allowing the orbital volume to expand anteriorly. Lateral canthotomy alone does not sufficiently increase the orbital volume; inferior cantholysis and sometimes superior cantholysis are also required. Surgical relief of the increased orbital pressure is a priority. Although IOP is elevated in the setting of traumatic orbital hemorrhage, the elevation reflects the increased orbital pressure and is not indicative of glaucoma (although angle-closure glaucoma can rarely occur following retrobulbar hemorrhages).

If a tight orbit has been ruled out, then a mechanism other than an ischemic compartment syndrome should be sought to explain the visual loss. The circumstances suggest indirect trauma to the optic nerve. The shock wave from trauma is transmitted through the orbital contents and can result in significant injury. Patients with this disorder usually have a history of blunt trauma to the frontal region or rapid deceleration of the cranium and often have experienced loss of consciousness associated with head trauma. Thin-section CT scans of the orbital apex and anterior clinoid process demonstrate fractures through or adjacent to the optic canal in most cases.

Management

The proper management of neurogenic visual loss after blunt head trauma is controversial. No treatment, high-dose corticosteroids, and surgical decompression of the optic canal are all currently considered to be reasonable options. Interest in high-dose methylprednisolone (30 mg/kg loading dose and 15 mg/kg every 6 hours) in traumatic optic neuropathy is supported by the success of this regimen in the National Acute Spinal Cord Injury Study II, wherein the regimen was found to produce significant improvement in patients treated within 8 hours of injury. As the steroid is given in such megadoses, the therapeutic effect appears to be based on the steroid's antioxidant, rather than anti-inflammatory, properties. The success seen with methylprednisolone as therapy for spinal cord injuries may not be applicable to the treatment of traumatic optic neuropathy, however; trial data for optic nerve injuries are lacking.

For a time, interest focused on surgical decompression of the optic canal in patients in whom high-dose steroids failed. Decompression of the medial wall of the bony optic canal through a transethmoidal sphenoidal route undertaken within 5 days of injury was purported to return vision to patients with indirect traumatic optic neuropathy. However, the optimal management of traumatic optic neuropathy remains unresolved because no large randomized studies have been carried out. A recent multicenter, prospective, non-randomized study failed to demonstrate clear benefit for either corticosteroid therapy or optic canal decompression. Successful results with steroid therapy or surgical treatment remain anecdotal, and a number of traumatic optic neuropathy cases have documented significant visual improvement without therapy.

Joseph MP, Lessell S, Rizzo J, Momose KJ. Extracranial optic nerve decompression for traumatic optic neuropathy. *Arch Ophthalmol.* 1990;108:1091–1093.

Levin LA, Beck RW, Joseph MP, Seiff S, Kraker R. The treatment of traumatic optic neuropathy: the International Optic Nerve Trauma Study. *Ophthalmology.* 1999;106:1268–1277.

Levin LA, Joseph MP, Rizzo JF III, Lessell S. Optic canal decompression in indirect optic nerve trauma. *Ophthalmology.* 1994;101:566–569.

Steinsapir KD, Goldberg RA. Traumatic optic neuropathy. *Surv Ophthalmol.* 1994;38:487–518.

CHAPTER **7**

Orbital Surgery

Surgical Spaces

There are 5 surgical spaces within the orbit (Fig 7-1):

1. the *subperiorbital (subperiosteal) surgical space,* which is the potential space between the bone and the periorbita
2. the *extraconal surgical space* (peripheral surgical space), which lies between the periorbita and the muscle cone with its fascia
3. the *intraconal surgical space* (central surgical space), which lies within the muscle cone
4. the *episcleral (sub-Tenon's) surgical space,* which lies between Tenon's capsule and the globe
5. the *subarachnoid surgical space,* which lies between the optic nerve and the nerve sheath

Orbital lesions may involve more than 1 space, and an orbital pathologic process may require a combination of approaches. Incisions to reach these surgical spaces via anterior or lateral orbitotomies are shown in Figure 7-2.

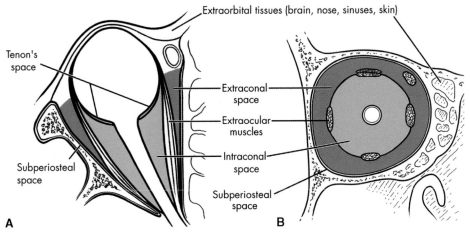

Figure 7-1 Surgical spaces of the orbit. **A,** Axial view. **B,** Coronal view. *(Reproduced with permission from Nerad JA. The Requisites in Ophthalmology: Oculoplastic Surgery. Philadelphia: Mosby; 2001:350.)*

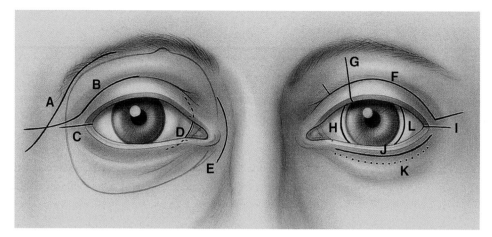

Figure 7-2 Sites of surgical entry into the orbit. *A,* Older Stallard-Wright lateral orbitotomy. *B,* Newer eyelid crease lateral orbitotomy. *C,* Canthotomy lateral orbitotomy. *D,* Transcaruncular medial orbitotomy. *E,* Frontoethmoidal (Lynch) medial orbitotomy. *F,* Upper eyelid crease anterior orbitotomy. *G,* Vertical eyelid split superomedial orbitotomy. *H,* Medial bulbar conjunctival orbitotomy. *I,* Lateral canthotomy anterior orbitotomy. *J,* Subciliary inferior orbitotomy. *K,* Transconjunctival inferior orbitotomy. *L,* Lateral bulbar conjunctival orbitotomy. *(Illustration by Christine Gralapp after a drawing by Jennifer Clemens.)*

Anterior Orbitotomy

Superior Approach

More orbital lesions are located in the superoanterior part of the orbit than in any other location. Lesions in this area can usually be reached through a transcutaneous or transconjunctival route. The surgeon must take care to avoid damaging the levator and superior oblique muscles, trochlea, lacrimal gland, and sensory nerves and vessels leaving or entering the orbit along the superior orbital rim.

Transcutaneous routes

The *transseptal route* provides entry into the extraconal surgical space. The upper eyelid crease is an excellent skin incision location for this route because this crease provides good surgical exposure and the scar is hidden.

For the *subperiosteal route,* skin incisions in the upper eyelid crease also offer good access to the superior orbital rim, where the periosteum can be incised, and superior cosmesis to incisions adjacent to the eyebrow. After making an upper eyelid crease incision, the surgeon can readily obtain access to the superior orbital rim by dissecting superiorly in the postorbicularis fascial plane. Exposure of the superior orbital rim allows entry into the subperiosteal space. By initially keeping the periorbita intact, the surgeon protects the orbital structures from the plane of dissection and excludes orbital fat from the surgical field.

Upper eyelid crease incisions may also be used for entry into the medial intraconal space, which requires exposure of the medial edge of the levator muscle and dissection through the intermuscular septum extending from the superior rectus to the medial rectus muscles. This approach may be used for exposure and fenestration of the retrobulbar optic nerve in cases of idiopathic intracranial hypertension.

Occasionally, a coronal scalp flap is used to expose superior orbital lesions. The purpose of this route is to avoid visible scars on the face; however, alopecia often occurs along the incision, and balding in men may expose the scar later. This route is most helpful for transcranial orbitotomies and for extensive lesions of the superior orbit and sinuses that require bone removal for access. Although the coronal incision has been used to gain access for lateral orbitotomy, this incision requires extensive elevation of the temporalis muscle, which may result in cosmetically significant temporal wasting postoperatively.

Harris GJ, Logani SC. Eyelid crease incision for lateral orbitotomy. *Ophthal Plast Reconstr Surg.* 1999;151:(9)–16.

Stewart WB, Levin PS, Toth BA. Orbital surgery. The technique of coronal scalp flap approach to lateral orbitotomy. *Arch Ophthalmol.* 1988;106:1724–1726.

Transconjunctival route

Incisions in the superior conjunctiva can be used to reach the superonasal, episcleral, intraconal, or extraconal surgical spaces, but dissection must be carried out medial to the levator muscle so that postoperative ptosis can be prevented.

Vertical eyelid splitting

Vertical splitting of the upper eyelid at the junction of the medial and central thirds allows extended transconjunctival exposure for the removal of superior medial intraconal tumors. The surgeon incises the eyelid and levator aponeurosis vertically to allow exposure of the superomedial intraconal space. Realignment of the tarsal plate and aponeurosis with vertical closure prevents postoperative ptosis and eyelid retraction, which are likely to occur if the levator muscle is transected horizontally.

Kersten RC, Kulwin DR. Vertical lid split orbitotomy revisited. *Ophthal Plast Reconstr Surg.* 1999;15(6):425–428.

Inferior Approach

The inferior approach is suitable for masses that are visible or palpable in the inferior conjunctival fornix of the lower eyelid, as well as for deeper inferior extraconal orbital masses. The surgeon can gain access to intraconal lesions by dissecting between the inferior rectus and the lateral rectus muscles. The inferior oblique muscle inserts over the macula and may be identified and retracted while intraconal lesions are accessed. This route is also used to approach the orbital floor for fracture repair or decompression.

Transcutaneous routes

An infraciliary blepharoplasty incision in the lower eyelid and dissection beneath the orbicularis muscle to expose the inferior orbital septum and inferior orbital rim minimize visible scarring. An incision in the lower eyelid crease can provide the same exposure but it leaves a slightly more obvious scar. However, placement of the incision in the eyelid crease reduces the risk of scar contracture and ectropion. The surgeon can then incise the septum to expose the extraconal surgical space but must take care to avoid cutting lower eyelid tissue perpendicular to normal skin lines because cutting this tissue disrupts lymphatic drainage and causes persistent lymphedema postoperatively.

For the *subperiosteal route,* a skin incision beneath the eyelashes or in the lower eyelid crease allows exposure of the rim, where the periosteum can be incised so that the floor of the orbit is exposed. Fractures of the orbital floor are reached by the subperiosteal route. Incisions made directly over the orbital rim leave a more objectionable scar.

Transconjunctival route

The transconjunctival approach (Fig 7-3) has largely replaced the transcutaneous route for exposure of tumors in the inferior orbit and for management of fractures of the orbital floor and medial wall (Fig 7-4). To reach the extraconal surgical space and the orbital floor, the surgeon may make an incision through the inferior conjunctiva and lower eyelid retractors. Exposure of the floor is optimized when this incision is combined with a lateral canthotomy and cantholysis. Incision of the bulbar conjunctiva and Tenon's capsule allows entry to the episcleral surgical space, and if the inferior rectus is retracted, the intraconal surgical space can be accessed.

Medial Approach

When dissecting in the medial orbit, the surgeon should be careful to avoid damaging the medial canthal tendon, lacrimal canaliculi and sac, trochlea, superior oblique tendon and muscle, inferior oblique muscle, and sensory nerves and vessels along the medial aspect of the superior orbital rim.

Transcutaneous route

Tumors within or near the lacrimal sac, frontal or ethmoidal sinuses, and medial rectus muscle can be approached through a skin incision (Lynch, or frontoethmoidal, incision) placed vertically just medial to the insertion of the medial canthal tendon (approximately 9–10 mm medial to the medial canthal angle). This route usually is used to enter the subperiosteal space. The medial canthal tendon can be reflected with the periosteum and, therefore, does not need to be incised. Superomedial intraconal lesions can be approached through a medial upper eyelid crease incision. The superior oblique tendon must be identified, and then dissection is carried out medial to the medial horn of the levator muscle, providing access to the intraconal space.

Pelton RW, Patel BC. Superomedial lid crease approach to the medial intraconal space: a new technique for access to the optic nerve and central space. *Ophthal Plast Reconstr Surg.* 2001;17(4):241–253.

Transconjunctival route

An incision in the bulbar conjunctiva allows entry into the extraconal surgical space. If the medial rectus is detached, the surgeon can enter the intraconal surgical space to

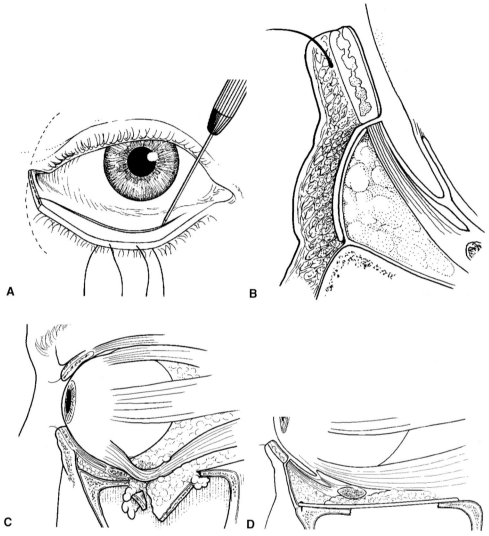

Figure 7-3 Inferior transconjunctival approach to the orbital floor. **A,** Canthotomy, cantholysis, and conjunctival incision. **B,** Plane of dissection anterior to the orbital septum. **C,** Tissue trapped in fracture. **D,** Reconstruction of orbital floor with implant after release of entrapped tissue. *(Reproduced with permission from Nerad JA. The Requisites in Ophthalmology: Oculoplastic Surgery. Philadelphia: Mosby; 2001:335–336.)*

expose the region of the anterior optic nerve for examination, biopsy, or decompression. If the posterior optic nerve or muscle cone needs to be visualized well, a combined lateral/medial orbitotomy can be performed. A lateral orbitotomy with removal of the lateral orbital wall to allow the globe to be displaced temporally is followed by a medial orbitotomy with detachment of the medial rectus muscle to provide good exposure of the posterior intraconal surgical space. A canthotomy incision combined with elevation of overlying soft tissue provides good exposure of the rim.

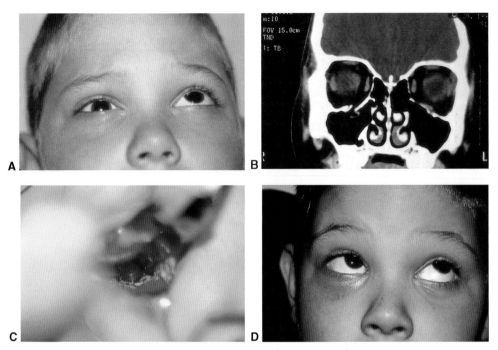

Figure 7-4 A, Marked restriction of elevation of the right eye in a young child with white-eyed blowout fracture. **B,** Coronal CT demonstrates right orbital floor trapdoor fracture. The inferior rectus muscle is displaced beneath the fracture into the maxillary sinus. **C,** Transconjunctival exploration of the orbital floor. The inferior rectus muscle can be seen entrapped in the fracture line. **D,** Restoration of elevation following release of the entrapped muscle. *(Courtesy of Robert C. Kersten, MD.)*

Transcaruncular route

An incision through conjunctiva immediately lateral to the caruncle allows excellent exposure of the medial periosteum. Dissection carried medially, just posterior to the lacrimal sac, allows access to the subperiosteal space along the medial wall. Incision and elevation of the medial periorbita allow exposure of the medial orbital wall. This incision has the advantage of providing better cosmetic results than the traditional frontoethmoidal, or Lynch, incision, but the surgeon must be careful to protect the lacrimal canaliculi and to remain posterior to the lacrimal apparatus. The combination of the transcaruncular route with an inferior transconjunctival incision allows extensive exposure of the inferior and medial orbit. This approach provides excellent access for repair of medial wall fractures, for medial orbital bone decompression, and for drainage of medial subperiosteal abscesses.

Shorr N, Baylis HI, Goldberg RA, Perry JD. Transcaruncular approach to the medial orbit and orbital apex. *Ophthalmology.* 2000;107(8):1459–1463.

Tsirbas A, Kazim M, Close L. Endoscopic approach to orbital apex lesions. *Ophthal Plast Reconstr Surg.* 2005;21(4):271–275.

Lateral Approach

Lesions in the anterior intraconal space lateral to the optic nerve may be exposed through either an upper eyelid crease incision (as discussed earlier) or a lateral canthotomy incision. A canthotomy incision allows exposure of the lateral orbital rim, and dissecting through the intermuscular septum either above or below the lateral rectus muscle and posterior to the equator of the globe provides access to the retrobulbar space. The retrobulbar optic nerve may be reached in this fashion and fenestrated in cases of idiopathic intracranial hypertension.

Kersten RC, Kulwin DR. Optic nerve sheath fenestration through a lateral canthotomy incision. *Arch Ophthalmol.* 1993;111:870–874.

Lateral Orbitotomy

A lateral orbitotomy is usually indicated when a lesion is located within the lateral intraconal space, behind the equator of the globe, or in the lacrimal gland fossa, particularly when a benign mixed tumor of the lacrimal gland is suspected. As the orbits are more shallow in children than in adults, extensive exposure of the orbits without the need for bone removal is possible in children. The traditional S-shaped Stallard-Wright skin incision, extending from beneath the eyebrow laterally and curving down along the zygomatic arch, allowed good exposure of the lateral rim but left a more noticeable scar. It has largely been replaced for lateral orbital exposure by newer approaches, through either an upper eyelid crease incision or a lateral canthotomy incision. Both of these approaches allow subcutaneous undermining and exposure of the lateral orbital rim and anterior portion of the zygomatic arch with reflection of the temporalis muscle.

As mentioned previously, in patients with shallow orbits, a lesion may be adequately exposed through the upper eyelid crease incision or the lateral canthotomy approach without the need for removal of the bony lateral wall; the same possibility exists when the lesion is located more anteriorly in the lacrimal fossa. If a lesion cannot be adequately exposed, an oscillating saw is used to remove the bone of the lateral rim to expose the underlying periorbita, which is then opened. An operating microscope is often useful during intraorbital surgery, especially if dissection proceeds inside the muscle cone. Good exposure of the intraconal surgical space can be achieved with retraction of the lateral rectus muscle. Tumors can occasionally be prolapsed into the incision by application of gentle pressure over the eyelids. A cryosurgical probe or Allis forceps can be useful in providing firm traction on encapsulated tumors. In cavernous hemangiomas, a suture through the lesion allows not only traction but also slow decompression of the tumor to facilitate its removal.

Complete hemostasis should be accomplished before closure. A drain may be placed through the skin to reach the deep orbital tissues. The lateral orbital rim is usually replaced and may be sutured in place through predrilled tunnels in the rim. Alternatively, the surgeon may plate or fixate the lateral orbital rim by firmly suturing the investing periosteum. The overlying tissues are then returned to their normal positions and sutured. The use of steel wire is avoided because it can cause artifacts on follow-up computed tomographic scans. The surgeon loosely closes the periosteum to allow postoperative hemorrhage to decompress.

Radical surgery, such as exenteration or extensive resection with potential for significant functional morbidity, should not be performed on the basis of a frozen-section biopsy report. The surgeon should await the permanent-section histopathology report and discuss the matter further with the patient before proceeding with disfiguring or disabling surgery. For lacrimal lesions thought to be malignant, biopsies are usually performed and an anterior approach through the orbital septum is used. Concern over soft tissue seeding with benign mixed or malignant lacrimal gland tumors has led some authors to recommend primary excisional biopsy of suspected epithelial tumors of the lacrimal gland (see under the heading Epithelial Tumors of the Lacrimal Gland in Chapter 5).

Corticosteroids may be administered intravenously at the start of the operation and continued for several days postoperatively to reduce orbital edema. Intravenous antibiotics may also be given preoperatively and continued for 48 hours postoperatively if the sinuses are entered during the orbital surgery. Otherwise, prophylactic systemic antibiotics are usually not necessary in orbital surgery.

Goldberg RA, Shorr N, Arnold AC, Garcia GH. Deep transorbital approach to the apex and cavernous sinus. *Ophthal Plast Reconstr Surg.* 1998;14:336–341.

Kersten RC. Lateral canthotomy incision for lateral orbitotomy. *Ophthal Plast Reconstr Surg.* 1999;15:19.

Shields JA, Shields CL, Epstein JA, Scartozzi R, Eagle RC Jr. Review: primary epithelial malignancies of the lacrimal gland: the 2003 Ramon L. Font lecture. *Ophthal Plast Reconstr Surg.* 2004;20(1):10–21.

Orbital Decompression

Historically, the primary indication for orbital decompression in thyroid ophthalmopathy was reduced vision caused by pressure of swollen extraocular muscles on the optic nerve. However, since surgical techniques have improved, the deformity of exophthalmos is now also considered an indication in many cases. The goal of orbital decompression is to allow the enlarged muscles to expand into periorbital spaces. This expansion relieves pressure on the optic nerve (and its blood supply) and reduces proptosis.

Decompression historically involved removal of the medial orbital wall and much of the orbital floor to allow orbital tissues to expand into the ethmoid and maxillary sinuses. The approach was made through the maxillary sinus (Caldwell-Luc) or transcutaneous anterior orbitotomy incision. The approach currently favored by most orbital surgeons is a transconjunctival incision combined with a lateral cantholysis to disinsert and evert the lower eyelid. Extension of this incision superonasally with a transcaruncular approach allows excellent access to the medial orbital wall. A transnasal endoscopic approach to the medial orbit via the ethmoid sinus may also be useful. To allow further decompression into the infratemporal fossa, the surgeon may remove the lateral orbital wall or reposition it outward. Burring down the medial surface of the lateral wall and the sphenoid wing results in additional decompression. This procedure is usually combined with the medial orbital decompression.

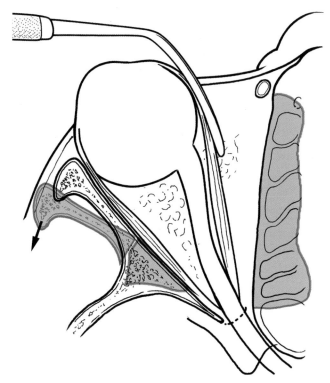

Figure 7-5 "Balanced" orbital decompression: medial and lateral (shaded areas). *(Modified from McCord CD Jr. Orbital decompression for Graves' disease: exposure through lateral canthal and inferior fornix incision.* Ophthalmology. *1981;88:526.)*

In patients with enlarged restricted inferior rectus muscles, orbital floor decompression may exacerbate globe ptosis, upper eyelid retraction, and vertical globe excursion because of prolapse of the enlarged inferior rectus muscle into the maxillary sinus. Recently, surgeons have advocated a balanced decompression of the medial and lateral orbital walls, which leaves the floor intact in these cases (Fig 7-5). Removal of retrobulbar fat at the time of decompression further reduces proptosis. Although exacerbation of eyelid retraction, vertical strabismus, and globe ptosis can be minimized with this approach, limitation of lateral excursion may occur because of prolapse of a tight medial rectus muscle into the decompressed ethmoid sinus. Decompression through the orbital roof into the anterior cranial fossa is rarely advisable. Craniofacial surgical techniques used to move the orbital bones forward can increase the effectiveness of decompression in particularly severe cases. Recent years have seen increased interest in removing orbital fat to decrease orbital volume, with or without associated bony decompression.

Garrity JA, Fatourechi V, Bergstralh EJ, et al. Results of transantral orbital decompression in 428 patients with severe Graves' ophthalmopathy. *Am J Ophthalmol.* 1993;116:533–547.

Goldberg RA. The evolving paradigm of orbital decompression surgery [editorial]. *Arch Ophthalmol.* 1998;116:95–96.

Kacker A, Kazim M, Murphy M, Trokel S, Close LG. "Balanced" orbital decompression for severe Graves' orbitopathy: technique with treatment algorithm. *Otolaryngol Head Neck Surg.* 2003;128(2):228–235.

Nadeau S, Pouliot D, Molgat Y. Orbital decompression in Graves' orbitopathy: a combined endoscopic and external lateral approach. *J Otolaryngol.* 2005;34(2):109–115.

Shepard KG, Levin PS, Terris DJ. Balanced orbital decompression for Graves' ophthalmopathy. *Laryngoscope.* 1998;108(11 Pt 1):1648–1653.

Trokel S, Kazim M, Moore S. Orbital fat removal. Decompression for Graves orbitopathy. *Ophthalmology.* 1993;100(5):674–682.

White WA, White WL, Shapiro PE. Combined endoscopic medial and inferior orbital decompression with transcutaneous lateral orbital decompression in Graves' orbitopathy. *Ophthalmology.* 2003;110(9):1827–1832.

Postoperative Care

Measures used to reduce postoperative edema are elevation of the head, iced compresses on the eyelids, administration of systemic steroids, and placement of a drain (if used, the drain is removed in 24–36 hours). Visual acuity should be checked at frequent intervals in the first 12 hours after surgery. Systemic antibiotics may be given. Patching of the operative site should be discouraged because it can delay diagnosis of a postoperative hemorrhage. Ice packs minimize swelling and still allow frequent observation of the operative site and vision monitoring.

Special Surgical Techniques in the Orbit

Fine-needle aspiration biopsy (FNAB) may have value in selected cases of lymphoid lesions, secondary tumors invading the orbit from the sinuses, suspected metastatic tumors, and blind eyes with optic nerve tumors. The technique is not very effective for obtaining tissue from fibrous lesions, from which it is difficult to aspirate cells. Although FNAB has not been considered a good technique for biopsy of lymphoproliferative disorders, it may assist in the diagnosis of selected cases when used with flow cytometry with monoclonal antibodies or polymerase chain reaction analysis.

FNAB is performed with a 4 cm 22- or 23-gauge needle attached to a syringe in a pistol-grip syringe holder. The needle is passed through the skin or conjunctiva. If necessary, the needle can be guided into the tumor by ultrasonography or computed tomography. Cells (and occasionally a small block of tissue) are aspirated from the lesion. A skilled cytologist is required to study the specimen. See BCSC Section 4, *Ophthalmic Pathology and Intraocular Tumors,* for further discussion of FNAB.

Masses or traumatic injuries may involve the skull base, including posterior and superior aspects of the orbit. Advanced surgical techniques provide access to these areas via a frontotemporal-orbitozygomatic approach. Such operations often require the combined efforts of the orbital surgeon, neurosurgeon, and otorhinolaryngologist. These techniques allow removal of tumors such as meningiomas, hemangiomas, hemangiopericytomas, schwannomas, and gliomas that might not otherwise be resectable. In addition, the frontotemporal-orbitozygomatic approach provides access to the intracranial optic canal for decompression.

McDermott MW, Durity FA, Rootman J, Woodhurst WB. Combined frontotemporal-orbitozygomatic approach for tumors of the sphenoid wing and orbit. *Neurosurgery.* 1990; 26:107–116.

Complications of Orbital Surgery

The surgeon can reduce complications from orbital surgery by performing a complete preoperative evaluation, choosing the appropriate approach, obtaining adequate exposure, carefully manipulating the tissues, maintaining good hemostasis, and consulting with a neurosurgeon or otorhinolaryngologist (or both) when appropriate.

Decreased or lost vision is a serious complication of surgery that may be caused by excessive traction on the globe and optic nerve, contusion of the optic nerve, or hemorrhage, which leads to increased orbital pressure and consequent ischemic injury to the optic nerve. A patient who has severe orbital pain postoperatively should be evaluated immediately for possible orbital hemorrhage. If this pain is associated with decreased visual acuity, proptosis, ecchymosis, increased intraocular pressure, and an afferent pupillary defect, the surgeon should consider immediately opening the wound and evacuating the hematoma.

Hypoesthesia over the distribution of the second division of cranial nerve V may follow orbital floor decompression. Other complications, such as downward displacement of the globe and postoperative exacerbation of upper eyelid retraction, were discussed previously. Motility disorders are encountered in up to one third of patients after orbital decompression, but most of these patients had preexisting restrictive myopathy.

Other complications of orbital surgery include extraocular muscle damage, ptosis, neuroparalytic keratopathy, pupillary changes, vitreous hemorrhage, detached retina, hypoesthesia of the forehead, keratitis sicca, cerebrospinal fluid leak, and infection.

Kersten RC, Nerad JA. In: Tasman W, Jaeger EA, eds. *Duane's Clinical Ophthalmology.* Philadelphia: Lippincott-Raven; 2005:chap 5.

CHAPTER 8

The Anophthalmic Socket

It is occasionally necessary to remove an eye or the contents of an orbit to enhance patient comfort and cosmesis, to protect the vision in the fellow eye, or to safeguard life. With loss of an eye, the patient can suffer depression or a degraded self-image. The ophthalmologist can assist the patient both before and after anophthalmic surgery by providing reassurance and psychological support. Discussions of the procedure, the rehabilitation process, and expected functional changes can help the patient with adjustment. With very few exceptions, the monocular patient may resume the full range of home, vocational, and athletic activities.

When resuming full activity, however, patients should take a cautious approach to allow adjustment to the changes in perception. The loss of depth perception and visual field may limit a patient's ability to perform as a commercial pilot or driver or to operate hazardous equipment safely. The ophthalmologist can help safeguard the remaining eye through regular follow-up examinations and the prescription of polycarbonate safety glasses for full-time wear.

Brady FB. *A Singular View: The Art of Seeing with One Eye.* 6th ed. Vienna, VA: Michael O. Hughes; 2004, www.asingularview.com.

Czeisler CA, Shanahan TL, Klerman EB, et al. Suppression of melatonin secretion in some blind patients by exposure to bright light. *N Engl J Med.* 1995;332:6–11.

The indications for anophthalmic surgery are diverse, and the procedure of choice varies. *Enucleation* involves removal of the entire globe while preserving other orbital tissues. *Evisceration* is the removal of the intraocular contents (lens, uvea, retina, vitreous, and sometimes cornea), leaving the sclera and extraocular muscles intact. *Exenteration* refers to the removal of all or parts of the orbital tissues including the globe. The cosmetic goals in anophthalmic surgery are to minimize any condition that draws attention to the anophthalmos. Surgical efforts to produce orbital and eyelid symmetry and to promote good prosthetic position and motility enhance cosmesis.

Enucleation

Enucleation allows for the complete histologic examination of the eye and optic nerve, possibly influencing subsequent treatment and contributing to medical knowledge. It also reduces the concern that surgery might contribute to the risk of sympathetic ophthalmia in the fellow eye. Enucleation is always the procedure of choice if the nature of the intraocular pathology is unknown.

Enucleation is indicated for primary intraocular malignancies not amenable to alternative modes of therapy such as external-beam or proton-beam irradiation or episcleral plaque brachytherapy. Retinoblastoma and choroidal melanoma are the ocular tumors that most commonly require enucleation. Evisceration should not be performed in cases of suspected intraocular malignancy. When enucleation is performed for an intraocular tumor, the surgeon must take care to avoid penetrating the globe during surgery, and he or she must handle the globe gently to minimize the risk of disseminating tumor cells. In cases of suspected retinoblastoma, the surgeon should obtain a long segment of optic nerve with the enucleation specimen to increase the chances of completely resecting the tumor. A lateral canthotomy during enucleation surgery may provide the desired surgical exposure.

Blind eyes with opaque media should be suspected of harboring an occult neoplasm unless another cause of ocular disease can be surmised. Although blind or phthisical eyes are not at increased risk for malignancy, a tumor can occasionally be the cause of globe degeneration. Ultrasonography is useful in evaluating these eyes and planning proper management.

In severely traumatized eyes, enucleation within the first 14 days of the injury may be considered if the risk of sympathetic ophthalmia and harm to the remaining eye is judged to be greater than the likelihood of recovering useful vision in the traumatized eye. Sympathetic ophthalmia is thought to be a delayed hypersensitivity immune response to the uveal antigens. The condition can occur from 9 days to 50 years after corneoscleral perforation. The incidence of sympathetic ophthalmia in fellow eyes following penetrating ocular trauma in eyes that were not enucleated has been estimated at 0.19%. Enucleation with complete removal of the uveal pigment may be beneficial in preventing a subsequent immune response. However, the infrequency of sympathetic ophthalmia, coupled with improved medical therapy for uveitis, has made early enucleation strictly for prophylaxis a debatable practice. In addition, it has been demonstrated that the majority of severely injured eyes do not subsequently require removal for pain and therefore can be treated by being fit with a cosmetic scleral shell, which provides excellent cosmesis and motility. Follow-up visits are required so that the fellow eye can be examined for signs of inflammation, the presence of which requires prompt medical therapy. Although there is some conflicting evidence, removal of an eye that has already stimulated sympathetic ophthalmia is unlikely to prevent progression of the disease.

Painful eyes without useful vision can be managed with enucleation or evisceration. Patients with end-stage neovascular glaucoma, chronic uveitis, or previously traumatized blind eyes can obtain dramatic relief from discomfort and improved cosmesis with either procedure. For debilitated patients unable to undergo surgery and rehabilitation, retrobulbar injection of ethanol may provide adequate pain relief. Retrobulbar injection of chlorpromazine (Thorazine) has also been reported to reduce pain. In a disfigured eye without pain, however, it is generally advisable to initially consider a trial of a cosmetic scleral shell. If tolerated, scleral shells give superior cosmesis and motility.

Guidelines for Enucleation

A functionally and aesthetically acceptable anophthalmic socket must have the following components:

- an orbital implant of sufficient volume centered within the orbit
- a socket lined with conjunctiva or mucous membrane with fornices deep enough to hold a prosthesis
- eyelids with normal appearance and adequate tone to support a prosthesis
- good transmission of motility from the implant to the overlying prosthesis
- a comfortable ocular prosthesis that looks similar to the normal eye

Enucleation can be performed satisfactorily under local or general anesthesia; however, most patients prefer general anesthesia or sedation when an eye is removed.

Enucleation in Childhood

Enucleation in early childhood, as well as congenital anophthalmos or microphthalmos, may lead to underdevelopment of the involved bony orbit with secondary facial asymmetry. Orbital soft tissue volume is a critical determinant of orbital bone growth. When enucleation is necessary in childhood, a large implant should be used to replace orbital volume. An adult-sized implant should be placed as soon as possible to encourage symmetric orbital bone growth. Volume loss in the adult anophthalmic socket may be adequately replaced by a 20–22 mm sphere implant. Rarely should an implant smaller than 18 mm be used even in the very young.

Autogenous dermis-fat grafts are used successfully as anophthalmic implants in children. These grafts appear to grow along with the expanding orbit. The opposite effect has been observed in adults, in whom loss of volume generally occurs when dermis-fat grafts are used as primary anophthalmic implants.

Heher KL, Katowitz JA, Low JE. Unilateral dermis-fat graft implantation in the pediatric orbit. *Ophthal Plast Reconstr Surg.* 1998;14:81–88.

Orbital Implants

The function of an implant is to replace lost orbital volume, to maintain the structure of the orbit, and to impart motility to the overlying ocular prosthesis.

Implants used today are usually either spheres or buried implants with front surface projections to which the extraocular muscles can be attached in various ways. Spherical implants may be grouped according to the materials from which they are manufactured: *inert materials,* such as glass, silicone, or methylmethacrylate; and *biointegrated materials,* such as porous polyethylene or hydroxyapatite. The latter are designed to be incorporated by soft tissue ingrowth into the socket.

Inert spherical implants provide comfort and low rates of extrusion but transfer motility to the prosthesis only through passive movement of the socket. Buried motility implants with front surface projections push the overlying prosthesis with a direct force and probably improve prosthetic motility. The front surface projections, however, may pinch the conjunctiva between the implant and the prosthesis, leading to a painful socket or erosion over the implant.

Hydroxyapatite and porous polyethylene implants allow for drilling and placement of a peg to integrate the prosthesis directly with the moving implant. Pegging is usually carried out 6–12 months after enucleation. Although pegged porous implants offer excellent motility, they also have a higher rate of postoperative exposure. A magnetic coupling post developed for the porous polyethylene implant eliminates exposed hardware extending into the implant and appears to decrease the complication rate with prosthetic integration. Most porous implants are never pegged to integrate with the prosthesis, with adequate motility. A nonporous sphere implant is an appropriate choice in patients not requiring implant integration. In this case, the function of the porous implants is similar to that of any other spherical implant. As porous implants are significantly more expensive, nonporous implants are as good a choice for patients for whom pegging will not be considered.

Locations for implants are either within Tenon's capsule or behind posterior Tenon's capsule in the muscle cone. Spheres may be covered with other materials such as homologous sclera or autogenous fascia, which serve as further barriers to migration and extrusion. Secure closure of Tenon's fascia over the anterior surface of an anophthalmic implant is an important barrier to later extrusion.

Extraocular muscles should not be crossed over the front surface of a sphere implant or purse-stringed anteriorly because the implant migrates when the muscles slip off the anterior surface. Muscles sutured into the normal anatomical locations, either directly to the implant or to homologous sclera or autogenous fascia surrounding the implant, allow superior motility and prevent migration.

Following enucleation surgery, an acrylic or silicone conformer is placed in the conjunctival fornices to maintain the conjunctival space that will eventually accommodate the prosthesis. An anophthalmic socket without a conformer or prosthesis in place can contract in a matter of days, preventing placement of the prosthesis.

Prostheses

An ocular prosthesis is fitted within 4–8 weeks after enucleation. The ideal prosthesis is custom-fit to the exact dimensions of the orbit after postoperative edema has subsided. Premade, or stock, eyes are less satisfactory cosmetically, and they limit prosthetic motility. In addition, they may trap secretions between the prosthesis and the socket.

The American Society of Ocularists is an international nonprofit professional and educational organization founded by technicians specializing in the fabrication and fitting of custom ocular prosthetics.

Custer PL, Kennedy RH, Woog JJ, Kaltreider SA, Meyer DR. Orbital implants in enucleation surgery: a report by the American Academy of Ophthalmology. *Ophthalmology.* 2003;110:2054–2061.

Custer PL, Trinkhaus KM, Fornoff J. Comparative motility of hydroxyapatite and alloplastic enucleation implants. *Ophthalmology.* 1999;106:513–516.

Edelstein C, Shields CL, De Potter P, Shields JA. Complications of motility peg placement for the hydroxyapatite orbital implant. *Ophthalmology.* 1997;104:1616–1621.

Jordan DR. Complications of motility peg placement in hydroxyapatite implants. *Ophthalmol.* 1998;105:1128–1129.

Su GW, Yen MT. Current trends in managing the anophthalmic socket after primary enucleation and evisceration. *Ophthal Plast Reconstr Surg.* 2004;20:274–280.

Intraoperative Complications of Enucleation

Removal of the wrong eye

This is one of the most feared complications in ophthalmology. Taking a "time out" to reexamine the chart, the operative permit, and the patient with ophthalmoscopy in the operating room immediately before enucleation is of critical importance. Marking the skin near the eye to be enucleated and having the patient point to the involved eye give further assurance.

Ptosis and extraocular muscle damage

Avoiding excessive dissection near the orbital roof and apex reduces the chance of damaging the extraocular muscles or their innervation.

Evisceration

Evisceration involves the removal of the contents of the globe, leaving the sclera, extraocular muscles, and optic nerve intact. Evisceration should be considered *only* if the presence of an intraocular malignancy has been ruled out.

Advantages of Evisceration

- *Less disruption of orbital anatomy.* Thus, the chance of injury to extraocular muscles and nerves and atrophy of fat is reduced with less dissection within the orbit. The relationships between the muscles, globe, eyelids, and fornices remain undisturbed.
- *Good motility of the prosthesis.* The extraocular muscles remain attached to the sclera.
- *Better treatment of endophthalmitis.* Evisceration is preferred by some surgeons in cases of endophthalmitis, because extirpation and drainage of the ocular contents can occur without invasion of the orbit. The chance of contamination of the orbit with possible subsequent orbital cellulitis or intracranial extension is therefore theoretically reduced.
- *A technically simpler procedure.* Performing this less invasive procedure may be important when general anesthesia is contraindicated or when bleeding disorders increase the risk of orbital dissection.
- *Lower rate of migration, extrusion, and reoperation.*

Disadvantages of Evisceration

Although not all surgeons agree on the exact indications for enucleation and evisceration, it should be emphasized that evisceration should never be performed if a tumor is suspected. It has been suggested that sympathetic ophthalmia may rarely be caused by a reaction to residual uveal tissue in the eviscerated socket, although an initial report of 4 cases more than 25 years ago has not been subsequently confirmed by additional case reports. Finally, evisceration affords a less complete specimen for pathologic examinations.

Levine MR, Pou CR, Lash RH. Evisceration: is sympathetic ophthalmia a concern in the new millennium? The 1998 Wendell Hughes Lecture. *Ophthal Plast Reconstr Surg.* 1999;15:4–8.

Techniques of Evisceration

Evisceration can be performed either with retention of the cornea or with excision of the cornea. The cornea can be retained if it is of normal thickness and shows no active corneal disease. The corneal epithelium and endothelium should be removed at the time of surgery. If there is mild thinning of the cornea, a bridge flap of conjunctiva and Tenon's capsule can be brought down from the bulbar area just above the cornea and sutured over the cornea. This technique has the advantage of allowing placement of a larger implant, thus enhancing orbital volume. The disadvantage is that the cornea may erode eventually, and extrusion of the implant can result. Regardless of the technique used for evisceration, all visible pigmented uvea should be removed before the implant is placed.

If there is active disease in the cornea, the cornea should be excised and the implant sutured within the sclera. Posterior relaxing incisions of the sclera (radially in each quadrant or concentric to optic nerve) may be utilized to allow placement of a larger implant.

Lucarelli MJ, Kaltreider SA. Advances in evisceration and enucleation. *Focal Points: Clinical Modules for Ophthalmologists.* San Francisco: American Academy of Ophthalmology; 2004, module 6.

Massry GG, Holds JB. Evisceration with scleral modification. *Ophthal Plast Reconstr Surg.* 2001;17:42–47.

Anophthalmic Socket Complications and Treatment

Deep Superior Sulcus

Deep superior sulcus deformity is caused by decreased orbital volume (Fig 8-1). The surgeon can correct this deformity by increasing the orbital volume through placement of a secondary implant subperiosteally on the orbital floor. This implant pushes the initial implant and superior orbital fat upward to fill out the superior sulcus. If a relaxed lower eyelid is present, it is tightened, usually with lid shortening at the lateral canthus. This procedure elevates the prosthesis and superior orbital fat to fill out the superior sulcus deformity. Dermis-fat grafts may be implanted in the upper eyelid to fill out the sulcus, but eyelid contour and function may be damaged and the graft may undergo resorption. A final way to correct superior sulcus deformity is to replace the original implant with a larger secondary anophthalmic implant.

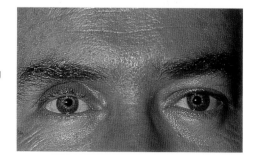

Figure 8-1 Superior sulcus deformity following enucleation of right eye.

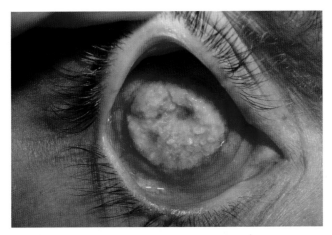

Figure 8-2 Large exposure of the porous polyethylene orbital implant in a patient who had undergone evisceration for trauma. *(Courtesy of Martin Devoto, MD.)*

Contracture of Fornices

Preventing contracted fornices includes preserving as much conjunctiva as possible and limiting dissection in the fornices. Placing extraocular muscles in the normal anatomical positions also minimizes shortening of the fornices. The patient should wear a conformer as continuously as possible postoperatively to minimize conjunctival shortening. Conformers and prostheses should not be removed for periods greater than 24 hours. The prosthesis can be removed frequently and cleaned in the presence of infection but should be replaced promptly after irrigation of the socket.

Exposure and Extrusion of Implant

Implants may extrude if placed too far forward or if closure of anterior Tenon's fascia is not satisfactory. Postoperative infection, poor wound healing, poorly fitting prostheses or conformers, and pressure points between the implant and prosthesis may also contribute to extrusion of the implant. Exposed implants are subject to infection. Although small defects over porous implants may rarely close spontaneously, most exposures should be covered with scleral patch grafts or autogenous tissue grafts to promote conjunctival healing (Fig 8-2).

A dermis-fat graft may be used when a limited amount of conjunctiva remains in the socket. This graft increases the net amount of conjunctiva available as the conjunctiva reepithelializes over the front surface of the dermis. Unpredictable reabsorption of volume is a serious drawback to the dermis-fat graft technique in adults. As stated earlier, dermis-fat grafts in children appear to continue to grow along with the surrounding orbit and may help stimulate orbital development if enucleation is required during infancy or childhood.

Contracted Sockets

Causes of contracted sockets include

- radiation treatment (usually as treatment of the tumor that necessitated removal of the eye)
- extrusion of an enucleation implant

- severe initial injury (alkali burns or extensive lacerations)
- poor surgical techniques (excessive sacrifice or destruction of conjunctiva and Tenon's capsule; traumatic dissection within the socket causing excessive scar tissue formation)
- multiple socket operations
- removal of the conformer or prosthesis for prolonged periods

Sockets are considered to be contracted when the fornices are too small to retain a prosthesis (Fig 8-3). Socket reconstruction procedures involve incision or excision of the scarred tissues and placement of a graft to enlarge the fornices. Full-thickness mucous membrane grafting is preferred because it allows the grafted tissue to match conjunctiva histologically. Buccal mucosal grafts may be taken from the cheeks (beware of damaging the duct to the parotid gland) or from the upper lip, lower lip, or hard palate. Goblet cells and mucus production are preserved.

Contracture of the fornices alone (more common with the inferior fornix) usually is associated with milder degrees of socket contracture. In these cases, the buccal mucosal graft is placed in the defect, and a silicone sheet is attached by sutures to the superior or inferior orbital rim, depending on which fornix is involved. In 2 weeks, the sheet may be removed and a prosthesis placed.

Anophthalmic Ectropion

Lower eyelid ectropion may result from the loosening of lower eyelid support under the weight of a prosthesis. Frequent removal of the prosthesis or a larger prosthesis accelerates the development of lid laxity. Tightening the lateral or medial canthal tendon may remedy the situation. Surgeons may combine ectropion repair with correction of eyelid retraction by recessing the inferior retractor muscle layer and grafting mucous membrane tissue in the inferior fornix.

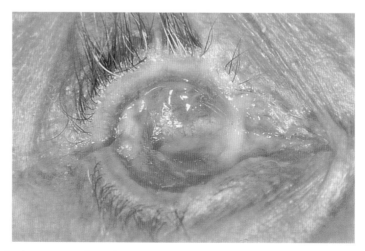

Figure 8-3 Socket contraction of right anophthalmic orbit. Note obliteration of conjunctival fornices. Patient is unable to wear an ocular prosthesis.

Anophthalmic Ptosis

Ptosis of the anophthalmic socket results from superotemporal migration of sphere implants, cicatricial tissue in the upper fornix, or damage to the levator muscle or nerve. Small amounts of ptosis may be managed by modification of the prosthesis. Greater amounts of ptosis require tightening of the levator aponeurosis. This procedure is best done under local anesthesia with intraoperative adjustment of eyelid height and contour, because mechanical forces may cause the surgeon to underestimate true levator function. Ptosis surgery usually improves a deep sulcus by bringing the preaponeurotic fat forward. Frontalis suspension is usually a less acceptable procedure because there is no visual drive to stimulate contracture of the frontalis muscle to elevate the eyelid.

Lash Margin Entropion

Lash margin entropion, trichiasis, and ptosis of the eyelashes are common in the anophthalmic socket. Contracture of fornices or cicatricial tissue near the lash margin contributes to these abnormalities. Horizontal tarsal incisions and rotation of the lash margin (such as the Wies procedure) may correct the problem. In more severe cases, splitting of the eyelid margins at the gray line with mucous membrane grafting to the eyelid margin may correct the entropic lash margin.

Cosmetic Optics

The style of frames and tinted lenses chosen for spectacles can help camouflage residual defects in reconstructed sockets. Plus (convex) lenses or minus (concave) lenses may be placed in the glasses in front of the prosthesis so that the apparent size of the prosthesis is changed. Prisms in the glasses may be used to change the apparent vertical position of the prosthesis.

Kaltreider SA, Lucarelli MJ. A simple algorithm for selection of implant size for enucleation and evisceration: a prospective study. *Ophthal Plast Reconstr Surg.* 2002;18:336–341.

Neuhaus R, Hawes MJ. Inadequate inferior cul-de-sac in the anophthalmic socket. *Ophthalmology.* 1992;99:153–157.

Smit TJ, Koornneef L, Zonneveld FW, Groet E, Otto AJ. Computed tomography in the assessment of the postenucleation socket syndrome. *Ophthalmology.* 1990;97:1347–1351.

Smit TJ, Koornneef L, Zonneveld FW, Groet E, Otto AJ. Primary and secondary implants in the anophthalmic orbit: preoperative and postoperative computed tomographic appearance. *Ophthalmology.* 1991;98:106–110.

Exenteration

Exenteration involves the removal of the soft tissues of the orbit, including the globe.

Considerations for Exenteration

Exenteration should be considered in the following circumstances:

- *Destructive tumors extending into the orbit from the sinuses, face, eyelids, conjunctiva, or intracranial space* (Fig 8-4). However, exenteration is not indicated for all such tumors: some are responsive to radiation, and some have extended too far to be completely removed by surgical excision.

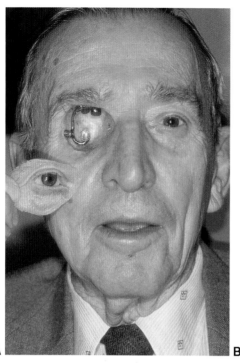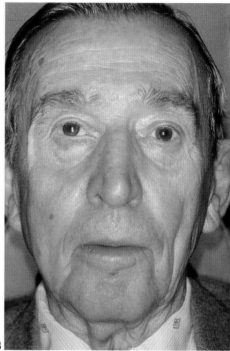

A   B

Figure 8-4 Orbital exenteration and osseointegrated prosthesis. **A,** Exenterated socket for sebaceous cell carcinoma. **B,** Prosthesis in place, retained with magnets attached to bone-anchored framework. *(Courtesy of Jeffrey A. Nerad, MD.)*

- *Intraocular malignant melanomas or retinoblastomas that have extended outside the globe (if evidence of distant metastases is excluded).* When local control of the tumor would benefit the nursing care of the patient, exenteration is indicated.
- *Malignant epithelial tumors of the lacrimal gland.* Although the procedure is somewhat controversial, these tumors usually require extended exenteration with radical bone removal of the roof, lateral wall, and floor.
- *Sarcomas and other primary orbital malignancies that do not respond to nonsurgical therapy.* Some tumors such as rhabdomyosarcomas that were previously treated by exenteration are now initially treated by radiation and chemotherapy.
- *Fungal infection.* Subtotal or total exenteration may be necessary for the management of orbital phycomycosis, which occurs most commonly in patients who are diabetic or immunosuppressed. However, attention is now being focused on achieving control through more limited debridement of involved orbital tissues.

Types of Exenteration

Exenterations vary in the amount of tissue that is removed. Following are the types of exenteration:

- *Subtotal.* The eye and adjacent intraorbital tissues are removed so that the lesion is locally excised (leaving periorbita and part or all of eyelids). This technique is used for some locally invasive tumors, for debulking of disseminated tumors, or for partial treatment in selected patients.

- *Total.* All intraorbital soft tissues, including periorbita, are removed, with or without the skin of the eyelids.
- *Extended.* All intraorbital soft tissues are removed, together with adjacent structures (usually bony walls and sinuses).

Following removal of the orbital contents, the bony socket may be allowed to spontaneously granulate and epithelialize or may be covered by a split-thickness skin graft, which may be placed onto bare bone or over a temporalis muscle or temporoparietal fascial flap.

The technique selected depends on the pathologic process. The goal is to remove all lesions along with appropriate margins of adjacent tissue while retaining as much healthy tissue as possible.

Bartley GB, Garrity JA, Waller RR, Henderson JW, Ilstrup DM. Orbital exenteration at the Mayo Clinic: 1967–1986. *Ophthalmology.* 1989;96:468–474.

Goldberg RA, Kim JW, Shorr N. Orbital exenteration: results of an individualized approach. *Ophthal Plast Reconstr Surg.* 2003;19:229–236.

Günalp I, Gündüz K, Dürük K. Orbital exenteration: a review of 429 cases. *Int Ophthalmol.* 1996;19:177–184.

Levin PS, Dutton JJ. A 20-year series of orbital exenteration. *Am J Ophthalmol.* 1991;112:496–501.

Yeatts RP, Marion JR, Weaver RG, Orkubi GA. Removal of the eye with socket ablation: a limited subtotal exenteration. *Arch Ophthalmol.* 1991;109:1306–1309.

PART II

Periocular Soft Tissues

CHAPTER 9

Anatomy

Face

The surgeon who undertakes surgical manipulation of the face should clearly understand its anatomy. The structural planes of the face include skin, subcutaneous tissue, the *superficial musculoaponeurotic system (SMAS)* and mimetic muscles, the deep facial fascia, and the plane containing the facial nerve, parotid duct, and buccal fat pad.

The skin has 2 layers: the *epidermis,* consisting of superficial stratified squamous epithelium; and the *dermis,* consisting of connective tissue containing blood vessels, lymphatics, pilosebaceous glands, and sweat glands.

The subcutaneous fat lies beneath the dermis, except in the eyelid. Connective tissue septa divide the subcutaneous fat into lobules. The thickness of the subcutaneous fat varies from person to person and from one area of the face to another. The cheeks, temples, and neck have the thickest subcutaneous fat.

The superficial facial fascia, an extension of the superficial cervical fascia in the neck, invests the facial mimetic muscles (platysma, zygomaticus major, zygomaticus minor, and orbicularis oculi), making up the SMAS (Fig 9-1). The SMAS distributes facial muscle contractions facilitating facial expression. These muscle actions are transmitted to the skin by ligamentous attachments located between the SMAS and the dermis. The SMAS is also connected to the underlying bone by a network of fibrous septa and ligaments. Thus, facial support is transmitted from the deep fixed structures of the face to the overlying dermis. Two major components of this system are the osteocutaneous ligaments (orbitomalar, zygomatic, and mandibular) and the ligaments formed by a condensation of superficial and deep facial fasciae (parotidocutaneous and masseteric). As these ligaments become attenuated in conjunction with facial dermal elastosis, facial aging becomes apparent. Dissection and repositioning of the SMAS have important implications for facial cosmetic surgery. Face-lifting techniques to improve facial descent can plicate or resect and advance the SMAS.

As the SMAS continues superiorly over the zygomatic arch, it becomes continuous with the superficial temporalis fascia (also called the *temporoparietal fascia*); farther superiorly, the SMAS becomes continuous with the galea aponeurotica. Although clinically these layers are distinct, the terminology for this area is confusing. Interior to the loose areolar tissue and the temporoparietal fascia, the deep temporalis fascia of the temporal muscle splits and envelops the temporal fat pad, creating deep and superficial layers of the deep temporalis fascia. Figure 9-1B helps clarify these layers.

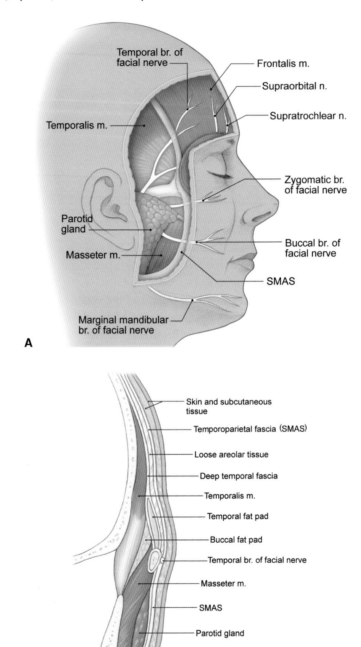

Figure 9-1 **A,** Superficial musculoaponeurotic system (SMAS). Note that the facial nerve branches inferior to the zygomatic arch are deep to the SMAS. **B,** Coronal section of face. The temporal branch of the facial nerve is found within the superficial portion of the temporal parietal fascia (extension of the SMAS). *(Illustrations by Christine Gralapp.)*

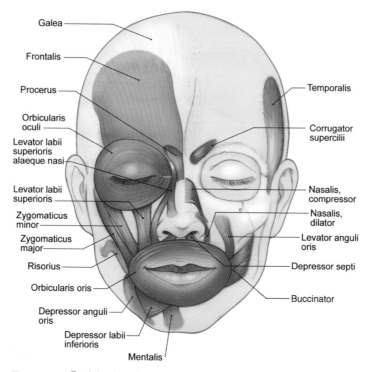

Figure 9-2 Facial mimetic muscles. *(Illustration by Christine Gralapp.)*

The mimetic muscles (Fig 9-2) can be grouped into those of the upper face and those of the lower face. In the upper face, the frontalis, corrugator, and procerus muscles animate the forehead and glabella. The orbicularis oculi depresses the eyebrows and closes the eyelids. The frontalis elevates the eyebrows, and contraction of the muscle causes transverse forehead rhytids.

In the lower face, mimetic muscles can be further categorized as superficial or deep. The superficial mimetic muscles that receive their neurovascular supply on the posterior surfaces include the platysma, zygomaticus major, zygomaticus minor, and risorius. The deep mimetic muscles receive their neurovascular supply anteriorly and include the buccinator, mentalis, and levator anguli oris. Remembering the location of innervation helps the surgeon determine safe surgical planes. Other facial muscles include the orbicularis oris, the levator labii superioris, the levator labii superioris alaeque nasi, the depressor anguli oris and the depressor labii inferioris, the masseter, and the temporalis.

In the neck, the superficial cervical fascia and platysma are continuous with the SMAS, and the deep cervical fascia is found on the superficial surface of the strap muscles, superior to the hyoid bone. The deep cervical fascia overlies the myelohyoid muscle and extends superiorly over the body of the mandible. The parotidomasseteric fascia is a continuation of the deep cervical fascia of the neck. The facial nerve lies deep to this thin layer in the lower face. In the temporal region, above the zygomatic arch, this layer is continuous with the deep temporal fascia, and the facial nerve (frontal branch) lies superficial to this fascial layer.

The facial nerve, cranial nerve VII (CN VII), which innervates the mimetic muscles, divides into 5 major branches within or deep to the parotid gland (Fig 9-3): temporal (frontal), zygomatic, buccal, marginal mandibular, and cervical. Landmarks identifying the depth of the nerve have special significance. In general, dissection deep to the SMAS and deep to the seventh cranial nerve (on top of the deep temporalis fascia) in the upper face and temporal region avoids the frontal nerve, whereas dissection superficial to the SMAS and superficial to the plane of the facial nerve (especially anterior to the parotid gland) avoids the facial nerve branches in the lower face.

In the *temporal area,* the frontal branch of CN VII (see Fig 9-3) crosses the zygomatic arch and courses superomedially in the deep layers of the temporoparietal fascia (also known as *superficial temporalis fascia* or *SMAS*). The temporoparietal fascia bridges the SMAS of the lower face to the galea aponeurosis of the upper face. Deep to the temporoparietal fascia, a dense, immobile fascia termed the *deep temporal fascia* overlies the temporalis muscle (see Fig 9-1B). Dissection along this fascia allows mobilization of the temporal forehead while avoiding the overlying frontal branch of the facial nerve. This is an important anatomical principle in brow- and forehead-lifting procedures.

In the *lower face,* the facial nerve branches, sensory nerves, vascular networks, and parotid gland and duct are deep to the SMAS (see Fig 9-1). Dissection just superficial to the SMAS, parotid gland, and parotidomasseteric fascia in the lower face avoids injury to all of these structures.

The face receives its sensory innervation from the 3 branches of the fifth cranial nerve: V_1, ophthalmic; V_2, maxillary; and V_3, mandibular. Damage to these nerves causes

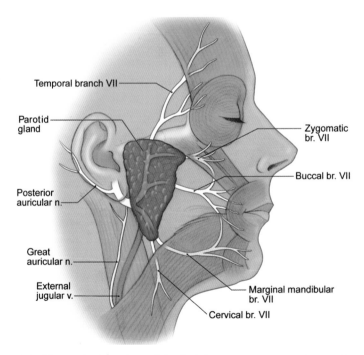

Figure 9-3 Five major branches of the facial nerve. *(Illustration by Christine Gralapp.)*

numbness and paresthesia. Fortunately, overlapping of the distal branches makes permanent sensation loss unusual unless injury occurs at the proximal neurovascular bundles or with extensive distal disruption, as can be seen with a bicoronal incision.

Eyelids

For discussion purposes, the eyelids can be conveniently divided into the following 7 structural layers:

- skin and subcutaneous tissue
- muscles of protraction
- orbital septum
- orbital fat
- muscles of retraction
- tarsus
- conjunctiva

Figures 9-4 and 9-5 detail the anatomy of the eyelids.

Skin and Subcutaneous Tissue

Eyelid skin is the thinnest of the body and is unique in having no subcutaneous fat layer. Because the thin skin of the eyelids is subjected to constant movement with each blink, the laxity that often occurs with age is not surprising. In both the upper and the lower eyelids, the pretarsal tissues are normally firmly attached to the underlying tissues, whereas the preseptal tissues are more loosely attached, creating potential spaces for fluid accumulation. The contours of the eyelid skin are defined by the *eyelid crease* and the *eyelid fold*. The upper eyelid crease approximates the attachments of the levator aponeurosis to the pretarsal orbicularis bundles and skin. This site is near or at the level of the superior border of the tarsus. The upper eyelid fold consists of the loose preseptal skin and subcutaneous tissues above the confluence of the levator aponeurosis and the septum.

Racial variation can be noted in the location of the eyelid crease and eyelid fold. The Asian eyelid normally has a relatively low upper lid crease because, in contrast to the supratarsal fusion seen in the non-Asian lid, the orbital septum in the Asian eyelid fuses with the levator aponeurosis between the eyelid margin and the superior border of the tarsus. This also allows preaponeurotic fat to occupy a position more inferior and anterior in the eyelid. Although the lower eyelid crease is less well defined than the upper eyelid crease, these racial differences are apparent in the lower eyelid as well.

Protractors

The orbicularis oculi muscle is the main protractor of the eyelid. Contraction of this muscle, which is innervated by CN VII, narrows the palpebral fissure. Specific portions of this muscle also constitute the lacrimal pump.

The orbicularis muscle is divided into *pretarsal, preseptal,* and *orbital* parts (Fig 9-6). These divisions are both anatomical and physiological. The palpebral (pretarsal and preseptal) parts are integral to involuntary eyelid movements (blink), whereas the orbital portion is

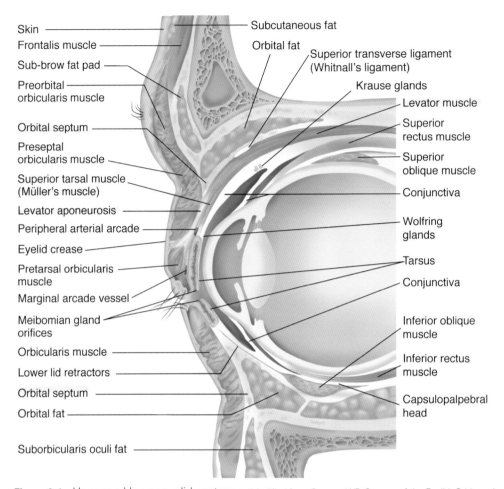

Skin
Frontalis muscle
Sub-brow fat pad
Preorbital orbicularis muscle
Orbital septum
Preseptal orbicularis muscle
Superior tarsal muscle (Müller's muscle)
Levator aponeurosis
Peripheral arterial arcade
Eyelid crease
Pretarsal orbicularis muscle
Marginal arcade vessel
Meibomian gland orifices
Orbicularis muscle
Lower lid retractors
Orbital septum
Orbital fat
Suborbicularis oculi fat

Subcutaneous fat
Orbital fat
Superior transverse ligament (Whitnall's ligament)
Krause glands
Levator muscle
Superior rectus muscle
Superior oblique muscle
Conjunctiva
Wolfring glands
Tarsus
Conjunctiva
Inferior oblique muscle
Inferior rectus muscle
Capsulopalpebral head

Figure 9-4 Upper and lower eyelid anatomy. *(Modified from Stewart WB.* Surgery of the Eyelid, Orbit, and Lacrimal System. *Ophthalmology Monograph 8, vol 2. San Francisco: American Academy of Ophthalmology; 1994:23, 85. Illustration by Cyndie C. H. Wooley.)*

primarily involved in forced eyelid closure. The pretarsal parts of the upper and lower eyelid orbicularis arise from deep origins at the posterior lacrimal crest and superficial origins at the anterior limb of the medial canthal tendon. Near the common canaliculus, the deep heads of the pretarsal orbicularis fuse to form a prominent bundle of fibers known as *Horner's muscle* (or *Horner's tensor tarsi*), which runs just behind the posterior arm of the canthal tendon. Horner's muscle continues posteriorly to the posterior lacrimal crest, just behind the posterior arm of the medial canthal tendon. The upper and lower eyelid segments of the pretarsal orbicularis fuse in the lateral canthal area to become the lateral canthal tendon.

The preseptal orbicularis arises from the upper and lower borders of the medial canthal tendon. The inferior preseptal muscle arises as a single head from the common tendon. In the upper eyelid, the preseptal muscle has an anterior head from the common tendon and a posterior head from both the superior and posterior arms of the tendon. Laterally, the preseptal muscles form the lateral palpebral raphe.

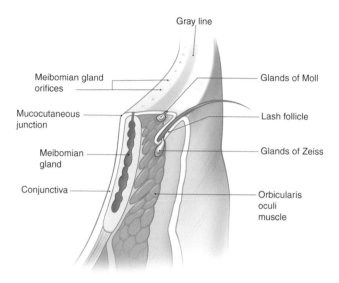

Figure 9-5 Eyelid margin anatomy. *(Illustration by Christine Gralapp.)*

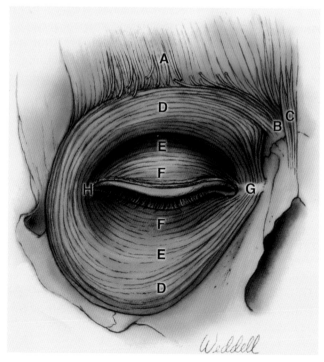

Figure 9-6 Orbicularis muscle and related musculature. *A,* Frontalis muscles; *B,* corrugator supercilii muscle; *C,* procerus muscle; *D,* orbicularis muscle (orbital portion); *E,* orbicularis muscle (preseptal portion); *F,* orbicularis muscle (pretarsal portion); *G,* medial canthal tendon; *H,* lateral canthal tendon. *(Adapted from Beard C. Ptosis. 3rd ed. St Louis: Mosby; 1981. Modified by Cyndie Wooley.)*

The orbital portions of the orbicularis muscle arise from the anterior limb of the medial canthal tendon, the orbital process of the frontal bone, and the frontal process of the maxillary bone in front of the anterior lacrimal crest. Its fibers form a continuous ellipse and insert just below the point of origin. Near the eyelid margin, a specialized bundle of striated muscle, the *muscle of Riolan,* lies more posterior than the main portion of the orbicularis and creates the gray line. The muscle of Riolan may play a role in meibomian glandular discharge, blinking, and the position of the eyelashes.

Dutton J. *Atlas of Clinical and Surgical Orbital Anatomy.* Philadelphia: Saunders; 1994:116–117.

Muzaffar AR, Mendelson BC, Adams WP Jr. Surgical anatomy of the ligamentous attachments of the lower lid and lateral canthus. *Plast Reconstr Surg.* 2002;110:873–884.

Wulc AE, Dryden RM, Khatchaturian T. Where is the gray line? *Arch Ophthalmol.* 1987;105:1092–1098.

Orbital Septum

The orbital septum, a thin multilayered sheet of fibrous tissue, arises from the periosteum over the superior and inferior orbital rims at the arcus marginalis. In the upper eyelid, the orbital septum fuses with the levator aponeurosis 2–5 mm above the superior tarsal border in non-Asians. In the lower eyelid, the orbital septum fuses with the capsulopalpebral fascia at or just below the inferior tarsal border. The fused capsulopalpebral orbital septum complex, along with a small contribution from the inferior tarsal smooth muscle, inserts on the posterior and anterior tarsal surfaces as well as the tapered inferior border of the tarsus. As a result of aging, the septum in both the upper and the lower eyelids may become quite attenuated. Thinning of the septum and laxity of the orbicularis muscle contribute to anterior herniation of the orbital fat in the aging eyelid.

Meyer DR, Linberg JV, Wobig JL, McCormick SA. Anatomy of the orbital septum and associated eyelid connective tissues. Implications for ptosis surgery. *Ophthal Plast Reconstr Surg.* 1991;7:104–113.

Orbital Fat

Orbital fat lies posterior to the orbital septum and anterior to the levator aponeurosis (upper lid) or the capsulopalpebral fascia (lower lid). In the upper lid, there are 2 fat pockets: nasal and central. In the lower lid, there are 3 fat pockets: nasal, central, and temporal. These pockets are surrounded by thin fibrous sheaths that are forward continuations of the anterior orbital septal system. The central orbital fat pad is an important landmark in both elective eyelid surgery and lid laceration repair because it lies directly behind the orbital septum and in front of the levator aponeurosis.

Retractors

The retractors of the upper eyelid are the levator muscle with its aponeurosis and the superior tarsal muscle *(Müller's muscle).* In the lower eyelid, the retractors are the capsulopalpebral fascia and the inferior tarsal muscle.

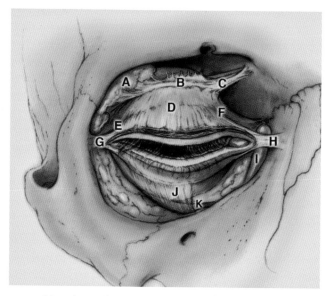

Figure 9-7 Deeper eyelid and anterior orbital structures from anterior view. *A*, Lacrimal gland; *B*, superior transverse ligament (Whitnall's ligament); *C*, superior oblique tendon sheath; *D*, levator aponeurosis; *E*, lateral horn; *F*, medial horn; *G*, lateral canthal tendon; *H*, medial canthal tendon; *I*, lacrimal sac; *J*, lower eyelid retractors; *K*, inferior oblique muscle. *(Adapted from Beard C. Ptosis. 3rd ed. St Louis: Mosby; 1981. Modified by Cyndie Wooley.)*

Upper eyelid retractors

The levator muscle originates in the apex of the orbit, arising from the periorbita of the lesser wing of the sphenoid, just above the annulus of Zinn. The muscular portion of the levator is approximately 40 mm long; the aponeurosis is 14–20 mm in length. The superior transverse ligament *(Whitnall's ligament)* is a sleeve of elastic fibers around the levator muscle located in the area of transition from levator muscle to levator aponeurosis (Fig 9-7).

Whitnall's ligament functions primarily as a suspensory support for the upper eyelid and the superior orbital tissues. The ligament also acts as a fulcrum for the levator, transferring its vector force from an anterior–posterior to a superior–inferior direction. Its analogue in the lower eyelid is *Lockwood's ligament.* Medially, Whitnall's ligament attaches to connective tissue around the trochlea and superior oblique tendon. Laterally, it forms septa through the stroma of the lacrimal gland, then arches upward to attach to the inner aspect of the lateral orbital wall approximately 10 mm above the lateral orbital tubercle, with a small group of fibers extending inferiorly to insert onto the lateral retinaculum. Whitnall's ligament has sometimes been confused with the horns of the levator aponeurosis and mistakenly illustrated as a structure to be cut during ptosis surgery. However, the horns of the levator aponeurosis lie more inferior and toward the canthi. The lateral horn inserts onto the lateral orbital tubercle; the medial horn inserts onto the posterior lacrimal crest. The lateral horn of the levator aponeurosis is strong, and it divides the lacrimal gland into orbital and palpebral lobes, attaching firmly to the orbital tubercle. The medial horn of the aponeurosis is more delicate and forms loose connective attachments to the posterior aspect of the medial canthal tendon and to the posterior lacrimal crest.

As the levator aponeurosis continues toward the tarsus, it divides into an anterior and posterior portion a variable distance above the superior tarsal border. The anterior portion is composed of fine strands of aponeurosis that insert into the septa between the pretarsal orbicularis muscle bundles and skin. These fine attachments are responsible for the close apposition of the pretarsal skin and orbicularis muscle to the underlying tarsus. The upper eyelid crease is formed by the most superior of these attachments and by contraction of the underlying levator complex. The upper eyelid fold is created by the overhanging skin, fat, and orbicularis muscle superior to the crease.

The levator muscle is innervated by the superior division of the third cranial nerve, which also supplies the superior rectus muscle. A superior division palsy, resulting in ptosis and decreased upgaze, implies an intraorbital disruption of the third cranial nerve.

Codère F, Tucker NA, Renaldi B. The anatomy of Whitnall ligament. *Ophthalmology.* 1995;102:2016–2019.

Stasior GO, Lemke BN, Wallow IH, Dortzbach RK. Levator aponeurosis elastic fiber network. *Ophthal Plast Reconstr Surg.* 1993;9:1–10.

The posterior portion of the levator aponeurosis inserts firmly onto the anterior surface of the lower half of the tarsus. It is most firmly attached approximately 3 mm above the eyelid margin and is only very loosely attached to the superior 2–3 mm of the tarsus. Disinsertion, dehiscence, or rarefaction of the aponeurosis following ocular surgery or due to intraocular inflammation, eyelid trauma, or senescence may give rise to ptosis.

Müller's muscle originates in the undersurface of the levator aponeurosis approximately at the level of Whitnall's ligament, 12–14 mm above the upper tarsal margin. This sympathetically innervated smooth muscle extends inferiorly to insert along the upper eyelid superior tarsal margin. This muscle provides approximately 2 mm of elevation of the upper eyelid; if it is interrupted (as in Horner syndrome), mild ptosis results. Müller's muscle is firmly attached to the adjacent conjunctiva posteriorly, especially just above the superior tarsal border. The peripheral arterial arcade is found between the levator aponeurosis and Müller's muscle, just above the superior tarsal border. This vascular arcade serves as a useful surgical landmark to identify Müller's muscle.

Lower eyelid retractors

The capsulopalpebral fascia in the lower eyelid is analogous to the levator aponeurosis in the upper eyelid. The fascia originates as the capsulopalpebral head from attachments to the terminal muscle fibers of the inferior rectus muscle. The capsulopalpebral head divides as it encircles the inferior oblique muscle and fuses with the sheath of the inferior oblique muscle. Anterior to the inferior oblique muscle, the 2 portions of the capsulopalpebral head join to form Lockwood's suspensory ligament. The capsulopalpebral fascia extends anteriorly from this point, sending strands to the inferior conjunctival fornix. The capsulopalpebral fascia inserts onto the inferior tarsal border, just after it fuses with the orbital septum.

The inferior tarsal muscle in the lower eyelid is analogous to Müller's muscle. The poorly developed inferior tarsal muscle runs posterior to the capsulopalpebral fascia. The smooth muscle fibers are most abundant in the area of the inferior fornix.

Tarsus

The tarsi are firm dense plates of connective tissue that serve as the skeleton of the eyelids. The upper eyelid tarsal plates measure 10–12 mm vertically in the center of the eyelid; the maximum lower eyelid tarsal plate measurement is 4 mm. The tarsal plates have rigid attachments to the periosteum through the canthal tendons medially and laterally. The tarsal plates may become horizontally displaced with age as a result of stretching of the medial and lateral supporting tendons. Both tarsal plates are usually 1 mm thick and taper at the medial and lateral ends as they approach the canthal tendons. Located within the tarsus, the meibomian, or tarsal, glands are holocrine sebaceous glands.

Conjunctiva

The conjunctiva is composed of nonkeratinizing squamous epithelium. It forms the posterior layer of the eyelids and contains the mucin-secreting goblet cells and the accessory lacrimal glands of Wolfring and Krause. The accessory lacrimal glands are found in the subconjunctival tissue mainly in the upper and lower eyelids. The glands of Wolfring are found primarily along the non-marginal tarsal borders, and the glands of Krause are found in the fornices.

Additional Anatomical Considerations

Connective tissue

Suborbicularis fat pads Deep to orbicularis muscle overlying the maxillary and zygomatic periosteum is a plane of nonseptate fat called the suborbicularis oculi fat (SOOF). This fat is analogous to the superiorly located retro-orbicularis oculi fat (ROOF), which is situated deep to the eyebrow and extends into the eyelid, where it merges with postorbicularis fascia in the upper eyelid.

The SOOF plays an important role in the aging process of gradual gravitational descent of the midfacial soft tissues. Studies and surgical procedures suggest that elevation of the SOOF into its previous anatomical position restores more youthful contours in the lower eyelid and midfacial soft tissues.

Similarly, the sub-brow fat pad undergoes gravitational descent, compounding a redundant upper eyelid skin fold. The displaced sub-brow fat pad can be confused with a coexisting redundant upper eyelid fold and prominent prolapsed upper eyelid preaponeurotic fat pad. An adequate functional and aesthetic result requires that, in addition to skin and eyelid fat adjustment, blepharoplasty address the descended sub-brow fat pad.

Lucarelli MJ, Khwarg SI, Lemke BN, Kozel JS, Dortzbach RK. The anatomy of midfacial ptosis. *Ophthal Plast Reconstr Surg.* 2000;16:7–22.

Mendelson BC, Muzaffar AR, Adams WP Jr. Surgical anatomy of the midcheek and malar mounds. *Plast Reconstr Surg.* 2002;110:885–896.

Canthal tendons The configuration of the palpebral fissure is maintained by the medial and lateral canthal tendons in conjunction with the attached tarsal plates. The 2 origins of the medial canthal tendon from the anterior and posterior lacrimal crests fuse just temporal to the lacrimal sac and then again split into an upper limb and a lower limb that attach to the upper and lower tarsal plates. The attachment of the tendon to the periosteum overlying the anterior lacrimal crest is diffuse and strong; the attachment to the posterior lacrimal crest is more delicate but important in maintaining apposition of the eyelids to the globe, allowing the puncta to lie in the tear lake.

The lateral canthal tendon attaches at the lateral orbital tubercle on the inner aspect of the orbital rim. It splits into superior and inferior branches that attach to the respective tarsal plates. Cutting, stretching, or disinsertion of either of the canthal tendons usually causes cosmetic or functional problems such as telecanthus and horizontal eyelid laxity. Horizontal eyelid instability is frequently the result of lateral canthal lengthening. Therefore, surgical correction should be directed at shortening the lateral canthus, rather than resecting the normal eyelid in the palpebral fissure. The lateral canthal tendon usually inserts 2 mm higher than does the medial canthal tendon, giving the normal horizontal palpebral fissure an upward slope medial to lateral. When the lateral canthal tendon inserts inferior to the medial canthal tendon, an antimongoloid slant occurs.

Eyelid margin

The eyelid margin is the confluence of the mucosal surface of the conjunctiva, the edge of the orbicularis, and the cutaneous epithelium. Along the margin are eyelashes and glands, which provide protection for the ocular surface. The mucocutaneous junction of the eyelid margin is often erroneously referred to as the *gray line*. The actual gray line is clearly visible in most patients. It consists of an isolated section of pretarsal orbicularis muscle (Riolan) just anterior to the tarsus. The actual mucocutaneous junction is located posterior to the meibomian gland orifices on the eyelid margin (see Fig 9-5). The horizontal palpebral fissure is approximately 30 mm long. The main portion of the margin, called the *ciliary margin,* has a rather well-defined anterior and posterior edge. Medial to the punctum, the eyelid is thinner because of the lack of ciliary follicles.

Wulc AE, Dryden RM, Khatchaturian T. Where is the gray line? *Arch Ophthalmol.* 1987;105:1092–1098.

Eyelashes

There are approximately 100 eyelashes in the upper eyelid and 50 in the lower eyelid. The lashes usually originate in the anterior aspect of the eyelid margin just anterior to the tarsal plate and form 2 or 3 irregular rows. A few cilia may be found in the caruncle.

Meibomian glands

The meibomian glands originate in the tarsus and number approximately 25 in the upper eyelid and 20 in the lower eyelid. During the second month of gestation, both the eyelashes and the meibomian glands differentiate from a common pilosebaceous unit. This dual potentiality explains why, following trauma or chronic irritation, a lash follicle may develop from a meibomian gland *(acquired distichiasis)*. Similarly, an extra row of lashes arising from the meibomian orifices may be present from birth *(congenital distichiasis)*.

Vascular and lymphatic supply

The extensive vascularity of the eyelids promotes healing and helps defend against infection. The arterial supply of the eyelids comes from 2 main sources: (1) the internal carotid artery by way of the ophthalmic artery and its branches (supraorbital and lacrimal) and (2) the external carotid artery by way of the arteries of the face (angular and temporal). Collateral circulation between these 2 systems is extensive, anastomosing throughout the upper and lower eyelids and forming the marginal and peripheral arcades in the eyelids.

The marginal arterial arcade should not be confused with the peripheral arterial arcade. In the upper eyelid, the marginal arcade lies 2 mm superior to the margin, near the follicles of the cilia and anterior to the tarsal plate. The peripheral arcade lies superior to the tarsus, between the levator aponeurosis and Müller's muscle (see Fig 9-4). The lower eyelid often has only 1 arterial arcade, located at the inferior tarsal border.

Eyelid venous drainage may be divided into pretarsal and posttarsal. The *pretarsal* tissues drain into the angular vein medially and into the superficial temporal vein laterally. *Posttarsal* drainage is into the orbital veins and the deeper branches of the anterior facial vein and pterygoid plexus. Lymphatic vessels serving the medial portion of the eyelids drain into the submandibular lymph nodes. Lymph channels serving the lateral portions of the eyelids drain first into the superficial preauricular nodes and then into the deeper cervical nodes.

Nerve supply

Sensory innervation to the eyelids is provided by branches of the first and second divisions of CN V. Branches of the frontal nerve (from V_1), the supratrochlear and the supraorbital, innervate the forehead and medial periocular region. The lacrimal nerve also joins with V_1 and supplies the superior lateral quadrant of the periocular region. Branches of the maxillary nerve (V_2) innervate the lower eyelid, cheek, and inferior lateral orbital region. The medial skin of the eyelids, the medial canthus, the lacrimal sac, and the caruncle are innervated by the infratrochlear nerve, a branch of the third division of V_1, the nasociliary nerve. The motor nerve supply to the eyelids is provided by CN III, CN VII, and the sympathetic nerves.

CHAPTER **10**

Principles of Facial and Eyelid Surgery

Proper patient selection, adequate preoperative evaluation, and meticulous surgical techniques enhance surgical outcome and help ensure predictable results. A basic understanding of wound healing and postoperative infection is mandatory.

Patient Preparation

Facial and eyelid surgery should be approached with care. Adequate preoperative preparation includes properly informing the patient of the proposed benefit as well as the potential complications of the procedure. Although a surgeon might wish to put the patient at ease by using such words as *routine* or *simple,* downplaying possible problems is inappropriate and misleading. Such reassurances imply that surgery is free of complications when, in actuality, significant complications—including facial nerve paralysis and loss of vision—are potential risks.

The patient should be encouraged to read, understand, and sign an operative consent in the relaxed atmosphere of the ophthalmologist's office. It is preferable to obtain this consent prior to the day of surgery. Patient anxiety or preoperative medication may make informed consent on the day of surgery difficult or impossible. The patient must have an opportunity to discuss with the surgeon any concerns about the procedure or the operative permit.

Careful attention to the patient's general medical problems is mandatory, whether or not such conditions are related to the planned surgery. Patients who are pregnant should wait until well after delivery before proceeding with cosmetic surgery. Also, every patient should be asked about any history of bleeding diatheses or use of anticoagulants (eg, warfarin sodium [Coumadin]); antiplatelet agents, including aspirin; or nonsteroidal anti-inflammatory drugs (NSAIDs), because use of platelet inhibitors before surgery may lead to severe intraoperative or postoperative bleeding, with resultant cosmetic and functional adverse sequelae. Hence, anticoagulants such as warfarin are usually discontinued in patients 4 days before elective surgery, if approved by the primary care physician. Aspirin, because of its irreversible platelet inhibitory function, should be stopped at least 5 days before elective surgery. NSAIDs, which are reversible platelet inhibitors, should be stopped at least 72 hours before surgery. Prothrombin time and partial thromboplastin time may be useful tests if coagulation status is a concern. Patients with a more complicated history of poor clotting should receive a preoperative hematologic consultation.

Patients should also be asked about their use of over-the-counter preparations (eg, Ginkgo biloba, vitamin E). As the popularity of alternative medicine has increased, so has the number of patients who use herbal and supplemental medicines. These herbal and supplemental medicines are generally considered natural and therefore harmless by the lay population. It is interesting to note that 30% of all modern conventional medicines are derived from plants. Vitamin C has been shown to stimulate wound healing and diminish postoperative bruising. Medical students typically learn that the origin of digitalis is the foxglove plant, which is quite natural but also quite dangerous if used incorrectly. Guidelines from the American Society of Anesthesiologists suggest that all herbal medicines without formal study be discontinued 2–3 weeks before any elective surgical procedure. Table 10-1 lists commonly used herbal and supplemental medicines that patients should consider discontinuing before anesthesia and surgery.

Table 10-1 Common Herbal and Supplemental Medicines to Consider Discontinuing Before Surgery

Herbal/Supplemental Medicine	Reason to Consider Discontinuation Preoperatively
Chondroitin	Has chemical composition similar to that of heparin
Glucosamine	May mimic human insulin and cause hypoglycemia
Ma huang (Ephedra sinica)	Associated with cardiac dysrhythmias, stroke, or death if used with some general anesthetic agents
Echinacea (Echinacea purpurea)	Potently inhibits cytochrome P-450 and can potentiate toxicity of drugs metabolized through this pathway; also, may adversely affect wound healing
Ginkgo (Ginkgo biloba)	Can inhibit platelet-activation factor and cause spontaneous hemorrhaging; should not be used with anticoagulants
Goldenseal (Hydrastis canadensis)	Can increase blood pressure or precipitate electrolyte imbalance; inhibits cytochrome P-450 metabolism
Milk thistle (Silybum marianum)	Can lead to volume depletion
Ginseng (Panax ginseng)	May cause hypertension and also may have an antiplatelet effect that is irreversible
Kava kava (Piper methysticum)	Potentiates the effects of barbiturates and benzodiazepines, causing excessive sedation. Also, associated with possible severe liver injury (Food and Drug Administration)
Garlic (Allium sativum)	Can inhibit platelet aggregation and should not be taken with other coagulation inhibitors or aspirin
Saw palmetto (Serenoa repens)	Possibly increases risk of intraoperative hemorrhage
St John's Wort (Hypericum perforatum)	Has been associated with cardiovascular collapse on induction of anesthesia (applies to long-term use)
Valerian (Valeriana officinalis)	Inhibits cytochrome P-450 enzyme system
Ginger (Zingiber officinale)	Potently inhibits thromboxane synthetase enzyme, leading to prolongation of bleeding time
Eicosapentaenoic acid (fish oil)	Inhibits platelet aggregation
Vitamin E	Decreases platelet adherence (and aggregation in patients with abnormal platelets, eg, diabetic patients)

Source: Ang-Lee MK, Moss J, Yuan CS. Herbal medicines and perioperative care. *JAMA.* 2001;286:208–216.

Patients who smoke should discontinue smoking several weeks before surgery, particularly those patients requiring large reconstructive flaps or cosmetic face-lifts. Nicotine has a vasoconstrictive effect and reduces the oxygen-carrying capacity of the blood cells. Nicotine replacement is not a helpful option, as the same effect is produced.

The patient's ethnic origin should be considered as well, preoperatively. Individuals of Hispanic, Asian, or African background may respond to surgery or laser treatment with postinflammatory hyperpigmentation (PIH), which can be minimized by pretreatment with bleaching creams or solutions and continuation of this treatment as needed postoperatively. Hypertrophic scarring can occur in patients of any ethnic background, but keloid formation (the scar extends beyond the margins of the wound and does not spontaneously regress) is most common in black patients. The patient's surgical history and family history can be helpful in predicting this possibility.

Cahill RA, McGreal GT, Crowe BH, et al. Duration of increased bleeding tendency after cessation of aspirin therapy. *J Am Coll Surg.* 2005;200:564–573.

Few patients undergo surgery without some degree of apprehension, which can be minimized with the following measures:

- preoperative counseling regarding the anticipated sequence of events, including the surgical procedure and postoperative care
- careful attention to any general medical problems of the patient
- an ongoing calm, reassuring attitude on the part of the surgeon, nursing staff, and administrative personnel

Anesthesia

Local anesthesia with patient cooperation allows the surgeon to assess lid margin height during eyelid surgery, improving accuracy in ptosis repair and eyelid retraction procedures. Anesthesia may be obtained by local infiltration, regional block, or a combination of these 2 techniques. However, local infiltration is usually adequate. Patient safety and comfort are priorities; therefore, the smallest amount of the lowest concentration of anesthetic agent that will provide the desired effect should be used. Administering epinephrine with the anesthetic agent prolongs the anesthetic duration and decreases the rate of systemic absorption, but potential cardiac side effects must be considered. Also, epinephrine enhances hemostasis, provided that the surgeon is willing to wait for approximately 10 minutes between injection and incision for maximum vasoconstriction. Adding hyaluronidase to the anesthetic solution improves dispersion of the anesthetic agent within soft tissue. Buffering of the local anesthetic with sodium bicarbonate may decrease the pain experienced by patients during local infiltration.

Oral sedation used in conjunction with local or regional blocks is considered by the Joint Commission on Accreditation of Healthcare Organizations (JCAHO) as *mild sedation,* which does not require full monitoring. The patient can easily respond to verbal commands, and the status of the respiratory and cardiovascular systems is not affected.

Oral diazepam (Valium) 2.5–5 mg administered 30 to 60 minutes before the surgery can be helpful in anxious patients. Flumazenil (Romazicon) is a benzodiazepine antagonist that specifically inhibits the central action of drugs like diazepam and chlordiazepoxide (Librium). For the treatment of oversedation, flumazenil can be given, 0.1–0.2 mg intravenously (IV) every few minutes up to a total dose of 1 mg. Clonidine (Catapres) is a centrally acting alpha$_2$ agonist that produces a pleasant anxiolytic effect and also decreases the systolic blood pressure without significantly increasing the risk of orthostatic hypotension (no peripheral action).

Tumescent anesthesia, developed by Jeffrey Klein, MD, has been a nice addition to our armamentarium for large facial flaps, face-lifting procedures, and neck liposuction. Intraoperative hemostasis and patient safety and comfort are significantly improved. Tumescent anesthesia can be used in place of general anesthesia in many patients and is the preferred method for some surgeons.

There is no standard dilution of lidocaine and epinephrine, but the following combination works well as a local anesthetic or in combination with general anesthesia: 25 cc of 1% lidocaine (Xylocaine) (10 mg/mL) can be mixed with 0.5 cc of epinephrine along with 6.25 cc sodium bicarbonate (1 mEq/mL) in 500 cc of warmed 0.9% sodium chloride solution. Approximately 100–200 cc of this mixture is used for tumescent anesthesia of the face and neck preoperatively. The surgeon should be well versed in the use of this solution and the potential adverse reactions.

Conscious sedation requires monitoring of the electrocardiogram, the pulse oximeter, and the vital signs by experienced personnel throughout the procedure, as well as establishment of IV access for quick handling of any emergency, all of which increase the margin of safety. Monitored IV sedation is a helpful adjunct for more prolonged or invasive procedures. The use of selective hypnotics and analgesics can decrease the patient's anxiety level and enhance the effectiveness of local anesthesia.

General anesthesia is usually necessary for longer, more complex facial surgeries or for procedures on children. Any family history of an unexplained anesthetic death should alert the surgeon to the possibility of malignant hyperthermia (MH), necessitating a preoperative anesthesiology consultation. Malignant hyperthermia is a potentially life-threatening intraoperative complication triggered by particular anesthetic agents. Although MH is more common in association with musculoskeletal ocular conditions, such as ptosis or strabismus, the clinical use of skeletal muscle biopsy results as a predictor of MH is controversial. See BCSC Section 1, *Update on General Medicine,* or Section 6, *Pediatric Ophthalmology and Strabismus,* for fuller discussions of MH, including treatment protocols.

Postoperative Care

Postoperatively, both the patient and the home caregivers should be given detailed oral and written instructions. Patients who are given any sedative medications should refrain for 24 hours from any activity requiring cognitive or coordination skills. Incisions should be covered with a bland antibiotic ointment so that an infection barrier is created, crusting can be reduced, and the postoperative appearance of the scar improved. To reduce the risk of tissue necrosis or infection, patients and caregivers must pay attention to the wound hygiene of grafts and flaps. Careful follow-up and appropriately timed suture removal are essential.

Postoperative pain is generally managed with hydrocodone 5 mg and acetaminophen 500 mg (Vicodin) or with codeine 30 mg and acetaminophen 325 mg (Tylenol #3). Codeine generally causes more problems with nausea than does hydrocodone, but both medications can cause this unpleasant side effect. For nausea, promethazine (Phenergan) suppositories 25 mg or Ondansetron hydrochloride (Zofran) 8–16 mg every 6 hours sublingually can be given. Ondansetron is effective but significantly more expensive than Phenergan. Metoclopramide (Reglan) 10–20 mg PO every 4 hours also can be helpful and is sedating. For the treatment of more significant pain, oxycodone HCl 5 mg and acetaminophen 500 mg (Percocet) can be used. Occasionally, patients require morphine sulfate (MS Contin) twice per day or oxycodone HCl controlled release (OxyContin) 2 or more times per day. Morphine and oxycodone are respiratory depressants that may also cause hypotension. The tablets should not be crushed, broken, or chewed. In patients who take more than 4 grams per day of medications containing acetaminophen, hepatic toxicity can develop.

For more extensive discussion of surgical considerations, see Chapter 15, Perioperative Management in Ocular Surgery, in BCSC Section 1, *Update on General Medicine.*

Eccarius SG, Gordon ME, Parelman JJ. Bicarbonate-buffered lidocaine-epinephrine-hyaluronidase for eyelid anesthesia. *Ophthalmology.* 1990;97:1499–1501.

Heiman-Patterson TD. Malignant hyperthermia. *Semin Neurol.* 1991;11:220–227.

Heller J, Gabbay JS, Ghadjar K, et al. Top-10 list of herbal and supplemental medicines used by cosmetic patients: what the plastic surgeon needs to know. *Plast Reconstr Surg.* 2006;117(2):436–447.

Iverson RE. Sedation and analgesia in ambulatory settings. *Plast Reconstr Surg.* 1999;104(5): 1559–1564.

Kaye AD, Kucera I, Sabar R. Perioperative anesthesia clinical considerations of alternative medicines. *Anesthesiol Clin North America.* 2004;22:125–139.

Klein JA. *Tumescent Technique: Tumescent Anesthesia & Microcannular Liposuction.* St Louis: Mosby; 2000.

CHAPTER **11**

Classification and Management of Eyelid Disorders

Like the orbit, the eyelids can be affected by a variety of congenital, acquired, infectious, inflammatory, neoplastic, and traumatic conditions. These disorders and their management are discussed in this chapter. In addition, the eyelids are subject to various positional abnormalities and involutional changes; these disorders are discussed in Chapter 12.

Congenital Anomalies

Congenital anomalies of the eyelid may be isolated or associated with other eyelid, facial, or systemic anomalies. Careful evaluation of patients in cases of hereditary syndromes is helpful before proceeding with treatment. Most congenital anomalies of the eyelids occur during the second month of gestation because of a failure of fusion or an arrest of development. The majority of the defects described in this section are rare. (See also BCSC Section 6, *Pediatric Ophthalmology and Strabismus.*)

Blepharophimosis Syndrome

This eyelid syndrome is an autosomal dominantly inherited blepharophimosis, usually presenting with telecanthus (widened intercanthal distance), epicanthus inversus (fold of skin extending from the lower to upper eyelid), and severe ptosis. Additional findings may include lateral lower eyelid ectropion secondary to vertical lid deficiency, a poorly developed nasal bridge, hypoplasia of the superior orbital rims, lop ears, and hypertelorism (Fig 11-1).

Surgical modification may be performed in 1 surgery or multiple surgeries. Timing of the repair is based first on the eyelid function and then on eyelid appearance. Visually disruptive ptosis is addressed promptly. Whether performed simultaneously with the ptosis repair or separately, the medial canthal repositioning will place traction on the upper eyelid and potentially magnify the ptosis. Repair of the ptosis usually requires frontalis suspension for adequate lift. Multiple Z-plasties or Y-V-plasties, sometimes combined with transnasal wiring of the elongated medial canthal tendons, are used to modify the telecanthus and epicanthus. Additional procedures may be needed to correct associated problems such as ectropion or hypoplasia of the orbital rims.

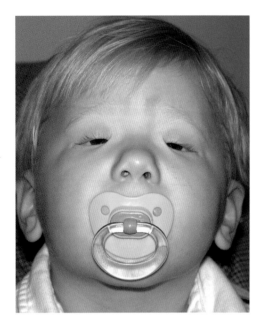

Figure 11-1 Blepharophimosis syndrome. *(Courtesy of Jill Foster, MD.)*

Anderson RL, Nowinski TS. The five-flap technique for blepharophimosis. *Arch Ophthalmol.* 1989;107:448–452.

Beckingsale PS, Sullivan TJ, Wong VA, Oley C. Blepharophimosis: a recommendation for early surgery in patients with severe ptosis. *Clin Experiment Ophthalmol.* 2003;31:138–142.

Bell R, Murday VA, Patton MA, Jeffrey S. Two families with blepharophimosis/ptosis/epicanthus inversus syndrome have mutations in the putative forkhead transcription factor *FOXL2*. *Genet Test.* 2001;5:335–338.

Small KW, Stalvey M, Fisher L, et al. Blepharophimosis syndrome is linked to chromosome 3q. *Hum Mol Genet.* 1995;4(3):443–448.

Congenital Ptosis of the Upper Eyelid

Congenital ptosis of the upper eyelid is discussed in Chapter 12 as part of a general review of all types of blepharoptosis.

Congenital Ectropion

In rare cases, congenital ectropion occurs as an isolated finding. It is more often associated with blepharophimosis syndrome, Down syndrome, or ichthyosis. Congenital ectropion is caused by a vertical insufficiency of the anterior lamella of the eyelid and, if severe, may give rise to chronic epiphora and exposure keratitis. Mild congenital ectropion usually requires no treatment. If it is severe and symptomatic, congenital ectropion is treated like a cicatricial ectropion, with horizontal tightening of the lateral canthal tendon and vertical lengthening of the anterior lamella by means of a full-thickness skin graft.

A complete eversion of the upper eyelids occasionally occurs in newborns (Fig 11-2). Topical lubrication and short-term patching of both eyes may be curative. Full-thickness sutures or a temporary tarsorrhaphy is used when necessary. Possible causes include inclusion conjunctivitis, anterior lamellar inflammation or shortage, or Down syndrome.

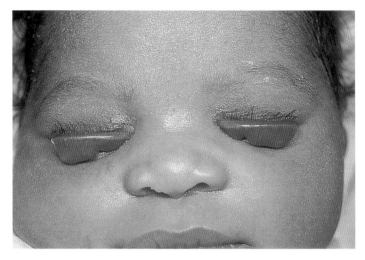

Figure 11-2 Congenital eyelid eversion. *(Courtesy of Thaddeus S. Nowinski, MD.)*

Euryblepharon

Euryblepharon is a unilateral or bilateral horizontal widening of the palpebral fissure sometimes associated with blepharophimosis syndrome. Euryblepharon usually involves the lateral portion of the lower eyelids and is associated with both vertical shortening and horizontal lengthening of the involved eyelids (Figs 11-3, 11-4). The palpebral fissure often has an antimongoloid slant because of inferiorly displaced lateral canthal tendon. Impaired blinking, poor closure, and lagophthalmos may result in exposure keratitis. If symptoms necessitate treatment, reconstruction may include lateral canthal repositioning along with suspension of the suborbicularis oculi fat to the lateral orbital rim so that the lower eyelid is supported. If excess horizontal length is still apparent, a lateral tarsal strip or eyelid margin resection may be added. Skin grafts may occasionally be necessary.

Ankyloblepharon

Ankyloblepharon is partial or complete fusion of the eyelids by webs of skin (see Fig 11-3). These webs can usually be opened with scissors after the web is clamped for a few seconds with a hemostat.

Epicanthus

Epicanthus is a medial canthal fold that may result from immature midfacial bones or a fold of skin and subcutaneous tissue (Fig 11-5; also see Fig 11-3). The condition is usually bilateral. An affected child may appear esotropic because of decreased scleral exposure nasally *(pseudostrabismus)*. Traditionally, 4 types of epicanthus are described:

- *epicanthus tarsalis* if the fold is most prominent in the upper eyelid
- *epicanthus inversus* if the fold is most prominent in the lower eyelid
- *epicanthus palpebralis* if the fold is equally distributed in the upper and lower eyelids

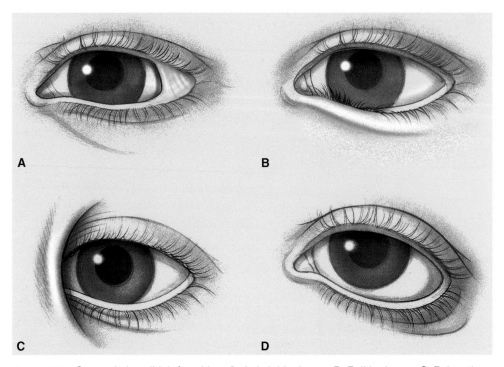

Figure 11-3 Congenital eyelid deformities. **A,** Ankyloblepharon. **B,** Epiblepharon. **C,** Epicanthus. **D,** Euryblepharon. *(Illustration by Christine Gralapp.)*

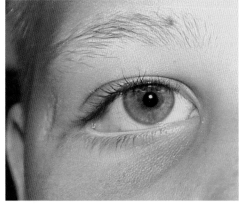

Figure 11-4 Euryblepharon. *(Courtesy of Jill Foster, MD.)*

- *epicanthus supraciliaris* if the fold arises from the eyebrow region running to the lacrimal sac

Epicanthus tarsalis can be a normal variation of the Asian eyelid, whereas epicanthus inversus is frequently associated with blepharophimosis syndrome.

Most forms of epicanthus resolve with normal growth of the facial bones. If no associated eyelid anomalies are present, treatment should be delayed until the face achieves maturity. Epicanthus inversus, however, rarely disappears with facial growth. Most cases of isolated epicanthus requiring treatment respond well to linear revisions such as Z-plasty

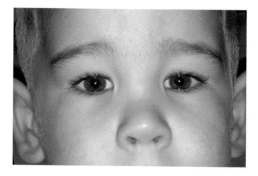

Figure 11-5 Epicanthal folds. *(Courtesy of Jill Foster, MD.)*

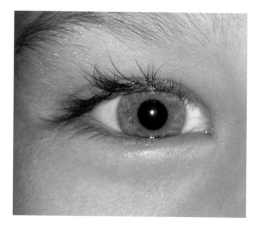

Figure 11-6 Epiblepharon. *(Courtesy of Jill Foster, MD.)*

or Y-V-plasty. Epicanthus tarsalis in the Asian patient may be eliminated by a Y-V-plasty with or without construction of an upper eyelid crease.

Epiblepharon

In epiblepharon, the lower eyelid pretarsal muscle and skin ride above the lower eyelid margin to form a horizontal fold of tissue that causes the cilia to assume a vertical position (Fig 11-6; also see Fig 11–3). The eyelid margin, therefore, is in normal position with respect to the globe. Epiblepharon is most common in Asian children.

The cilia often do not touch the cornea except in downgaze; therefore, epiblepharon may not require surgical treatment because it tends to diminish with the maturation of the facial bones, and the lashes rarely cause corneal staining. However, epiblepharon occasionally results in keratitis; in that case, the excess skin and muscle fold should be excised just inferior to the eyelid margin (in the case of the lower eyelid) and the skin edges approximated.

Congenital Entropion

In contrast with epiblepharon, eyelid margin inversion is present in congenital entropion (Fig 11-7). Developmental factors that lead to this rare condition include lower eyelid retractor dysgenesis, structural defects in the tarsal plate, and relative shortening of the posterior lamella. Congenital entropion often does not improve spontaneously and may

Figure 11-7 Congenital entropion. *(Courtesy of Jill Foster, MD.)*

require surgical correction. Congenital entropion may be repaired through removal of a small amount of the skin and orbicularis along the subciliary portion of the eyelid, in conjunction with a suture that advances the lower eyelid retractors onto the tarsus.

Tarsal kink of the upper eyelid is an unusual form of congenital entropion. It may be repaired by incision of the kink combined with a marginal rotation.

Bartley GB, Nerad JA, Kersten RC, Maguire LJ. Congenital entropion with intact lower eyelid retractor insertion. *Am J Ophthalmol.* 1991;112:437–441.

Dailey RA, Harrison AR, Hildebrand PL, Wobig JL. Levator aponeurosis disinsertion in congenital entropion of the upper eyelid. *Ophthal Plast Reconstr Surg.* 1999;15:360–362.

Congenital Distichiasis

Distichiasis is a rare, sometimes hereditary condition in which an extra row of eyelashes is present in place of the orifices of the meibomian glands. Congenital distichiasis occurs when embryonic pilosebaceous units improperly differentiate into hair follicles (Fig 11-8). Treatment of this condition is indicated if the patient is symptomatic or if evidence of corneal irritation is present. Lubricants and soft contact lenses may be sufficient, but electrolysis, radiofrequency epilation, or cryoepilation may be offered as an alternative. Eyelid splitting with electrolysis, radiofrequency epilation, or cryoepilation or surgical removal of the abnormal follicles may still allow preservation of the normal eyelashes.

Vaughn GL, Dortzbach RK, Sires BS, Lemke BN. Eyelid splitting with excision or microhyfercation for distichiasis. *Arch Ophthalmol.* 1997;115:282–284.

Congenital Coloboma

A coloboma is an embryologic cleft that is usually an isolated anomaly when it occurs in the medial upper eyelid. When found in the lower eyelid, however, the coloboma is frequently associated with other congenital conditions such as facial clefts (eg, Goldenhar syndrome) and lacrimal deformities. A true coloboma includes a defect in the eyelid margin (Fig 11-9).

Full-thickness defects affecting up to one third of the eyelid can usually be repaired through the creation of a rectangular surgical wound between the eyelid crease line and

Figure 11-8 Congenital distichiasis. *(Courtesy of Jill Foster, MD.)*

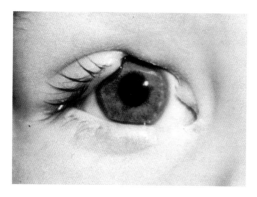

Figure 11-9 True coloboma of upper eyelid.

the eyelid margin. The cut edges of the tarsus are then advanced along the eyelid crease line and repaired with direct closure. A lateral cantholysis may provide additional horizontal relaxation. Almost all large defects can be repaired with use of a variation of the lateral canthal semicircular flap (see Eyelid Defects Involving the Eyelid Margin later in this chapter).

Eyelid-sharing procedures that occlude the visual axis should be avoided in children unless no other reconstructive alternative will preserve the eye, as these patients may develop deprivation amblyopia.

Congenital Eyelid Lesions

Capillary hemangioma

Although capillary hemangiomas sometimes occur as congenital eyelid lesions, most are not apparent at birth. Rather, they usually appear over the first weeks or months of life. Hemangiomas may also involve the orbit (see under Vascular Tumors in Chapter 5). They are associated with a high incidence of amblyopia; therefore, treatment is recommended for patients who present with occlusion of the visual axis, anisometropia, or strabismus, as well as for those with lesions causing significant disfigurement. In the typical natural course of capillary hemangioma, the lesion occurs shortly after birth, increases in size until the patient is 1-year-old, and then decreases over the next 4–5 years.

Intralesional corticosteroid injection is the current treatment of choice in patients whose vision is threatened by a hemangioma limited to the eyelid. If there is more widespread involvement, systemic steroids may be given. Intralesional steroids may act by rendering the tumor's vascular bed more sensitive to the body's circulating catecholamines. This technique is relatively safe, simple, and repeatable. However, rare cases of eyelid necrosis, embolic retinal vascular occlusion, and systemic adrenal suppression may occur following even a single injection. Treatment with systemic steroids eliminates the risks attributed to the injection delivery but increases the systemic dosage and risk of systemic side effects. Topical treatment with clobetasol propionate has also been reported to successfully shrink eyelid hemangiomas. However, topical treatment does not eliminate the risks of systemic steroid exposure. Interferon-α is usually reserved for life-threatening or sight-threatening lesions because of the risk of serious adverse effects. Surgical excision may be used on well-circumscribed lesions. Using the carbon-dioxide laser as an incisional device is helpful for controlling bleeding. Topical lasers may be used on the superficial (1–2 mm) layers of the skin to diminish the redness of a lesion. However, cutaneous lasers do not penetrate deeply enough to shrink a visually disabling lesion.

Cruz OA, Zarnegar SR, Myers SE. Treatment of periocular capillary hemangioma with topical clobetasol propionate. *Ophthalmology.* 1995;102(12):2012–2015.

Kushner, BJ. Intralesional corticosteroid injection for infantile adnexal hemangioma. *Am J Ophthalmol.* 1982;93:496–506.

Ruttum MS, Abrams GW, Harris GJ, Ellis MK. Bilateral retinal embolization associated with intralesional corticosteroid injection for capillary hemangioma of infancy. *J Pediatr Ophthalmol Strabismus.* 1993;30:4–7.

Cryptophthalmos

Cryptophthalmos is a rare condition that presents with partial or complete absence of the eyebrow, palpebral fissure, eyelashes, and conjunctiva (Fig 11-10). The partially developed adnexa are fused to the anterior segment of the globe. Cryptophthalmos may be unilateral or bilateral. Histologically, the levator, orbicularis, tarsus, conjunctiva, and meibomian glands are attenuated or absent; thus, attempts at reconstruction are difficult. Severe ocular defects are present in the underlying eye.

Acquired Eyelid Disorders

Chalazion

Chalazion, a type of focal inflammation of the eyelids, can result from an obstruction of the meibomian glands (an internal posterior hordeolum). This disorder is often associated with rosacea and chronic blepharitis. This common disorder may occasionally be confused with a malignant neoplasm.

The meibomian glands are oil-producing sebaceous glands located in the tarsal plates of both upper and lower eyelids. If the gland orifices on the eyelid margin become plugged,

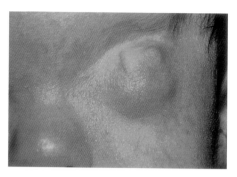

Figure 11-10 Cryptophthalmos.

the contents of the glands (sebum) are released into the tarsus and the surrounding eyelid soft tissue. This elicits an acute inflammatory response accompanied by pain and erythema of the skin. The exact role of bacterial agents (most commonly *Staphylococcus aureus*) in the production of chalazia is not clear. Histopathologically, these lesions are characterized by chronic lipogranulomatous inflammation.

Treatment

In the acute inflammatory phase, treatment consists of warm compresses and appropriate eyelid hygiene. Although topical antibiotic or anti-inflammatory ocular medications can be used, they may have minimal effect in resolving a chalazion. Acute secondary infection may be treated with an antibiotic directed at skin flora. Doxycycline or tetracycline given for systemic effect may be appropriate when a case requires long-term suppression of meibomian gland inflammation associated with ocular rosacea. Patients should be counseled about the possible side effects of systemically administered antibiotics.

Occasionally, chalazia become chronic and cystlike, requiring surgical management to facilitate clearing of the inflammatory mass. If the greatest inflammatory response is on the posterior eyelid margin, an incision through tarsus and conjunctiva is appropriate for drainage. Sharp dissection and excision of all necrotic material, including the posterior cyst wall, are indicated. This results in a posterior marsupialization of the chalazion (Fig 11-11). Caution is needed for the removal of inflammatory tissue at the eyelid margin or adjacent to the punctum. In the rare cases in which the greatest inflammatory response is anterior, incision through the skin and orbicularis muscle, with appropriate removal of granulomatous tissue, is possible. Pathologic examination is appropriate for atypical or recurrent chalazia. Local injection of corticosteroids in chalazia resistant to conservative management can cause temporary depigmentation of the overlying skin and is not as effective as surgical treatment. Combining excision with steroid injection into the excisional bed results in a 95% resolution rate.

Epstein GA, Putterman AM. Combined excision and drainage with intralesional corticosteroid injection in the treatment of chronic chalazia. *Arch Ophthalmol.* 1988;106:514–516.

Hordeolum

An acute infection (usually staphylococcal) can involve the sebaceous secretions in the glands of Zeis *(external hordeolum,* or *stye)* or the meibomian glands *(internal*

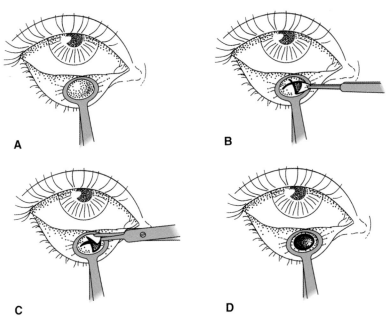

Figure 11-11 Excision of chalazion. **A,** After a clamp is placed around the chalazion, a blade is used to make a vertical incision into the tarsus. **B,** Cruciate incision of conjunctiva and cyst wall. **C,** Flaps are excised with a scissors. **D,** Defect is allowed to heal by secondary intention. *(Illustration by Jeanne C. Koelling.)*

hordeolum). In the case of external hordeola, the infection often appears to center around an eyelash follicle, and the eyelash can be plucked to promote drainage. Spontaneous resolution often occurs. If needed, assiduous application of hot compresses and topical antibiotic ointment is usually curative. Rarely, hordeola may progress to true superficial cellulitis, or even abscesses, of the eyelid. In such cases, systemic antibiotic therapy and possible surgical incision and drainage may be required.

Eyelid Edema

Swelling of the eyelids may be caused by local conditions such as insect bites or allergy or by systemic conditions such as cardiovascular disease, renal disease, certain collagen vascular diseases, or Graves disease. Cerebrospinal fluid leakage into the orbit or eyelids following trauma may mimic eyelid edema. Lymphedema may be present after the lymphatic drainage system from the eyelid is interrupted.

Floppy Eyelid Syndrome

Floppy eyelid syndrome is characterized by chronic papillary conjunctivitis; easily everted, flaccid upper eyelids; and nonspecific irritative symptoms (Fig 11-12). Associations have been reported with obesity, keratoconus, eyelid rubbing or mechanical pressure, hyperglycemia, and sleep apnea. A marked decrease in the number of elastin fibers in the tarsus has been reported. Often, patients have a history of sleeping prone; a mechanical upper eyelid eversion can result from contact with a pillow or bed sheets. Initial conservative treatment with viscous lubrication and patching or an eyelid shield is helpful. Frequently, horizontal tightening of the eyelid is indicated. Sleep studies are recommended to rule out sleep apnea.

A   **B**

Figure 11-12 Floppy eyelid syndrome. **A,** Eyelash malposition, characteristic of floppy eyelid syndrome. **B,** Easy eversion of loose eyelid, characteristic of floppy eyelid syndrome. *(Courtesy of Jill Foster, MD.)*

Netland PA, Sugrue SP, Albert DM, Shore JW. Histopathologic features of the floppy eyelid syndrome. *Ophthalmology.* 1994;101:174–181.

Eyelid imbrication syndrome is pathophysiologically similar to floppy eyelid syndrome in that a lax upper eyelid is present in both sydromes. However, in eyelid imbrication syndrome, the upper eyelid does not easily evert and the tarsal plate is normal. The upper eyelid overrides the lower eyelid margin during eyelid closure, resulting in chronic conjunctivitis. Management consists of topical lubrication in mild cases. In more severe cases, horizontal tightening of the upper eyelid is indicated.

Karesh JW, Nirankari VS, Hameroff SB. Eyelid imbrication: an unrecognized cause of chronic ocular irritation. *Ophthalmology.* 1993;100:883–889.

Trichotillomania

Trichotillomania is an impulse control disorder most commonly seen in preteen or teenage girls. It is characterized by the repeated desire to pull out hairs, frequently eyebrows or eyelashes. Diagnosis may be elusive, as affected patients usually deny the cause. Characteristically, multiple hairs are broken off and regrowing at different lengths. Applying ophthalmic ointment to the affected area sometimes helps diagnosis and treatment by allowing hairs to regrow. Habit reversal therapy or oral treatment with selective serotonin reuptake inhibitors may be effective, as employed in the treatment of obsessive-compulsive behavior.

Eyelid Neoplasms

Numerous benign and malignant cutaneous neoplasms may develop in the periocular skin, arising from the epidermis, dermis, or eyelid adnexal structures. However, most lesions, whether benign or malignant, develop from the epidermis, the rapidly growing superficial layer of the skin. Although many of these lesions may occur elsewhere on the body, their appearance and behavior in the eyelids may be unique owing to the particular characteristics of eyelid skin and the specialized adnexal elements. The malignant lesions most frequently affecting the eyelids are basal cell carcinoma, squamous cell carcinoma, sebaceous cell carcinoma, and melanoma. Because clinical judgment is not as exact as pathologic diagnosis, histopathologic examination of suspected cutaneous malignancies is generally recommended.

Clinical Evaluation of Eyelid Tumors

The history and physical examination of eyelid lesions offer important clues regarding the likelihood of malignancy. Predisposing factors in the development of skin cancer include

- a history of prior skin cancer
- excessive sun exposure, especially blistering sunburn during adolescence
- previous radiation therapy
- history of smoking
- Celtic or Scandinavian ancestry, with fair skin, red hair, blue eyes
- immunosupression

Signs suggesting eyelid malignancy are

- slow, painless growth of a lesion
- ulceration, with intermittent drainage, bleeding, and crusting
- irregular pigmentary changes
- destruction of normal eyelid margin architecture (especially meibomian orifices) and loss of cilia
- heaped-up, pearly, translucent margins with central ulceration
- fine telangiectasias
- loss of fine cutaneous wrinkles

Palpable induration extending well beyond visibly apparent margins suggests tumor infiltration into the dermis and subcutaneous tissue.

Lesions near the puncta should be evaluated for punctal or canalicular involvement. Probing and irrigation may be required for exclusion of lacrimal system involvement or as preparation for surgical resection.

Large lesions should be palpated for evidence of fixation to deeper tissues or bone. In addition, regional lymph nodes should be palpated for evidence of metastases in cases of suspected squamous cell carcinoma, sebaceous carcinoma, malignant melanoma, or Merkel cell carcinoma. Lymphatic tumor spread may produce rubbery swelling along the line of the jaw or in front of the ear. Restriction of ocular motility and proptosis suggest orbital extension of an eyelid malignancy. The function of cranial nerves VII and V is assessed so that any deficiencies possibly indicating perineural tumor spread can be detected. Perineural invasion is a feature of squamous cell carcinoma. Systemic evidence of liver, pulmonary, bone, or neurological involvement should be sought in cases of sebaceous adenocarcinoma or melanoma of the eyelid.

It is important to obtain photographs prior to treatment of the lesion. If photographs cannot be obtained, drawings and measurements are recorded for future comparison.

The following discussions of eyelid neoplasms are intended to provide a brief overview of the most prevalent lesions. For more extensive coverage and additional clinical and pathologic photographs, see BCSC Section 4, *Ophthalmic Pathology and Intraocular Tumors.*

Cook BE Jr, Bartley GB. Epidemiologic characteristics and clinical course of patients with malignant eyelid tumors in an incidence cohort in Olmsted County, Minnesota. *Ophthalmology.* 1999;106:746–750.

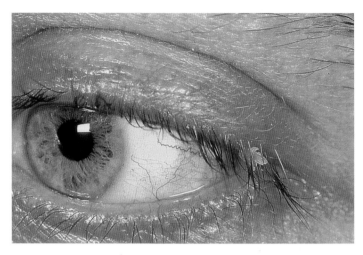

Figure 11-13 Squamous papilloma, or acrochordon.

Benign Eyelid Lesions

Epithelial hyperplasias

The terminology used by dermatopathologists to describe various benign epithelial proliferations is continuing to evolve and can be confusing. It is helpful to group the various benign epithelial proliferations under the clinical heading of *papillomas*. (This designation does not necessarily imply any association with the papillomavirus.) Clinical and histopathologic characterizations of the various benign epithelial proliferations overlap considerably. Included within this group are seborrheic keratosis; pseudoepitheliomatous hyperplasia; verruca; acrochordon (skin tag, fibroepithelial polyp, squamous papilloma; Fig 11-13); basosquamous acanthoma; squamous acanthoma; and many others. These benign epithelial proliferations can all be managed with shave excision at the dermal–epidermal junction.

Seborrheic keratosis is a common example of the various acquired benign eyelid papillomas (Fig 11-14). It tends to affect middle-aged and elderly patients. Its clinical appearance varies; it may be sessile or pedunculated and have varying degrees of pigmentation and hyperkeratosis. On facial skin, seborrheic keratosis typically appears as a smooth, greasy, stuck-on lesion. On the thinner eyelid skin, this lesion can be more lobulated, papillary, or pedunculated with visible excrescences on its surface. Even large lesions of this type remain totally superficial. They can be managed by shave excision at the dermal–epidermal junction. Deep excision is unnecessary, and the residual flat surface reepithelializes rapidly. Shaving a seborrheic keratosis from the thin eyelid skin may be more challenging.

Pseudoepitheliomatous hyperplasia is not a discrete lesion but rather refers to a pattern of reactive changes in the epidermis that may occur overlying areas of inflammation or neoplasia.

Verruca vulgaris, caused by epidermal infection with the human papillomavirus (type 6 or 11), rarely occurs in thin eyelid skin (Fig 11-15). Cryotherapy may eradicate the lesion and minimizes the risk of viral spread.

A *cutaneous horn* is a clinically descriptive, nondiagnostic term referring to *exuberant hyperkeratosis.* This chronic lesion may be associated with a variety of benign or malignant histopathologic processes, including seborrheic keratosis, verruca vulgaris, and squamous or basal cell carcinoma. Biopsy of the base of the cutaneous horn is required to establish a definitive diagnosis.

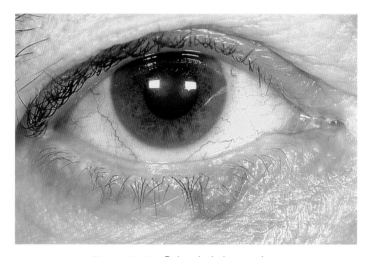

Figure 11-14 Seborrheic keratosis.

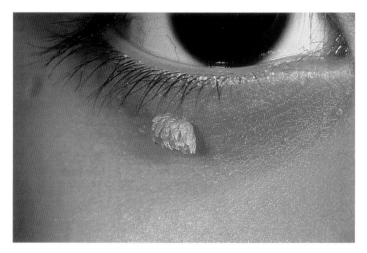

Figure 11-15 Verruca vulgaris (wart).

Benign epithelial lesions

Cysts of the epidermis are the second most common type of benign periocular cutaneous lesions, accounting for approximately 18% of excised benign lesions. Most of these are *epidermal inclusion cysts,* which arise from the infundibulum of the hair follicle, either spontaneously or following traumatic implantation of epidermal tissue into the dermis (Fig 11-16). The lesions are slow-growing, elevated, round, and smooth. They often have a central pore, indicating the remaining pilar duct. Although these cysts are often called *sebaceous cysts,* they are actually filled with keratin. Rupture of the cyst wall may cause an inflammatory foreign body reaction. The cysts may also become secondarily infected. Recommended treatment for small cysts is marsupialization, excising around the periphery of the cyst but leaving the base of the cyst wall to serve as the new surface epithelium. Larger or deeper cysts may require a complete excision of the cyst, in which case the cyst wall should be removed intact so that recurrence can be avoided.

Multiple tiny epidermal inclusion cysts are called *milia.* Milia may appear spontaneously, following trauma, or during the healing phase of a bullous disease process. They are particularly common in newborn infants. Generally, milia resolve spontaneously, but they may be marsupialized with a sharp blade or needle. Multiple confluent milia may be treated with topical retinoic acid cream.

A less common epidermal cyst is the *pilar,* or *trichilemmal, cyst.* These cysts are clinically indistinguishable from epidermal inclusion cysts but tend to occur in areas containing large and numerous hair follicles. Approximately 90% of pilar cysts occur on the scalp; in the periocular region, they are generally found in the eyebrows. The cysts are filled with desquamated epithelium, and calcification occurs in approximately 25% of these cysts.

Molluscum contagiosum is a viral infection of the epidermis that often involves the eyelid in children (Fig 11-17). Occasionally, multiple exuberant lesions appear in adult patients with acquired immunodeficiency syndrome (AIDS). The lesions are characteristically waxy and nodular, with a central umbilication. They may produce an associated follicular conjunctivitis. Treatment is observation, excision, controlled cryotherapy, or curettage, with care taken to avoid damaging eyelash follicles or the eyelid margin and causing depigmentation of the skin.

Xanthelasmas are yellowish plaques that occur commonly in the medial canthal areas of the upper and lower eyelids (Fig 11-18). They represent collections of lipid-laden

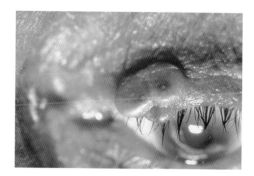

Figure 11-16 Epidermal inclusion cyst. *(Courtesy of Robert C. Kersten, MD.)*

Figure 11-17 Molluscum lesion of eyelid. *(Courtesy of Jill Foster, MD.)*

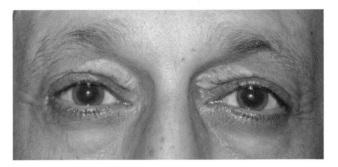

Figure 11-18 Xanthelasma. *(Courtesy of Jill Foster, MD.)*

macrophages in the superficial dermis and subdermal tissues. Although xanthelasmas usually occur in patients with normal serum cholesterol levels, they are sometimes associated with hypercholesterolemia or congenital disorders of lipid metabolism. When excising these lesions, the surgeon must be careful to avoid removing too much of the anterior lamella of the eyelids, because doing so can lead to cicatricial ectropion. Once excised, xanthelasma may recur. Other treatment options include serial excision, CO_2 laser ablation, or topical 100% trichloroacetic acid. Deep extension into the orbicularis muscle can occur, in which case the lesion may not be amenable to surface ablative therapies.

Benign Adnexal Lesions

The term *adnexa* refers to skin appendages that are located within the dermis but communicate through the epidermis to the surface. They include oil glands, sweat glands, and hair follicles. The eyelid contains both the specialized eyelashes and the normal vellus hairs found on skin throughout the body. Periocular adnexal oil glands include the *meibomian glands* within the tarsal plate, the *glands of Zeis* associated with eyelash follicles, and normal *sebaceous glands* that are present as part of the pilosebaceous units in the skin hair. Sweat glands in the periocular region include the *eccrine sweat glands,* which have a general distribution throughout the body and are responsible for thermal regulation, and the eccrine glands with apocrine secretion (the *glands of Moll*) associated with the eyelid margin.

Lesions of oil gland origin

Chalazion and hordeolum These common eyelid lesions are discussed earlier in this chapter under Acquired Eyelid Disorders.

Sebaceous hyperplasia Sebaceous gland hyperplasia presents as multiple small yellow papules that may have central umbilication. They tend to occur on the forehead and cheeks and are common in patients older than 40 years. These lesions may sometimes be mistaken for basal cell carcinoma because of their tendency for central umbilication and fine telangiectasias. However, they are cream-colored and are soft on palpation. They may result from chronic dermatitis and can also be seen in patients with rosacea. Patients with multiple acquired sebaceous gland adenomas, adenomatoid sebaceous hyperplasia, or basal cell carcinomas with sebaceous differentiation have an increased incidence of visceral malignancy *(Muir-Torre syndrome)* and should be evaluated accordingly.

When sebaceous gland hyperplasia occurs in the meibomian glands in the tarsal plate, the eyelids may become thickened and ectropic. This condition may coexist with chronic blepharitis, and the possibility of sebaceous gland carcinoma must be considered.

Sebaceous adenoma This rare tumor appears as a yellowish papule on the face, scalp, or trunk and may mimic a basal cell carcinoma or seborrheic keratosis.

Tumors of eccrine sweat gland origin

Eccrine hidrocystoma Eccrine hidrocystomas are common cystic lesions 1–3 mm in diameter that occur in groups and tend to cluster around the lower eyelids and canthi and on the face. They are considered to be ductal retention cysts, and they often enlarge in conditions such as heat and increased humidity, which stimulate perspiration. Treatment consists of surgical excision.

Syringoma Benign eccrine sweat gland tumors found commonly in young females, syringomas present as multiple small, waxy, pale yellow nodules 1–2 mm in diameter on the lower eyelids (Fig 11-19). Syringomas can also be found in the axilla and sternal region. They become more apparent at the time of puberty. Because the eccrine glands are located within the dermis, these lesions lie too deep to allow shave excision. Removal requires complete surgical excision, which is often best accomplished in a staged fashion.

Eccrine spiradenoma An uncommon benign tumor that appears as a solitary nodule 1–2 cm in diameter and that may be tender and painful. It tends to occur in early adulthood, and eyelid involvement is rare. Treatment is surgical excision.

Eccrine acrospiroma Also called *clear cell hidradenoma,* this rare tumor occurs as a solitary nodular lesion that is usually mobile beneath the skin. Treatment is surgical excision.

Pleomorphic adenoma This rare benign tumor occurs most commonly in the head and neck region and may involve the eyelids. Histologically, the tumor is identical to the pleomorphic adenoma of the salivary and lacrimal glands (discussed in Chapter 5). Treatment is complete surgical excision at the time of the primary exploration.

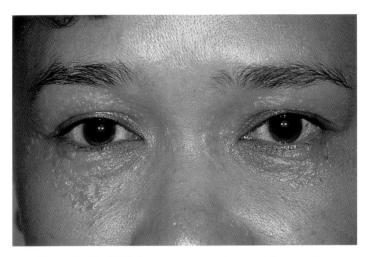

Figure 11-19 Syringomas. *(Courtesy of Robert C. Kersten, MD.)*

Tumors of apocrine sweat gland origin

Apocrine hidrocystoma A very common solitary smooth cyst arising from the glands of Moll along the eyelid margin, apocrine hidrocystoma is considered a true adenoma of the secretory cells of Moll rather than a retention cyst (Fig 11-20). These lesions typically are translucent or bluish, and they transilluminate. They may be multiple and often extend deep beneath the surface, especially in the canthal regions. Treatment for superficial cysts is marsupialization. Deep cysts require complete excision of the cyst wall. Apocrine hidrocystomas are also known as *cystadenomas* or *sudoriferous cysts.*

Cylindroma Cylindromas are rare tumors that may be solitary or multiple and may be dominantly inherited. Lesions are dome-shaped, smooth, flesh-colored nodules of varying size and tend to affect the scalp and face. They may occur so profusely in the scalp that the scalp is entirely covered with lesions, in which case they are called *turban tumors.* Treatment is surgical excision, but it may prove difficult if there are multiple lesions over a large surface area.

Tumors of hair follicle origin

Several rare benign lesions may arise from the eyelashes, eyebrows, or vellus hairs in the periocular region.

Trichoepitheliomas These lesions are small flesh-colored papules with occasional telangiectasias that occur on the eyelids or forehead (Fig 11-21). Histopathologically, trichoepitheliomas appear as basaloid islands and keratin cysts with immature hair follicle structures. If keratin is abundant, these lesions may clinically resemble an epidermal inclusion cyst. The individual histologic picture may be difficult to differentiate from that of basal cell carcinoma. Simple excision is curative.

Trichofolliculoma A trichofolliculoma is a single, sometimes umbilicated, lesion found mainly in adults. Histopathologically, it represents a squamous cystic structure containing keratin and hair shaft components.

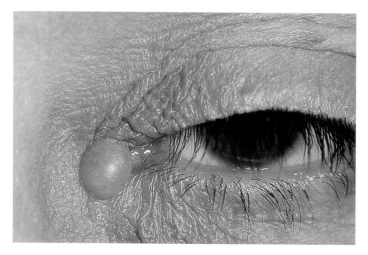

Figure 11-20 Apocrine hidrocystoma. *(Courtesy of Robert C. Kersten, MD.)*

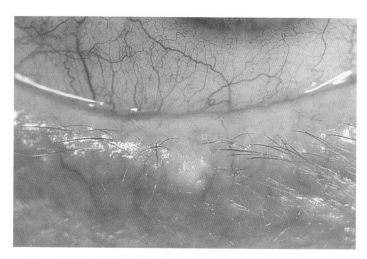

Figure 11-21 Trichoepithelioma. *(Courtesy of Jeffrey A. Nerad, MD.)*

Trichilemmoma Another type of solitary lesion that occurs predominantly in adults, trichilemmomas resemble verrucae. Histopathologically, they show glycogen-rich cells oriented around hair follicles.

Pilomatricoma These lesions most often affect young adults and usually occur in the eyebrow and central upper eyelid as a reddish purple subcutaneous mass attached to the overlying skin (Fig 11-22). They may become quite large. The tumor is composed of islands of epithelial cells surrounded by basophilic cells with shadow cells. Excision is curative.

Benign Melanocytic Lesions

Melanocytic lesions of the skin arise from 3 sources: nevus cells, dermal melanocytes, and epidermal melanocytes. Virtually any benign or malignant lesion may be pigmented, and

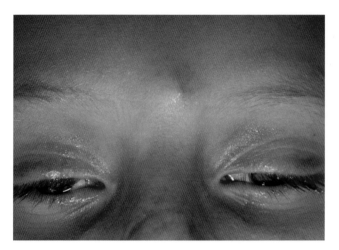

Figure 11-22 Pilomatricoma of glabella. *(Courtesy of Jill Foster, MD.)*

lesions of melanocytic origin do not necessarily have visible pigmentation. For example, seborrheic keratoses are frequently pigmented, and basal cell carcinomas are occasionally pigmented, especially if they arise in persons with darker skin. In contrast, dermal nevi typically have no pigmentation in Caucasians. Melanocytes are normally found distributed at the dermal–epidermal junction throughout the skin. Melanocytes are similar to nevus cells, but nevus cells are arranged in clusters and have ultrastructural differences. Both nevus cells and melanocytes give rise to a number of benign lesions.

In addition to the individual lesions described next, diffuse eyelid skin hyperpigmentation called *melasma,* or *chloasma,* can occur in women who are pregnant or using oral contraceptives; in families with an autosomal dominant trait; and in patients with chronic atopic eczema, rosacea, and other inflammatory dermatoses.

Nevi

Nevi are the third most common benign lesions encountered in the periocular region (after papillomas and epidermal inclusion cysts). They arise from *nevus cells,* which are incompletely differentiated melanocytes found in clumps in the epidermis and dermis and in the junction zone between these 2 layers. Nevi are not apparent clinically at birth but begin to appear during childhood and often develop increased pigmentation at the time of puberty.

All nevi tend to undergo evolution during life through 3 stages: *junctional* (located in the basal layer of the epidermis at the dermal–epidermal junction), *compound* (extending from the junctional zone up into the epidermis and down into the dermis), and *dermal* (caused by involution of the epidermal component and persistence of the dermal component). In children, nevi arise initially as junctional nevi, which are typically flat, pigmented macules. Beyond the second decade, most nevi become compound, at which stage they appear as elevated, pigmented papules. Later in life, the epidermal pigmentation is lost and the compound nevus remains as an elevated but minimally pigmented or amelanotic lesion. By age 70 virtually all nevi have become dermal nevi and have lost pigmentation.

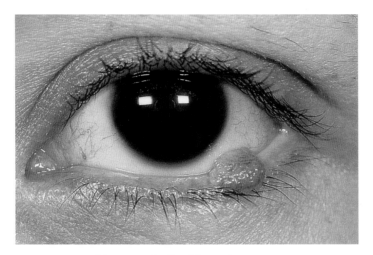

Figure 11-23 Eyelid margin nevus.

Nevi are frequently found on the eyelid margin, characteristically molded to the ocular surface (Fig 11-23). Asymptomatic benign nevi require no treatment, but malignant transformation of a junctional or compound nevus can rarely occur. Nevi may become symptomatic if they rub on the ocular surface or enlarge and obstruct vision. They are managed with shave excision or wedge resection of the eyelid margin.

Freckle

An *ephelis,* or *freckle,* is a small, flat, brown spot on the skin. Ephelides appear from hyperpigmentation of the basal layer of the epidermis. The number of epidermal melanocytes is not increased, but they extrude more than the usual amount of pigment into the epidermal basal cell layer. Ephelides are common in fair-skinned persons, and the hue of the ephelis darkens with sunlight exposure. These small, circumscribed macules usually appear on the malar areas, but they occasionally present on the eyelids or conjunctiva. No treatment is necessary other than sun protection.

Lentigo simplex

Simple lentigines are flat, pigmented spots larger in diameter than ephelides. Occurring throughout life, lentigo simplex is not apparently related to sun exposure. This type of lentigo also differs from a freckle in that the number of epidermal melanocytes is increased, and melanin is found in adjacent basal keratinocytes. Individual lesions are evenly pigmented and measure a few millimeters in diameter. Eyelid lentigines may be associated with Peutz-Jeghers syndrome (autosomal dominant polyposis of the intestinal tract). No treatment is necessary for lentigo simplex. Melanin-bleaching preparations may achieve cosmetic improvement.

Traboulsi EI, Maumanee IH. Periocular pigmentation in the Peutz-Jeghers syndrome. *Am J Ophthalmol.* 1986;102(1):126–127.

Solar lentigo

Multiple solar lentigines may occur in older persons, in which case they are called *senile lentigo,* or, incorrectly, *liver spots.* Chronic sun exposure produces pigmented macules with an increased number of melanocytes. Solar lentigines are uniformly hyperpigmented and somewhat larger than simple lentigines. The dorsum of the hands and the forehead are the most frequently affected areas. No treatment is necessary, but sun protection is recommended. Melanin-bleaching preparations or cryotherapy may help fade the pigmentation of solar lentigines.

Blue nevus

A blue nevus is a dark blue-gray to blue-black, slightly elevated lesion that may be congenital or may develop during childhood. The blue nevus arises from a localized proliferation of dermal melanocytes. The dome-shaped, dark lesions beneath the epidermis are usually 10 mm or less in diameter. Although the malignant potential is extremely low, these lesions are generally excised.

Dermal melanocytosis

Also known as *nevus of Ota,* this diffuse, congenital blue nevus of the periocular skin most often affects persons of African, Hispanic, or Asian descent, especially females. Dermal melanocytes proliferate in the region of the first and second dermatomes of cranial nerve V. The eyelid skin is diffusely brown or blue, and pigmentation may extend to the adjacent forehead. Approximately 5% of cases are bilateral. When patchy slate gray pigmentation also appears on the episclera and uvea, as occurs in two thirds of affected patients, the condition is known as *oculodermal melanocytosis* (Fig 11-24). Although malignant transformation may occur, especially in white patients, no prophylactic treatment is recommended. Approximately 1 in 400 patients with oculodermal melanocytosis develops a uveal malignant melanoma.

Premalignant Epidermal Lesions

Actinic keratosis

Actinic keratosis is the most common precancerous skin lesion. It usually affects elderly persons who have a fair complexion and a history of chronic sun exposure (Fig 11-25).

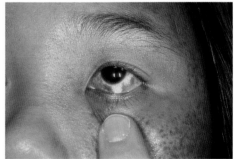

Figure 11-24 Oculodermal melanocytosis. *(Courtesy of Jerry Popham, MD.)*

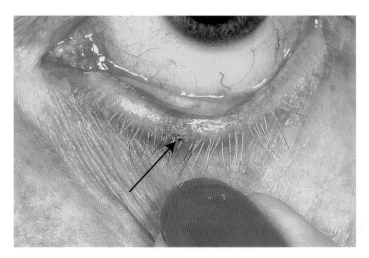

Figure 11-25 Actinic keratosis *(arrow)*.

These lesions are typically round, scaly, keratotic plaques that on palpation have the texture of sandpaper. They often develop on the face, head, neck, forearms, and dorsum of the hands. These lesions are in a state of continual flux, increasing in size and darkening in response to sunlight exposure and remitting with reduced sun exposure. It has been reported that up to 25% of individual actinic keratoses spontaneously resolve over a 12-month period, although new lesions tend to develop continually. The risk of malignant transformation from a given actinic keratosis is only 0.24% per year, but over extended follow-up, a patient with multiple actinic keratoses has a 12%–16% incidence of squamous cell carcinoma. Squamous cell carcinomas arising from actinic keratoses are thought to be less aggressive than those developing de novo.

For lesions arising in the periocular region, incisional or excisional biopsy is recommended to establish a definitive diagnosis. Excision or cryodestruction is recommended. Alternatively, extensive lesions may be treated with topical 5-fluorouracil or imiquimod cream.

Gupta AK, Davey V, McPhail H. Evaluation of the effectiveness of imiquimod and 5-fluorouracil for the treatment of actinic keratosis: critical review and meta-analysis of efficacy studies. *J Cutan Med Surg.* 2005;9:209–214.

In Situ Epithelial Malignancies

Bowen disease

The term *Bowen disease* refers to squamous cell carcinoma in situ of the skin. These lesions typically appear as elevated nonhealing erythematous lesions. They may present with scaling, crusting, or pigmented keratotic plaques. Pathologically, the lesions demonstrate full-thickness epidermal atypia without dermal invasion. In 5% of patients, Bowen disease may progress to vertically invasive squamous cell carcinoma; therefore, complete surgical

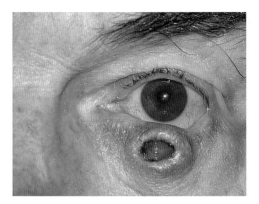

Figure 11-26 Keratoacanthoma.

excision is advised. Alternatively, cryotherapy of Bowen disease may be used, especially in larger areas of involvement.

Keratoacanthoma

Although keratoacanthoma was previously considered to be a benign self-limiting lesion, many authors now regard this entity as a low-grade squamous cell carcinoma. The lesion usually begins as a flesh-colored papule on the lower eyelid that develops rapidly into a dome-shaped nodule with a central keratin-filled crater and elevated rolled margins (Fig 11-26). Keratoacanthomas typically occur in middle-aged and elderly patients and show an increased incidence in immunosuppressed patients. Gradual involution over the course of 3–6 months has often been observed. The abundant keratin production in the center of the lesion may incite a surrounding inflammatory reaction, which may play a role in ultimate resolution. At present, incisional biopsy followed by complete surgical excision is recommended.

Grossniklaus HE, Wojno TH, Yanoff M, Font RL. Invasive keratoacanthoma of the eyelid and ocular adnexa. *Ophthalmology.* 1996;103:937–941.

Premalignant Melanocytic Lesions

Lentigo maligna

Also known as *Hutchinson melanotic freckle* or *precancerous melanosis,* lentigo maligna is a flat, irregularly shaped, unevenly pigmented, slowly enlarging lesion that typically occurs on the malar regions in older white persons. Unlike senile or solar lentigo, characteristics of lentigo maligna include significant pigmentary variation, irregular borders, and progressive enlargement. These characteristics reflect a radial, intraepidermal, uncontrolled growth phase of melanocytes, which in 30%–50% of patients eventually progresses to nodules of vertically invasive melanoma.

The area of histopathologic abnormality frequently extends beyond the visible pigmented borders of the lesion; in the periocular region, cutaneous lentigo maligna of the eyelid may extend onto the conjunctival surface, where the lesion appears identi-

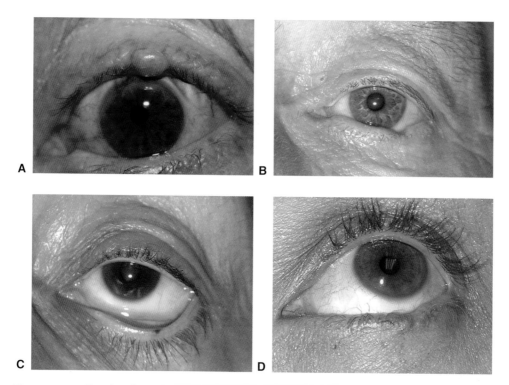

Figure 11-27 Basal cell carcinoma. **A,** Nodular. **B,** Ulcerative. **C,** Pigmented. **D,** Sclerosing. *(Courtesy of Jill Foster, MD.)*

cal to primary acquired melanosis. Excision with adequate surgical margins is recommended, with permanent sections for final monitoring. Close observation for recurrence is warranted.

Marines HM, Patrinely JR. Benign eyelid tumors. In: Liesegang TJ, ed. *Ophthalmology Clinics of North America.* Philadelphia: Saunders; 1992;5:243–260.

Malignant Eyelid Tumors

Basal cell carcinoma

Basal cell carcinoma, the most common eyelid malignancy, accounts for approximately 90%–95% of malignant eyelid tumors. Basal cell carcinomas are often located on the lower eyelid margin (50%–60%) and near the medial canthus (25%–30%). Less commonly, they may occur on the upper eyelid (15%) and lateral canthus (5%). Basal cell carcinoma may have many different clinical manifestations in the eyelid (Fig 11-27).

Patients at most risk for basal cell carcinoma are fair-skinned, blue-eyed, red-haired or blond, middle-aged and older people with English, Irish, Scottish, or Scandinavian ancestry. They may have a history of prolonged sun exposure during the first 2 decades of life. A history of cigarette smoking also increases the risk of basal cell carcinoma. Patients with prior basal cell carcinomas have a higher probability of developing additional skin cancers.

Basal cell carcinoma is being increasingly seen in younger patients, and discovery of malignant eyelid lesions in these patients or those with a positive family history should prompt inquiry into possible systemic associations such as basal cell nevus syndrome or xeroderma pigmentosum. *Basal cell nevus syndrome (Gorlin syndrome)* is an uncommon autosomal dominant multisystem disorder characterized by multiple nevoid basal cell carcinomas, which appear early in life, and associated with skeletal anomalies, especially of the mandible, maxilla, and vertebrae. *Xeroderma pigmentosum* is a rare autosomal recessive disorder characterized by extreme sun sensitivity and a defective repair mechanism for ultraviolet light–induced DNA damage in skin cells.

Nerad JA, Whitaker DC. Periocular basal cell carcinoma in adults 35 years of age and younger. *Am J Ophthalmol.* 1988;106:723–729.

Nodular basal cell carcinoma, the most common clinical appearance of basal cell carcinoma, is a firm, raised, pearly nodule that may be associated with telangiectasia and central ulceration. Histopathologically, tumors of this form demonstrate nests of basal cells that originate from the basal cell layer of the epithelium and may show peripheral palisading. As the nests of atypical cells break through to the surface of the epithelium, central necrosis and ulceration may occur.

A less common and more aggressive basal cell carcinoma is the *morpheaform,* or *fibrosing,* type. These lesions may be firm and slightly elevated. The margins of the tumor may be indeterminate on clinical examination. Histopathologically, these lesions do not show peripheral palisading but rather occur in thin cords that radiate peripherally. The surrounding stroma may show proliferation of connective tissue into a pattern of fibrosis. Morpheaform tumors behave more aggressively than nodular basal cell carcinomas.

Basal cell carcinoma may simulate chronic inflammation of the eyelid margin and is frequently associated with loss of eyelashes (madarosis). *Multicentric* or *superficial* basal cell carcinoma may be mistaken for chronic blepharitis and can silently extend along the eyelid margin.

Blasi MA, Giammaria D, Balestrazzi E. Immunotherapy with imiquimod 5% cream for eyelid nodular basal cell carcinoma. *Am J Ophthalmol.* 2005;140:1136–1139.

Margo CE, Waltz K. Basal cell carcinoma of the eyelid and periocular skin. *Surv Ophthalmol.* 1993;38:169–192.

Miller SJ. Biology of basal cell carcinoma (parts I and II). *J Am Acad Dermatol.* 1991;24: 1–13, 161–175.

Management A biopsy is necessary to confirm any clinical suspicion of basal cell carcinoma (Fig 11-28). The most accurate diagnosis can be ensured if every incisional biopsy provides tissue that

- is representative of the clinically evident lesion
- is of adequate size for histologic processing
- is not excessively traumatized or crushed
- contains normal tissue at the margin to show the transitional area

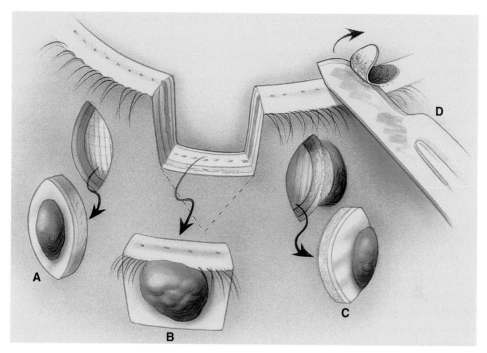

Figure 11-28 Techniques of eyelid biopsy. *A*, Excisional biopsy. *B*, Full-thickness eyelid biopsy. *C*, Incisional or punch biopsy including normal skin. *D*, Shave biopsy of eyelid margin lesion. *(Illustration by Christine Gralapp.)*

An *incisional biopsy* can be used as a confirmatory office procedure for suspected malignant tumors. The site of the incisional biopsy should be photographed or sketched with measurements because the site may heal so well that the original location of the tumor becomes difficult to find for subsequent additional tumor removal.

An *excisional biopsy* is reasonable when eyelid lesions are small and do not involve the eyelid margin or when eyelid margin lesions are centrally located, away from the lateral canthus or lacrimal punctum. However, histopathologic monitoring of tumor borders to ensure complete excision is mandatory. The borders of any excisional biopsy should be marked in case the excision is incomplete and further resection is thus necessary. Excisional biopsies should be oriented vertically so that closure does not put vertical traction on the eyelid. If the margins of the excised portion of the eyelid are positive for residual tumor cells, the involved area of the eyelid should be reexcised, with surgical monitoring of the margins by Mohs' micrographic technique (discussed later) or by frozen-section technique.

Occasionally, histopathologic examination of a clinically complete excision of a presumably benign lesion reveals an unsuspected basal cell carcinoma extending to the margins of resection. If reexamination of the patient at the slit lamp reveals no detectable residual lesion, the physician may elect to observe the patient closely for recurrence. The importance of rigorous follow-up, especially for medial canthal excisional sites, must be stressed to the patient. Interestingly, less than half of incompletely excised basal cell carcinomas have been found to recur over inclusive long-term follow-up.

Anscher M, Montana G. Management of periocular basal cell carcinoma. II, Radiotherapy. *Surv Ophthalmol.* 1993;38:203–210.

Leshin B, Yeatts P. Management of periocular basal cell carcinoma. I, Mohs' micrographic surgery. *Surv Ophthalmol.* 1993;38:193–203.

Warren RC, Nerad JA, Carter KD. Punch biopsy technique for the ophthalmologist. *Arch Ophthalmol.* 1990;108:778–779.

Surgery is the treatment of choice for all basal cell carcinomas of the eyelid. Surgical excision affords the advantages of complete tumor removal with histologic control of the margins. Excision has a lower recurrence rate than any other treatment modality. It also offers superior cosmetic results in most cases. Finally, surgery usually offers rapid resolution.

Caution: Basal cell carcinomas that arise in the medial canthal area and vertical mid-face *(H zone)* are more likely to be deeply infiltrative than those arising from the eyelid margins. Therefore, primary nonsurgical treatments such as radiation therapy or cryotherapy should be avoided with canthal tumors, because these techniques offer no way to define the limits of the lesion.

When basal cell carcinomas involve the medial canthal area, the lacrimal drainage system may have to be removed in order to completely eradicate the tumor. If the lacrimal drainage system has been removed for tumor eradication, reconstruction of the lacrimal outflow system should not be undertaken until it is established that the patient is tumor-free. This reduces the possibility that unsuspected residual basal cell carcinoma will gain access to the nasal cavity through a surgically created conjunctivodacryocystorhinostomy tract.

Orbital invasion of basal cell carcinoma is particularly common in cases that have been inadequately treated, in clinically neglected tumors, or in morpheaform tumors. Orbital exenteration may be required in such cases. Retrospective studies show that the mortality rate from ocular adnexal basal cell carcinoma is 3%. The vast majority of patients who died from basal cell carcinoma had disease that started in the canthal areas, had undergone prior radiation therapy, or had clinically neglected tumors.

Howard GR, Nerad JA, Carter KD, Whitaker DC. Clinical characteristics associated with orbital invasion of cutaneous basal cell and squamous cell tumors of the eyelid. *Am J Ophthalmol.* 1992;113:123–133.

Histological examination of the margins of an excised malignant tumor should be performed to check for complete tumor excision. Frozen-section techniques permit such examination during the course of surgery. After the clinically apparent tumor has been removed, the surgeon should also excise strips that are 1–2 mm wide from the adjacent tissue for frozen-section examination. Alternatively, the surgeon may excise the clinically apparent tumor along with 1–2 mm of clinically uninvolved tissue, and then send the entire specimen, oriented on a drawing, to the pathologist. The pathologist then samples the margins with frozen-section technique.

Reconstruction is undertaken when all margins are found to be tumor-free. Some tumors have subcutaneous extensions that are not recognized clinically. Consequently, the surgeon must always be prepared to do a much larger reconstruction than originally anticipated from the surface appearance of the tumor.

To ensure complete removal of recurrent, deeply infiltrated, or morpheaform tumors and tumors in the medial canthal region, dermatologists with special training often use *Mohs' micrographic surgery.* Tissue may be removed in thin layers that provide a 3-dimensional mapping of the tumor excision. Mohs' micrographic tumor resection is most commonly used in the resection of morpheaform basal cell carcinoma and squamous cell carcinoma.

Micrographic excision preserves the maximal amount of healthy tissue while providing the best insurance of complete cancer removal. Preoperative planning between the micrographic surgeon and oculoplastic reconstructive surgeon allows for most efficient patient care. In some cases, micrographic excision may allow the preservation of a globe, whereas conventional surgical techniques might indicate the need for exenteration. However, a major limitation of Mohs' micrographic surgery is in identifying margins of the tumor when the tumor has invaded orbital fat.

Following Mohs' micrographic surgery, the eyelid should be reconstructed by standard oculoplastic procedures. Urgent reconstruction is not critical, but surgery should be performed expeditiously. Early surgery affords maximum protection for the globe and allows reconstruction to take place while the remaining eyelid margins are still fresh. At times, it is not possible to proceed with immediate reconstruction. In such cases, the cornea should be protected by patching or temporarily suturing the remaining eyelids closed over the globe. Reconstruction then proceeds once the surgical team is assembled and the medical situation stabilized. Spontaneous granulation may be a treatment alternative when small defects are encountered. Best results have been reported for defects of the medial canthus, particularly when the defect extends equally above and below the medial canthal tendon.

Mohs FE. Micrographic surgery for the microscopically controlled excision of eyelid cancers. *Arch Ophthalmol.* 1986;104:901–909.

Waltz K, Margo CE. Mohs' micrographic surgery. *Ophthalmol Clin North Am.* 1991;4:153–163.

The recurrence rate following *cryotherapy* is higher than that following surgical therapy for well-circumscribed nodular lesions. When cryotherapy is used to treat more diffuse sclerosing lesions, the recurrence rate is unacceptably high. Consequently, this modality of treatment is avoided for canthal lesions, recurrent lesions, lesions greater than 1 cm in diameter, and morpheaform lesions. Further, since cryotherapy may lead to depigmentation and tissue atrophy, it should not be used when final cosmesis is important. Accordingly, cryotherapy for eyelid basal cell carcinoma is generally reserved for patients who are otherwise unable to tolerate surgery, such as elderly patients confined to bed or those with serious medical conditions that prevent surgical intervention.

Radiation therapy should also be considered only a palliative treatment that should generally be avoided for periorbital lesions. In particular, it should not be used for canthal lesions in view of the risk of orbital recurrence. As with cryotherapy, histologic margins cannot be evaluated with radiation treatment. The recurrence rate following radiation treatment is higher than that following surgical treatment. Moreover, recurrence after radiation is more difficult to detect, occurs at a longer interval after initial treatment, and is more difficult to manage surgically because of the altered healing of previously irradiated tissues.

Complications of radiation therapy include cicatricial changes in the eyelids, lacrimal drainage scarring with obstruction, keratitis sicca, and radiation-induced malignancy. Radiation-induced injury to the globe may also occur if the globe is not shielded during treatment. See also BCSC Section 4, *Ophthalmic Pathology and Intraocular Tumors*.

Squamous cell carcinoma

Squamous cell carcinoma of the eyelid is 40 times less common than basal cell carcinoma, but it is biologically more aggressive. Tumors can arise spontaneously or from areas of solar injury and actinic keratosis, and they may be potentiated by immunodeficiency (Fig 11-29). The treatment modalities available for squamous cell carcinoma are similar to those for basal cell carcinoma. Mohs' micrographic resection or surgical excision with wide margins and frozen sections is preferred because of the potentially lethal nature of this tumor. Squamous cell carcinoma may metastasize through lymphatic transmission, blood-borne transmission, or direct extension, often along nerves. Recurrences of squamous cell carcinoma should be treated with wide surgical resection, possibly including orbital exenteration, and may require collaboration with a head and neck cancer surgeon.

Reifler DM, Hornblass A. Squamous cell carcinoma of the eyelid. *Surv Ophthalmol.* 1986;30:349–365.

Sebaceous adenocarcinoma

Carcinoma of the sebaceous glands is a highly malignant and potentially lethal tumor that arises from meibomian glands of the tarsal plate; from glands of Zeis associated with the eyelashes; or from sebaceous glands of the caruncle, eyebrow, or facial skin. Unlike basal cell or squamous cell carcinoma, sebaceous gland carcinoma occurs more frequently in females and originates twice as often in the upper eyelid, reflecting the greater numbers of meibomian and Zeis glands there. Multicentric origin is common, and separate upper and lower eyelid tumors occur in 6%–8% of patients. The tumor often exhibits a yellow coloration as a result of lipid material within the neoplastic cells. Patients are commonly older than 50 years, but these tumors have been reported in younger patients.

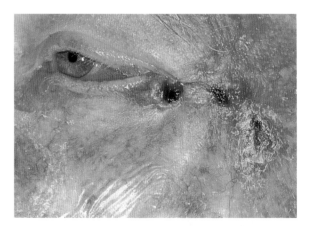

Figure 11-29 Squamous cell carcinoma of the eyelid. *(Courtesy of Jeffrey A. Nerad, MD.)*

These tumors often masquerade as benign eyelid diseases. Clinically, they may simulate chalazia, chronic blepharitis, basal cell or squamous cell carcinoma, ocular cicatricial pemphigoid, superior limbic keratoconjunctivitis, or pannus associated with adult inclusion conjunctivitis. Typically, effacement of the meibomian gland orifices with destruction of follicles of the cilia occurs, leading to loss of lashes (Fig 11-30).

A feature of sebaceous carcinoma is the tendency for the tumor within the tarsal plate to progress to an intraepidermal growth phase, which may extend over the palpebral and bulbar conjunctiva. A fine papillary elevation of the tarsal conjunctiva may indicate pagetoid spread of tumor cells; intraepithelial growth may replace corneal epithelium as well. Sebaceous secretions from the intraepithelial cancer cells may cause marked conjunctival inflammation and injection.

A nodule that initially simulates a chalazion but later causes loss of eyelashes and destruction of the meibomian gland orifices is characteristic of sebaceous gland carcinoma. Such a lesion warrants biopsy. Solid material from a chalazion that has been surgically excised more than once should be submitted for histopathologic examination. Because the rate of histopathologic misdiagnosis is high among general pathologists, the clinician should maintain suspicion based on clinical findings and request special stains (lipid) or outside consultation. Any chronic unilateral blepharitis could also raise the possibility of sebaceous gland carcinoma.

Because eyelid margin sebaceous carcinomas originate in the tarsal plate or the eyelash margin, superficial shave biopsies may reveal chronic inflammation but miss the underlying tumor. A full-thickness eyelid biopsy with permanent sections may be required to assist the correct diagnosis. Alternatively, full-thickness punch biopsy of the tarsal plate may be diagnostic.

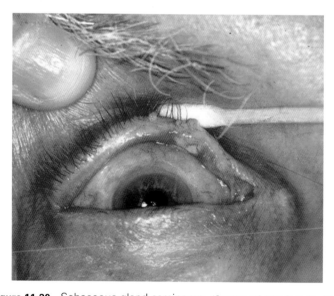

Figure 11-30 Sebaceous gland carcinoma. *(Courtesy of John B. Holds, MD.)*

Wide surgical excision is mandatory for adequate treatment of sebaceous adenocarcinoma. Mohs' micrographic surgery has been used in some cases, but skip areas, pagetoid spread, and polycentricity characteristic of these tumors demand considerable caution. Map biopsies of the conjunctiva are helpful to eliminate the potential of pagetoid spread. If pagetoid spread is present, cryotherapy may be used. Orbital exenteration may be considered for recurrent or large tumors invading through the orbital septum (see Chapter 8). These tumors usually metastasize to regional lymph nodes but may rarely spread hematogenously or through direct extension. Radiation therapy is usually not appropriate, as sebaceous carcinomas are relatively radioresistant.

Sentinel lymph node (SLN) biopsy is considered for patients with eyelid sebaceous cell carcinoma with high-risk features (recurrent lesions or extensive involvement of the eyelid or orbit); conjunctival or eyelid melanoma with a Breslow thickness greater than 1 mm; or Merkel cell carcinoma of the eyelid. (Melanoma and Merkel cell carcinoma are discussed later.) With the exception of basal cell carcinoma, cancers of the eyelid and conjunctiva typically metastasize to the regional lymph nodes, and regional metastasis commonly occurs before metastasis to distant sites. Sentinel lymph node biopsy has evolved as a technique for identifying early subclinical, microscopic regional lymph node metastasis for many solid tumors throughout the body. The identification of microscopic regional nodal metastases may indicate that more extensive therapy is warranted. It can also provide prognostic information to the physician and patient.

Kass LG, Hornblass A. Sebaceous carcinoma of the ocular adnexa. *Surv Ophthalmol.* 1989;33:477–490.

Khan JA, Doane JF, Grove AS Jr. Sebaceous and meibomian carcinomas of the eyelid: recognition, diagnosis, and management. *Ophthal Plast Reconstr Surg.* 1991;7:61–66.

Lisman RD, Jakobiec FA, Small P. Sebaceous carcinoma of the eyelids. The role of adjunctive cryotherapy in the management of conjunctival pagetoid spread. *Ophthalmology.* 1989;96:1021–1026.

Nijhawan N, Ross MI, Diba R, Gutstein BF, Ahmadi MA, Esmaeli B. Experience with sentinel lymph node biopsy for eyelid and conjunctival malignancies at a cancer center. *Ophthal Plast Reconstr Surg.* 2004;20:291–295.

Wilson MW, Fleming JC, Fleming RM, Haik BG. Sentinel node biopsy for orbital and ocular adnexal tumors. *Ophthal Plast Reconstr Surg.* 2001;17(5):338–344.

Malignant melanoma

Malignant melanoma accounts for approximately 5% of cutaneous cancers. The incidence of malignant melanoma has been steadily increasing over the last half century. Multiple factors, including sunlight exposure, genetic predisposition, and environmental mutagens, have been implicated in this increase. Cutaneous melanomas may develop de novo or from preexisting melanocytic nevi or lentigo maligna. Although malignant melanoma accounts for about 5% of all skin cancers, primary cutaneous malignant melanoma of the eyelid skin is rare (<1% of eyelid malignancies). Melanomas should be suspected in any patient with an acquired pigmented lesion beyond the first 2 decades of life. Melanomas typically have variable pigmentation with darker and lighter hues within the lesion. They usually have irregular borders and may also ulcerate and bleed.

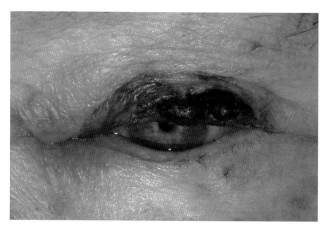

Figure 11-31 Upper eyelid melanoma. *(Courtesy of Jill Foster, MD.)*

There are 4 clinicopathologic forms of cutaneous melanoma:

- lentigo maligna melanoma
- nodular melanoma
- superficial spreading melanoma
- acrolentiginous melanoma

The eyelid is most often involved by either lentigo maligna melanoma or nodular melanoma.

Lentigo maligna melanoma represents the invasive vertical malignant growth phase that occurs in 10%–20% of patients with lentigo maligna. It accounts for 90% of head and neck melanomas. Clinically, the invasive areas are marked by nodule formation within the broader flat tan to brown irregular macule. The eyelid is usually involved by secondary extension from the malar region, and pigmentation may progress over the eyelid margin and onto the conjunctival surface. Surgical excision is recommended for a premalignant lentigo maligna and is mandatory in patients with lentigo maligna melanoma.

Nodular melanoma (Fig 11-31) accounts for approximately 10% of cutaneous melanomas. These tumors may be amelanotic, but they are extremely rare on the eyelids. The vertical invasive growth phase is the initial presentation of these lesions, and they are therefore likely to have extended deeply by the time of the initial diagnosis.

Treatment for cutaneous melanoma includes wide surgical excision with histologic assurance (by means of permanent sections) of complete tumor removal. Regional lymph node dissection or SLN biopsy may be performed in patients with melanomas that show microscopic evidence of vascular or lymphatic involvement or Breslow thickness >1 mm. Complete preoperative metastatic workup is indicated for tumors with thickness greater than 1.5 mm. Thin lesions (<0.75 mm) confer a 5-year survival rate of 98%; thicker lesions (>4 mm) with ulceration confer a survival rate of less than 50%. Because tumor thickness has strong prognostic implications, a biopsy should be performed on these lesions, specifically, a biopsy with a disposable punch that allows a core to be taken through the full depth of the tumor. Biopsy of these lesions does not increase the risk of metastatic spread.

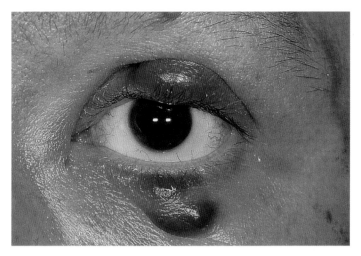

Figure 11-32 Kaposi sarcoma.

Although cryotherapy may have a role in the treatment of acquired melanomas in the conjunctiva, it should not be considered for treatment of cutaneous melanoma.

> Boulos PR, Rubin PA. Cutaneous melanomas of the eyelid. *Semin Ophthalmol.* 2006;21: 195–206.
> Grossniklaus HE, McLean IW. Cutaneous melanoma of the eyelid: clinicopathologic features. *Ophthalmology.* 1991;98:1867–1873.

Kaposi sarcoma

This previously rare tumor presents as a chronic reddish dermal mass and is a frequent manifestation of AIDS (Fig 11-32). The conjunctival lesions can be mistaken for foreign-body granuloma or cavernous hemangioma. The lesion is composed of spindle cells of probable endothelial origin. It may be treated with cryotherapy, excision, radiation, or intralesional chemotherapeutic agents. Kaposi sarcoma may regress with adequate anti-viral treatment of the HIV infection.

> Shuler JD, Holland GN, Miles SA, Miller BJ, Grossman I. Kaposi sarcoma of the conjunctiva and eyelids associated with the acquired immunodeficiency syndrome. *Arch Ophthalmol.* 1989;107:858–862.

Merkel cell carcinoma

The Merkel cell is part of the dendritic (neuroendocrine) cell population of the skin. Studies suggest that, as a slowly adapting mechanoreceptor, it has a role in mediating the sense of touch. Merkel cells can give rise to malignant neoplasms, one tenth of which occur in the eyelid and periocular area and manifest as painless erythematous nodules, with overlying telangiectatic blood vessels. Merkel cell carcinoma can mimic other malignant lesions; thus, the diagnosis can be difficult. One third of the tumors recur after excision, and there is a high rate of metastasis. The estimated 5-year survival rate is 38%. Initial treatment should be aggressive and include surgical resection, with consideration of post-operative radiation and/or chemotherapy.

Peters GB, Meyer DR, Shields JA, et al. Management and prognosis of Merkel cell carcinoma of the eyelid. *Ophthalmology.* 2001;108:1575–1579.

Eyelid Trauma

Injury of the eyelid may be divided into blunt and penetrating trauma. Cardinal rules in the management of eyelid trauma include the following:

- Take a careful history.
- Record the best acuity for each eye.
- Thoroughly evaluate the globe and orbit.
- Obtain appropriate radiologic studies.
- Have a detailed knowledge of eyelid and orbital anatomy.
- Ensure the best possible primary repair.

Blunt Trauma

Ecchymosis and edema are the most common presenting signs of blunt trauma. Patients should be evaluated for intraocular injury with a thorough biomicroscopic evaluation and a dilated fundus examination. Computed tomography, both axial and direct coronal, may be necessary to determine whether an orbital fracture is present (see Chapter 6).

Penetrating Trauma

A detailed knowledge of eyelid anatomy helps the surgeon in repairing a penetrating eyelid injury and often reduces the need for secondary repairs. Generally, the treatment of eyelid lacerations depends on the depth and location of the injury.

Lacerations not involving the eyelid margin

Superficial eyelid lacerations involving just the skin and orbicularis muscle usually require only skin sutures. To avoid unnecessary scarring, follow the basic principles of plastic repair. These include conservative debridement of the wound, use of small-caliber sutures, eversion of the wound edges, and early suture removal.

The presence of orbital fat in the wound means that the orbital septum has been violated. Superficial or deep foreign bodies should be searched for meticulously before these deeper eyelid lacerations are repaired. Copious irrigation washes away contaminated material in the wound. Orbital fat prolapse in an upper eyelid wound is an indication for levator exploration. A lacerated levator muscle or aponeurosis must be carefully repaired so that the levator can best return to its pretrauma function. Upper eyelid lagophthalmos and tethering to the superior orbital rim are common if the orbital septum is inadvertently incorporated into the laceration repair. Orbital septum lacerations should not be sutured. Meticulous closure of overlying eyelid skin and orbicularis muscle is adequate in all cases and avoids possible vertical shortening of the sutured orbital septum.

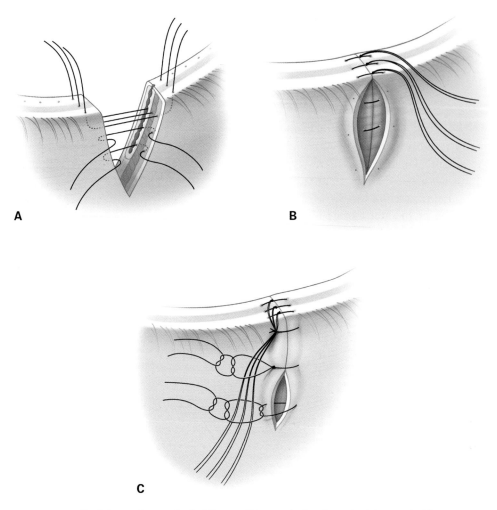

Figure 11-33 Eyelid margin repair. **A,** The eyelid margin is aligned with resorbable tarsus-to-tarsus sutures, and the lash line, gray line, and mucocutaneous junction are aligned with eyelid margin sutures. **B,** The tarsal sutures are tied and cut; the eyelid margin sutures are tied and left long. **C,** The skin surface of the eyelid is sewn closed, with the skin sutures used to tie down the tails of the margin sutures. *(Modified from Nerad JA. The Requisites in Ophthalmology: Oculoplastic Surgery. Philadelphia: Mosby; 2001:319. Illustration by Christine Gralapp.)*

Lacerations involving the eyelid margin

Repair of eyelid margin lacerations requires precise suture placement and critical suture tension so that notching of the eyelid margin is minimized. Many techniques have been described, but the most important principle is that tarsal approximation must be made in a meticulous, direct manner (Fig 11-33). Eyelid margin closure may be accomplished by 2 or 3 sutures for alignment through the lash line, the meibomian gland plane, and (optionally) the gray line. Surgeons differ as to whether they place the tarsal or the eyelid margin sutures first. Precise anatomical alignment of the margin and secure tarsal closure are the goals, and many variations of techniques are acceptable. To avoid corneal epithelial disruption, the tarsal sutures should not extend through the conjunctival surface, especially in the upper eyelid. The eyelid margin closure should result in a moderate eversion of the well-approximated wound edges. Resorbable buried sutures may be used in the margin as an alternative to the permanent externally tied sutures.

Trauma involving the canthal soft tissue

Trauma to the medial or lateral canthal areas is usually the result of horizontal traction on the eyelid, which causes an eyelid avulsion at the lid's weakest points, the medial or lateral canthal tendon. Careful review of the patient's history often confirms that an object or finger engaged the eyelid soft tissue in the central aspect of the eyelid, with subsequent horizontal traction of the eyelid. Hence, lacerations in the medial canthal area demand evaluation of the lacrimal drainage apparatus, which is often involved in an avulsion injury. Canalicular involvement is usually confirmed by inspection and gentle probing. The examiner can assess the integrity of the inferior and superior limbs of medial or lateral canthal tendons by grasping each lid with toothed forceps and tugging away from the injury while palpating the insertion of the tendon. Even trivial medial canthal injuries can result in canalicular lacerations.

Medial canthal tendon avulsion should be suspected when there is a rounding of the medial canthal tendon and acquired telecanthus. Attention to the posterior portion of the tendon's attachment to the posterior lacrimal crest is critical.

Treatment of medial canthal tendon avulsions depends on the nature of the avulsion. If the upper or lower limb is avulsed but the posterior attachment of the tendon is intact, the avulsed limb may be sutured to its stump or to the periosteum overlying the anterior lacrimal crest. If the entire tendon, including the posterior portion, is avulsed but there is no naso-orbital fracture, the avulsed tendon should be wired through small drill holes in the ipsilateral posterior lacrimal crest. If the entire tendon is avulsed and there is a naso-orbital fracture, transnasal wiring or plating is necessary after reduction of the fracture. A Y-shaped miniplate may be fixed anteriorly on the nasal bone, with posterior extension into the orbit. The suture is sewn through the severed tendons and passed through the holes in the miniplate. This technique is particularly helpful when the bone of the posterior lacrimal crest is missing.

Devoto MH, Kersten RC, Teske SA, Kulwin DR. Simplified technique for eyelid margin repair. *Arch Ophthalmol.* 1997;115:566–567.

Howard GR, Nerad JA, Kersten RC. Medial canthoplasty with microplate fixation. *Arch Ophthalmol.* 1992;110:1793–1797.

Shore JW, Rubin PA, Bilyk JR. Repair of telecanthus by anterior fixation of cantilevered miniplates. *Ophthalmology.* 1992;99:1133–1138.

A 3-dimensional perspective is crucial in the evaluation and repair of canthal lacerations—that is, to ensure optimal functional and cosmetic repair, the surgeon must always keep in mind the horizontal, vertical, and anteroposterior position of the canthal angle and medial canthal tendon. The different configurations of the medial and lateral canthal angles must also be considered. Whereas the lateral canthal angle is sharp, the medial canthal angle is slightly rounded. Failure to appreciate this difference gives rise to postoperative cosmetic and functional problems.

Secondary Repair

Secondary repair of eyelid trauma usually requires treatment of cicatricial changes that result from either the initial trauma or the subsequent surgical repair. Revision of scars may require simple fusiform excision with primary closure or a more complex rearrangement of tissue. The location of a particular scar in relation to the relaxed skin tension lines (which correspond to the facial wrinkles in most cases) determines the best technique or combination of techniques to use. An elliptical excision of the scar is most useful for revision of scars that follow the relaxed skin tension lines. Single Z-plasty or multiple Z-plasty reconstructive techniques can be used for the revision of scars that do not conform to relaxed skin tension lines.

Free skin grafts alone or in combination with various flaps are used when tissue has been lost. Although any non–hair-bearing skin can be used, full-thickness postauricular or preauricular skin is the most commonly used donor site for lower and upper eyelid reconstruction. Ipsilateral or contralateral upper eyelid, supraclavicular or subclavicular areas, and even brachial or inner thigh areas are all potential donor sites for eyelid reconstruction.

Tarsoconjunctival grafts are good substitutes for posterior lamella eyelid defects when both the tarsal plate and the conjunctiva are deficient. Buccal mucosa may be used when only the conjunctiva is insufficient. Hard palate composite grafts have also become increasingly popular for posterior lamella defects in the lower eyelid. However, they should be avoided as a tarsal replacement in the upper eyelid because of the presence of keratinized epithelium, which can irritate the cornea.

Before treatment is considered for traumatic ptosis, the patient should be observed for 6 months or until no further spontaneous return of function occurs. An exception to this rule may be in a young child, in whom the possibility of deprivation amblyopia may necessitate early surgery to clear the visual axis.

Dog and Human Bites

Tearing and crushing injuries occur secondary to dog or human bites. Partial-thickness and full-thickness eyelid lacerations, canthal avulsions, and canalicular lacerations are common. Serious facial and intracranial injury is possible, especially in infants, as bites generate hundreds of pounds of force per square inch. Irrigation and early wound repair are mandatory, and tetanus and rabies protocols should be observed. Systemic antibiotics are recommended.

Bartley GB. Periorbital animal bites. *Focal Points: Clinical Modules for Ophthalmologists.* San Francisco: American Academy of Ophthalmology; 1992, module 3.

Burns

Burns of the eyelid are rare. Eyelid burns generally occur in patients who have sustained significant burns over large surface areas of the body. Often these patients are semiconscious or heavily sedated and require protection of the ocular surface to prevent corneal exposure, ulceration, and infection. Lubricating antibiotic eyedrops and ointments, moisture chambers, and frequent evaluation of both the globes and the eyelids are part of the early treatment of these patients. Once cicatricial changes begin in the eyelids, a relentless and rapid deterioration of the patient's ocular status often ensues secondary to cicatricial eyelid retraction, lagophthalmos, and corneal exposure. If tarsorrhaphies are used, they should always be more extensive than seems to be immediately necessary. Unfortunately, with progression of the cicatricial traction, even the most aggressive eyelid adhesions may dehisce. In the past, skin grafting was usually delayed until the cicatricial changes stabilized, but the early use of full-thickness skin grafts and various types of flaps can effectively reduce ocular morbidity in selected patients.

Kulwin DR, Kersten RC. Management of eyelid burns. *Focal Points: Clinical Modules for Ophthalmologists.* San Francisco: American Academy of Ophthalmology; 1990, module 2.

Meyer DR, Kersten RC, Kulwin DR, Paskowski JR, Selkin RP. Management of canalicular injury associated with eyelid burns. *Arch Ophthalmol.* 1995;113:900–903.

Eyelid and Canthal Reconstruction

The following discussion of eyelid reconstruction applies to defects resulting from tumor resection as well as congenital and traumatic defects. Several methods may be appropriate for reconstruction of a particular eyelid defect. The surgeon's choice of procedure depends on the age of the patient, the character of the eyelids, the size and position of the defect, and personal experience and preference. Priorities in eyelid reconstruction are

- development of a stable eyelid margin
- provision of adequate vertical eyelid height
- adequate eyelid closure
- smooth, epithelialized internal surface
- maximum cosmesis and symmetry

The following general principles guide the practice of eyelid reconstruction:

- Reconstruct either the anterior or the posterior eyelid lamella, but not both, with a graft; 1 of the layers must provide the blood supply (pedicle flap). A graft placed on a graft has a high likelihood of failure.
- Maximize horizontal tension and minimize vertical tension.
- Maintain sufficient and anatomical canthal fixation.
- Match like tissue to like tissue.
- Narrow the defect as much as possible before sizing a graft.
- Choose the simplest technique.
- Get help from a subspecialist if you need it.

Eyelid Defects Not Involving the Eyelid Margin

Defects not involving the eyelid margins can be repaired by direct closure if this procedure does not distort the eyelid margin. If undermining does not allow direct closure, advancement or transposition of flaps of skin may be used. Tension of closure should be directed horizontally so that secondary deformity can be avoided; vertical tension may cause eyelid retraction or ectropion. Avoidance of vertical tension requires placement of vertically oriented incision lines.

If the defect is too large to be closed primarily, several advancement or transposition techniques of local skin flaps may be used. The flaps most commonly used are rectangular advancement, rotation, and transposition. Flaps usually provide the best tissue match and aesthetic result but require planning in order to minimize secondary deformities. Although skin grafting procedures are generally easier to perform, the final texture, contour, and cosmesis are typically better with flaps.

Anterior lamella upper eyelid defects are best repaired with full-thickness skin grafts from the contralateral upper eyelid. Preauricular or postauricular skin grafts may be used, but their greater thickness may limit upper eyelid mobility. Lower eyelid defects are best filled with preauricular or retroauricular skin grafts. If skin is not available from the upper eyelids or auricular areas, full-thickness grafts may be obtained from the supraclavicular fossa or the inner upper arm. It is important to avoid placement of hair-bearing skin grafts near the eyes.

Use of split-thickness grafts should be avoided in eyelid reconstruction. They are recommended only in the treatment of severe burns of the face when adequate full-thickness skin is not available.

Patrinely JR, Marines HM, Anderson RL. Skin flaps in periorbital reconstruction. *Surv Ophthalmol.* 1987;31:249–261.

Teske SA, Kersten RC, Devoto MH, Kulwin DR. The modified rhomboid transposition flap in periocular reconstruction. *Ophthal Plast Reconstr Surg.* 1998;14:360–366.

Eyelid Defects Involving the Eyelid Margin

Small upper eyelid defects

Small defects involving the upper eyelid margin can be repaired by direct closure if this technique does not place too much tension on the wound (Fig 11-34). Direct closure is usually employed when 33% or less of the eyelid margin is involved; if a larger area is involved, advancement of adjacent tissue or grafting of distant tissue may be required. The surgeon can cut the superior limb of the lateral canthal tendon to allow 3–5 mm of medial mobilization of the remaining lateral eyelid margin, taking care to avoid the lacrimal ductules in the lateral third of the upper eyelid. Removal or destruction of these ductules may lead to dry eye problems. Postoperatively, the eyelid appears tight and ptotic because of traction, but it relaxes over several weeks.

Moderate upper eyelid defects

Moderate defects of the upper eyelid margin (33%–50% involvement) can be repaired by advancement of the lateral segment of the eyelid. The lateral canthal tendon is incised, and a semicircular skin flap is made below the lateral portion of the eyebrow and canthus to allow for further mobilization of the eyelid. Tarsal-sharing procedures in the upper eyelid may also be employed.

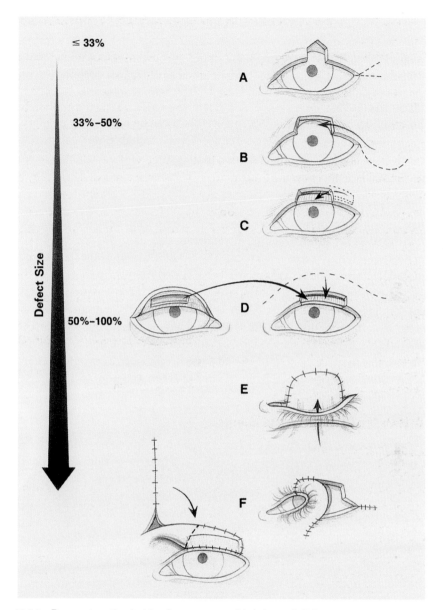

Figure 11-34 Reconstructive ladder for upper eyelid defect. *A,* Primary closure with or without lateral canthotomy or superior cantholysis. *B,* Semicircular flap. *C,* Adjacent tarsoconjunctival flap and full-thickness skin graft. *D,* Free tarsoconjunctival graft and skin flap. *E,* Full-thickness lower eyelid advancement flap (Cutler-Beard). *F,* Lower eyelid switch flap or median forehead flap. *(Illustration by Christine Gralapp.)*

Large upper eyelid defects

Upper eyelid defects involving more than 50% of the upper eyelid margin require advancement of adjacent tissues. With an incision below the lower eyelid tarsus, a full-thickness lower eyelid flap is moved into the defect of the upper eyelid by advancement of the flap behind the remaining lower eyelid margin *(Cutler-Beard procedure)*. This procedure, however, results in a thick and relatively immobile upper eyelid. Alternatively, a free tarsoconjunctival graft taken from the contralateral upper eyelid can be positioned and covered with a skin-muscle flap if adequate redundant upper eyelid skin is present.

Small lower eyelid defects

Small defects of the lower eyelid (<33% involvement) can be repaired by primary closure (Fig 11-35). In addition, the inferior crus of the lateral canthal tendon can be released so that there is an additional 3–5 mm of medial mobilization of the remaining lateral eyelid margin.

Moderate lower eyelid defects

Semicircular advancement or rotation flaps, which have been described for upper eyelid repair, can be used for reconstruction of moderate defects in the lower eyelid as well. The flap most commonly used in such cases is a modification of the Tenzel semicircular rotation flap. Tarsoconjunctival autografts harvested from the underside of the upper eyelid may be transplanted into the lower eyelid defect for reconstruction of the posterior lamella of the eyelid. When tarsal grafts are being harvested, the marginal 4–5 mm height of tarsus is preserved. This prevents distortion of the donor eyelid margin. Tarsoconjunctival autografts may be covered with skin flaps of various types. Cheek elevation may also be required so that vertical traction on the lid and ectropion can be avoided. Alternatively, a tarsoconjunctival flap developed from the upper eyelid and a full-thickness skin graft can also be used.

Large lower eyelid defects

Defects involving more than 50% of the lower eyelid margin can be repaired by advancement of a tarsoconjunctival flap from the upper eyelid into the posterior lamellar defect of the lower eyelid. The anterior lamella of the reconstructed eyelid is then created with an advancement skin flap or, in most cases, a free skin graft taken from the preauricular or postauricular area *(modified Hughes procedure)*. The modified Hughes procedure therefore results in placement of a bridge of conjunctiva from the upper eyelid across the pupil for several weeks. The vascularized pedicle of conjunctiva is then released in a staged, second procedure once the lower eyelid flap is revascularized. Eyelid-sharing techniques should be avoided in children, as these patients may develop deprivation amblyopia. Large rotating cheek flaps *(Mustardé procedure)* can work well for repair of large anterior lamellar defects, but they require some tarsal substitute such as a free tarsoconjunctival autograft, hard palate mucosa, or a Hughes flap for posterior lamella replacement. Both the Mustardé cheek rotation flap and the Tenzel semicircular rotation flap frequently result in a rounded lateral canthus. The surgeon can reduce this problem by creating a very high incision toward the lateral end of the eyebrow where the incision emanates from the lateral commissure. Free tarsoconjunctival autografts from the upper eyelid covered with a vascularized skin flap have been used to repair large defects as well. This type of procedure has the advantage of requiring only 1 surgical stage and avoids even temporary occlusion of the visual axis.

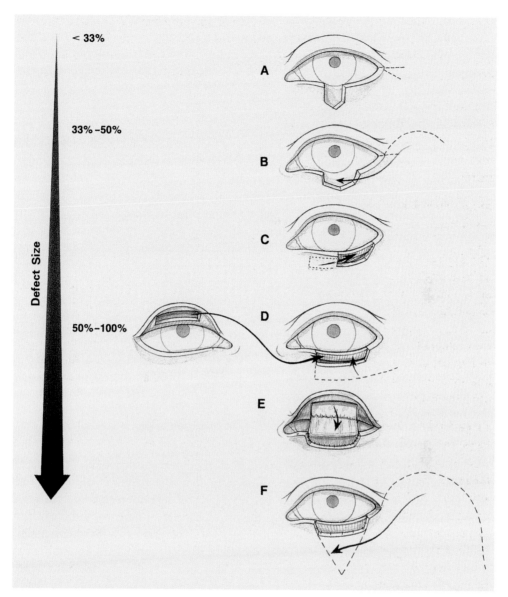

Figure 11-35 Reconstructive ladder for lower eyelid defect. *A,* Primary closure with or without lateral canthotomy or superior cantholysis. *B,* Semicircular flap. *C,* Adjacent tarsoconjunctival flap and full-thickness skin graft. *D,* Free tarsoconjunctival graft and skin flap. *E,* Tarsoconjunctival flap from upper eyelid and skin graft (Hughes procedure). *F,* Composite graft with cheek advancement flap (Mustardé flap). *(Illustration by Christine Gralapp.)*

Lateral Canthal Defects

Laterally based transposition flaps of upper eyelid tarsus and conjunctiva can be used for large lower eyelid defects extending to the lateral canthus. These flaps can be covered with free skin grafts. Semicircular advancement flaps of skin can also be used to repair defects extending to the lateral canthal area. Sometimes, strips of periosteum and temporalis fascia left attached at the lateral orbital rim can be swung over and attached to the remaining lateral eyelid margins for reconstruction of the entire lateral canthal posterior lamella. A Y-shaped pedicle flap of periosteum is optimal to reconstruct the entire lateral canthal posterior lamella.

Medial Canthal Defects

The medial canthal area lends itself to a variety of reconstructive methods. Spontaneous granulation of anterior lamellar defects has been used with varying success. Full-thickness skin grafting or flap reconstructions are more widely accepted repair techniques for medial canthal defects. When full-thickness medial eyelid defects are present, the medial canthal attachments of the remaining eyelid margin must be fixed to firm periosteum or bone. This fixation may be accomplished with heavy permanent suture, wire, or titanium miniplates. Defects involving the lacrimal drainage apparatus are more complex and require simultaneous microsurgical reconstruction and possible silicone intubation or marsupialization. If extensive sacrifice of the canaliculi has occurred in the resection of a tumor, the patient may have to tolerate epiphora until recurrence of the tumor is no longer a risk. Until tumor recurrence is ruled out, it is critical to avoid lacrimal surgery that could create a pathway for tumor to spread into the nose or sinuses. After a recurrence-free period of up to 5 years (based on clinical judgment), the patient may undergo a conjunctivodacryocystorhinostomy with a Jones tube to eliminate the epiphora.

Howard GR, Nerad JA, Kersten RC. Medial canthoplasty with microplate fixation. *Arch Ophthalmol.* 1992;110:1793–1797.

Lowry JC, Bartley GB, Garrity JA. The role of second-intention healing in periocular reconstruction. *Ophthal Plast Reconstr Surg.* 1997;13:174–188.

Full-thickness skin grafts offer an excellent method of reconstruction of the medial canthus compared with the cicatrix resulting from spontaneous granulation. The full-thickness grafts are thin enough to allow for early detection of tumor recurrence. However, every effort should be made at the time of tumor resection to minimize the risk of recurrent medial canthal tumors. Frozen sections and wide margins or Mohs' micrographic resection techniques minimize the risk of recurrent medial canthal tumors and the risk of orbital or lacrimal extension of these tumors. Large medial canthal defects of anterior lamellar structures may be reconstructed through the transposition of forehead or glabellar flaps. However, such flaps have the disadvantage of being thick, thereby making early detection of recurrences difficult. In addition, they often require second-stage thinning in order to achieve the best cosmetic result. Mohs' micrographic resection of tumors offers the highest cure rates for eradication of medial canthal epithelial malignancies.

Spinelli HM, Jelks GW. Periocular reconstruction: a systematic approach. *Plast Reconstr Surg.* 1993;91:1017–1024.

CHAPTER **12**

Periocular Malpositions and Involutional Changes

Evaluation of all eyelid anomalies requires an assessment of what structural alterations are present. Determining whether the abnormality is associated with anterior lamella (skin and orbicularis muscle) or posterior lamella (tarsus and conjunctiva) facilitates treatment planning.

Ectropion

Ectropion (Fig 12-1) is an outward turning of the eyelid margin and may be classified as

- congenital
- involutional
- paralytic
- cicatricial
- mechanical

The majority of cases seen in a general ophthalmology practice are involutional, with horizontal eyelid laxity being the primary cause. Congenital ectropion of the eyelid is rare. Treatment errors and recurrences will be minimized if each case is accurately diagnosed before treatment is undertaken.

> Goldberg RA, Neuhaus RW. Eyelid malpositions associated with skin and conjunctival disease. *Ophthalmol Clin North Am.* 1992;5:227–241.

Congenital Ectropion
Congenital ectropion is discussed in Chapter 11, under the heading Congenital Anomalies.

Involutional Ectropion
Involutional ectropion results from tissue relaxation, with horizontal eyelid laxity usually in the medial or lateral canthal tendons. If untreated, this condition usually leads to loss of eyelid apposition to the globe, with eversion of the eyelid margin. Chronic conjunctival inflammation with hypertrophy and keratinization results.

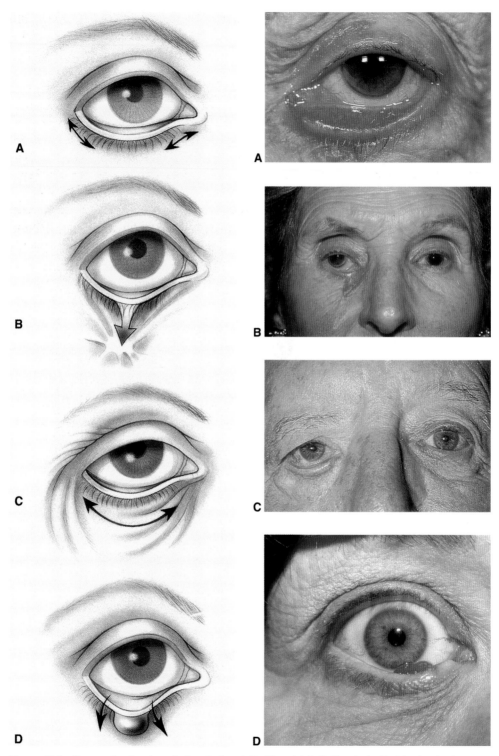

Figure 12-1 Types of ectropion. **A,** Involutional. **B,** Cicatricial. **C,** Paralytic. **D,** Mechanical. *(Illustrations by Christine Gralapp. Photographs A and B courtesy of James R. Patrinely, MD; photograph D courtesy of Robert C. Kersten, MD.)*

Involutional ectropion usually occurs in the lower eyelid, probably because of the added effects of gravity on a horizontally lax lower eyelid. Horizontal laxity of the eyelid caused by disinsertion or stretching of the inferior limbs of the canthal tendons, especially laterally, is a common feature in involutional ectropion.

In cases of mild medial eyelid ectropion with punctal malposition, thermal cautery of the conjunctiva has historically been used and is still utilized in selected cases to cause inward rotation of the eyelid margin. However, recurrence of the ectropion is common. As an alternative surgical procedure, horizontal fusiform excision of conjunctiva and eyelid retractors 4 mm inferior to the puncta, with closure utilizing inverting sutures (*medial spindle procedure,* Fig 12-2A), usually corrects the punctal malposition. In cases with associated horizontal eyelid laxity, eyelid lateral canthal tightening may be used in conjunction with this operation.

If the involutional ectropion is more severe and involves more than the punctum, one of the following types of surgical procedures is generally used: (1) horizontal eyelid shortening, including horizontal resection of the lateral eyelid, plication of the canthal tendons,

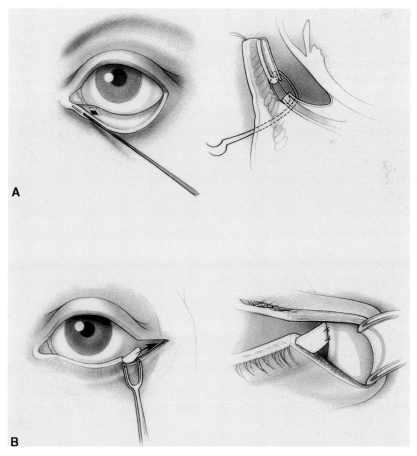

Figure 12-2 **A,** Medial spindle procedure: outline of excision of conjunctiva and retractors. **B,** Lateral tarsal strip procedure: anchoring of tarsal strip to periosteum inside lateral orbital rim. *(Illustration by Christine Gralapp.)*

and lateral canthoplasty (*tarsal strip procedure,* Fig 12-2B); or (2) reinsertion of the lower eyelid retractors.

Before selecting the procedure or combinations of procedures to use, the surgeon must take into account not only the etiologic factors but also the presence or absence of punctal malposition and secondary contraction of the anterior lamella. Combining more than 1 type of procedure to correct involutional ectropion is not unusual.

Horizontal eyelid shortening

Horizontal tightening can be achieved via a full-thickness excision of the eyelid just medial to the lateral canthal angle *(Bick procedure).* Resection of the eyelid in this location may cause rounding and medial displacement of the lateral canthal angle. Repair of the eyelid defect following full-thickness resection is similar to the process described in Chapter 11 for a full-thickness eyelid margin laceration (see Fig 11-35).

Laxity of the lower limb of the medial canthal tendon can be diagnosed by demonstration of excessive lateral movement of the lower punctum with lateral eyelid traction. Lateral canthal tendon laxity or disinsertion can be similarly detected. Repair of medial canthal laxity is difficult at best. After placing a probe in the canaliculus for identification, the surgeon makes an infraciliary incision from the medial canthal angle temporally 4–5 mm beyond the puncta. The anterior origin of the medial canthal tendon and its inferior limb are then plicated with a 5–0 nonabsorbable mattress suture. This technique is often complicated by a kinking of the canaliculus or distraction of the punctum away from the globe, with secondary epiphora.

Horizontal eyelid laxity may be treated by direct shortening of the lateral canthal tendon or the lateral edge of the tarsal plate. The horizontally shortened lateral canthal tendon is reattached to the lateral orbital rim periosteum. This does not compromise the horizontal dimension of the palpebral fissure and maintains a sharp, correctly positioned lateral canthal angle.

Repair of lower eyelid retractors

Retractor laxity, disinsertion, or dehiscence may be associated with ectropion, especially when the eyelid is completely everted, a condition known as *tarsal ectropion.* Attenuation or disinsertion of the inferior retractors may occur as an isolated defect or may accompany horizontal laxity in involutional ectropion. When both defects are present, repair of the retractors can be combined with a horizontal tightening of the eyelid. Reattachment of the retractors can be initiated directly through a conjunctival approach to advance the lower eyelid retractors to the inferior border of tarsus.

Long-standing involutional ectropion with contraction of the anterior lamella (skin) usually requires horizontal tightening of the eyelid combined with midface lifting or full-thickness skin grafting. (See discussion under the heading Cicatricial Ectropion.)

Dailey RA, Jones LT. Rejuvenation of the aging face. *Focal Points: Clinical Modules for Ophthalmologists.* San Francisco: American Academy of Ophthalmology; 2003, module 11.

Jordan DR, Anderson RL. The lateral tarsal strip revisited. *Arch Ophthalmol.* 1989;107:604–606.

Nowinski TS, Anderson RL. The medial spindle procedure for involutional medial ectropion. *Arch Ophthalmol.* 1985;103:1750–1753.

Tse DT, Kronish JW, Buus D. Surgical correction of lower-eyelid tarsal ectropion by reinsertion of the retractors. *Arch Ophthalmol.* 1991;109:427–431.

Paralytic Ectropion

Paralytic ectropion usually follows temporary or permanent seventh nerve paralysis or palsy. Concomitant upper eyelid lagophthalmos (incomplete closure of the eyelids) is usually present secondary to paralytic upper eyelid orbicularis dysfunction. Poor blinking and eyelid closure lead to chronic ocular surface irritation resulting from inferior corneal exposure together with poor tear film replenishment and distribution. Chronically stimulated reflex secretors (main or accessory lacrimal glands) along with atonic eyelids account for the frequent complaint of tearing in these patients. Eyelid excursion during the blink cycle is further limited in the setting of vertical eyelid shortening or Graves ophthalmopathy with eyelid retraction or proptosis.

Neurological evaluation may be indicated to determine the cause of the seventh nerve paralysis. In cases resulting from stroke or intracranial surgery, clinical evaluation of corneal sensation is indicated because neurotrophic keratitis combined with paralytic lagophthalmos results in increased risk of corneal decompensation.

Lubricating drops, viscous tear supplementation, ointments, taping of the temporal half of the lower eyelid, or moisture chambers may be used alone or in combination. Such measures may be the only treatment necessary, especially for temporary paralysis. In long-term or permanent paralysis of the lower eyelid, tarsorrhaphy, medial or lateral canthoplasties, skin grafts, suspension procedures, and horizontal tightening procedures are useful in selected patients.

Tarsorrhaphies can be performed either medially or laterally. An adequate temporary tarsorrhaphy (1–3 weeks) can be achieved with nonabsorbable suture placement between the upper and lower eyelid margins without disruption of the eyelid epithelium. A permanent tarsorrhaphy first requires careful removal of the epithelium along the upper and lower eyelid margins. The surgeon should exercise caution to avoid the lash follicles. Next, absorbable sutures are placed to unite the raw surfaces of the upper and lower eyelids (Fig 12-3). In general, patients dislike the permanent tarsorrhaphy from a functional and cosmetic perspective. This procedure should be avoided if possible, except in patients with recalcitrant corneal disease from exposure. Placement of a gold weight in the upper eyelid and repair of horizontal eyelid laxity or ectropion generally allow the patient to avoid permanent tarsorrhaphy.

Occasionally, a fascia lata or silicone suspension sling of the lower eyelid may be indicated. Lower eyelid vertical elevation may be useful in reducing exposure of the lower one third of the cornea. This elevation may be accomplished through inferior retractor muscle recession combined with full-thickness hard palate mucosal graft or ear cartilage graft.

Gold weight loading of the upper eyelid is currently the most commonly performed procedure for the treatment of paralytic lagophthalmos. The appropriate gold weight size can be selected through a process of preoperatively taping various sizes of weights to the upper eyelid skin to determine which one best achieves adequate relaxed eyelid closure while limiting eyelid ptosis in primary gaze. A standard upper eyelid incision is made through skin and orbicularis muscle. The gold weight is then sutured to the anterior surface of the tarsal plate. The gold weight implant (average weight, 0.8–1.6 g) reduces but does not usually eliminate lagophthalmos and corneal exposure. A 2.2-g

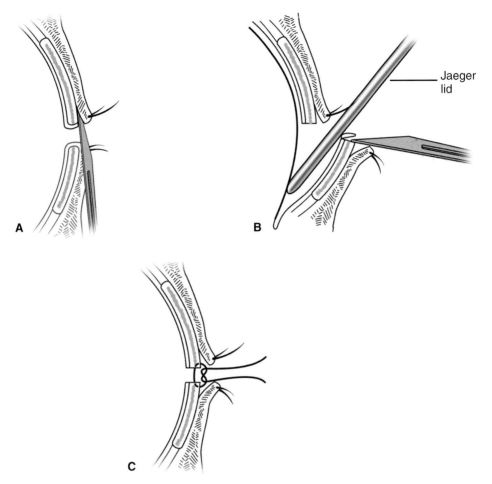

Figure 12-3 Tarsorrhaphy. **A,** Eyelid is split 2–3 mm deep. **B,** Epithelium is carefully removed along the upper and lower eyelid margins; the lash follicles are avoided. **C,** The raw surfaces are then united with absorbable sutures. *(Illustration by Christine Gralapp.)*

gold weight can be placed behind the orbital septum, superior to the tarsus, to avoid the inevitable mass effect of the pretarsal area if cosmesis is a concern. Implanted eyelid springs to provide dynamic eyelid closure are infrequently used because of limited long-term success.

Gilliland G, Wobig JL, Dailey RA. A modified surgical technique in the treatment of facial nerve palsies. *Ophthal Plast Reconstr Surg.* 1998;14:94–98.

Tower RN, Dailey RA. Gold weight implantation: a better way? *Ophthal Plast Reconstr Surg.* 2004;20(3):202–206.

Townsend DJ. Eyelid reanimation for the treatment of paralytic lagophthalmos: historical perspectives and current applications of the gold weight implant. *Ophthal Plast Reconstr Surg.* 1992;8:196–201.

Cicatricial Ectropion

Cicatricial ectropion of the upper or lower eyelid may occur secondary to thermal or chemical burns, mechanical trauma, surgical trauma, or chronic actinic skin damage. Cicatricial ectropion can also be caused by chronic inflammation of the eyelid from dermatologic conditions such as rosacea, atopic dermatitis, eczematoid dermatitis, or herpes zoster infections. Treatment of the underlying cause along with conservative medical protection of the cornea is essential as primary management. Cicatricial ectropion of the lower eyelid is usually treated in a 3-step procedure:

1. Vertical cicatricial traction is surgically incised and relaxed.
2. The eyelid is horizontally tightened with a lateral tarsal strip operation.
3. The anterior lamella is vertically lengthened via a midface lift or full-thickness skin graft.

Treatment of cicatricial ectropion or retraction of the upper eyelid usually requires only augmentation of the vertically shortened anterior lamella with a full-thickness skin graft.

Although skin from the opposite upper eyelid is the best color and texture match for skin grafting, this source is usually inadequate except in patients with significant dermatochalasis. Postauricular skin is the next most desirable donor site for eyelid reconstruction.

Mechanical Ectropion

Mechanical ectropion is usually caused by the effect of gravity on bulky tumors of the eyelid. Fluid accumulation, herniated orbital fat, or poorly fitted spectacles may also provide a mechanical component for lower eyelid ectropion.

Entropion

Entropion is an inversion of the eyelid margin. Lower eyelid entropion (usually involutional) is much more common than upper eyelid entropion (usually cicatricial). Entropion may be unilateral or bilateral and is often classified into the following categories:

- congenital
- acute spastic
- involutional
- cicatricial

More than 100 procedures have been described to correct entropion, and as in ectropion, causes must be identified before the most appropriate type of procedure can be selected.

Congenital Entropion

Congenital entropion is discussed in Chapter 11, under Congenital Anomalies.

Acute Spastic Entropion

This condition follows ocular irritation or inflammation. It is most common after intraocular surgery in a patient who had unrecognized or mild involutional eyelid changes preoperatively.

Sustained eyelid orbicularis muscle contraction causes inward rotation of the eyelid margin. A cycle of increasing entropion caused by corneal irritation secondary to the preexisting entropion perpetuates the problem. The acute entropion usually resolves when the irritation/entropion cycle is broken by treatment of both the underlying cause and the entropion.

Taping of the inturned eyelid to evert the margin, cautery, or various suture techniques afford temporary relief for most patients (Fig 12-4). However, because underlying involutional changes are usually present in the eyelid, additional definitive surgical repair may be needed to permanently correct the entropion. In selected cases, botulinum toxin type A (Botox) can be used to paralyze the overriding preseptal orbicularis muscle.

Involutional Entropion

Involutional entropion is usually associated with the lower eyelids. The factors, alone or in combination, thought to play a role in the development of involutional entropion are horizontal laxity of the eyelid, attenuation or disinsertion of eyelid retractors, and overriding of the preseptal orbicularis. Horizontal laxity can be detected by a poor tone of the eyelid (*snapback test*) and ability to pull the eyelid more than 6 mm from the globe. Such laxity is a result of involutional stretching of the medial and lateral canthal tendons. Normally, the lower eyelid retractors maintain the lower eyelid margin in proper orientation. However, attenuation of the eyelid retractors (capsulopalpebral fascia and inferior tarsal muscle) in the lower eyelids allows the inferior border of the tarsus to ride forward and superiorly with the eyelid margin rotating inward (Fig 12-5). Several clinical clues may be present to indicate disinsertion of the retractors:

- a white subconjunctival line several millimeters below the inferior tarsal border caused by the leading edge of the detached retractors
- an inferior fornix that is deeper than usual

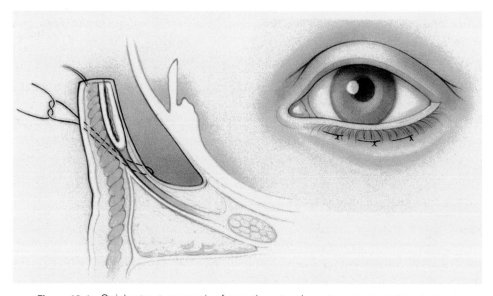

Figure 12-4 Quickert suture repair of spastic entropion. *(Illustration by Christine Gralapp.)*

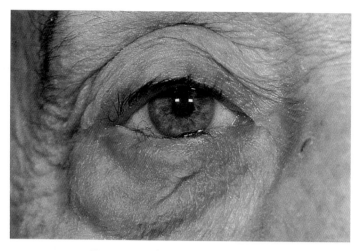

Figure 12-5 Involutional entropion.

- ptosis of the lower eyelid (lower eyelid is higher than normal)
- little or no inferior movement of the lower eyelid on downgaze

Superior migration of the preseptal orbicularis is detected by observation of the preseptal orbicularis as the patient squeezes his or her eyes closed after the entropic eyelid has been placed in its normal position (overriding orbicularis). Involutional changes in the orbital soft tissues may also contribute to involutional entropion by reducing the lower eyelid posterior support.

Procedures to repair involutional entropion of the lower eyelid generally fall into 1 of 3 groups: temporizing measures, horizontal tightening procedures, and repair of the retractors. Often, a combination of procedures must be used to minimize recurrence. Trichiasis, or misdirected lashes, may need specific treatment either in conjunction with the entropion repair or subsequently if lashes remain misdirected after proper positioning of the eyelid margin.

Temporizing measures

Suture techniques (Quickert sutures—see Fig 12-4) are occasionally useful as temporizing measures in involutional entropion, but these procedures by themselves are associated with high recurrence rates. Thermal cautery is rarely successful as a means of tightening the anterior lamella.

Horizontal eyelid tightening

Horizontal tightening of the eyelid at the lateral canthus stabilizes the eyelid and often corrects the entropion. The lateral tarsal strip operation is useful (see Fig 12-2B).

Repair of retractors

The Quickert suture repair is a fast but often temporary means of reinserting the retractors. The surgeon can combine this procedure with horizontal shortening to increase the success rate of the repair. Direct exploration and repair of lower eyelid retractor defects through a skin incision (Fig 12-6) or transconjunctival approach (Fig 12-7) are designed

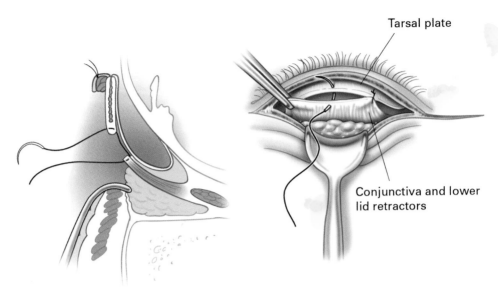

Figure 12-6 Retractor repair of involutional entropion. *(Illustration by Christine Gralapp.)*

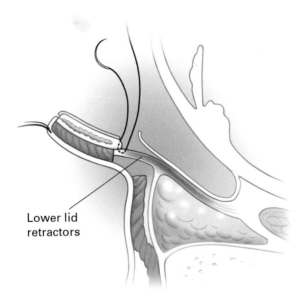

Figure 12-7 Retractor repair *(transconjunctival approach).*
(Illustration by Christine Gralapp.)

to stabilize the inferior border of the tarsus. The retractor reinsertion operation is usually combined with a lateral canthal tightening of the eyelid. When retractor reinsertion
is performed using an incision through the skin and orbicularis muscles at or near the
inferior tarsal border, the incisional scar helps prevent postoperative orbicularis override.
A small amount of preseptal orbicularis muscle can also be removed in selected patients

who have a large amount of override. Reinsertion of the retractor performed through the skin in conjunction with a lateral tarsal strip operation corrects all 3 etiologic factors in involutional entropion and is the combined approach of choice for many surgeons.

Barnes JA, Bunce C, Olver JM. Simple effective surgery for involutional entropion suitable for the general ophthalmologist. *Ophthalmology.* 2006;113(1):92–96.

Dresner SC, Karesh JW. Transconjunctival entropion repair. *Arch Ophthalmol.* 1993;111:1144–1148.

Seiff SR, Carter SR, Tovilla-Canales JL, Choo PH. Tarsal margin rotation with posterior lamella superadvancement for the management of cicatricial entropion of the upper eyelid. *Am J Ophthalmol.* 1999;127:67–71.

Cicatricial Entropion

Cicatricial entropion is caused by vertical tarsoconjunctival contracture and internal rotation of the eyelid margin with resulting irritation of the globe from inturned cilia or the keratinized eyelid margin (Fig 12-8). A variety of conditions may lead to cicatricial entropion, including *autoimmune* (cicatricial pemphigoid), *inflammatory* (Stevens-Johnson syndrome), and *infectious* diseases (trachoma, herpes zoster) and *surgical* (enucleation, posterior-approach ptosis correction) and *traumatic* (thermal or chemical burns, scarring) conditions. The long-term use of topical glaucoma medications, especially miotics, may cause chronic conjunctivitis with vertical conjunctival shortening and secondary cicatricial entropion.

The patient's history along with a simple diagnostic test (digital eversion) usually distinguishes cicatricial entropion from involutional entropion. Digital eyelid traction to attempt to return the eyelid to a normal anatomical position corrects the abnormal margin position in involutional entropion but not in cicatricial entropion. Inspection of the posterior aspect of the eyelid reveals subtle to severe scarring of the tarsal conjunctiva in cases of cicatricial entropion.

Effectiveness of treatment in cicatricial entropion depends primarily on cause and severity. When the cause is autoimmune or inflammatory disease, the prognosis

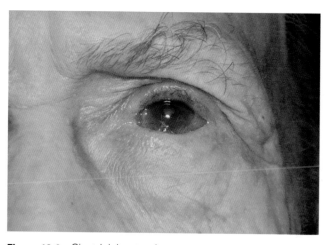

Figure 12-8 Cicatricial entropion. *(Courtesy of Roger A. Dailey, MD.)*

is guarded because of frequent disease progression; when the cause is prior surgery or trauma, the prognosis is generally good because the process tends to be localized and reversible. Infectious causes fall somewhere in between.

Successful management of cicatricial entropion depends on thoughtful preoperative evaluation to determine the cause, severity, and prominent features in each patient. The goal of treatment is to eliminate the chronic ocular irritation by removing the lashes and keratinized tissue from contact with the cornea. Cicatricial entropion usually requires surgery, but lubricating drops and ointments, barriers to symblepharon formation, and cryotherapy are sometimes useful adjuncts. Indeed, surgery is contraindicated during the acute phase of autoimmune diseases, and topical and systemic medications are more appropriate until the disease stabilizes.

When there is only slight inversion of the margin (with or without trichiasis) and little distortion of other eyelid structures, resection of anterior lamellar tissue with or without mucous membrane grafting may be curative. The anterior lamellar repositioning slides the offending tissues away from the eye.

The tarsal fracture operation is useful in cases of mild to moderate cicatricial entropion (marginal entropion) in the upper or lower eyelid (Fig 12-9). In this situation, lashes abrade the cornea, and careful examination shows that the ciliary eyelid margin has lost its square edges and is rotated posteriorly. A posterior horizontal tarsal incision is made 2 mm inferior to the eyelid margin. This full-thickness tarsal incision allows the eyelid margin to be fractured away from the globe in an everted position. The eyelid position is stabilized with everting sutures.

For marginal rotation to be effective, the tarsus should be intact and of reasonably good quality. Because it is advisable not to violate the conjunctiva in patients with active autoimmune disease, medical management of the inflammatory condition with systemic and topical anti-inflammatory medications is desirable. When surgery is indicated,

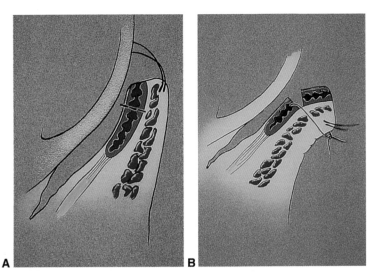

Figure 12-9 **A,** Tarsotomy. **B,** Margin rotation for cicatricial entropion.

maximal inflammatory suppression is achieved with pulsed systemic anti-inflammatory medications (corticosteroids and immunosuppressive agents).

Because it is usually scarred and distorted in patients with severe cicatricial entropion, the involved tarsus generally needs to be replaced. In the upper eyelid, tarsoconjunctival grafts are useful tarsal substitutes; in the lower eyelid, autogenous ear cartilage, preserved scleral grafts, and hard palate mucosa have been used.

D'Ostroph AO, Dailey RA. Cicatricial entropion associated with chronic dipivefrin application. *Ophthal Plast Reconstr Surg.* 2001;17:328–331.

Heiligenhaus A, Shore JW, Rubin PAD, Foster CS. Long-term results of mucous membrane grafting in ocular cicatricial pemphigoid: implications for patient selection and surgical considerations. *Ophthalmology.* 1993;100:1283–1288.

Kersten RC, Kleiner FP, Kulwin DR. Tarsotomy for the treatment of cicatricial entropion with trichiasis. *Arch Ophthalmol.* 1992;110:714–717.

Symblepharon

A symblepharon is an adhesion between conjunctival surfaces. Symblepharon can occur as a result of inflammation, trauma, or previous surgery. Conjunctival Z-plasties are sometimes effective for localized contracted linear adhesions when vertical lengthening of the involved tissue is the primary objective. More extensive symblepharon formation requires a full-thickness conjunctival graft or flap or a partial-thickness buccal mucous membrane graft. The preferred technique for managing symblepharon formation associated with cicatricial entropion is determined by the area of conjunctiva involved in the entropion.

Trichiasis

Trichiasis is an acquired misdirection of the eyelashes. The method used for treating trichiasis is usually dictated by the pattern (segmental or diffuse) of the misdirected lashes and the quality of the posterior lamella of the involved eyelid. Inturned lashes not associated with involutional entropion are usually seen in cases of posterior lamellar scarring (marginal cicatricial entropion). If the eyelid margin is misdirected, treatment should be directed at correcting the entropion.

Mechanical Epilation

The usual method for initially treating a few misdirected lashes is removal with forceps under the slit lamp. Following mechanical removal of the eyelash, recurrence is anticipated in 3–4 weeks because of eyelash regrowth. Short cilia regrowth is often mechanically more irritating to the cornea than mature longer lashes.

Electrolysis

Standard electrolysis is still used for the treatment of trichiasis. However, the recurrence rate is high, adjacent normal lashes may be damaged, and scarring of the adjacent eyelid margin tissue can worsen the problem. Radiofrequency epilation with an insulated probe is an excellent alternative to electrolysis because the success rate is high and the collateral damage is minimal, which limits scarring. Radiofrequency epilation is discussed later in this section.

Cryotherapy

Segmental trichiasis can be treated with a nitrous oxide probe. Cryotherapy is an in-office procedure that requires only local infiltrative anesthesia. The involved area is frozen for approximately 20 seconds, allowed to thaw, and then refrozen for 20 seconds (double freeze–thaw technique). The lashes are mechanically removed with forceps after treatment. Edema lasting several days, loss of skin pigmentation, notching of the eyelid margin, and possible interference with goblet cell function are disadvantages of cryotherapy. This method may be combined with various surgical techniques and repeated if offending lashes persist or recur.

Argon Laser

Argon laser treatment of trichiasis is less effective than cryotherapy but useful when only a few scattered eyelashes require ablation or when the stimulation of larger areas of inflammation is undesirable. The reported single-treatment success rate is 45%–80%. After local anesthesia is administered, a 100-μm spot size is directed at the lash base for 0.1–0.2 seconds at 1000–2000 milliwatts (mW) of power.

Radiofrequency Epilation

The radiofrequency unit allows treatment of each trichitic eyelash. A partially insulated needle tip is inserted along the shaft of the cilia to the cilia's base, and then the radiofrequency signal is delivered for approximately 1 second on cut mode at a very low power setting to destroy the hair follicle. When the needle tip is removed, the lash should remain attached to it. The single-session success rates range from 56% to 90%, and additional treatment sessions are commonly necessary.

Surgery

Full-thickness pentagonal resection with primary closure may be considered when trichiasis is confined to a segment of the eyelid. A cantholysis with or without a semicircular advancement flap (see Eyelid Defects Involving the Eyelid Margin in Chapter 11) may be useful with more extensive full-thickness resections. When entropion is present, the treatment is dictated by the severity of the entropion.

Bartley GB, Bullock JD, Olsen TG, Lutz PD. An experimental study to compare methods of eyelash ablation. *Ophthalmology.* 1987;94:1286–1289.

Dutton JJ, Tawfik HA, DeBacker CM, Lipham WJ. Direct internal eyelash bulb extirpation for trichiasis. *Ophthal Plast Reconstr Surg.* 2000;16:142–145.

Kezirian GM. Treatment of localized trichiasis with radiosurgery. *Ophthal Plast Reconstr Surg.* 1993;9:260–266.

Blepharoptosis

The term *ptosis* refers to drooping or inferodisplacement of any anatomical structure. This shortened form is often used in place of the more accurate term, *blepharoptosis,* to describe drooping or inferodisplacement of the upper eyelid.

Two helpful classification systems are used to describe upper eyelid ptosis. It may be categorized by onset: congenital or acquired. Alternatively, it may be classified by the cause: myogenic, aponeurotic, neurogenic, mechanical, or traumatic. The most common type of *congenital* ptosis results from a poorly developed levator muscle (myogenic cause); the most common type of *acquired* ptosis is caused by stretching or even disinsertion of the levator aponeurosis (aponeurotic cause).

Blepharoptosis is a common cause of reversible peripheral visual loss. Although the superior visual field is primarily involved, central vision can also be affected. Many patients with ptosis complain of difficulty with reading because the ptosis is worsened in downgaze. Such exacerbation of ptosis in downgaze is caused by relaxation of the frontalis muscle, whose chronic contracture might have been masking full expression of the ptosis in primary gaze. Blepharoptosis has also been shown to decrease the overall amount of light reaching the macula and therefore can reduce visual acuity as well, especially at night.

Bergin DJ. *Management and Surgery of Congenital and Acquired Ptosis.* Continuing Ophthalmic Video Education. San Francisco: American Academy of Ophthalmology; 1990.

Meyer DR, Rheeman CH. Downgaze eyelid position in patients with blepharoptosis. *Ophthalmology.* 1995;102:1517–1523.

Evaluation

The ocular, medical, and surgical history of a patient helps determine whether surgical repair of ptosis is appropriate for that individual. The surgeon should be aware of any history of dry eye syndrome and should temper any blepharoptosis repair in the presence of significant dry eye problems. Patients should be questioned about their coagulation status (see Chapter 10). Other pertinent historical queries should include the presence of thyroid eye disease, previous eye or eyelid surgery, and prior periorbital trauma.

The patient's history usually distinguishes congenital from acquired ptosis. Patients with congenital or acquired blepharoptosis may be aware of a family history of the condition. Marked variability in the degree of ptosis during the day and complaints of diplopia should suggest ocular myasthenia gravis (MG). Complaints of dysphonia, dyspnea, dysphagia, or proximal muscle weakness suggest systemic MG.

Physical Examination

Physical examination of the ptosis patient begins with 4 clinical measurements:

- vertical palpebral fissure height
- margin–reflex distance

- upper eyelid crease position
- levator function (upper eyelid excursion)

The physician can record these data by means of a drawing of the cornea, the pupil size, and the position of the upper and lower eyelids in relation to these structures (Fig 12-10).

Vertical interpalpebral fissure height

The vertical interpalpebral fissure is measured at the widest point between the lower eyelid and the upper eyelid. This measurement is taken with the patient fixating on a distant object in primary gaze.

Margin–reflex distance

The margin–reflex distance (MRD), which is the distance from the upper eyelid margin to the corneal light reflex in primary position, is probably the single most effective measurement in describing the amount of blepharoptosis. The light reflex may be obstructed by the eyelid in severe cases of ptosis and therefore have a zero or negative value. If the patient complains of visual obstruction while reading, the MRD should also be checked in the reading position. Lower eyelid retraction (or scleral show) should be noted separately as the *margin–reflex distance 2 (MRD2)*. The MRD2 is the distance from the corneal light reflex to the lower eyelid margin. The sum of the MRD1 and the MRD2 should equal the vertical interpalpebral fissure height.

Upper eyelid crease position

The distance from the upper eyelid crease to the eyelid margin is measured. Because the insertion of fibers from the levator muscle into the skin contributes to formation of the upper eyelid crease, high, duplicated, or asymmetric creases may indicate abnormal insertions or disinsertions of the levator aponeurosis. The crease is usually elevated in patients with involutional ptosis. The upper eyelid crease is often shallow or absent in patients with congenital ptosis. The upper eyelid crease is typically lower or obscured in the Asian eyelid, with or without ptosis.

Levator function

The levator function is estimated by measuring the upper eyelid excursion from downgaze to upgaze with frontalis muscle function negated. Fixating the brow with digital pressure can help the examiner take care to minimize contributions from accessory elevators of the

Palpebral fissure height	9.5	7.5
Margin–reflex distance	+4	+2
Upper eyelid crease	8	11
Levator function	15	14

Figure 12-10 Example of ptosis data sheet.

eyelids such as the frontalis muscle. Failure to negate the influence of the frontalis muscle results in incorrect evaluations of true levator function. Accurate analysis of the amount of levator function is crucial in determining the cause and treatment plan (Fig 12-11).

Frueh BR, Musch DC. Evaluation of levator muscle integrity in ptosis with levator force measurement. *Ophthalmology.* 1996;103:244–250.

Other

Physical examination also includes checking head position, chin elevation, brow position, and brow action in attempted upgaze. These features help show the patient how blepharoptosis affects function. The quantity and quality of the tear film and the presence or absence of lagophthalmos must be evaluated and documented as part of the initial evaluation. Lagophthalmos and poor tear film quantity or quality may predispose a patient to complications of ptosis repair such as dryness and exposure keratitis. The examiner should also note the presence or absence of a normal Bell's phenomenon and assess whether corneal sensation is normal; these factors may also affect the treatment plan.

Variation in the amount of blepharoptosis with extraocular muscle or jaw muscle movements *(synkinesis)* must also be assessed. Synkinesis may be seen in Marcus Gunn jaw-winking ptosis, aberrant regeneration of the oculomotor nerve or the facial nerve, and some types of Duane syndrome. The examiner should attempt to elicit synkinesis as part of the evaluation of patients with congenital blepharoptosis or those with possible aberrant regeneration.

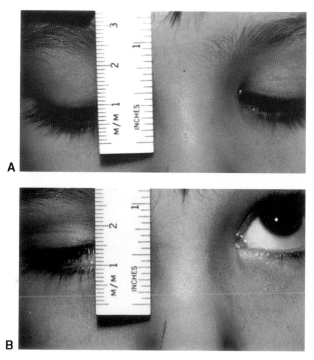

Figure 12-11 Measurement of levator excursion. **A,** Downgaze. **B,** Upgaze.

The position of the ptotic eyelid in downgaze should be checked as an aid in differentiating between congenital and acquired causes. The congenitally ptotic eyelid is typically higher in downgaze than the contralateral, normal eyelid, as a result of eyelid lag. The congenitally ptotic eyelid may also manifest lagophthalmos. In contrast, the affected eyelid in acquired involutional ptosis remains ptotic in all positions of gaze and may even worsen in downgaze with relaxation of the frontalis muscle.

The ophthalmologist must assess visual function and refractive error in all cases of congenital or childhood ptosis in order to identify and treat the child with concomitant amblyopia resulting from anisometropia, high astigmatism, strabismus, or occlusion of the pupil. Amblyopia occurs in approximately 20% of patients with congenital ptosis. Extraocular muscle function should also be assessed because extraocular muscle dysfunction associated with blepharoptosis occurs in various congenital conditions (combined superior rectus/levator muscle maldevelopment, congenital oculomotor palsy) and acquired conditions (ocular or systemic MG, chronic progressive external ophthalmoplegia, oculopharyngeal dystrophy, and oculomotor palsy with or without aberrant regeneration).

In addition, pupillary examination is important in the evaluation of ptosis. Pupil abnormalities are present in some acquired and congenital conditions associated with ptosis (eg, Horner syndrome, cranial nerve III palsy). Miosis that is most apparent in dim illumination is one finding in Horner syndrome; mydriasis is seen in some cases of oculomotor nerve palsy.

External examination may reveal other abnormalities as well. For example, severe bilateral congenital ptosis may be associated with telecanthus, epicanthus inversus, flattening of the superior orbital rim, horizontal shortening of the eyelids, and hypoplasia of the nasal bridge. These findings characterize an autosomal dominant condition known as *blepharophimosis syndrome* (discussed in Chapter 11, under the heading Congenital Anomalies).

Ancillary tests

Visual field testing with the eyelids untaped (in the natural, ptotic state) and taped (artificially elevated as if the blepharoptosis has been repaired) helps determine the patient's level of functional visual impairment. Comparison of the taped visual field with the untaped visual field gives an estimate of the superior visual field improvement that can be anticipated following surgery. Visual field testing and external full-face photography may be required as a part of the initial evaluation in order to distinguish *functional* from *cosmetic* blepharoptosis repair.

Meyer DR, Stern JH, Jarvis JM, Lininger LL. Evaluating the visual field effects of blepharoptosis using automated static perimetry. *Ophthalmology.* 1993;100:651–659.

Pharmacologic testing may be helpful in confirming the clinical diagnosis of Horner syndrome. Because cocaine blocks the reuptake of norepinephrine at the neuromuscular junction, topical application of 4%–10% cocaine to a normal eye increases the availability of norepinephrine to the iris dilator muscle and results in pupillary dilation. In contrast, the pupil affected by Horner syndrome fails to dilate after application of cocaine, because of the absence of norepinephrine in the synaptic cleft (Fig 12-12). A variety of other pharmacologic tests may help localize the lesion causing the Horner syndrome (see BCSC

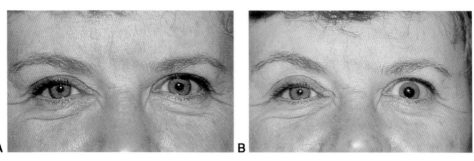

Figure 12-12 Horner syndrome. **A,** Before instillation of topical cocaine. **B,** Pupil of normal left eye dilates after instillation of cocaine, but right pupil does not respond. *(Courtesy of Robert C. Kersten, MD.)*

Section 5, *Neuro-Ophthalmology*). Although the differentiation among first-, second-, and third-order neuron dysfunction in the cause of Horner syndrome is important to the patient's general medical assessment, this information does not affect the choice of treatment for the ptosis. Third-order neuron dysfunction resulting in Horner syndrome is typically benign. Neuron dysfunction of the first or second order, however, is more often associated with malignant neoplasms such as an apical lung (Pancoast) tumor, aneurysm, or dissection of the carotid artery.

Because blepharoptosis is the most common presenting sign of MG, the ophthalmologist may order or perform tests to rule out this diagnosis in appropriate patients. Fluctuating ptosis that seems to worsen with fatigue or prolonged upgaze, especially when accompanied by diplopia or other clinical manifestations of systemic MG, is an indication for further diagnostic testing. Testing with edrophonium chloride (Tensilon), an acetylcholinergic agent, has traditionally been used to diagnose MG. In the myasthenic patient whose acetylcholine receptors have been compromised through autoimmune destruction, the infusion of edrophonium chloride typically results in improvement in the ptosis or motility. Clinicians administering the Tensilon test should be aware of potential adverse effects such as lacrimation, salivation, flushing, abdominal cramping, bradycardia, or even respiratory arrest and should be prepared to administer atropine and other appropriate care in case of adverse reactions. (The Tensilon test is described more fully in BCSC Section 5, *Neuro-Ophthalmology.*)

The *ice pack test* is an alternative approach that has few potential side effects and that may obviate routine Tensilon testing in the diagnosis of MG. The ice pack test is a simple procedure that can be performed in the office. An ice pack is applied to the patient's eyelid(s) for about 2 minutes. If MG is present, the ptosis often improves because of the enhancement of neuromuscular transmission that occurs with inhibition of acetylcholinesterase under cold conditions Some neuro-ophthalmologists use a sleep test as well. For this test, the patient lies in a darkened room (approximately 30 minutes), after which the ophthalmologist examines the patient. Rest or sleep improves myasthenic ptosis. Cold conditions also reduce weakness; thus, the ice pack test is actually a combination of cold plus rest and presumably more effective than other approaches.

Yet another alternative to Tensilon testing is the *acetylcholine receptor antibody test,* a serum assay designed to detect the autoimmune antibody responsible for the destruction of the muscle motor end-plate receptors in patients with MG. Binding antibodies are detectable in about 90% of patients with systemic MG and in about 70% of patients with ocular myasthenia. The ophthalmologist should be aware that some laboratories set their reference ranges artificially high, thus essentially assessing for systemic MG. The antibody levels in ocular myasthenia are presumably lower. Therefore, the detection of very small amounts of acetylcholine receptor antibodies may be suggestive of ocular MG. Of course, there have been several reports of patients who have significant generalized disease and a low level of antibodies and other cases in which patients have only modest ocular involvement and a very high level of antibodies.

Classification

As discussed earlier, ptosis may be classified according to the time of onset or the underlying abnormality. Most cases of congenital ptosis result from a localized myogenic dysgenesis. Most cases of acquired ptosis result from involutional stretching or disinsertion of the levator aponeurosis (aponeurotic abnormality). The cause of blepharoptosis is therefore commonly presumed to be myogenic in congenital ptosis and aponeurotic in acquired ptosis, and these cases are often referred to simply as *congenital* or *acquired ptosis*. However, a more specific and accurate classification system is based on a defined underlying abnormality and includes the additional categories of neurogenic, mechanical, and traumatic ptosis.

Clark BJ, Kemp EG, Behan WM, Lee WR. Abnormal extracellular material in the levator palpebrae superioris complex in congenital ptosis. *Arch Ophthalmol.* 1995;113:1414–1419.

Myogenic ptosis

Congenital myogenic ptosis results from dysgenesis of the levator muscle. Instead of normal muscle fibers, fibrous or adipose tissue is present in the muscle belly, diminishing the ability of the levator to contract and relax. Therefore, congenital ptosis caused by maldevelopment of the levator muscle is characterized by decreased levator function, eyelid lag, and sometimes lagophthalmos (Fig 12-13). The amount of levator function is an indication of the amount of normal muscle. Congenital myogenic ptosis with an associated poor Bell's phenomenon or vertical strabismus may indicate concomitant maldevelopment of the superior rectus muscle (*double elevator palsy,* or *monocular elevation deficiency*). The upper eyelid crease is often not present or is poorly formed. In general, the crease is less well developed in cases of more severe ptosis.

Acquired myogenic ptosis is uncommon and results from localized or diffuse muscular disease such as muscular dystrophy, chronic progressive external ophthalmoplegia, MG, or oculopharyngeal dystrophy. Because of the underlying muscle dysfunction, surgical correction may be difficult. The choice of surgical technique is most often based on the amount of levator function. Surgical procedures directed toward levator shortening are more effective in patients whose levator function is relatively good. If the levator function is relatively poor, frontalis suspension can be carried out by various surgical techniques designed to attach the eyelid to the frontalis muscle so that elevation of the brow results in elevation of the eyelid. Although shortening of the levator muscle aponeurosis or frontalis

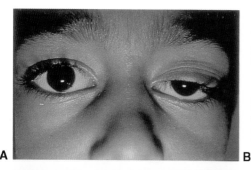
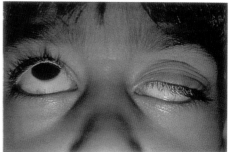

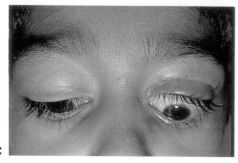

Figure 12-13 Bilateral asymmetric congenital ptosis. **A,** Note margin–reflex distance (MRD = 5.0 mm OD, 1.0 mm OS). Normal = 4.5 mm. **B,** Upgaze accentuates ptosis. **C,** Downgaze exhibits eyelid lag. *(Courtesy of Robert C. Kersten, MD.)*

suspension may help raise the eyelid to a functional level just above the pupil, too much elevation can lead to secondary keratitis due to lagophthalmos and exposure. Therefore, a compromise between cosmetic and functional results is sometimes required. Associated orbicularis oculi dysfunction in patients with myogenic blepharoptosis reduces the ability to close the eyelids and may further increase the risk of postoperative exposure keratitis. Silicone rod frontalis suspension may be more useful than other procedures if removal or adjustment of the sling is anticipated.

Holds JB, McLeish WM, Anderson RL. Whitnall's sling with superior tarsectomy for the correction of severe unilateral blepharoptosis. *Arch Ophthalmol.* 1993;111:1285–1291.

Aponeurotic ptosis

The levator aponeurosis transmits levator force to the eyelid. Thus, any disruption in its anatomy or function can lead to ptosis. *Congenital aponeurotic ptosis* is caused by failure of the aponeurosis to insert in its normal position on the anterior surface of the tarsus. This condition is characterized by good upper eyelid excursion and a high or indistinct upper eyelid crease. It is a rare cause of congenital ptosis and may be associated with birth trauma, especially in deliveries requiring forceps.

Acquired aponeurotic ptosis is the most common of all forms of blepharoptosis. It is caused by stretching or dehiscence of the levator aponeurosis or disinsertion from its normal position. Common causes are involutional attenuation or repetitive traction on the eyelid. Such repetitive traction may result from frequent eye rubbing or wearing of rigid contact lenses. Aponeurotic ptosis may also be caused or exacerbated by intraocular surgery or eyelid surgery through multiple mechanisms (Fig 12-14).

Eyelids with aponeurotic defects characteristically have a high or absent upper eyelid crease secondary to upward displacement or loss of the insertion of levator fibers into the skin. Thinning of the eyelid superior to the upper tarsal plate is often an associated finding and may allow visualization of the iris through the eyelid. Because the levator muscle itself

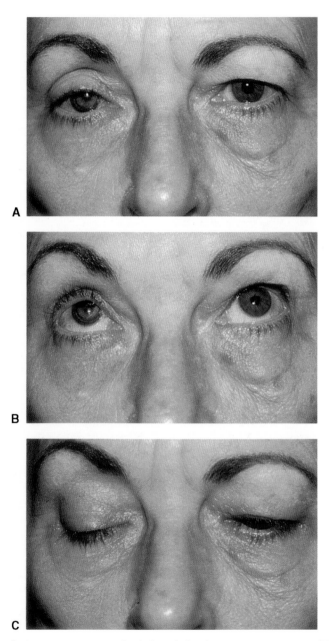

Figure 12-14 **A,** Levator aponeurosis defect following cataract surgery. Similar aponeurotic ptosis can occur following various other intraocular and eyelid surgical procedures as well. **B,** Excellent levator function on upgaze. **C,** Depression is greater than normal (eyelid drop) in downgaze.

is healthy, levator function in aponeurotic ptosis is usually normal (approximately 15 mm). Acquired aponeurotic ptosis may worsen in the reading position and therefore interfere with the patient's ability to read as well as limit the superior visual field. Table 12-1 compares acquired aponeurotic ptosis with congenital myogenic ptosis.

Kersten RC, de Conciliis C, Kulwin DR. Acquired ptosis in the young and middle-aged adult population. *Ophthalmology.* 1995;102:924–928.

Neurogenic ptosis

Congenital neurogenic ptosis is caused by innervational defects that occur during embryonic development. This condition is relatively rare and is most commonly associated with congenital cranial nerve III (CN III) palsy, congenital Horner syndrome, or the Marcus Gunn jaw-winking syndrome.

Congenital oculomotor nerve (CN III) palsy is manifested as blepharoptosis together with inability to elevate, depress, or adduct the globe. The pupils may also be dilated. This nerve palsy may be partial or complete, but blepharoptosis is very rarely an isolated finding in CN III palsy. It is uncommon to find aberrant innervation in congenital CN III palsies. Management of strabismus and amblyopia is difficult in many cases of congenital third nerve palsy; moreover, management of the associated ptosis is also complicated. The ptosis repair usually requires a frontalis suspension procedure, which often leads to some degree of lagophthalmos. As a result of the lagophthalmos, poor motility of the globe, and poor postoperative eyelid excursion, postoperative management may be complicated by diplopia, exposure keratitis, and corneal ulceration.

Malone TJ, Nerad JA. The surgical treatment of blepharoptosis in oculomotor nerve palsy. *Am J Ophthalmol.* 1988;105:57–64.

Congenital Horner syndrome is a manifestation of an interrupted sympathetic nervous chain and may cause mild ptosis associated with miosis, anhidrosis, and decreased pigmentation of the iris on the involved side. The mild blepharoptosis of Horner syndrome is due to an innervational deficit to the sympathetic Müller's muscle, an eyelid elevator second in importance to the levator muscle. Decreased sympathetic tone to the lower eyelid tarsal muscle, the analogue of Müller's muscle in the upper eyelid, results in elevation of the lower eyelid, sometimes called *lower eyelid ptosis*. The combined upper and lower eyelid ptosis decreases the vertical interpalpebral fissure and may falsely suggest enophthalmos. The pupillary miosis is most apparent in dim illumination, when the contralateral pupil dilates more effectively (see under the earlier subheading "Ancillary tests").

Table 12-1 Blepharoptosis Comparison

	Congenital Myogenic Ptosis	Acquired Aponeurotic Ptosis
Palpebral fissure height	Mild to severe ptosis	Mild to severe ptosis
Upper eyelid crease	Weak or absent crease in normal position	Higher than normal crease
Levator function	Reduced	Near normal
Downgaze	Eyelid lag	Eyelid drop

Congenital neurogenic ptosis may also be synkinetic. Marcus Gunn jaw-winking syndrome is the most common form of congenital synkinetic neurogenic ptosis (Fig 12-15). In this synkinetic syndrome, the unilaterally ptotic eyelid elevates with jaw movements. The movement that most commonly causes elevation of the ptotic eyelid is lateral mandibular movement to the contralateral side. This phenomenon is usually first noticed by the mother when she is feeding or nursing the baby. This synkinesis is thought to be caused by aberrant connections between the motor division of CN V and the levator muscle. Infrequently, this syndrome is associated with abnormal connections between other cranial nerves and CN III. Some forms of Duane retraction syndrome also cause elevation of a ptotic eyelid with movement of the globe. This congenital syndrome is also thought to result from aberrant nerve connections.

Acquired neurogenic ptosis results from interruption of normally developed innervation and is most often secondary to an acquired CN III palsy, to an acquired Horner syndrome, or to MG.

Delineation of the cause of acquired oculomotor nerve palsy is important. Distinction must be made between *vasculopathic* and *compressive* causes. The majority of acquired oculomotor palsies are vasculopathic and associated with diabetes, hypertension, or arteriosclerotic disease. Typically, vasculopathic acquired CN III palsies do not include pupillary abnormalities, and they resolve spontaneously with satisfactory levator function within 3 months. If a pupil-sparing third nerve palsy fails to resolve spontaneously within 3–6 months, further workup for a compressive lesion is indicated. However, if a patient presents with a CN III palsy involving the pupil, an immediate workup (including neuroimaging) should commence in order to rule out a compressive neoplastic or aneurysmal lesion. Surgical correction of ptosis related to CN III palsy usually requires

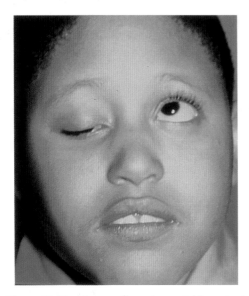 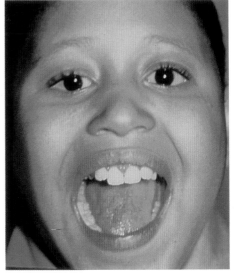

Figure 12-15 Marcus Gunn jaw-winking ptosis (synkinesis linking cranial nerve V to cranial nerve III). *(Courtesy of Jeffrey A. Nerad, MD.)*

frontalis suspension and should be reserved for patients in whom strabismus surgery allows single binocular vision in a useful field of gaze.

As discussed previously, the ice pack test, acetylcholine receptor antibody assay, or Tensilon test is indicated when the history or clinical examination suggests MG. Myasthenia gravis is an autoimmune disorder in which autoantibodies attack the receptors of the neuromuscular junction. The disease is most often generalized and systemic. Approximately 10% of patients with MG have thymomas; thus, scanning should be considered for all patients with MG to rule out these lesions. Early manifestation of MG is often ophthalmic, with ptosis being the most common presenting sign. Diplopia is also common. When the effects of MG are isolated to the periocular musculature, the condition is called *ocular myasthenia gravis.* Other autoimmune disorders may occur in myasthenic patients. For example, Graves disease occurs in 5%–10% of patients with MG.

The ptosis of ocular myasthenia often responds poorly to systemic anticholinesterase medications or steroids. Neuro-ophthalmologic consultation is useful in the evaluation and treatment of difficult cases. Surgical treatment of blepharoptosis in the myasthenic patient should be delayed until medical improvement has been maximized. Because of the variability of levator function, frontalis suspension is usually preferred. (See BCSC Section 5, *Neuro-Ophthalmology,* for further discussion.)

Sethi KD, Rivner MH, Swift TR. Ice pack test for myasthenia gravis. *Neurology.* 1987;37:1383–1385.

Wong JF, Theriault JF, Bouzouaya C, Codère F. Marcus Gunn jaw-winking phenomenon: a new supplemental test in the preoperative evaluation. *Ophthal Plast Reconstr Surg.* 2001;17:412–418.

Other, more unusual, causes of acquired neurogenic ptosis include myotonic dystrophy, chronic progressive external ophthalmoplegia, Guillain-Barré syndrome, oculopharyngeal dystrophy, and iatrogenic botulism. Botulinum toxin injection in the forehead or orbital region to ameliorate benign essential blepharospasm or to reduce facial rhytids may result in infiltration of the neurotoxin into the levator muscle complex. The resultant neurogenic ptosis is temporary, usually resolving after a few weeks.

Mechanical ptosis

Mechanical ptosis usually refers to the condition in which a neoplasm weighs or pulls down the upper eyelid, resulting in inferodisplacement. It may be caused by a *congenital abnormality,* such as plexiform neuroma or hemangioma, or by an *acquired neoplasm,* such as a large chalazion or basal cell or squamous cell carcinoma. Postsurgical or posttraumatic edema may result in temporary mechanical ptosis.

Traumatic ptosis

Blunt or sharp trauma to the levator aponeurosis or the levator muscle may also cause ptosis. The underlying histologic defects may be a combination of myogenic, aponeurotic, and cicatricial elements. Eyelid lacerations exposing preaponeurotic fat indicate that the orbital septum has been transected and suggest the possibility of damage to the levator aponeurosis. Exploration of the levator muscle or aponeurosis is indicated in these patients if levator function is diminished or ptosis is present. Orbital and neurosurgical procedures may also lead to traumatic ptosis. Because such ptosis may resolve or improve spontaneously, the ophthalmologist normally observes the patient for approximately 6 months before considering surgical intervention.

Pseudoptosis

Pseudoptosis—apparent eyelid drooping—should be differentiated from *true* ptosis. An eyelid may appear to be abnormally low in various conditions, including hypertropia, enophthalmos, microphthalmos, anophthalmos, phthisis bulbi, or a superior sulcus defect secondary to trauma or other causes. Contralateral upper eyelid retraction may also simulate ptosis. The term *pseudoptosis* is also sometimes used to describe *dermatochalasis,* the condition in which excess upper eyelid skin overhangs the eyelid margin, transects the pupil, and gives the appearance of a true ptosis of the eyelid margin (Fig 12-16).

Treatment of Ptosis

Ptosis repair is a challenging oculoplastic surgical procedure that requires correct diagnosis, thoughtful planning, thorough understanding of eyelid anatomy, and good surgical technique. Although an inexperienced ptosis surgeon (and sometimes even the patient) may think that ptosis repair is straightforward and predictable, the experienced ptosis surgeon realizes and anticipates the potential complexities.

After the patient has been evaluated and the cause and nature of the ptosis have been determined, treatment plans may be formulated. Blepharoptosis that causes significant superior visual field loss or difficulties with reading is considered a functional problem,

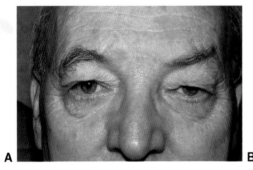
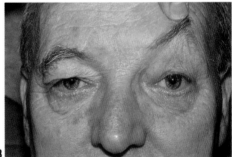

A

B

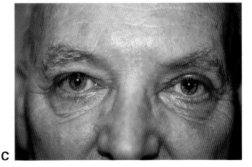

C

Figure 12-16 **A,** Patient with apparent ptosis of left upper eyelid. **B,** Manual elevation of dermatochalasis reveals this to be pseudoptosis; the underlying palpebral fissure is actually within normal limits. **C,** Clearance of visual axis is achieved following blepharoplasty alone. *(Courtesy of Robert C. Kersten, MD.)*

and correction of this defect often improves the ability of patients to perform the activities of daily living. In many instances, ptosis is considered to be a cosmetic issue, causing a tired or sleepy appearance in the absence of a true visual function deficit. Because ptosis repair is often an elective surgical procedure, it is particularly important for the surgeon to have a preoperative discussion with the patient to communicate the alternatives, potential risks, and benefits.

Nonsurgical treatment options are unusual but may include devices called *eyelid crutches,* which are attached to eyeglass frames. Eyelid crutches are occasionally useful in patients with acquired neurogenic and myogenic ptosis in whom surgical correction could lead to severe exposure-related corneal defects. Taping the upper eyelid open during appropriate times is also a simple, but often impractical, treatment method. These methods have largely been supplanted by better homologous and synthetic materials for frontalis suspension.

Surgical procedures designed to correct ptosis fall into 3 broad categories and should be directed toward correction of the underlying pathologic condition (Fig 12-17). The 3 categories of surgical procedures most commonly used in ptosis repair are

- external (transcutaneous) levator advancement
- internal (transconjunctival) levator/tarsus/Müller's muscle resection approaches
- frontalis muscle suspensions

The amount and type of ptosis and the degree of levator function are the most common determining factors in the choice of the surgical procedure for blepharoptosis repair. The surgeon's comfort level and experience with various procedures is also an important factor. In patients with good levator function, surgical correction is generally directed toward the levator aponeurosis: the levator muscle is the most potent and most useful elevator of the eyelid in most patients. However, if levator function is poor or absent, frontalis muscle suspension techniques become the preferred repair procedures.

External (transcutaneous) levator advancement surgery is most commonly used when levator function is normal and the upper eyelid crease is high. In this setting, the levator muscle itself is normal, but the levator aponeurosis (its tendinous attachment to the tarsal plate) is stretched or pulled loose (disinserted). The levator aponeurosis is approached from the outside of the eyelid through the upper eyelid crease. This approach is the one used most commonly for acquired aponeurotic ptosis repair and is particularly useful because it allows the surgeon to remove excess eyelid skin (dermatochalasis) at the same time. Typically, the levator aponeurosis is attenuated or stretched and requires advancement. Occasionally, the surgeon must reduce the redundant aponeurosis to avoid a thickened or irregular eyelid. In some cases, the distal end of the aponeurosis may be found to be higher than its normal position on the lower anterior surface of the tarsus. Reinsertion of the aponeurosis usually produces an excellent result.

The *internal (transconjunctival)* approach to ptosis repair may be directed toward Müller's muscle, the tarsus, or the levator aponeurosis. Müller's muscle resections may be indicated when the sympathetic nerve supply to this smooth muscle has been interrupted, as in Horner syndrome. This type of muscle resection is also used by some surgeons on patients who have an adequate upper eyelid position following instillation of a drop of

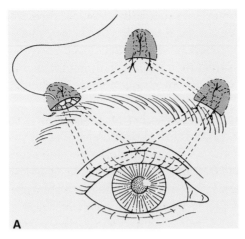

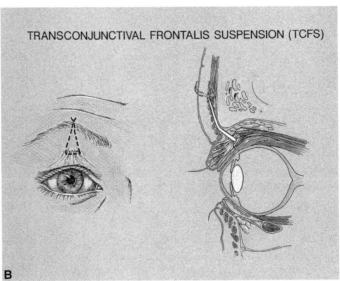

TRANSCONJUNCTIVAL FRONTALIS SUSPENSION (TCFS)

Figure 12-17 **A,** Frontalis suspension: Crawford method. **B,** Transconjunctival frontalis suspension. *(Part A reprinted by permission from Stewart WB.* Surgery of the Eyelid, Orbit, and Lacrimal System. Ophthalmology Monograph 8, vol 2. San Francisco: American Academy of Ophthalmology; 1994:120. Part B from Dailey RA, Wilson DJ, Wobig JL. Transconjunctival frontalis suspension [TCFS]. Ophthal Plast Reconstr Surg. *1991;7:289–297.)*

2.5% phenylephrine hydrochloride. Müller's muscle resections are typically used for repair of minimal ptosis (<2 mm) and are thought by most to be superior to the Fasanella-Servat procedure (tarsoconjunctival müllerectomy) in maintaining eyelid contour and preserving the superior tarsal border. The Fasanella-Servat ptosis repair procedure, though also directed toward small amounts of ptosis, requires removal of the superior tarsal border.

When levator function is essentially absent, the surgeon should consider utilizing the accessory elevators of the eyelid in ptosis repair. This type of surgery is most commonly required in congenital ptosis with poor levator function or in various forms of neurogenic ptosis with poor levator function.

Most patients with significant ptosis automatically elevate the forehead and brow on the affected side in an attempt to raise the eyelid and clear the visual axis; however, this maneuver is normally very inefficient because of the elasticity of the eyelid skin. In *frontalis suspension surgery* (the most common solution to this problem), the eyelid is suspended directly from the frontalis muscle so that movement of the brow is efficiently transmitted to the eyelid. Thus, the patient is able to elevate the eyelid by using the frontalis muscle to lift the brow. Frontalis suspension can be performed transcutaneously or transconjunctivally (see Fig 12-17).

Autogenous tensor fascia lata, banked fascia lata, and synthetic materials have been used for this purpose. *Autogenous fascia lata* has shown the best long-term results but requires harvesting and additional surgery. Generally, patients need to be at least 3 years old or weigh 35 pounds or more. *Banked fascia lata* may be obtained from a variety of sources and obviates the need for additional operative sites and harvesting. However, this material may incite immune reactions or inflammation and have poorer long-term outcomes than autogenous tissue. *Synthetic materials* such as polytetrafluoroethane (GORE-TEX) and silicone rods are being increasingly used and may improve eyelid elasticity and allow easier adjustment or removal if necessary.

There is some controversy about whether bilateral frontalis suspension should be performed in patients with unilateral ptosis. Unilateral frontalis suspension results in asymmetry in downgaze because of upper eyelid lag induced by the sling. Bilateral surgery may improve the patient's symmetry, especially in downgaze, but it subjects the normal eyelid to surgery and its attendant risks. The decision to modify a normal eyelid in an attempt to gain symmetry must be discussed by the surgeon and patient (or the parents if the patient is a child).

Complications

The most common complication of blepharoptosis surgery is undercorrection. This has led some ptosis surgeons to use adjustable suture techniques or to advocate early adjustment in the office during the first postoperative week when indicated. Judgment is required to differentiate true undercorrection from apparent undercorrection resulting from postoperative edema. Other potential complications include overcorrection, unsatisfactory or asymmetric eyelid contour, scarring, wound dehiscence, eyelid crease asymmetry, conjunctival prolapse, tarsal eversion, and lagophthalmos with resultant exposure keratitis. Lagophthalmos following ptosis repair is most common in patients with decreased levator function. This condition is usually temporary, but it requires treatment with lubricating drops or ointments until it resolves.

Callahan MA, Beard C. *Beard's Ptosis.* 4th ed. Birmingham, AL: Aesculapius; 1990.

Dailey RA, Wilson DJ, Wobig JL. Transconjunctival frontalis suspension (TCFS). *Ophthal Plast Reconstr Surg.* 1991;7:289–297.

Dortzbach RK, Kronish JW. Early revision in the office for adults after unsatisfactory blepharoptosis correction. *Am J Ophthalmol.* 1993;115:68–75.

Loff HJ, Wobig JL, Dailey RA. Transconjunctival frontalis suspension: a clinical evaluation. *Ophthal Plast Reconstr Surg.* 1999;15(5):349–354.

Eyelid Retraction

Eyelid retraction is present when the upper eyelid is displaced superiorly or the lower eyelid, inferiorly, exposing sclera between the limbus and the eyelid margin. Lower eyelid retraction may also be a normal anatomical variant in patients with shallow orbits or certain genetic orbital or eyelid characteristics. Retraction of the eyelids often leads to lagophthalmos and exposure keratitis. The effects of these conditions can range from ocular irritation and discomfort to vision-threatening corneal decompensation.

Eyelid retraction can have local, systemic, or central nervous system causes. The most common causes of eyelid retraction are thyroid-associated orbitopathy (TAO), recession of the vertical rectus muscles, overly aggressive skin excision in blepharoplasty, and overcompensation for a contralateral ptosis (in accordance with Hering's law).

TAO is the most common cause of both superior and inferior eyelid retraction, as well as the most common cause of unilateral or bilateral proptosis (Fig 12-18). Because proptosis commonly coexists with and may mimic eyelid retraction in patients with TAO, these conditions must be distinguished from each other through eyelid measurements and exophthalmometry. A common finding in thyroid-related eyelid retraction is lateral flare. In this condition, the eyelid retraction is more severe laterally than medially, resulting in an abnormal upper eyelid contour that appears to flare along the lateral half of the eyelid margin. The histopathological changes in the eyelid in TAO are secondary to inflammatory infiltration and fibrous contraction of the eyelid retractors. The sympathetically innervated eyelid retractor muscles (Müller's muscle in the upper eyelid and the analogous eyelid retractor muscle in the lower eyelid) are preferentially affected by the inflammation and fibrosis of TAO (see Chapter 4 for a more extensive discussion of thyroid-associated orbitopathy).

Eyelid retraction may also be caused by recession of the vertical rectus muscles, owing to anatomical connections between the superior rectus and the levator muscles in the upper eyelid and between the inferior rectus muscle and capsulopalpebral fascia in

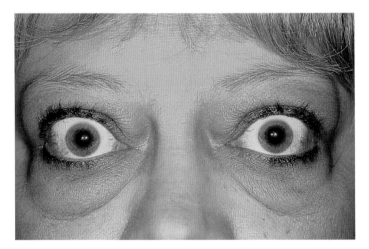

Figure 12-18 Thyroid-associated eyelid retraction. *(Courtesy of Roger A. Dailey, MD.)*

the lower eyelid. Eyelid retraction, therefore, is a common side effect of vertical muscle recession surgery.

Another common cause of eyelid retraction (especially of the lower eyelids) is excessive resection of skin during cosmetic lower blepharoplasty. This surgical complication is more common in patients with preexisting lower eyelid laxity and may even manifest as frank ectropion. Endoscopic midface lifting or full-thickness skin grafting may be required to correct this iatrogenic deformity. Conservative excision of skin in lower blepharoplasty along with concomitant correction of any lower eyelid laxity minimizes the risk of this problem.

Overcompensation for a contralateral ptosis (Hering's law) may also give the appearance of upper eyelid retraction. The surgeon must distinguish this condition from true eyelid retraction by observing the position of the supposedly retracted eyelid while the contralateral, presumably ptotic eyelid is either manually elevated or occluded.

Meyer DR, Wobig JL. Detection of contralateral eyelid retraction associated with blepharoptosis. *Ophthalmology*. 1992;99:366–375.

Parinaud syndrome is an example of eyelid retraction caused by a central nervous system lesion. Congenital eyelid retraction may also occur as a rare, isolated entity.

Treatment of Eyelid Retraction

Management of eyelid retraction is based on the etiologic factors underlying the retraction. Artificial tears, lubricants, and ointments may be sufficient to protect the cornea and minimize symptoms in cases of mild eyelid retraction. With time, mild eyelid retraction following lower blepharoplasty or in TAO frequently resolves spontaneously. A variety of surgical techniques have been developed to correct eyelid retraction if the condition fails to resolve spontaneously or if the eyelid retraction causes an immediate threat to vision or the cornea. Various techniques involve release or recession of the eyelid retractors, with or without the use of spacers or grafts.

Eyelid retraction in TAO can be managed by means of several surgical procedures. Unless there is severe exposure keratopathy, surgical intervention is indicated only after serial measurements have established stability of the disease over at least 6 months. Upper eyelid retraction can be corrected by excision or recession of Müller's muscle (anterior or posterior approach), recession of the levator aponeurosis with or without hang-back sutures, measured myotomy of the levator muscle, or insertion of a spacer between the distal end of the levator aponeurosis and the tarsus. Spacers may include fascia lata, donor sclera, ear cartilage, or alloplastic materials.

If the patient has lateral flare (common in TAO), a small eyelid-splitting lateral tarsorrhaphy combined with recession of the upper and lower eyelid retractors can improve the upper eyelid contour. This technique should be used only if the release of the lateral horn of the levator aponeurosis has failed to correct the flare, because lateral tarsorrhaphy may limit the patient's lateral visual field.

Surgical correction of lower eyelid retraction is also directed by the etiologic factors or deficiency underlying the retraction. *Anterior lamellar deficiency* (eg, excess skin resection from blepharoplasty) requires recruitment of vertical skin by means of a direct or endoscopic midface lift or addition of skin via a full-thickness skin graft. *Middle lamellar deficiency* (eg, posttraumatic septal scarring) requires scar release and possible placement of a rigid spacer graft. *Posterior lamellar deficiency* from congenital scarring or conjunctival shortage (eg, ocular cicatricial pemphigoid) may require a full-thickness mucous membrane graft.

Severe retraction of the lower eyelids, common in patients with TAO, requires grafting of spacer materials between the lower eyelid retractors and the inferior tarsal border. Autogenous auricular cartilage or hard palate mucosa is a good spacer material for this type of surgery. Preserved sclera and fascia lata have also been used, but autogenous materials are less likely to produce a significant inflammatory reaction. Some form of horizontal eyelid or lateral canthal tightening or elevation is also often required. Because horizontal tightening of the lower eyelid in a patient with proptosis may exacerbate the eyelid retraction, this technique requires caution.

Bartley GB. The differential diagnosis and classification of eyelid retraction. *Ophthalmology.* 1996;103:168–176.

Ben Simon GJ, Mansury AM, Schwarcz RM, Modjtahedi S, McCann JD, Goldberg RA. Transconjunctival Müller muscle recession with levator disinsertion for correction of eyelid retraction associated with thyroid-related orbitopathy. *Am J Ophthalmol.* 2005;140:94–99.

Elner VM, Hassan AS, Frueh BR. Transconjunctival Müller muscle recession with levator disinsertion for correction of eyelid retraction associated with thyroid-related orbitopathy. *Am J Ophthalmol.* 2006;141:233.

Kersten RC, Kulwin DR, Levartovsky S, Tiradellis H, Tse DT. Management of lower-lid retraction with hard-palate mucosa grafting. *Arch Ophthalmol.* 1990;108:1339–1343.

Facial Dystonia

Benign Essential Blepharospasm

Benign essential blepharospasm is a bilateral focal dystonia that affects approximately 300 of every 1 million people. The condition is characterized by increased blinking and involuntary spasms of the orbicularis oculi, procerus, and corrugator muscles. The spasms generally start as mild twitches and progress over time to forceful contractures. The involuntary episodes of forced blinking or contracture may severely limit the patient's ability to drive, read, or perform activities of daily living. With time, this condition can progress until the patient is functionally blind as a result of episodic inability to open the eyelids. Women are affected more frequently than men. The age of onset is usually over 40 years. Neuroimaging is rarely indicated in the workup because the diagnosis is made clinically. Severe dry eye syndrome may also result in contracture of the periorbital musculature and must be differentiated from benign essential blepharospasm.

Other muscles of the face may also be involved with blepharospasm. The cause of blepharospasm is unknown; however, it is probably of central origin, in the basal ganglia. Blepharospasm can be managed by medical or surgical approaches. Oral medications have very limited usefulness.

Anderson RL, Patel BC, Holds JB, Jordan DR. Blepharospasm: past, present, and future. *Ophthal Plast Reconstr Surg.* 1998;14:305–317.

Hallett M, Daroff RB. Blepharospasm: report of a workshop. *Neurology.* 1996;46:1213–1218.

Botulinum toxin injection

Repeated periodic injection of botulinum toxin type A (Botox) is the treatment of choice for benign essential blepharospasm. Botulinum toxin is a potent neurotoxin derived from *Clostridium botulinum*. Botulinum toxin type A alters receptor proteins in the presynaptic neuron, inhibiting the release of acetylcholine. Injection of this agent at therapeutic doses results in chemical denervation and localized muscle paralysis. Botulinum toxin injection is typically effective but temporary. Average onset of action is 2–3 days, and average peak effect occurs at about 7–10 days following injection. Duration of effect also varies but is typically 3–4 months, at which point recurrence of the spasms and reinjection can be anticipated.

Botulinum toxin type B (BTX-B; Myobloc) is an antigenically distinct serotype of toxin produced by the bacteria *Clostridium botulinum* that also exerts its effects at the neuromuscular junction. Botulinum toxin type B cleaves a protein component of the soluble *N*-ethylmaleimide–sensitive factor attachment protein (SNAP) receptor (SNARE) complex. This blocks the release of acetylcholine into the neuromuscular junction. Compared with botulinum toxin type A, type B seems to have a quicker onset and greater diffusion in the tissues. Also, its dosage is significantly different from that of type A, and its duration of action is shorter. However, patients treated with type B generally experience more discomfort at injection, and their ultimate satisfaction rates are lower. For patients who show decreased clinical response or who fail to respond to treatment with type A, the type B form of botulinum toxin appears to be a safe and effective alternative.

Orbicularis oculi subtotal myectomy and facial nerve ablation are considered secondary procedures for patients unresponsive to botulinum therapy. Surgical subtotal myectomy may result in improved patient responsiveness to botulinum toxin therapy. Complications associated with botulinum toxin injection include bruising, blepharoptosis, ectropion, epiphora, diplopia, lagophthalmos, corneal exposure, and superficial punctate keratitis. These adverse reactions are usually transient and typically result from spread of the toxin to adjacent muscles.

Alster TS, Lupton JR. Botulinum toxin type B for dynamic glabellar rhytides refractory to botulinum toxin type A. *Dermatol Surg.* 2003;29:516–518.

Baumann L, Black L. Botulinum toxin type B (Myobloc). *Dermatol Surg.* 2003;29:496–500.

Dutton JJ, Buckley EG. Long-term results and complications of botulinum A toxin in the treatment of blepharospasm. *Ophthalmology.* 1988;95:1529–1534.

Price J, Farish S, Taylor H, O'Day J. Blepharospasm and hemifacial spasm: randomized trial to determine the most appropriate location for botulinum toxin injections. *Ophthalmology.* 1997;104:865–868.

Surgical myectomy

This treatment is reserved for patients who are poorly responsive to botulinum therapy and incapacitated by the spasms. Meticulous removal of orbicularis fibers in the upper and lower eyelids, including the orbital as well as palpebral portions of the muscle, can be an effective and permanent treatment for blepharospasm. Complications of surgical myectomy include lagophthalmos, chronic lymphedema, or periorbital contour deformities. Limited myectomy is helpful in patients with less-severe disease.

Many patients with blepharospasm have an associated dry eye condition that may be aggravated by any treatment modality that decreases eyelid closure. This is most common in patients after surgical myectomy. Punctal plugs or occlusion, artificial tears, ointments, moisture chamber shields, and tinted spectacle lenses may help minimize discomfort from ocular surface problems.

Surgical ablation of the facial nerve

Though effective in eliminating blepharospasm, this treatment has been largely discontinued. Recurrence rates may be as high as 30%, and hemifacial paralysis frequently results from facial nerve dissection. Subsequent complications include brow ptosis, inadequate eyelid closure, and weakness of the lower face. The results obtained with facial nerve dissection are, therefore, less satisfactory than those of direct orbicularis oculi myectomy. Some surgeons have had greater success with microsurgical ablation of selected facial nerve branches.

Frueh BR, Musch DC, Bersani TA. Effects of eyelid protractor excision for the treatment of benign essential blepharospasm. *Am J Ophthalmol.* 1992;113:681–686.

Gillum WN, Anderson RL. Blepharospasm surgery. An anatomical approach. *Arch Ophthalmol.* 1981;99:1056–1062.

McCord CD Jr, Coles WH, Shore JW, Spector R, Putnam JR. Treatment of essential blepharospasm. Comparison of facial nerve avulsion and eyebrow–eyelid muscle stripping procedure. *Arch Ophthalmol.* 1984;102:266–268.

Muscle relaxants and sedatives

Muscle relaxants and sedatives are rarely of great value in the primary treatment of the essential blepharospasm patient. Oral medications such as orphenadrine (Norflex) 100 mg once or twice daily or lorazepam (Ativan) 0.5–1.0 mg or clonazepam (Klonopin) 0.5–1.0 mg once to twice daily are sometimes effective in suppressing mild cases of essential blepharospasm, prolonging the interval between botulinum toxin therapy or helping dampen lower facial dystonia (Meige syndrome) associated with essential blepharospasm. Psychotherapy has little or no value for the patient with blepharospasm.

Hemifacial Spasm

Blepharospasm should be differentiated from hemifacial spasm. Hemifacial spasm is characterized by intermittent synchronous gross contractures of the entire side of the face and is rarely bilateral. Unlike essential blepharospasm, the spasms are present during sleep. Hemifacial spasm is often associated with ipsilateral facial nerve weakness. In most cases, the cause of hemifacial spasm is vascular compression of the facial nerve at the brain stem. Magnetic resonance imaging (MRI) often documents the ectatic vessel. MRI also helps rule out other lesions (eg, pontine glioma) that may be the cause in 1% of cases. Neurosurgical decompression of the facial nerve may be curative in hemifacial spasm. Periodic injection of botulinum toxin is another treatment option. Aberrant regeneration after facial nerve palsy also presents with unilateral aberrant synkinetic facial movements. The history (eg, previous Bell palsy, trauma) and clinical examination are distinctive.

Involutional Periorbital Changes

Dermatochalasis

Dermatochalasis refers to redundancy of eyelid skin and is often associated with orbital fat protrusion or prolapse *(steatoblepharon).* Though more common in older patients, dermatochalasis can also occur in middle-aged people, particularly if a familial predisposition exists. Dermatochalasis of the upper eyelids is often associated with an indistinct or lower-than-normal eyelid crease. It also may be associated with true ptosis of the upper eyelids (Fig 12-19).

Significant dermatochalasis of the upper lids leads to complaints of a heavy feeling around the eyes, brow ache, complaint of eyelashes in the visual axis, and, eventually, reduction in the superior visual field. Dermatochalasis is often made worse by associated brow ptosis, especially if patients do not use their frontalis muscle to elevate the brows to relieve visual obscuration by the excess skin. Lower lid dermatochalasis is considered a cosmetic issue unless the excess skin and prolapsed fat are so severe that the patient cannot be fit with bifocals.

Blepharochalasis

Although blepharochalasis is not an involutional change, it is included in this discussion because it can simulate, and must be differentiated from, dermatochalasis. Rather, blepharochalasis is a rare familial variant of angioneurotic edema. It typically occurs in younger persons, most commonly young females, and is characterized by idiopathic episodes of inflammatory edema of the eyelids. Because of the recurrent bouts of inflammation and edema, the eyelid skin of a patient with blepharochalasis becomes thin and wrinkled, simulating the appearance of dermatochalasis. In addition, true ptosis, herniation of the orbital lobe of the lacrimal gland, atrophy of the orbital fat pads, and prominent eyelid vascularity may be associated with blepharochalasis secondary to the repeated attacks of edema. Surgical repair of the eyelid skin changes and ptosis that result from blepharochalasis may be

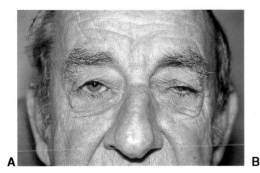

A B

Figure 12-19 A, Patient with bilateral asymmetric drooping due to blepharoptosis and dermatochalasis. **B,** Elevation of more ptotic left upper eyelid reveals increased blepharoptosis on right, which had been masked by the effect of Hering's law of equal innervation to each levator muscle. *(Courtesy of Robert C. Kersten, MD.)*

complicated by repeated episodes of inflammation and edema, causing recurrence of the ptosis and other eyelid changes.

Collin JR. Blepharochalasis. A review of 30 cases. *Ophthal Plast Reconstr Surg.* 1991;7:153–157.

Blepharoplasty

Upper Eyelid

Upper eyelid blepharoplasty is one of the most commonly performed *functional* as well as *cosmetic* ophthalmic plastic surgical procedures. Involutional skin and structural changes often begin in the periorbital area, and they can obstruct the superior visual field. Blepharoplasty is frequently performed to relieve this obstruction. Functional indications for blepharoplasty are documented by means of external photography and visual field testing with and without manual eyelid elevation.

Patients undergoing blepharoplasty for cosmetic reasons may have different expectations than patients undergoing functional blepharoplasty. Thus, a thorough preoperative discussion of the anticipated results is critical to preoperative planning. The surgeon must educate the patient with regard to reasonable postoperative expectations. Cosmetic blepharoplasty is more commonly performed in relatively young patients with less dermatochalasis than is found in the elderly patient presenting with visual field obstruction.

Lower Eyelid

Lower eyelid blepharoplasty is rarely considered functional. The surgery would be considered functional if a patient's excess skin and fat completely covered the spectacle bifocals so that the patient was unable to read. For cosmetic lower lid surgery, satisfactory results often require skin rejuvenation with chemical peels or laser resurfacing in addition to surgical alterations of periocular structure. The preoperative discussion should clearly explain the reasonable expectations as well as risks. Patients should understand that aggressive resection of lower eyelid skin and fat may lead to eyelid retraction, ectropion, or a sunken, aged periorbital appearance.

Physical examination before upper blepharoplasty should include the following elements:

- a complete ocular examination including visual acuity testing and documentation
- visual field testing to demonstrate superior visual field defects if present
- evaluation of tear secretion or the tear film, which may be carried out through Schirmer testing, tear breakup time, or assessment of the adequacy of the tear meniscus
- evaluation of the forehead and eyebrows (including brow height and contour) to detect forehead and eyebrow ptosis; the surgeon should make careful observations when the patient's facial and brow musculature is relaxed
- notation of the position of the upper eyelid crease; the position of the upper eyelid crease varies according to genetic as well as involutional factors: the typical Asian upper eyelid crease is absent or significantly lower than that of the typical Caucasian eyelid, and the upper eyelid crease is usually 8–9 mm in Caucasian males and 9–11 mm in Caucasian females

Preoperative examination for lower blepharoplasty should also include

- testing of the elasticity and distractibility of the lower eyelid; the surgeon should be alert to the need for possible horizontal tightening of the lower eyelids as part of the lower blepharoplasty procedure
- notation and discussion of prominent supraorbital rims, if present; malar hypoplasia or relative exophthalmos may predispose the patient to postoperative scleral show following lower blepharoplasty; burring of the rim is not recommended

Preoperative examination for both upper and lower blepharoplasty should include

- assessment of the amount and areas of excess skin, as well as the amount and contours of prolapsed orbital fat, in the upper and lower eyelids
- evaluation for lagophthalmos; incomplete eyelid closure can lead to postoperative drying and exposure keratitis
- examination of periorbital bone contours and discussion of findings with the patient
- a detailed discussion of anticipated surgical results as well as possible surgical complications
- photographic documentation for medicolegal and other purposes

Dailey RA. Upper eyelid blepharoplasty. *Focal Points: Clinical Modules for Ophthalmologists.* San Francisco: American Academy of Ophthalmology; 1995, module 8.

Technique

Blepharoplasty begins with a thorough working knowledge of periorbital and eyelid anatomy (discussed in Chapter 9). In addition, just as the brow and glabellar areas affect the upper eyelids, the midfacial structures are influential in the position, tone, contour, and function of the lower eyelid and must be considered in the planning of lower eyelid surgery.

Preoperative planning should include marking excess skin for excision prior to the infiltration of local anesthetic. Often, the surgeon determines the amount of excess skin to be excised by using a pinch technique. For the upper lid, this involves placing 1 tip of the forceps in the eyelid crease. The other forceps tip is then advanced superiorly until the upper eyelid lashes begin to evert. The excess upper eyelid skin is then allowed to fall between the 2 tips of the forceps, and the tips are pinched together. Next, the surgeon uses a surgical marking pen to mark out the parameters of the excess upper eyelid skin. The marking pen is then used to draw out the existing upper eyelid crease or a new lid crease, as well as the superior border of the planned area of excision. Typically, this marking process results in the delineation of a crescent shape on the upper eyelid. To avoid excessive skin removal, the surgeon usually leaves 20 mm of skin remaining between the inferior border of the brow and the upper eyelid margin. To avoid lid retraction or ectropion, the surgeon must not be overly aggressive with skin resection in the lower lid.

Anesthesia for blepharoplasty is typically a combination of local infiltration of anesthetic agents and intravenous administration of sedatives. Often, a rapid-onset, short-duration agent such as lidocaine 1% with epinephrine 1:100,000 is mixed 50–50 with a slower-onset, longer-duration agent such as bupivacaine. A final epinephrine concentration of 1:200,000 is sufficient for maximizing pharmaceutical hemostasis while minimizing the risk of epinephrine toxicity. Injection is best accomplished with sedation before the patient is prepared and draped and prior to surgical scrubbing. This allows enough time for the epinephrine to cause vasoconstriction and thereby reduce the risk of significant perioperative bleeding. Additional local anesthetic and intravenous sedation may be administered intraoperatively if needed.

Upper blepharoplasty

Upper blepharoplasty begins with the surgeon making an incision in the lid crease and then following the area marked on the upper eyelid. The skin and underlying orbicularis oculi muscle are generally excised as a single flap because excising the tissues separately generally results in more bleeding. Surgeons may consider preservation of all or most of the orbicularis oculi muscle in patients with dry eye syndrome.

The orbital septum is incised exposing the underlying preaponeurotic fat pad. The surgeon may remove the fat by gently teasing it forward and excising it with scissors, cautery, or laser. When performed, resection of the preaponeurotic fat pad is carried no deeper than the boundary created by the superior orbital rim. Removal of fat deeper than the rim may result in a hollow superior sulcus. The medial upper eyelid fat pad is typically the most prolapsed and is opened and contoured or excised in a similar manner. However, because the medial palpebral blood vessels overlie the medial upper eyelid fat pads, the surgeon must exercise caution to avoid significant bleeding in this area. The upper eyelid crease is created by the attachments of the levator aponeurosis to the orbicularis muscle and skin near the upper tarsal border. Aging often results in elevation or loss of the upper eyelid crease. The surgeon can often correct a high, low, or absent eyelid crease during blepharoplasty by anchoring the eyelid skin to the levator aponeurosis with deep fixation sutures at the desired position. Alternatively, many surgeons rely on placement of the incision and excision of skin and muscle to manipulate the position of the upper eyelid crease. The upper eyelid skin can be closed with a running or subcuticular suture.

Lower blepharoplasty

Lower eyelid blepharoplasty, almost always performed for cosmetic purposes, is most often accomplished through a transconjunctival incision. At times, excess lower eyelid skin may necessitate skin excision through a transcutaneous incision. Skin removal during lower blepharoplasty carries a greater risk of lower eyelid contour abnormalities, retraction, or frank ectropion. Alternatively, excess skin can be tightened without excision through the precise application of laser skin resurfacing techniques or through chemical peeling with exfoliating solutions.

For transconjunctival surgery, preoperative evaluation defines the extent and location of lower eyelid fat prolapse and thus determines the boundaries of surgical excision. The surgery begins with retraction of the lower lid. The incision is created with a No. 15 blade, a monopolar cautery unit equipped with a Colorado needle, or the carbon-dioxide (CO_2) laser. The incision is begun just medial to the lower eyelid punctum so that damage to the lower canaliculus is avoided. The incision then courses laterally 2–3 mm below the inferior tarsal border across the length of the eyelid. It is carried through the conjunctiva and lower eyelid retractors so that access to the anterior face of the orbital fat pads is gained.

Dissection is then carried along the relatively avascular plane of the septum toward the inferior orbital rim. Dissection along the septum is also carried medially and laterally so that the central, medial, and lateral fat compartments are exposed. The medial fat compartment is separated from the central fat compartment by the inferior oblique muscle. The surgeon must be aware of the location of the inferior oblique muscle and work carefully around it to avoid damaging it during lower blepharoplasty. The medial fat pad of the lower eyelid, as in the upper eyelid, is paler than the more yellow lateral fat pads. The central fat compartment is separated from the lateral fat compartment by a fascial layer extending off the capsulopalpebral fascia: removal or incision of this fascial barrier may improve access to the lateral fat pad.

After the orbital septum overlying the fat pads has been exposed and opened, the surgeon may carefully and gradually excise the fat while repeatedly checking the external contour of the lower eyelid. To improve access to and removal of the fat, the surgeon can apply pressure gently on the globe. This pressure helps prolapse the fat forward. The surgeon discontinues excision when the visible fat remains at or slightly behind the inferior orbital rim when gentle pressure is applied to the globe. Typically, similar volumes of fat are removed from each lower eyelid. Excessive fat removal may give the lower eyelid a hollow appearance. Often, no fat needs to be resected. In these cases, the fat can be mobilized over the inferior orbital rim and held in position to the suborbicularis oculi fat (SOOF) by sutures of the surgeon's choosing. Maintaining maximal hemostasis throughout lower blepharoplasty is critical to the avoidance of vision-threatening complications. The conjunctival incision edges can usually be reapproximated without formal closure with sutures, although absorbable suture closure may occasionally be necessary if the conjunctival edges do not approximate naturally.

Complications

Loss of vision is the most dreaded complication of blepharoplasty. Almost every case of postblepharoplasty visual loss reported has been associated with *lower* blepharoplasty. Although blindness following eyelid surgery is rare, it has been reported to occur at a rate of between 1 in 2000 and 1 in 5000 cases. Such blindness is typically thought to be secondary to postoperative retrobulbar hemorrhage, with the increased intraorbital pressure resulting in ischemia due to compression of the ciliary arteries supplying the optic nerve. Other mechanisms of injury may also be present, however, including excessive iatrogenic retraction or idiopathic constriction of retrobulbar blood vessels in response to epinephrine in the local anesthetic. Orbital hemorrhage may result from injury to the deeper orbital blood vessels or from bleeding from the orbicularis muscle. Risk factors for this complication are TAO and blood dyscrasias (see Chapter 10). Postoperative pressure dressings should be avoided: they increase orbital pressure and obscure underlying problems. Finally, patients should be observed postoperatively so that possible orbital hemorrhage can be detected. Any patient complaining of significant pain, asymmetric swelling, or proptosis following surgery should be evaluated immediately. Visual dimming, darkness, or significant or asymmetric blurred vision following eyelid surgery may also be indicative of orbital hemorrhage and should be assessed and treated immediately.

Visual loss from orbital hemorrhage is an ophthalmic emergency. When compressive hemorrhage occurs in the orbit, the surgeon may decompress the orbit by opening the surgical wounds, performing lateral canthotomy with cantholysis, and administering high doses of intravenous corticosteroids. Anterior chamber paracentesis has no role in the management of orbital hemorrhage. In addition, medical glaucoma management is not useful because the increased intra*ocular* pressure reflects increased underlying intra*orbital* pressure. Lack of immediate response to these procedures may necessitate surgical decompression of the orbit with removal of the orbital floor or medial wall.

Diplopia secondary to injury of extraocular muscles is the next most severe complication of blepharoplasty. Diplopia may result from injury to the inferior oblique muscle, the inferior rectus muscle, or the superior oblique muscle. The inferior oblique muscle originates near the anterior lacrimal crest along the infraorbital rim and is anterior in the orbit. It separates and courses across the central and medial lower eyelid fat pads and may be injured during the removal of lower eyelid fatty tissue. The trochlea of the superior oblique muscle also may be injured by deep dissection in orbital fat in the superior nasal aspect of the upper eyelid.

Excessive removal of skin is a serious complication that can lead to lagophthalmos of the upper eyelids as well as cicatricial ectropion or retraction of the lower eyelids (Fig 12-20). Topical lubricants and massage may be helpful for managing mild postoperative lagophthalmos, retraction, or ectropion, all of which may resolve over time without further intervention. Injectable steroids (triamcinolone acetonide, 10 mg/mL [Kenalog-10]) can be used if a deep cicatrix contributes to the retraction. Severe cases require the use of free skin grafts, lateral canthoplasty, or release of scar tissue or eyelid retractors. Inferior scleral show can also result from septal scarring, orbicularis hematoma, and malar hypoplasia, even when minimal skin has been excised.

Baylis HI, Long JA, Groth MJ. Transconjunctival lower eyelid blepharoplasty. Technique and complications. *Ophthalmology.* 1989;96:1027–1032.

Baylis HI, Nelson ER, Goldberg RA. Lower eyelid retraction following blepharoplasty. *Ophthal Plast Reconstr Surg.* 1992;8:170–175.

Dailey RA. Upper eyelid blepharoplasty. *Focal Points: Clinical Modules for Ophthalmologists.* San Francisco: American Academy of Ophthalmology; 1995, module 8.

Hamra ST. The role of the septal reset in creating a youthful eyelid–cheek complex in facial rejuvenation. *Plast Reconstr Surg.* 2004;113:2124–2141.

Figure 12-20 Lower eyelid retraction following blepharoplasty. *(Courtesy of Roger A. Dailey, MD.)*

Jordan DR, Anderson RL, Thiese SM. Avoiding inferior oblique injury during lower blepharoplasty. *Arch Ophthalmol.* 1989;107:1382–1383.

Lowry JC, Bartley GB. Complications of blepharoplasty [major review]. *Surv Ophthalmol.* 1994;38:327–350.

Neuhaus RW. Complications of blepharoplasty. *Focal Points: Clinical Modules for Ophthalmologists.* San Francisco: American Academy of Ophthalmology; 1990, module 3.

Ophthalmic Procedures Assessment Committee. *Functional Indications for Upper and Lower Eyelid Blepharoplasty.* San Francisco: American Academy of Ophthalmology; 1994.

Brow Ptosis

Loss of elastic tissues and involutional changes of the forehead skin result in drooping of the forehead and, most noticeably, drooping of the eyebrows. This condition is known as *brow ptosis.* Visually significant brow ptosis may also result from facial nerve palsy. Brow ptosis frequently accompanies dermatochalasis and must be recognized as a factor that contributes to the appearance of aging in the periorbital area. Brow ptosis may become severe enough to affect the superior visual field. The patient often involuntarily attempts to compensate for this condition by chronic use of the frontalis muscle to elevate the eyebrows (Fig 12-21). Such chronic contracture of the frontalis muscle often leads to brow ache, headache, and prominent transverse forehead rhytids.

In most patients, the brow is located above the superior orbital rim. Generally, the female brow is higher and more arched than is the typical male brow. The brow is considered ptotic when it falls below the superior orbital rim. Measuring the distance in millimeters between the central brow and the superior orbital rim documents brow ptosis.

Treatment of Functional Brow Ptosis

Brow ptosis must be recognized and treated prior to or concomitant with the surgical repair of coexistent dermatochalasis of the eyelids. Because brow elevation results in a reduction of the amount of dermatochalasis present, it should be performed or simulated first when combined with upper blepharoplasty. Aggressive upper blepharoplasty in a patient with concomitant brow ptosis results in further depression of the brow. Functional brow ptosis may be corrected with browpexy or direct brow lift.

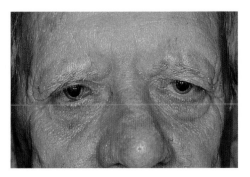 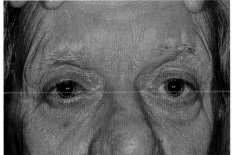

Figure 12-21 Brow ptosis.

Browpexy

Browpexy is performed through an upper eyelid blepharoplasty incision for mild to moderate brow ptosis. The sub-brow tissues are resuspended with sutures to the frontal bone periosteum above the orbital rim as part of a blepharoplasty.

McCord CD, Doxanas MT. Browplasty and browpexy: an adjunct to blepharoplasty. *Plast Reconstr Surg.* 1990;86:248–254.

Direct eyebrow elevation

The eyebrows can be elevated with incisions placed at the upper edge of the eyebrow. This procedure is useful for men and women with lateral eyebrow ptosis. When direct eyebrow elevation is used across the entire brow, it may result in an arch that is unacceptable in men. A conspicuous scar may occur, especially above the medial portion of the eyebrow, when the entire brow is lifted.

Kerth JD, Toriumi DM. Management of the aging forehead. *Arch Otolaryngol Head Neck Surg.* 1990;116:1137–1142.

Cosmetic Facial Surgery

Most ophthalmic plastic surgeons think that effective treatment of cosmetic and reconstructive upper eyelid problems must include consideration of eyebrow and forehead surgery. Likewise, effective lower eyelid cosmetic and reconstructive surgery must include consideration of midface and cheek surgery. Consequently, most ophthalmic plastic surgical fellowship programs in the United States include training in facial cosmetic and reconstructive surgery. It is important that any eyelid surgeon understand the surgical procedures discussed here. The performance of these procedures, however, generally requires special training, experience, and expertise.

The human face is an essential component of human communication. The aging face may communicate tiredness, depression, anger, or fear in an otherwise well-rested, well-adjusted, fully functioning person. To understand the problems and solutions of facial plastic surgery as they relate to communication and human beauty, the patient and surgeon must appreciate that our perception of the face and its communicative ability is based on the relative appearance and position of its parts in an additive fashion. The face is composed of smaller cosmetic units such as the forehead, eyelids, cheek, nose, lips, and neck. As we age, one or more of these cosmetic units undergo changes that lead to facial imbalance, disharmony, and ultimately miscommunication. If a single subunit has aged out of proportion to the rest of the face, as in dermatochalasis, a bilateral upper blepharoplasty produces a nice result. On the other hand, if the patient has concomitant aging changes of the mid and lower face and neck yet only undergoes lower eyelid blepharoplasty, the result will be far from satisfactory and will perpetuate further facial miscommunication, chronologic facial imbalance, and perceptual confusion.

Pathogenesis of the Aging Face

Factors that lead to involutional facial changes can be divided into 2 categories: intrinsic and extrinsic. *Intrinsic aging* refers to changes that occur as a result of chronologic aging. *Extrinsic aging* results from environmental factors such as cigarette smoke, ultraviolet radiation, wind, and gravity.

The facial contour and appearance is derived from soft tissue draped over underlying bone. The soft tissue component is composed of skin, subcutaneous fat, muscle, deeper fat pads, and fascial layers. The underlying structural element is composed of bone, cartilage, and teeth.

As the face ages, the soft tissue component moves inferiorly and the bone component loses mass. These changes leave relatively more soft tissue to hang from its attachments to the bone. Loss of subcutaneous fat, skin atrophy, and descent of facial fat pads compound this sagging-face phenomenon. Around the eyes, the lateral brow typically descends more than the medial brow, and this leads to temporal hooding. The orbital septum stretches, bulges, or dehisces, allowing fat to move forward. In the lower lid, midface descent produces the skeletonization of the infraorbital rim and increases the prominence of the orbital fat. This has been described as a *double convexity deformity.* This deformity also contributes to the increased prominence of the nasolabial fold. Sagging of the platysma muscle in the neck posterior to the mandibular ligament gives rise to jowling. The *turkey gobbler defect* in the neck is the result of redundant skin and separated medial borders of the platysma muscle at the midline.

Physical Examination of the Aging Face

Much of the surgeon's appraisal of the aging face can be obtained through close observation of the patient during the introduction and history phase of the initial meeting. From the top, so to speak, the surgeon should observe the hairstyle and hair thickness, the presence of bangs, the height of the hairline, the use of the frontalis, the position of the brow, the texture and quality of the facial skin, the presence and location of rhytids, telangiectasias, pigmentary dyschromia, and expressive furrows.

If chemical peeling or CO_2 laser resurfacing may be considered, the surgeon should also note the patient's Fitzpatrick skin type. There are 6 skin types in the Fitzpatrick skin type classification system, which denotes skin color and reaction of the skin to sun exposure. The higher the number, the greater the amount of skin pigment. Thus, Fitzpatrick type I refers to persons with minimal skin pigment and very fair skin. These individuals always burn with sun exposure and do not tan. Type VI represents individuals with markedly pigmented black skin, typically dark African American patients; they never burn and always tan.

In addition, the surgeon should assess eyelid skin and fat along with margin position relative to the pupil and cornea, presence or absence of horizontal lower lid laxity, midface position, presence of jowling, accumulation of subcutaneous fat in the neck, and chin position. He or she should note any nasal deformities and tip descent and broadening, as well as thinning of the lips. The surgeon may find a side view of the neck to be particularly helpful in determining the extent of aging. Preoperative photographs should be available in the operating room.

Facial Rejuvenation Surgery

Cosmetics, chemical peels, microdermabrasion, and laser resurfacing may be used to treat involutional and actinic facial skin changes. These relatively superficial procedures may precede or be combined with other surgical procedures that reposition deeper structures. It is important to remember that the upper eyelid appearance is inextricably linked to the position of the eyebrow. The same applies to the lower eyelid and midface as well as the lower face and neck. Subunits of the facial cosmetic superstructure cannot be viewed or manipulated individually but must be addressed in the context of the entire face and neck.

Laser Skin Resurfacing

Laser skin resurfacing, a technology popularized in the early 1990s, is designed to reduce wrinkles and enhance the texture and appearance of the facial and periorbital skin. A variety of lasers have been developed to perform laser resurfacing, with short-pulse CO_2 and Er:YAG lasers being the most widely used. Although the CO_2 laser had other medical applications for many years, its usefulness in skin resurfacing was originally limited because the laser caused peripheral thermal damage, resulting in scarring. By the early 1990s, the development of the ultrapulsed CO_2 laser allowed ablative skin resurfacing without the secondary thermal damage and scarring. The ultrapulsed laser is designed to deliver small pulses of high-energy laser to the skin. Pauses between the pulses allow cooling of the tissues in the treated area, minimizing the risk of secondary thermal damage. The Er:YAG laser has a nearly pure ablative effect on collagen and water-containing tissues, with a much smaller zone of thermal injury and much less heat transfer into the tissues than the CO_2 laser.

Laser resurfacing has been shown to be a useful adjunct to blepharoplasty, particularly lower blepharoplasty. The skin-shrinking, collagen-tightening effect of laser skin resurfacing often allows the surgeon to avoid making an external incision and removing skin. Accordingly, this may reduce the incidence of common complications of lower blepharoplasty, such as eyelid retraction, ectropion, lagophthalmos, or exposure keratitis. Many CO_2 laser units have interchangeable hand pieces that concentrate the laser energy and allow the laser to be used as a cutting instrument, or a type of scalpel. The laser scalpel can be beneficial to the ophthalmic surgeon because, when used appropriately, it allows nearly bloodless surgery in many patients and may reduce postoperative edema, ecchymosis, and healing time.

Safe and effective laser resurfacing requires special training. Additional understanding of skin, skin anatomy, laser physics, and perioperative care is crucial to a successful outcome. Ophthalmologists who receive training in intraocular laser use tend to feel comfortable with other laser modalities as well.

Laser skin resurfacing complications may include a variety of ophthalmic problems, such as lagophthalmos, exposure keratitis, corneal injury, and lower eyelid retraction.

Selection of appropriate patients is critical for successful laser skin resurfacing. Patients with a fair complexion and generally healthy, well-hydrated skin are ideal candidates. Patients with greater degrees of skin pigmentation can be safely treated, but additional care and caution are necessary. The darker the skin pigmentation, the greater the risk of postoperative inflammatory hyperpigmentation. Laser resurfacing is contraindicated in patients who have used isotretinoin (Accutane) within the past 12 months because reepithelialization is inhibited. Other contraindications include inappropriate, unrealistic expectations; collagen vascular disease such as active systemic lupus erythematosus; and significant uncorrected lower eyelid laxity.

Most surgeons treat patients preoperatively with suppressing doses of antiviral agents as prophylaxis against outbreaks of herpes simplex virus on the laser-resurfaced skin. Herpes simplex virus infection after laser resurfacing may lead to irreversible scarring. Antiviral prophylaxis should begin 1–2 days before the procedure and continue for 6–14 days after surgery. Antibiotic prophylaxis such as cephazolin or ciprofloxacin is generally used.

A desire to improve superficial skin characteristics and facial wrinkling without the prolonged period of healing and erythema seen with ablative laser skin resurfacing has led to the development of a variety of devices that use lasers, intense pulsed light, or radio-frequency to deliver energy to the skin. Treating the skin in these ways can produce even skin tone, remove cutaneous dyschromias or fine wrinkles, and even lift and smooth facial tissues. Each of these devices has its own list of risks and limitations, but in general, all of them offer some level of improvement in aspects of facial aging, with fewer risks and shorter recovery times than those of ablative laser skin resurfacing.

Goldbaum AM, Woog JJ. The CO_2 laser in oculoplastic surgery. *Surv Ophthalmol.* 1997;42:255–267.

Sullivan SA, Dailey RA. Complications of laser resurfacing and their management. *Ophthal Plast Reconstr Surg.* 2000;16:417–426.

Cosmetic Uses of Botulinum Toxin

The initial use of botulinum toxin in patients with blepharospasm and hemifacial spasm led to the observation that botulinum toxin reduces or eliminates some facial wrinkles. Use of botulinum toxin type A (Botox Cosmetic) for the treatment of upper facial wrinkles has become widespread, and Botox Cosmetic was approved by the Food and Drug Administration (FDA) in 2002 for use in the glabellar area to reduce or eliminate wrinkles. A number of "bootleg" Botox products are available. However, physicians should recognize the significant medicolegal risk of using a non–FDA-approved substance for injection.

The areas most amenable to neuromodulation, besides the glabella, are the forehead, lateral canthus (crow's-feet), perioral rhytids, and platysmal bands. Use of Botox Cosmetic for cosmetic improvement of areas beyond the glabella is currently considered off-label. The amount of botox required for injection in the forehead and platysmal bands, as well as the location of injection, varies significantly among patients and should be individualized.

The eyebrow can be chemically lifted when botulinum toxin is injected into the depressors of the eyebrow. The corners of the mouth can be elevated when botox is injected into the depressor anguli oris muscle. The onset of action, peak effect, and duration of effect of botulinum toxin for cosmetic purposes are the same as those noted earlier for botulinum toxin as therapy for benign essential blepharospasm. The complications are also the same as those listed for botulinum toxin for blepharospasm.

Upper Face Rejuvenation

Many surgical options are available to the surgeon, but our discussion includes 2 methods commonly used in cosmetic surgery: standard endoscopic brow lift and the pretrichial endoscopic approach.

Endoscopic brow and forehead lift: standard approach

Endoscopic techniques allow the surgeon to raise the brow and rejuvenate the forehead (fore-headplasty) through small incisions approximately 1 cm behind the hairline (Fig 12-22A). An endoscope protected by a hooded sleeve is attached through a fiber-optic light cord to a bright light source. A camera is also attached to the endoscope and is connected in turn to a video monitor. Dissection is accomplished with an endoscopic periosteal elevator, sharp scissors, suction, and monopolar cautery.

Typically, 2 parasagittal incisions are placed behind the hairline approximately 4–5 cm lateral to the midline incision. One 2-cm incision can be placed just posterior to the hairline in the midline, if necessary for dissection. Each of these incisions then is carried down to bone. Subperiosteal dissection is initially performed without the endoscope. A central subperiosteal space, or *optical pocket*, is developed posteriorly to the occiput and anteriorly to 1–2 cm above the superior orbital rim. This allows insertion of the hooded endoscope to complete the dissection in the area of the orbital rim. The supraorbital and supratrochlear neurovascular bundles are visualized and avoided. To eliminate glabellar lines, the surgeon strips the corrugator and procerus muscles or removes them altogether. The central subperiosteal pocket is used to release periosteum along the superior rim, and the temporal pockets allow release of periosteum along the lateral brow. Temporally, incisions are placed 2–3 cm behind and parallel to the hairline in the temporal fossa. Blunt dissection is carried down to the deep temporalis fascia. An ellipse of scalp is excised, and dissection is begun under direct visualization along the deep temporalis fascia. This pocket, deep to the temporoparietal fascia, is enlarged under endoscopic guidance. Dissection along the deep temporalis fascia spares the frontal branch of the facial nerve in the overlying temporoparietal fascia. The central and temporal pockets are joined through release of the conjoint fascia, which is firmly adherent tissue along the temporal lines.

Once elevation is completed, fixation and closure are the final steps. Fixation points are based on the preoperative brow position. Paracentral elevation increases the arch of the brow; central elevation lifts the glabella and medial brows. In the skull, holes are drilled with an appropriate-sized bit. Fixation screws anchor the periosteum to its new position (Fig 12-22B). The temporoparietal fascia is sutured to the deep temporalis fascia, providing temporal brow elevation and a surprising amount of central elevation as well. A suture that does not degrade for at least 6 weeks postoperatively should be used (eg, 3-0 Monocryl by Ethicon), as this appears to be the amount of time necessary to obtain good periosteal fixation. The wounds are closed with surgical staples.

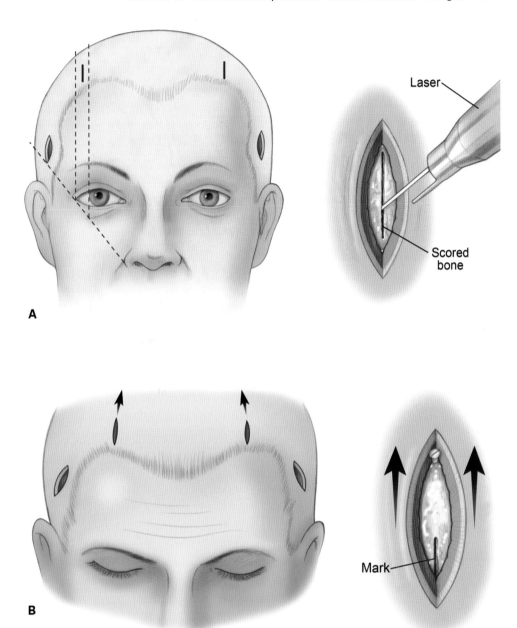

Figure 12-22 Standard endoscopic brow lift. **A,** CO_2 laser is used for incision of scalp and scoring of bone. **B,** The scalp is retracted posteriorly, and the fixation screw is placed at the posterior aspect of the incision. *(Illustrations by Christine Gralapp.)*

Other forms of fixation of the forehead flap are available, such as Tiseel fibrin sealant and Mitek bone anchors. Among the most commonly used devices are the Endotine Forehead soft tissue fixation device (Coapt Systems, Inc, Palo Alto, Calif), bone tunnels, and BioGlue Surgical Adhesive (CryoLife, Inc, Kennesaw, Ga).

Berkowitz RL, Jacobs DI, Gorman PJ. Brow fixation with the endotine forehead device in endoscopic brow lift. *Plast Reconstr Surg.* 2005;116:1761–1770.

Daniel RK, Tirkanits B. Endoscopic forehead lift: an operative technique. *Plast Reconstr Surg.* 1996;98:1148–1157.

Jones BM, Grover R. Endoscopic brow lift: a personal review of 538 patients and comparison of fixation techniques. *Plast Reconstr Surg.* 2004;113:1242–1250.

Putterman AM. *Cosmetic Oculoplastic Surgery.* 3rd ed. Philadelphia: Saunders; 1999.

Sidle DM, Loos BM, Ramirez AL, Kabaker SS, Maas CS. Use of BioGlue surgical adhesive for brow fixation in endoscopic browplasty. *Arch Facial Plast Surg.* 2005;7:393–397.

Endoscopic brow lift: pretrichial approach

The pretrichial approach is used in patients whose hairline is to be raised above 70 mm or in those worried about developing a high hairline. Access occurs through a pretrichial incision instead of the small skin incisions used with the standard approach. Periosteal release is performed endoscopically through incisions in the galea, frontalis muscle, and periosteum. An appropriate amount of forehead skin is resected, and the underlying frontalis and galea are plicated with a subsequent layered closure.

Midface Rejuvenation

The entire midface should be evaluated in a patient presenting for lower eyelid blepharoplasty. With age, cheek tissue descends and orbital fat herniates, creating the double-convexity deformity. Varying degrees of SOOF and midface elevation combined with conservative transconjunctival fat removal or redistribution restore youthful anterior projection of the midface, rendering a single smooth contour to the lower eyelid and midface region. A lower lid approach (infraciliary or transconjunctival) or a combined oral mucosal and temporal endoscopic approach may be used. These techniques of midfacial elevation allow the lower eyelid/midface unit to be fully addressed as part of facial rejuvenation.

SOOF lift: preperiosteal

SOOF lifts are indicated for cosmetic midface rejuvenation as well as for correction of mildly or moderately retracted or ectropic lower lids when anterior lamellar skin shortage is the main problem. In many of these cases, a full-thickness skin graft can be avoided. The elevation can occur in the subperiosteal or preperiosteal plane.

The midface is accessed through a transconjunctival, subciliary, or temporal scalp incision. One approach uses a conjunctival incision (with lateral canthotomy) immediately deep to the inferior tarsal border with dissection down to just below the inferior orbital rim. The orbit is not entered unless orbital fat is to be manipulated. The SOOF is visualized on the anterior maxillary surface (Fig 12-23). This fat is darker yellow and tougher in consistency than orbital fat. An incision is made between the periosteum and SOOF for the entire width of the infraorbital rim. Dissection continues inferiorly in

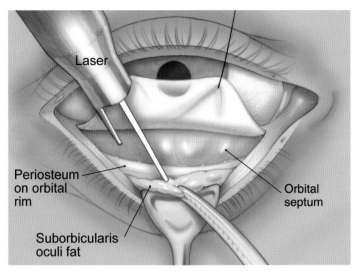

Figure 12-23 Preperiosteal approach to suborbicularis oculi fat (SOOF) lift. *(Illustration by Christine Gralapp.)*

the preperiosteal plane. The SOOF is elevated and secured to the arcus marginalis. The lateral canthal region is reformed and sutured to the lateral orbital rim. The transconjunctival wound can be left open.

Hoenig JA, Shorr N, Shorr J. The suborbicularis oculi fat in aesthetic and reconstructive surgery. *Int Ophthalmol Clin.* 1997;37:179–191.

Midface lift: subperiosteal

A subperiosteal midface lift is done in cases of more severe retraction of the lower eyelid. This lift is also commonly combined with brow lift or lower face-lift and can be done without a lateral canthal incision. The subperiosteal midface can be accessed from the lateral canthus, through a superior gingival sulcus incision so that a visible scar at the lateral canthus can be avoided, or through a temporal scalp incision.

The anterior maxillary surface is approached as discussed previously for the SOOF lift. In cosmetic cases, access is typically through a combined temporal scalp incision and gingival sulcus incision. A transconjunctival incision is also used and, in this case, the periosteum is incised 3–4 mm inferior to the orbital rim, leaving a rim of periosteum from which the cheek SOOF and periosteum will be suspended. A periosteal elevator is used to lift the periosteum from the maxilla and medial zygoma. The infraorbital neurovascular bundle is visualized and spared. Dissection extends to the piriform aperture medially, the superior alveolar ridge inferiorly, and the anterior border of the masseter muscle laterally. The periosteum is released with electrocautery or digital blunt dissection. The end point is a well-mobilized midface. The cheek is secured to the arcus marginalis medially and the intermediate temporalis fascia laterally. This multivector lift corrects the infraorbital depression secondary to SOOF descent and softens the nasolabial fold.

Endoscopic midface lift: subperiosteal

The endoscopic technique is used when significant elevation is needed and the patient has redundant forehead and mid-facial skin. There are 3 major steps. First, a temporal pocket is created as for standard endoscopic brow lifts (Fig 12-24A). Second, the midface is mobilized by subperiosteal dissection via either transconjunctival or superior gingival sulcus oral mucosal incision. The third step is elevation and suspension of the midface to the deep temporalis fascia with sutures passed through the temporal pocket (Fig 12-24B). The oral incision, if used, is closed with 4–0 chromic gut, with the remaining incisions closed as previously described.

Lower Face and Neck Rejuvenation

During preoperative evaluation, the entire face and neck should be considered as a single cosmetic unit. Correction of the cosmetic subunits of the upper and midface without the lower face and neck can create a chronologically out-of-balance appearance that is unacceptable to many patients. At the very least, these concerns must be discussed with the patient preoperatively along with surgical options.

Rejuvenation of the aging face requires a multitude of techniques. Peels, laser resurfacing, dermabrasion, liposculpting, and various other laser treatments can all augment the results following surgical intervention or even preclude incisional intervention.

Rhytidectomy

Credit for the first cosmetic full face-lift is generally given to Lexer, who performed the procedure in 1916. Today, the most common procedures include the classic (subcutaneous) rhytidectomy, the subcutaneous rhytidectomy with the superficial musculoaponeurotic system (SMAS), and the deep plane rhytidectomy. The classic rhytidectomy was the procedure of choice throughout most of the 1970s. The anatomical work of Mitz and Peyronie and the surgical approach of Skoog led surgeons to mobilize and secure the deeper SMAS layer, allowing better skin support and more lasting results. Rhytidectomies typically comprise surgical management of the neck including liposuction with or without platysmaplasty.

The 3 rhytidectomy procedures briefly discussed in this section differ mainly in the location and extent of dissection. Although the more superficial procedures are generally less likely to result in damage to the seventh cranial nerve, they are also less likely to produce lasting improvement and more likely to result in skin scarring. The more extensive procedures are more dangerous (ie, facial nerve injury) but the likelihood that they will produce dramatic, longer-lasting improvement is greater.

Classic (subcutaneous) rhytidectomy The standard face-lift incisions are marked. In men, a pretragal incision is made in the groove; a posttragal incision is generally used in women. The submental incision, if used, is placed 2 mm posterior to the submental crease.

Subcutaneous undermining of the skin is then initiated first with a blade and then with scissors. The more medial dissection can be visualized with direct illumination from a fiber-optic retractor or surgeon's headlight. Once this dissection is finished, attention is turned to the other side, where the same procedure is performed. The skin is then redraped

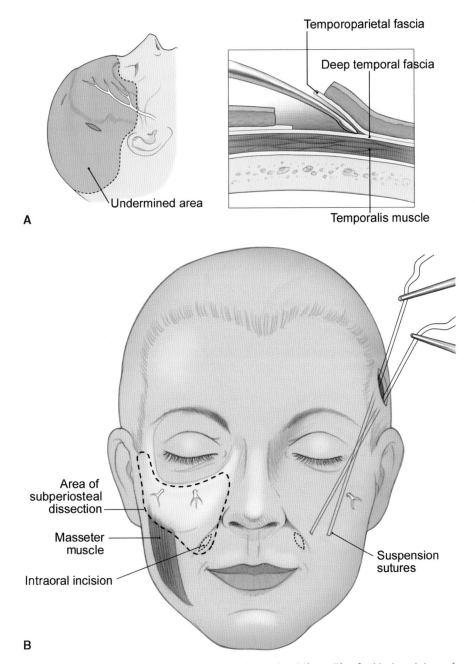

Figure 12-24 Endoscopic approach to subperiosteal midface lift. **A,** Undermining of temporoparietal fascia. **B,** Midface subperiosteal dissection and suture fixation. *(Illustrations by Christine Gralapp.)*

in a posterosuperior manner, and skin resection is initiated. Fixation sutures are placed, but there should be essentially no traction on the flap, particularly the postauricular portion, as it is the most susceptible to necrosis.

Complications of this technique are directly related to the extent of subcutaneous undermining. These complications are hematoma, seroma, skin necrosis, hair loss, paresthesias, motor deficits, incisional scarring, asymmetry, and contour irregularities. Hematoma is the leading face-lift complication, but patient dissatisfaction is the most common problem facing the facial surgeon postoperatively.

Subcutaneous rhytidectomy with SMAS Subcutaneous rhytidectomy with SMAS plication or resection differs from the classic rhytidectomy in that the SMAS is mobilized in some fashion along with subcutaneous dissection (Fig 12-25). Mobilization of the SMAS allows more skin to be repositioned with deep support for a more natural, less surgical appearance. Improvement of jowling and the appearance of the jaw line are enhanced.

Deep plane rhytidectomy The deep plane rhytidectomy also involves mobilization of the SMAS. The extent of SMAS dissection is greater than with the combined technique, but the extent of subcutaneous dissection over the SMAS is less. Dissection is extended to the mandible for greater mobilization. The edge of the SMAS flap is attached to the firm preauricular tissues (Fig 12-26). The lateral platysma in the neck is plicated, and excess skin is resected and closed without tension. Although the deep plane approach is

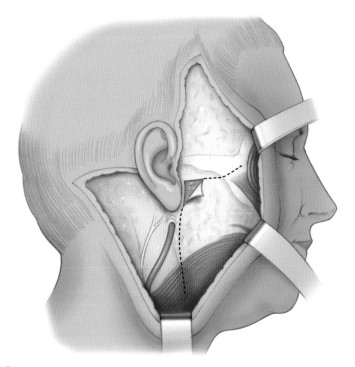

Figure 12-25 Subcutaneous rhytidectomy with superficial musculoaponeurotic system (SMAS). *(Illustration by Christine Gralapp.)*

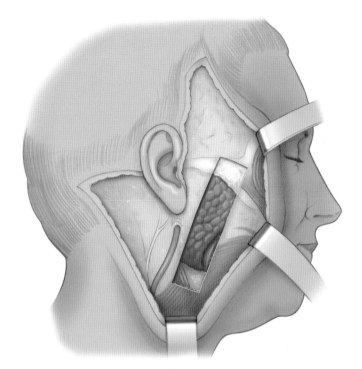

Figure 12-26 Deep plane rhytidectomy. *(Illustration by Christine Gral-app.)*

considered the most surgically demanding, troublesome subcutaneous hematomas occur less frequently.

Neck liposuction

Stab incisions, or *adits,* are made just posterior to the earlobe on each side and just anterior to the central submental crease. Microcannulas allow fat removal (Fig 12-27). A layer of fat is left on the dermis, and the liposuction cannula openings are always oriented away from the dermis to avoid injury to the vascular plexus deep to the dermis. In addition to abnormalities in skin quality, damage in this area can lead to unsightly scarring of the dermis of the underlying neck musculature. The adits are left open, and a compression bandage is worn for 1 week after the procedure.

Platysmaplasty

Platysmaplasty is performed to correct troublesome platysmal bands. A subcutaneous dissection is carried out in the preplatysmal plane centrally under the chin to the level of the thyroid cartilage (Fig 12-28A). As part of a rhytidectomy, lateral platysmal undermining and suspension may be performed. Midline platysma resection (Fig 12-28B) and reconstruction (Fig 12-28C) are performed if midline neck support is needed. A drain and a light compression dressing are placed. Postoperatively, the cervicomental angle is more acute, yielding a more youthful look.

Baker DC. Minimal incision rhytidectomy (short scar face lift) with lateral SMASectomy: evolution and application. *Aesthetic Surg J.* 2001;21:14–26.

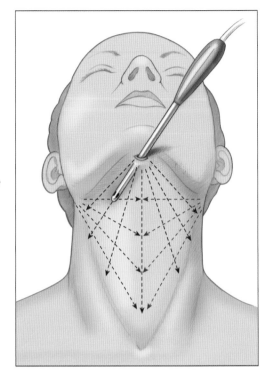

Figure 12-27 Neck liposuction. *(Illustration by Christine Gralapp.)*

Baker TJ, Stuzin JM. Personal technique of face lifting. *Plast Reconstr Surg.* 1997;100:502–508.

Baylis HI, Goldberg RA, Shorr N. The deep plane facelift: a 20-year evolution of technique. *Ophthalmology.* 2000;107:490–495.

Dailey RA, Jones LT. Rejuvenation of the aging face. *Focal Points: Clinical Modules for Ophthalmologists.* San Francisco: American Academy of Ophthalmology; 2003, module 11.

Kamer FM, Frankel AS. Deep plane face-lift for improvement of the lateral oral groove. *Facial Plast Surg Clin North Am.* 1997;5:23–28.

Kamer FM, Halsey W. The two-layer rhytidectomy. *Arch Otolaryngol.* 1981;107:450–453.

Klein JA. *Tumescent Technique: Tumescent Anesthesia & Microcannular Liposuction.* St Louis: Mosby; 2000.

Rees TD. The classic operation. In: Rees TD, LaTrenta GS, eds. *Aesthetic Plastic Surgery.* 2nd ed. Philadelphia: Saunders; 1994:683–707.

Conclusions

The periocular area, where most comprehensive ophthalmologists work, is part of a larger anatomical superstructure called the face. The primary function of this composite entity is communication. Changes that occur through aging, disease, or surgery alter messages transmitted by this entity. If a single subunit is changed without consideration of the other subunits, facial miscommunication, chronologic facial imbalance, and perceptual confusion can result. It is therefore incumbent upon the ophthalmic facial surgeon to understand the aging process, anatomy, and available surgical techniques before embarking

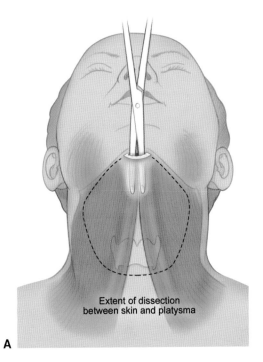

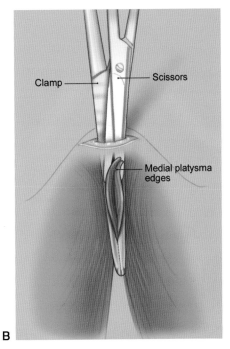

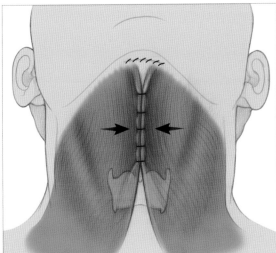

Figure 12-28 Cervicoplasty. **A,** Undermining of the skin. **B,** Resection of medial platysma. **C,** Platysmaplasty. *(Illustrations by Christine Gralapp.)*

on surgery that changes any portion of the face. Discussion of these issues with the patient preoperatively helps prevent patient dissatisfaction postoperatively.

PART III

Lacrimal System

CHAPTER 13

Development, Anatomy, and Physiology of the Lacrimal Secretory and Drainage Systems

Development

Secretory Apparatus

The lacrimal gland develops from multiple solid ectodermal buds in the anterior supero-lateral orbit. These buds branch and canalize, forming ducts and alveoli. The lacrimal glands are small and do not function fully until approximately 6 weeks after birth. This explains why newborn infants do not produce tears when crying.

Excretory Apparatus

By the end of the fifth gestational week, the nasolacrimal groove forms as a furrow lying between the nasal and maxillary prominence (Fig 13-1). In the floor of this groove, the nasolacrimal duct (NLD) develops from a linear thickening of ectoderm. A solid cord separates from adjacent ectoderm and sinks into the mesenchyme. The cord canalizes, forming the NLD and the lacrimal sac at its cranial end. The canaliculi are thought to form similarly from invaginated ectoderm continuous with the distal cord. Caudally, the duct extends intranasally, exiting within the inferior meatus. Canalization is usually complete around the time of birth. Failure of the caudal end to completely canalize results in congenital NLD obstruction. Obstruction at the distal end (the valve of Hasner) is present in approximately 50% of infants at birth. Patency usually occurs spontaneously within the first few months of life. As explained previously, lacrimation does not function normally until 6 weeks, and excessive tearing may not be immediately obvious if an obstruction exists.

Normal Anatomy

Secretory Apparatus

The main lacrimal gland is an exocrine gland located in the superior lateral quadrant of the orbit within the lacrimal gland fossa (Fig 13-2). Embryologic development of the lateral

259

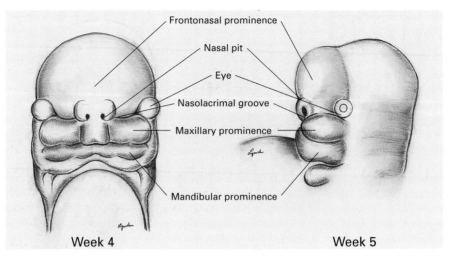

Figure 13-1 The development of the lacrimal drainage system between gestational weeks 4 and 5. *(Illustration by Lynda Van, PharmD.)*

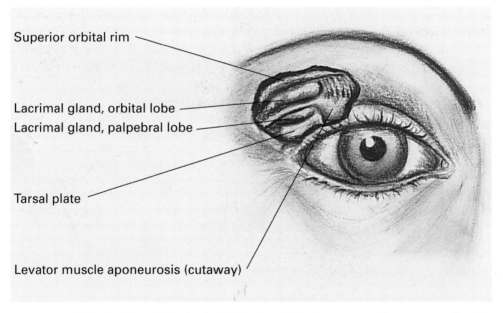

Figure 13-2 Relationship of the lacrimal gland and the levator muscle aponeurosis. The aponeurosis lies between the orbital and palpebral lobes of the lacrimal gland. *(Illustration by Lynda Van, PharmD.)*

horn of the levator aponeurosis indents the lacrimal gland and divides it anteriorly into orbital and palpebral lobes. The superior transverse ligament (Whitnall's ligament) inserts at the division of the 2 lobes, with some fibers also projecting onto the lateral orbital tubercle.

Eight to 12 major lacrimal ducts empty into the superior cul-de-sac approximately 5 mm above the lateral tarsal border after passing posterior to the aponeurosis, through

Müller's muscle, and finally through the conjunctiva. The ducts from the orbital portion run through and join the ducts of the palpebral lobe. Therefore, removal of or damage to the palpebral portion of the gland can seriously reduce secretion from the entire gland. This is the reason that biopsy of the lacrimal gland is generally performed on the orbital lobe.

Ocular surface irritation activates tear production from the lacrimal gland. The ophthalmic branch of the trigeminal nerve provides the sensory *(afferent)* pathway in this reflex tear arc. The *efferent* pathway is more complicated. Parasympathetic fibers, originating in the superior salivary nucleus of the pons, exit the brain stem with the facial nerve, cranial nerve VII (CN VII). Lacrimal fibers then leave CN VII as the greater superficial petrosal nerve and pass to the sphenopalatine ganglion. From there, they are thought to enter the lacrimal gland via the superior branch of the zygomatic nerve, via an anastomosis between the zygomaticotemporal nerve and the lacrimal nerve. Whether the anastomosis between the zygomaticotemporal and lacrimal nerves is uniformly present has been debated. What role, if any, the sympathetic nervous system plays in lacrimation is not well understood.

The accessory exocrine glands of Krause and Wolfring are located deep within the superior fornix and just above the superior border of the tarsus, respectively. Aqueous lacrimal secretion has traditionally been divided into basal low-level secretion and reflex secretion. Previously, it was argued that the accessory glands provided basal tear secretion and the lacrimal gland was responsible for reflex tearing. However, recent evidence suggests that all tearing may be reflex.

The tear film composition is as follows:

- Goblet cells within the conjunctiva provide the inner layer of the tear film by secreting mucin, which allows for even distribution of the tear film over the ocular surface.
- The main and accessory lacrimal gland secretions form the intermediate aqueous layer of the tear film.
- Meibomian glands produce the oily outer layer of the tear film, which reduces the evaporation of the underlying aqueous layer.

See BCSC Section 2, *Fundamentals and Principles of Ophthalmology*, for a more detailed discussion of the tear film.

Excretory Apparatus

The entrance to the lacrimal drainage system is through puncta located medially on the margin of both the upper and the lower eyelids (Fig 13-3). The lower puncta lie slightly farther lateral than the upper puncta. Normally, the puncta are slightly inverted, lying against the globe within the tear lake. Each punctum is surrounded by its respective ampulla, a fleshy elevation oriented perpendicular to the eyelid margin.

Each punctum leads to its respective canaliculus. The canaliculi are lined with non-keratinized, non–mucin-producing stratified squamous epithelium. They run roughly 2 mm vertically, and then turn 90° and run 8–10 mm medially to connect with the lacrimal

sac. In more than 90% of patients, the canaliculi combine to form a single common canaliculus before entering the lateral wall of the lacrimal sac.

The *valve of Rosenmüller* has traditionally been described as the structure that prevents tear reflux from the sac back into the canaliculi. The presence of a mucosal fold was
detected with electron microscopy. This fold (valve of Rosenmüller) presumably functions
as a 1-way valve. Additional studies suggest that the common canaliculus consistently
bends from a posterior to an anterior direction behind the medial canthal tendon before
entering the lacrimal sac at an acute angle. This bend, in conjunction with the fold of
mucosa, may play a role in blocking reflux.

Located in the anterior medial orbit, the lacrimal sac lies within a bony fossa that
is bordered by the anterior and posterior lacrimal crests, to which the medial canthal
tendon attaches. The medial canthal tendon is a complex structure composed of anterior
and posterior crura. The superficial head attaches to the anterior lacrimal crest; the deep
head (Horner's muscle), to the posterior lacrimal crest. The medial wall of the fossa (the
lamina papyracea) is composed of the lacrimal bone posteriorly and the frontal process

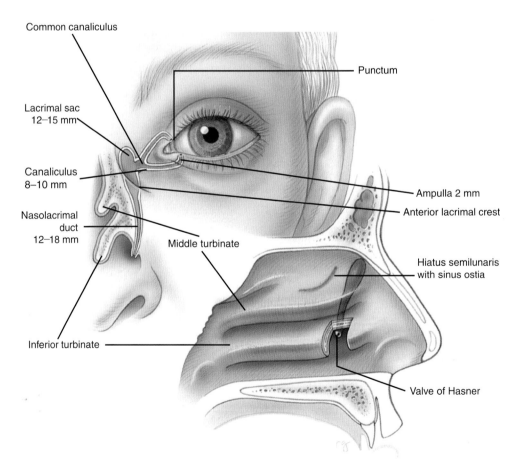

Figure 13-3 Normal anatomy of the lacrimal excretory system. Measurements are for adults. *(Illustration by Christine Gralapp.)*

of the maxilla anteriorly. Medial to the lamina papyracea is the middle meatus of the nose, sometimes with intervening ethmoid cells. The dome of the sac extends several millimeters above the medial canthal tendon. Superiorly, the sac is lined with fibrous tissue. This may explain why, in most cases, lacrimal sac distension extends inferior to the medial canthal tendon. Inferiorly, the lacrimal sac is continuous with the NLD. Additional structures that the surgeon should be aware of when operating in and around the lacrimal sac are the angular artery and vein, which lie 7–8 mm medial to the medial canthal angle and anastomose with the vascular systems of the face and orbit.

The NLD measures 12 mm or more in length. It travels through bone within the nasolacrimal canal, which initially curves in an inferior and slightly lateral and posterior direction. The NLD opens into the nose through an ostium under the inferior

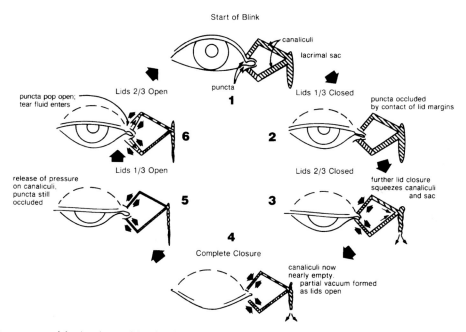

Figure 13-4 Mechanism of lacrimal drainage (Rosengren-Doane). Clockwise from top: *1,* At the start of the blink, the lacrimal drainage passages already contain tear fluid that has entered following the previous blink. *2,* As upper eyelid descends, the papillae containing the punctal openings elevate from the medial lid margin. By the time the upper eyelid has descended halfway, the papillae forcefully meet the opposing lid margin, effectively occluding the puncta and preventing fluid regurgitation. *3,* The remaining portion of lid closure acts to squeeze the canaliculi and sac through the action of the orbicularis oculi, forcing out the contained fluid via the nasolacrimal duct. *4,* At complete eyelid closure, the system is compressed and largely empty of fluid. *5,* At the beginning of the opening phase of a blink, the puncta are still occluded, and valving action at the inner end of canaliculi (and perhaps in the nasolacrimal duct) acts to prevent reentry of fluid or air. Compressive action ends and elastic walls of passages try to expand to their normal shape. This elastic force causes a partial vacuum or suction to form within the canaliculi and sac. *6,* Suction force holding punctal region of eyelid margin together is released when eyelid separation is sufficient. The punctal papillae suddenly pop apart at this point, opening the canaliculi for fluid entry, which occurs during the first few seconds after the blink. *(Modified from Doane MG. Blinking and the mechanics of the lacrimal drainage system. Ophthalmology. 1981;88:850.)*

turbinate (the inferior meatus), which is usually partially covered by a mucosal fold (the valve of Hasner; see Fig 13-3). Failure of this ostium to develop is, in most cases, the cause of congenital NLD obstruction. The exact configuration of the ostium varies, but it is located fairly anteriorly in the inferior nasal meatus, approximately 2.5 cm posterior to the naris.

Physiology

Evaporation accounts for approximately 10% of tear elimination in the young and for 20% or more in the elderly. Most of the tear flow is actively pumped from the tear lake by the actions of the orbicularis muscle. Several variations in the theoretical mechanism of the tear pump have been proposed. In the mechanism described by Rosengren-Doane, the contraction of the orbicularis provides the motive power (Fig 13-4). The contraction is thought to produce positive pressure in the tear sac, forcing tears into the nose. As the eyelids open and move laterally, negative pressure is produced in the sac. This pressure is initially contained by opposition of the eyelids and therefore the puncta. When the eyelids are fully opened, the puncta pop open and the negative pressure draws tears into the canaliculi. A weakened blink interferes with the normal lacrimal pumping mechanism and explains why some patients with partial facial nerve palsies experience epiphora.

CHAPTER **14**

Abnormalities of the Lacrimal Secretory and Drainage Systems

Treatment of lacrimal drainage obstruction differs according to the cause of the obstruction and whether the obstruction involves the puncta, canaliculi, lacrimal sac, or nasolacrimal duct (NLD). Because of differing pathophysiology and management, congenital and acquired abnormalities are addressed separately.

Congenital Lacrimal Drainage Obstruction

Evaluation

The evaluation of congenital tearing is straightforward in most cases: the patient's parents give a history of tearing or mucopurulent discharge (or both) beginning shortly after birth. In rare cases, distension of the sac is present, suggesting a congenital dacryocele. Otherwise, distinction should be made among the following characteristics:

- constant tearing with minimal mucopurulence, which suggests an upper system block caused by punctal or canalicular dysgenesis
- constant tearing with frequent mucopurulence and matting of the lashes, which suggests complete obstruction of the NLD
- intermittent tearing with mucopurulence, which suggests intermittent obstruction of the NLD, most likely the result of impaction of a swollen inferior nasal turbinate, such as in association with an upper respiratory tract infection

Office examination includes inspection of the eyelid margins for open puncta and evaluation for extrinsic causes of reflex hypersecretion, including sources of ocular surface irritation. These causes may include infectious conjunctivitis, epiblepharon, trichiasis, and congenital glaucoma. Inspection of the medial canthal region for a distended lacrimal sac, inflammation, or congenital defects such as an encephalocele is important. However, the single most important maneuver is digital pressure over the tear sac. A dome-shaped distension of the sac suggests congenital obstruction. If mucoid reflux is present, complete obstruction at the level of the NLD becomes the working diagnosis.

Punctal and Canalicular Agenesis and Dysgenesis

The medial eyelid margin should be carefully inspected for the presence of elevated lacrimal papillae. Close evaluation with magnification may reveal a punctum with a membranous occlusion in patients who were initially thought to have complete punctal agenesis. Membranes such as these can usually be opened without difficulty with a sharp probe or medium-caliber needle. Temporary intubation (discussed later in this section) or placement of a silicone plug may help prevent recurrence. If the punctum is truly absent, the surgeon may cut down through the eyelid margin in the expected area of the lateral canaliculus or perform retrograde probing through an open lacrimal sac with direct visualization of the common canalicular opening (common internal punctum). However, punctal agenesis is usually associated with the absence of underlying canalicular tissue. Occasionally, these maneuvers reveal the presence of a relatively mature canalicular system with a patent nasolacrimal sac and duct. In this case, intubation may be performed. Symptomatic patients with a single punctum frequently require surgery to relieve nasolacrimal rather than canalicular obstruction. Complete absence of the punctum and the canalicular system requires a conjunctivodacryocystorhinostomy (CDCR) when the patient is old enough to allow manipulation of and to care for the Jones tube. (CDCR is discussed later in this chapter under Acquired Obstruction.)

Lyons CJ, Rosser PM, Welham RA. The management of punctal agenesis. *Ophthalmology.* 1993;100:1851–1855.

Congenital Nasolacrimal Duct Obstruction

Congenital obstruction of the lacrimal drainage system, which is usually caused by a membranous block of the valve of Hasner covering the nasal end of the NLD, may be present in roughly 50% of newborn infants. Most obstructions open spontaneously within 4–6 weeks after birth. Such an obstruction becomes clinically evident in only 2%–6% of full-term infants at 3–4 weeks of age. Of these, one third have bilateral involvement. Approximately 90% of all symptomatic congenital NLD obstructions resolve in the first year of life.

Numerous management options are available, and they can loosely be divided into conservative (nonsurgical) and surgical. Conservative options include observation, lacrimal sac massage, and topical antibiotics. The long-term use of topical antibiotics may be needed to suppress chronic mucoid discharge with matting of the lashes.

When the obstruction fails to resolve with conservative measures, more invasive intervention may be required. Most often this consists of probing of the NLD in order to rupture a presumptive membrane occluding the NLD at the duct's exit in the nose (discussed in detail later in this chapter). In cases associated with airway obstruction or dacryocystitis, prompt treatment may be required. However, in uncomplicated cases, opinions differ regarding how long clinicians should continue with conservative management before probing.

As stated earlier, most cases of congenital NLD obstruction—including infants with clinical symptoms at 6 months—resolve in the first year of life. Several reports have suggested that delaying probing past 13 months of age may be associated with a decreased success rate. Most likely, the observed lower success rate of probing beyond 1 year was the result of a selection bias. By delaying probing until after 1 year of age, a number of patients resolve spontaneously. If probing were performed in these patients earlier than 1 year of age, these cases would be considered successfully managed with probing. Thus, the perceived success rate of later probing is lowered. Regardless, the more recent trend is for surgeons to observe these patients, with the hope of spontaneous resolution, until the patients approach 1 year of age.

Although the trend has been to perform probing with the patient under sedation if symptoms persist at 1 year of age, some advocate office probing earlier, usually at 6 months of age. In a younger child, probing in the office is more easily performed and topical anesthesia can be used, whereas children aged 1 year or older usually require general anesthesia. Probing with topical anesthetic is inexpensive and relatively safe in well-trained hands. Early office probing avoids the potential for months of mucopurulent discharge, and a visit to the operating room is not necessary. Some advocates of early office probing report that the pain associated with this procedure appears to be about the same as that of an immunization injection.

In some instances of congenital NLD obstruction, dacryocystitis may manifest as an acutely inflamed lacrimal sac with cellulitis of the overlying skin. This possibility should be discussed with the parents so that treatment with systemic antibiotics can be started promptly. Management of the pediatric patient is similar to that of the adult patient (discussed in detail later). Following resolution of the infectious process, elective probing should be performed promptly to prevent recurrence of the dacryocystitis.

Kassoff J, Meyer DR. Early office-based vs late hospital-based nasolacrimal duct probing. A clinical decision analysis. *Arch Ophthalmol.* 1995;113:1168–1171.

Katowitz JA, Welsh MG. Timing of initial probing and irrigation in congenital nasolacrimal duct obstruction. *Ophthalmology.* 1987;94:698–705.

Kushner BJ. Congenital nasolacrimal system obstruction. *Arch Ophthalmol.* 1982;100:597–600.

Kushner BJ. Early office-based vs late hospital-based nasolacrimal duct probing [editorial]. *Arch Ophthalmol.* 1995;113:1103–1104.

Probing and irrigation

Probing is a delicate surgical maneuver that is facilitated by immobilization of the patient and by shrinkage of the nasal mucosa with a topical vasoconstrictor, usually oxymetazoline hydrochloride (Afrin). Some clinicians avoid the use of cocaine in children because of the risk of cardiac toxicity. Others believe that cocaine can be safely administered if the concentration used is no higher than 4% and if it is not used in association with intranasal phenylephrine (Neo-Synephrine) or epinephrine.

When probing, the physician should recall that the upper system begins at the punctum, followed first by a 2-mm vertical segment and then by a horizontal segment of 8–10 mm (canaliculus). Punctal dilation is often needed to safely introduce a small Bowman probe (usually size 00 or smaller). The surgeon initially inserts the probe into the punctum perpendicular to the eyelid margin and then advances it down the canalicular system toward the medial canthal tendon while maintaining lateral traction with the opposite hand. Manual lateral traction of the eyelid straightens the canaliculus and decreases the risk of damage to the canalicular mucosa and creation of a false passage.

Resistance of passage of the probe, along with medial movement of the eyelid soft tissue ("soft stop"), causing wrinkling of the overlying skin, may signify canalicular obstruction. More commonly, resistance is simply due to a kink in the canaliculus created by bunching of the soft tissues in front of the probe tip. When kinking is encountered, withdrawing the probe and maintaining lateral horizontal traction while reprobing eliminate canalicular kinking (Fig 14-1). If the probe advances successfully through the common canalicular system and across the lacrimal sac, the medial wall of the lacrimal sac and adjacent lacrimal bone will be encountered, resulting in a tactile "hard stop."

The probe is then rotated superiorly against the brow until it lies adjacent to the supraorbital notch at the superior orbital rim and then directed posteriorly and slightly laterally as it is advanced down the NLD. If significant resistance is encountered at any point during the probing procedure, the probe should be withdrawn and the procedure attempted again. The distance from the punctum to the level of the inferior meatus in the infant is approximately 20 mm. Direct visualization of the probe tip is usually possible with the use of a nasal speculum and a fiber-optic headlight or endoscope along the lateral wall of the nose approximately 2.5 cm posterior to the naris. If the probe is not visualized, patency of the duct can be confirmed by irrigation with saline mixed with fluorescein. The fluorescein can be retrieved from the inferior meatus and visualized with a transparent suction catheter (Fig 14-2).

A single lacrimal probing is successful in opening a congenital NLD in 90% of patients who are 13 months old or younger. In adults, irrigation and probing are limited to the canalicular system for diagnostic purposes only. Probing of the NLD in adults is potentially traumatic and rarely effective in permanently relieving an obstruction. Merely puncturing the sometimes extensive scar tissue of the NLD only leads to contraction.

Intubation

Intubation is usually performed with a silicone stent and is indicated for children who have recurrent epiphora following nasolacrimal system probing or for older children when initial probing reveals significant stenosis or scarring. Intubation is also useful for

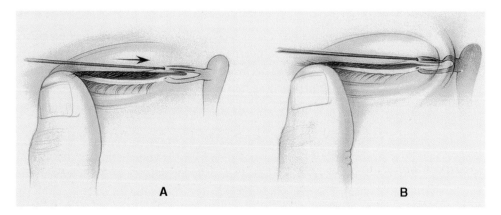

Figure 14-1 **A,** Bowman probe in right upper horizontal canaliculus. **B,** Attempted advancement of Bowman probe at site of canalicular atresia produces wrinkling of skin over the medial canthus. *(Illustration by Christine Gralapp.)*

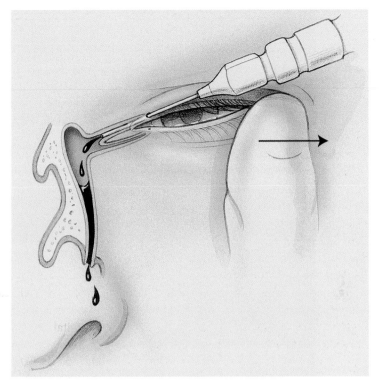

Figure 14-2 Irrigation of the nasolacrimal system. Dye is injected from the syringe, and patency of the system is confirmed by suctioning the dye from the inferior meatus of the nose. *(Illustration by Christine Gralapp.)*

upper system abnormalities such as canalicular stenosis and agenesis of the puncta. Nasolacrimal intubation after failed probing has a reported success rate of 69%–100%.

Many intubation techniques and types of intubation sets have been described. Figure 14-3 illustrates one of the more commonly utilized stents (Crawford stent). Keys to successful intubation include shrinkage of the nasal mucosa with a topical vasoconstrictor and adequate lighting with a fiber-optic headlight. In more difficult cases, an endoscope can be used, and turbinate infracture is sometimes performed. The silicone tubing can be secured by a simple square knot that allows removal of the tube through the canalicular system in a retrograde fashion. Alternatively, the silicone stent may be directly sutured to the lateral wall of the nose, or the limbs of the stent can be passed through either a silicone band or a sponge in the inferior meatus of the nose. These techniques allow the stent to be retrieved through the nose. Monocanalicular stents are also available (Fig 14-4). The monocanalicular stent is passed through a single punctum to the nasal cavity, where the end of the stent is simply cut and allowed to retract loosely into the nose. The proximal end has a smooth barb and is self-secured at the punctum. The monocanalicular stent is useful when the patient has only 1 patent canaliculus.

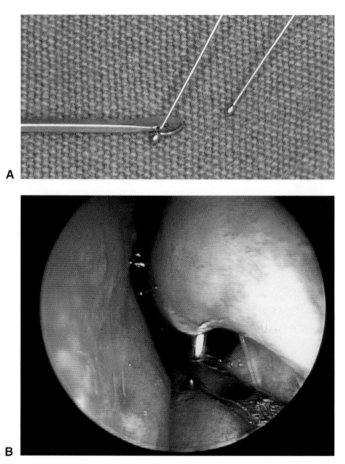

Figure 14-3 Crawford stent and hook. **A,** Hook engaging "olive tip" of stent. **B,** Intranasal view of engaged hook retrieving the stent. *(Reproduced with permission from Nerad JA.* The Requisites in Ophthalmology: Oculoplastic Surgery. *Philadelphia: Mosby; 2001:233.)*

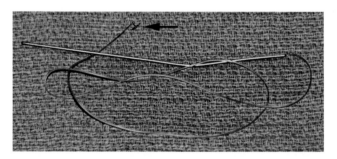

Figure 14-4 Monocanalicular stent. The metal probe is used as a guide during placement of the stent and allows the stent to be retrieved within the nasal passage. Tension can therefore be applied, aiding in soft tissue approximation. At the proximal end is a soft barb and collarette, which secure the stent within the punctum *(arrow)*. *(Courtesy of Timothy J. McCulley, MD.)*

Balloon dacryoplasty

Balloon catheter dilation of the nasolacrimal canal has been used successfully in congenital nasolacrimal obstruction. A collapsed balloon catheter is placed in a manner similar to probing and inflated inside the duct at multiple levels. Balloon dacryoplasty has reported success rates ranging from roughly 80% to 100%. Although these results seem promising, the role of this modality remains undefined in part because the necessary catheter equipment is expensive and simple probing has such a high success rate. Thus, balloon dacryoplasty is now generally limited to complicated cases or to recurrence following standard probing techniques.

Turbinate infracture

If the inferior turbinate seems to be impacted on the nasolacrimal duct at the time of probing and irrigation, medial infracturing of the inferior turbinate should be performed. This condition should be suspected in patients whose symptoms appear primarily related to upper respiratory tract infections, when swelling of the mucosa over the turbinate may cause intermittent obstruction of the inferior meatus. This procedure is most commonly performed as follows. The blunt end of a periosteal elevator is placed within the inferior meatus along the lateral surface of the inferior turbinate. The inferior turbinate is then rotated medially toward the septum (Fig 14-5). Fracturing the turbinate at its base

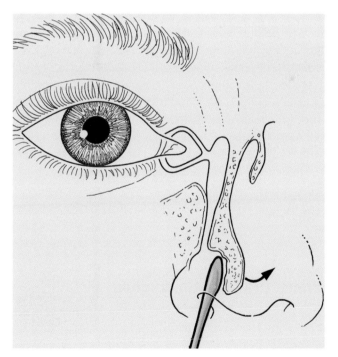

Figure 14-5 Infracture of inferior turbinate. A periosteal elevator is slipped into the inferior meatus and, using the lateral wall of the nose as a fulcrum, the elevator is pushed medially, fracturing the turbinate easily and creating a larger space for the exit of tears from the nasolacrimal duct. *(From Nerad JA. The Requisites in Ophthalmology: Oculoplastic Surgery. Philadelphia: Mosby; 2001:229.)*

significantly enlarges the inferior meatus and permits direct visualization of the lacrimal probe tip.

Wesley RE. Inferior turbinate fracture in the treatment of congenital nasolacrimal duct obstruction and congenital nasolacrimal duct anomaly. *Ophthalmic Surg.* 1985;16(6):368–371.

Dacryocystorhinostomy

Dacryocystorhinostomy (DCR) is usually reserved for children who have persistent epiphora following intubation and balloon dacryoplasty and for patients with extensive developmental abnormalities of the nasolacrimal drainage system that prevent probing and intubation. The details of DCR are discussed later in this chapter under Acquired Obstruction.

Mucoceles

Mucoceles may form within the lacrimal sac or within the nasal cavity as a consequence of congenital NLD obstruction. By definition, a mucocele is a mucous cyst, a mucous polypus, or a retention cyst of the lacrimal sac, paranasal sinuses, appendix, or gallbladder. Lacrimal sac distention, a type of mucocele, has been termed a *dacryocystocele* (Fig 14-6). It occurs when the NLD is obstructed and amniotic fluid or mucus (secreted by lacrimal sac goblet cells) is trapped in the tear sac. The dacryocystocele is initially sterile and may respond to conservative management with prophylactic topical antibiotics and massage. If there is no response in 1–2 weeks or if infection develops, probing of the lacrimal drainage system may be needed. Distention of the nasal mucosa into the nasal cavity at the level of an occluded valve of Hasner may also occur. These *nasal mucoceles* often extend inferiorly under the inferior turbinate, where they can be observed during nasal examination. Excision or marsupialization of the prolapsed distended duct with nasal endoscopy is often necessary. Urgent treatment may be needed if the condition is bilateral and causes airway obstruction.

In most cases, dacryocystoceles expand inferior to the medial canthal tendon. Congenital swelling above the medial canthal tendon, especially in the midline, should suggest alternate, often more serious, etiologies, such as a meningoencephalocele or dermoid. Proper imaging with computed tomography (CT) or magnetic resonance (MR) is mandatory to evaluate the patient for these more complex diagnoses.

Mansour AM, Cheng KP, Mumma JV, et al. Congenital dacryocele: a collaborative review. *Ophthalmology.* 1991;98:1744–1751.

Paysse EA, Coats DK, Bernstein JM, Go C, de Jong AL. Management and complications of congenital dacryocele with concurrent intranasal mucocele. *J AAPOS.* 2000;4:46–53.

Acquired Lacrimal Drainage Obstruction

Evaluation

History

Tearing patients can be loosely divided into 2 groups:

1. Those with hypersecretion of tears (lacrimation)
2. Those with impairment of drainage (epiphora)

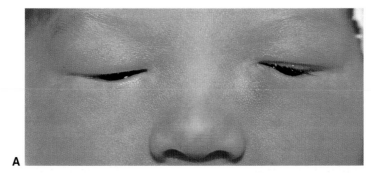

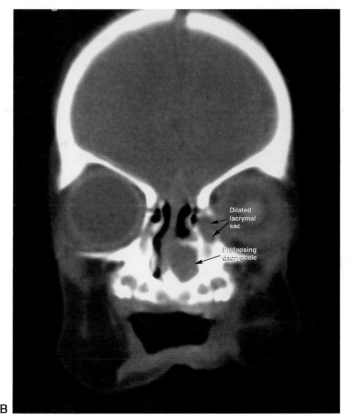

Figure 14-6 **A,** Left congenital dacryocystocele 1 week postpartum. **B,** Computed tomographic scan of a congenital dacryocele. *(Courtesy of Pierre Arcand, MD.)*

The initial step in evaluating the tearing patient is distinguishing the 2 conditions. The following list can help guide the examiner in the assessment of the patient with tearing:

- constant versus intermittent tearing
- periods of remission, or lack of
- unilateral condition or bilateral condition
- subjective ocular surface discomfort

- history of allergies
- use of topical medications
- probing as a child
- prior ocular surface infections
- prior sinus disease or surgery, midfacial trauma, or a nasal fracture
- previous episodes of lacrimal sac inflammation
- clear tears versus tears with discharge or blood (blood in the tear meniscus may indicate malignancy)

Examination

Systematic examination helps pinpoint the cause of tearing. Similar to taking the patient's history, the initial step of the examination is to distinguish patients with lacrimal drainage system obstruction and true epiphora from those with secondary hypersecretion.

Pseudoepiphora evaluation *Epiphora* is defined as overflow tearing. Some patients perceive their eyes as having too many tears but do not exhibit frank epiphora. These sensations are often caused by other ocular or eyelid abnormalities. For example, patients with dry eye may perceive foreign-body sensation or increased mucous production as excess tearing, but in reality they do not exhibit true overflow of tears over the lid margin or down the cheek. In assessing pseudoepiphora, the ophthalmologist should consider the following.

TEAR MENISCUS The size of the lacrimal lake as well as the presence of precipitated proteins and stringy mucus may indicate an abnormal tear film.

TEAR BREAKUP TIME The mucin layer of the tear film helps spread the other layers evenly over the corneal surface. This can be observed best after fluorescein has been placed in the conjunctival cul-de-sac. The patient is asked to open his or her eyes and refrain from blinking. The ophthalmologist then examines the tear film using a broad beam of the slit lamp. The normal time before breakup should be at least 15 seconds. Tear breakup in a rapid range (<10 sec) may indicate poor function of the mucin layer despite a sufficient amount of tears.

CORNEAL AND CONJUNCTIVAL EPITHELIUM EVALUATION Topical rose bengal detects subtle ocular surface abnormalities by staining devitalized conjunctival and corneal epithelium. Fluorescein staining in the inferior third of the cornea indicates more severe tear film malfunction with epithelial loss.

SCHIRMER I This test measures tear secretion. A strip of filter paper is placed without anesthetic in the inferior cul-de-sac for 5 minutes, and the amount of wetting is recorded. The normal amount is approximately 15 mm. Hypersecretion is considered when the filter strip is rapidly inundated with tears. However, excess secretion may occur in response to the irritation from the measuring strips themselves. Serial testing should be performed to confirm this assumption. Schirmer I is one of several variations of the Schirmer test; some clinicians prefer the basic Schirmer test (measured after instillation of a topical anesthetic drop), finding it more useful in determining tear production deficiency. See also BCSC Section 8, *External Disease and Cornea,* for further discussion of tear film abnormalities.

Patients should also be evaluated for mechanical irritation of the cornea. Corneal irritation from contact with eyelashes is a common cause of ocular irritation and secondary lacrimation. This can be seen in the setting of misdirected eyelashes (trichiasis) or eyelid malposition (entropion). Other ocular irritants include allergy; chronic infection, as seen, for example, with Chlamydia or Molluscum; and contact lens–related disease such as giant papillary conjunctivitis. Careful examination of the palpebral conjunctiva can aid in the identification of many such disorders.

Lacrimal outflow evaluation

Abnormal lacrimal outflow may result from problems in any number of structures. With eyelid malposition, tears might not have access to the puncta. Careful attention should be given to the eyelid and in particular the position of the puncta. Slit-lamp examination during the blink cycle may be needed to determine whether the punctum is properly positioned within the tear lake. Facial nerve dysfunction can result in a weakened or incomplete blink and may explain poor lacrimal pump function. Caruncular hypertrophy and conjunctival prolapse can also occlude the puncta, and the patient should be evaluated for these conditions. Punctal stenosis, occlusion, or aplasia can be present.

Lacrimal sac evaluation can be invaluable. Palpation with pressure on a distended lacrimal sac may cause reflux of mucoid or mucopurulent material through the canalicular system. This reflux confirms complete NLD obstruction, and no further diagnostic tests are needed if a lacrimal sac tumor is not suspected.

Routine nasal examination may uncover an unsuspected cause of the epiphora, such as an intranasal tumor, turbinate impaction, or chronic allergic rhinitis. These conditions may occlude the nasal end of the NLD.

Diagnostic tests

The clinical evaluation of the lacrimal drainage system was originally outlined by Lester Jones. Evaluation was in the form of a dye disappearance test followed by a Jones I and Jones II test. By using this sequence (with modifications) as a guide, the physician can frequently streamline diagnostic testing.

The *dye disappearance test (DDT)* is useful for assessing the presence or absence of adequate lacrimal outflow, especially in unilateral cases. It is more heavily relied upon in children, in whom lacrimal irrigation is impossible without deep sedation. Using a drop of sterile 2% fluorescein solution or a moistened fluorescein strip, the examiner instills fluorescein into the conjunctival fornices of each eye and then observes the tear film, preferably with the cobalt blue filter of the slit lamp. Persistence of significant dye and, particularly, asymmetric clearance of the dye from the tear meniscus over a 5-minute period indicate an obstruction. Bilateral delayed dye disappearance is illustrated in Figure 14-7. If the DDT result is normal, severe lacrimal drainage dysfunction is highly unlikely. However, intermittent causes of tearing such as allergy, dacryolith, or intranasal obstruction cannot be ruled out.

Wright MM, Bersani TA, Frueh BR, Musch DC. Efficacy of the primary dye test. *Ophthalmology.* 1989;96:481–483.

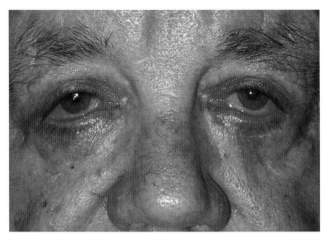

Figure 14-7 Dye disappearance test. *(Courtesy of Timothy J. McCulley, MD, and Robert C. Kersten, MD.)*

Table 14-1 **Results of Primary and Secondary Jones Tests**

Result		Interpretations
Jones I		
	Dye retrieved in nose	Patent system, probably normal physiological function
	Dye not retrieved in nose	False negative *or* physiological dysfunction, anatomic obstruction
Jones II		
	Dye in nose	Partial block at lower sac or duct
	Saline in nose	Punctal or canalicular stenosis or physiological dysfunction
	Regurgitation at opposite punctum with dye	Complete nasolacrimal duct obstruction
	Regurgitation at opposite punctum without dye	Complete common canaliculus obstruction

Modified from Stewart WB, ed. *Surgery of the Eyelid, Orbit, and Lacrimal System.* Ophthalmology Monograph 8, vol 3. San Francisco: American Academy of Ophthalmology; 1995:261.

The Jones I and Jones II tests have historically been used in the evaluation of epiphora. Table 14–1 shows the results obtained with both types of tests. Like the DDT, the *Jones I test,* or *primary dye test,* investigates lacrimal outflow under normal physiologic conditions. The examiner instills fluorescein into the conjunctival fornices and recovers it in the inferior nasal meatus by passing a cotton-tipped wire applicator into the region of the ostium of the NLD at 2 and 5 minutes. As this test occasionally yields abnormal results in normal patients, it is not uniformly performed.

The nonphysiologic *Jones II test* determines the presence or absence of fluorescein in the irrigating saline fluid retrieved from the nose. This test is performed as follows. The residual fluorescein is flushed from the conjunctival sac following an unsuccessful Jones I test. This is done so that the examiner can determine whether any reflux upon irrigation contains fluorescein. Irrigation of the lacrimal drainage system is performed with clear saline, which is retrieved from the inner aspect of the nose. Although some clinicians continue to use and rely on formal Jones testing, most have found retrieving the irrigating fluid from the nose to be technically difficult and have abandoned the test, proceeding instead with a simplified approach.

Lacrimal drainage system irrigation is most frequently performed immediately after a DDT to determine the level of lacrimal drainage system occlusion (Fig 14-8). After instillation of topical anesthesia, the lower eyelid punctum is dilated and any punctal stenosis noted. The irrigating cannula is placed in the canalicular system. To prevent canalicular kinking and difficulty in advancing the irrigating cannula, the clinician maintains lateral traction of the lower eyelid (see Fig 14-1). Canalicular stenosis or occlusion should be noted and confirmed by subsequent diagnostic probing. Once the irrigating cannula has been advanced into the horizontal canaliculus, clear saline is injected and the results noted. Careful observation and interpretation determine the area of obstruction without additional testing.

Difficulty advancing the irrigating cannula and an inability to irrigate fluid suggest *total canalicular obstruction.* If saline can be irrigated successfully but it refluxes through the upper canalicular system, and if no distension of the lacrimal sac is noted with palpation, *complete blockage of the common canaliculus* is suggested (Fig 14-9). Subsequent probing determines whether the common canalicular stenosis is total or whether it can be dilated. If mucoid material or fluorescein refluxes through the opposite puncta with possible palpable lacrimal sac distension, then the diagnosis is *complete NLD obstruction.* If saline irrigation is not associated with canalicular reflux or fluid passing down the NLD, then inflation of the lacrimal sac with significant patient discomfort will occur. This result confirms a complete NLD obstruction with a functional valve of Rosenmüller preventing reflux through the canalicular system. A combination of saline reflux through the opposite canaliculus and saline irrigation through the NLD into the nose may indicate a *partial NLD stenosis.*

If saline irrigation passes freely into the nose with no reflux through the canalicular system, a *patent nasolacrimal drainage system* is present. However, it is important to note that even though this irrigation is successful under a nonphysiological condition such as increased hydrostatic pressure on the irrigating saline, a *functional obstruction* may still be present. A dacryolith may also impair tear flow without blocking irrigation.

Diagnostic probing of the upper system (puncta, canaliculi, lacrimal sac) is useful in confirming the level of obstruction. In adults, this procedure can easily be performed with topical anesthesia. A small probe (00) should be used initially to detect any canalicular obstruction. If an obstruction is encountered, the probe is clamped at the punctum before withdrawal, thereby measuring the distance to the obstruction. A large probe may be useful to determine the extent of a partial obstruction, but the probe should not be forced through any area of resistance.

Diagnostic probing of the NLD has no place in adults because there are other means of diagnosing NLD obstruction. Also, probing in adults has limited therapeutic value, rarely producing lasting patency. In contrast, probing in infants is a useful and largely successful procedure. This reflects the differing pathophysiologies of congenital and acquired NLD obstruction, with the former often resulting from a thin membrane occluding the NLD and the latter from more extensive fibrosis of the duct itself.

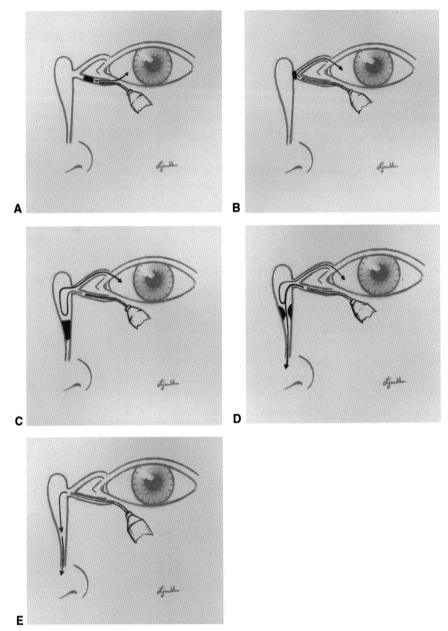

Figure 14-8 Lacrimal drainage system irrigation. **A,** Complete canalicular obstruction. The cannula is advanced with difficulty, and irrigation fluid refluxes from the same canaliculus. **B,** Complete common canalicular obstruction. A "soft stop" is encountered at the level of the lacrimal sac, and irrigated fluid refluxes through the opposite punctum. **C,** Complete nasolacrimal duct obstruction. The cannula is easily advanced to the medial wall of the lacrimal sac, "hard stop," and irrigation fluid refluxes through the opposite punctum. Often, the refluxed fluid contains mucus and/or purulence. With an intact valve of Rosenmüller, lacrimal sac distension without reflux of irrigation fluid may be encountered. **D,** Partial nasolacrimal duct obstruction. The cannula is easily placed, and irrigation fluid passes into the nose as well as refluxes through the opposite punctum. **E,** Patent lacrimal drainage system. The cannula is placed with ease, and most of the irrigation fluid passes into the nose. *(Illustration by Lynda Van, PharmD.)*

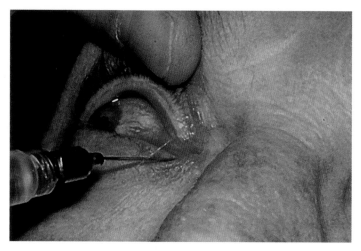

Figure 14-9 Reflux from opposite canaliculus caused by common canalicular obstruction. *(Courtesy of Robert C. Kersten, MD.)*

Nasal endoscopy allows for direct visualization of the lacrimal passages. Diagnostic endoscopy takes only a few minutes to perform and is helpful in the evaluation of the nasal anatomy and in the identification of disease processes. Endoscopy can be performed prior to surgical correction of NLD obstruction, particularly if direct visualization is difficult.

Contrast dacryocystography and *dacryoscintigraphy* aid in the evaluation of the anatomy and function of the lacrimal drainage system. They are used infrequently these days, primarily because alternate methods of evaluation are available such as simple irrigation and modern imaging techniques (CT and MRI). Also, they are not uniformly available at all institutions. Descriptions of contrast dacryocystography and dacryoscintigraphy are included here because these techniques are historically significant and because knowledge of them underscores an understanding of the normal lacrimal drainage system.

Contrast dacryocystography can add useful information by radiologically defining the lacrimal sac anatomy. Radiopaque dye is injected into the canalicular systems on 1 or both sides and is followed by imaging. Films taken at 10 minutes show any delay in drainage. Computerized digital subtraction improves imaging of the lacrimal system by removing the images of the surrounding bones (Fig 14-10). This information is especially helpful in determining the level of blockage, checking the extent of lacrimal sac maldevelopment, or detecting tumors. However, it is not helpful in determining lacrimal drainage physiology.

Dacryoscintigraphy, using gamma ray–emitting radionuclides such as technetium-99, can be used to evaluate the physiological flow of tears when true obstruction is difficult to differentiate from eyelid problems or other causes (Fig 14-11). A drop of radionuclide tracer technetium-99m in saline or technetium sulfur colloid is instilled in the conjunctival cul-de-sac, followed by imaging of the lacrimal system with a scintigram. Scintigraphy is useful in patients who show contradictory or inconsistent results with lacrimal drainage system irrigation but have a strong history of epiphora. Because the test is performed under normal physiological conditions, a functional obstruction can be determined more

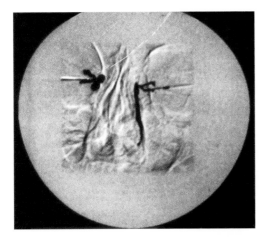

Figure 14-10 Computerized digital subtraction dacryocystogram in a patient with unilateral epiphora after facial trauma. Right lacrimal sac is dilated, and obstruction is visible at the sac–duct junction. The left side shows lacrimal system of normal caliber. *(Reproduced by permission from Stewart WB, ed. Surgery of the Eyelid, Orbit, and Lacrimal System. Ophthalmology Monograph 8, vol. 3. San Francisco: American Academy of Ophthalmology; 1995:262.)*

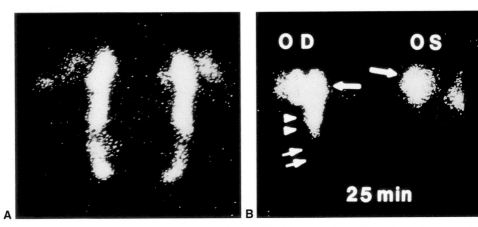

Figure 14-11 **A,** Normal lacrimal scintigraphy. **B,** Total nasolacrimal duct obstruction on the left (OS) with partial obstruction on the right (OD). *Arrows* = lacrimal sac. *(Courtesy of Robert C. Kersten, MD.)*

accurately. However, dacryoscintigraphy does not provide the fine anatomical detail as visualized with contrast dacryocystography.

Computed tomography and *magnetic resonance imaging* are useful following craniofacial injury, in congenital craniofacial deformities, or for suspected neoplasia. CT is superior in the evaluation of suspected bony abnormalities, such as fractures. It also allows for assessment of the position of the cribriform plate, thereby helping avoid injury and subsequent cerebrospinal fluid leak at the time of surgery. MRI is superior in the evaluation of suspected soft tissue disease, such as malignancy. Either CT or MRI may be helpful in evaluating concomitant sinus or nasal disease that may contribute to excess tearing.

Guzek JP, Ching AS, Hoang T-A, et al. Clinical and radiologic lacrimal testing in patients with epiphora. *Ophthalmology.* 1997;104:1875–1881.

Punctal Conditions

Several punctal abnormalities can result in epiphora. These include puncta that are too small (occlusion and stenosis) or too big (usually iatrogenic); and puncta that are malpositioned or occluded by adjacent structures.

Punctal stenosis and occlusion occur in numerous settings such as the following: congenital (discussed in more detail under Developmental Abnormalities), inflammatory (Stevens-Johnson syndrome or pemphigoid), infectious (herpetic), and iatrogenic (deliberate occlusion in the treatment of dry eye disease). Punctal stenosis may be treated by dilation, punctoplasty, or stenting. Most often the benefits of dilation are short-lived and punctoplasty is required. This is usually performed with a snip procedure, in which a small portion of the ampulla is excised. When stenosis recurs, stenting may be required during healing to prevent contraction. Treatment of complete occlusion consists of surgical canalization and, in most cases, stenting.

Abnormally large puncta can also cause epiphora, although this is somewhat counterintuitive. In this case, epiphora is thought to be the result of disruption of the lacrimal pump. The expanded opening prevents formation of an adequate seal when the eyes are closed. This in turn prevents formation of negative pressure, and suctioning of the tears does not occur. Punctal enlargement is almost exclusively the result of iatrogenic injury. Stenting of the lacrimal drainage system can result in "cheese-wiring" of the puncta and adjacent canaliculi. Therefore, patients with stents in place require periodic monitoring. Stents should be removed when punctal deformation is detected. Punctal enlargement can also result from overly aggressive punctoplasty and occasionally results from excision of adjacent neoplasms. Damage to the puncta should be avoided because no uniformly effective treatment is available. Attempts at reconstruction usually fail, leaving a CDCR as the only reasonable alternative. Fortunately, symptoms are rarely severe enough to necessitate performing this procedure.

In order to drain, tears must have access to the puncta. This access can be disrupted by a punctum that is malpositioned, such that the punctum no longer lies within the tear lake. In cases of epiphora secondary to punctal malposition, the anatomical abnormality must be corrected. Medial ectropion repair by resection of a horizontal ellipse of conjunctival and subconjunctival connective tissue below the punctum, with reapposition of the edges, rotates the punctum inward into the tear lake. This procedure may be combined with horizontal eyelid tightening if laxity is present. Frequently, punctal stenosis coexists and may require a punctoplasty.

Puncta may also become obstructed or malpositioned by adjacent structures, either a hypertrophied caruncle or conjunctiva (conjunctivochalasis). In most cases, this is easily corrected with excision of the abnormal caruncle or conjunctiva.

Canalicular Obstruction

Evaluation

Obstruction can occur within the common, upper, or lower canaliculus. Diagnostic canalicular probing may uncover a canalicular obstruction. *Partial obstruction* may be discovered during lacrimal system irrigation with partial fluid flow into the nose and partial reflux. *Total common canalicular obstruction* is characterized by flow from the lower to the upper canaliculus with no flow into the lacrimal sac during lacrimal system irrigation. After insertion, the lacrimal probe advances only about 8 mm from the punctum before encountering a tactile soft stop: the probe cannot be advanced beyond the total common canalicular obstruction. In normal conditions, a hard stop would be reached when the probe successfully passes through the open canalicular system into the lumen of the lacrimal sac and finally encounters the medial lacrimal sac and lacrimal bone. When common canalicular obstruction is present, lacrimal system irrigation results in a high-velocity reflux from the adjacent canaliculus (see Fig 14-9).

The clinician should keep in mind that what appears to be a partial obstruction may sometimes be a *total functional occlusion*. This can be seen with weakness of the lacrimal pump or inability of tears to pass through the partial obstruction under normal physiological conditions. Some functional obstructions may be overcome with irrigation by the creation of an abnormally high hydrostatic pressure.

Etiology

Lacrimal plugs Punctal and canalicular plugs come in a variety of shapes and sizes. As discussed in detail in this section, they are designed to obstruct the lacrimal outflow in the treatment of dry eye disease. Although any type of plug can result in obstruction, this is most commonly seen with a specific variety of canalicular plug, Herrick, which is placed deep within the canaliculus. Punctal plugs that are too small may migrate within the canaliculi and also result in obstruction. Even the temporary or absorbable variety has been known to result in a local inflammatory response and canalicular constriction. Canalicular probing is diagnostic. High-frequency ultrasound has also been used to identify silicone plugs causing obstructions within canaliculi. Once identified, the problematic plug can usually be surgically excised. Often, excision of a short segment of scarred canaliculus is required. The canaliculus is then repaired with reanastomosis over a stent. This technique is similar to reconstruction following trauma or after injury of the canaliculus during excision of a neoplasm.

White WL, Bartley GB, Hawes MJ, Linberg JV, Leventer DB. Iatrogenic complications related to the use of Herrick Lacrimal Plugs. *Ophthalmology.* 2001;108(10):1835–1837.

Medication Medications can occasionally cause canalicular obstruction. This is most often encountered with systemic chemotherapeutic agents (5-fluorouracil, docetaxel, idoxuridine). These drugs are secreted in the tears, and this results in inflammation and scarring of the canaliculi. If this condition is identified early—before the obstruction is complete—stents can be placed to stretch constricted canaliculi and also prevent progression while the patient completes his or her course of chemotherapy. Canalicular obstruction has also been reported to follow the use of topical medication (phospholine iodide, eserine), although this is less common.

Infection Numerous infections can cause canalicular obstruction. Most often obstruction occurs in the setting of more diffuse conjunctival infection (vaccinia virus, herpes simplex virus). Isolated canalicular infection (canaliculitis; discussed later) can similarly result in obstruction.

Inflammatory disease Inflammatory conditions such as pemphigoid, Stevens-Johnson syndrome, and graft-vs-host disease often cause loss of the puncta and/or canaliculi. However, because of concurrent dry eye disease, patients often do not suffer from epiphora.

Trauma Traumatic injury to the canaliculi can result in permanent damage if the injury is not managed appropriately soon after it occurs. This is discussed further in the section specifically addressing trauma.

Neoplasm When a neoplasm is present in the medial canthal area, complete resection may also include removal of the puncta and canaliculi. Complete tumor excision must be ascertained by histopathologic examination of excised tissue before connection of the lacrimal drainage system with the middle meatus is considered. When the distal lacrimal drainage system remains intact, the remaining portion of the canaliculi may be marsupialized to the conjunctival surface with or without intubation.

Management

Canalicular stenting *Intubation* or *stenting* of the lacrimal drainage system should be considered as first line therapy whenever possible. With symptomatic canalicular constriction but not occlusion, intubation of the nasolacrimal drainage system can usually be successfully performed.

Reconstruction Reconstruction of an obstructed canaliculus is often successful when only a few millimeters are involved. If a limited area of total occlusion is discovered near the punctum, the occluded canaliculus can be resected and the cut ends of the canaliculus anastomosed over a stent. When a focal obstruction is found distally or within the common canaliculus, trephining of the scarred segment establishes a patent lumen. Stenting is then required to prevent contracture and also to provide a scaffolding to direct proper epithelialization. Also, with removal of a punctal or canalicular plug, a small segment of scarred canaliculus is often excised, followed by reconstruction over a stent.

Canaliculodacryocystorhinostomy If obstruction is total at the common canaliculus, a canaliculodacryocystorhinostomy may be performed. In this procedure, the area of total common canalicular obstruction is removed and the remaining patent canalicular system is directly anastomosed to the lacrimal sac mucosa. Use of a silicone stent for the reconstructed canalicular system is an important part of this type of reconstruction. Because the failure rate of canalicular resection surgery for total obstruction is significant, Jones tube placement is a surgical alternative.

Conjunctivodacryocystorhinostomy When 1 or both canaliculi are severely obstructed, a conjunctivodacryocystorhinostomy (CDCR) may be required. This procedure is a complete bypass of the lacrimal drainage system. A CDCR is indicated when the canalicular abnormality is too severe and the canalicular system therefore cannot be used in the reconstruction of the tear outflow apparatus. A Pyrex glass (Jones tube) is placed through an opening created at the inferior half of the caruncle and then through an osteotomy site into the middle nasal meatus. A partial carunculectomy may need to be performed to prevent obstruction of the tube. The ocular end of the tube must be situated in the tear lake, whereas the nasal end must clear the anterior end of the middle turbinate. Subtotal resections of the anterior middle turbinate may be necessary. Different lengths of these tubes should be available at the time of surgery to obtain a tube that emerges clearly in the nose without abutting the nasal septum.

Postoperative care and complications, including obstruction of the tube with mucus and migration of the tube, can be troublesome. Forced inspiration, with the mouth and nose manually closed, creates significant airflow through the tube into the nasal airway and usually clears mucous debris and prevents obstruction. Patients should be instructed to perform this maneuver daily. They should also be informed that loss of the tube, even if only for a few days, may cause significant closure of the soft tissue tract of the Jones tube. Periodic removal and cleaning of the Jones tube in the office, followed by immediate replacement, may be needed. Jones tubes themselves often cause chronic foreign-body sensation and mucous production and may incite pyogenic granuloma formation. Despite these drawbacks, many patients with otherwise intractable epiphora are helped by this procedure. In patients who have problems with recurrent migration or loss of the tube, a frosted Jones tube (Weiss Scientific Glass Blowing Company, Portland, Ore) can be placed. There is also the Medpor-coated tube (Porex Corporation, Newnan, Ga), which allows for ingrowth of fibrous tissue into its outer covering. This ingrowth secures the tube in position.

Dailey RA, Tower RN. Frosted Jones Pyrex tubes. *Ophthal Plast Reconstr Surg.* 2005;21(3): 185–187.

Rosen N, Ashkenazi I, Rosner M. Patient dissatisfaction after functionally successful conjunctivodacryocystorhinostomy with Jones tube. *Am J Ophthalmol.* 1994;117:636–642.

Acquired Nasolacrimal Duct Obstruction

Nasolacrimal duct obstruction can usually be diagnosed with irrigation. There is a tendency for clinicians to assume that NLD obstruction is a relatively benign condition and proceed directly to a discussion of surgery. Although this is true in most cases, the alternate causes of NLD obstruction merit consideration.

Bartley GB. Acquired lacrimal drainage obstruction: an etiologic classification system, case reports, and a review of the literature, parts 1–3. *Ophthal Plast Reconstr Surg.* 1992;8: 237–249 and 1993;9:11–26.

Tucker N, Chow D, Stockl F, Codère F, Burnier M. Clinically suspected primary acquired nasolacrimal duct obstruction. Clinicopathologic review of 150 patients. *Ophthalmology.* 1997;104:1882–1886.

Etiology

Involutional stenosis Involutional stenosis is probably the most common cause of NLD obstruction in older persons. It affects women twice as frequently as men. Although the inciting event in this process is unknown, clinicopathologic study suggests that compression of the lumen of the NLD results from inflammatory infiltrates and edema. This may be the result of an unidentified infection or possibly an autoimmune disease. Management almost uniformly consists of DCR.

Dacryolith Dacryoliths or cast formation within the lacrimal sac can also produce obstruction of the NLD. Dacryoliths consist of shed epithelial cells, lipids, and amorphous debris with or without calcium. Most often no inciting event or abnormality is identified. Occasionally, infection with *Actinomyces israelii* or *Candida* species or long-term administration of topical medications such as epinephrine can lead to the formation of such a cast.

A dacryolith can form in patients with an otherwise normal lacrimal drainage system. When this occurs, patients often experience intermittent symptoms, depending on the location of the dacryolith. Dacryoliths also have a tendency to form with a preexisting obstruction; in this setting, symptoms are unremitting.

Acute impaction of a dacryolith in the NLD can produce lacrimal sac distension, which may be accompanied by substantial pain. Dacryoliths can be removed without difficulty during DCR.

Hawes MJ. The dacryolithiasis syndrome. *Ophthal Plast Reconstr Surg.* 1988;4:87–90.

Sinus disease Sinus disease often occurs in conjunction with and in other instances may contribute to the development of NLD obstruction. Patients should be asked about previous sinus surgery, as damage to the NLD sometimes results when the maxillary sinus ostium is being enlarged anteriorly.

Trauma Naso-orbital fractures may involve the NLD. Early treatment by fracture reduction with stenting of the entire lacrimal drainage system should be considered. However, such injuries are often not recognized or are initially neglected as more serious injuries are managed. In such cases, late treatment of persistent epiphora usually requires DCR. Injuries may also occur during rhinoplasty or endoscopic sinus surgery; the management of these injuries is similar to the treatment of injuries occurring with fractures.

Inflammatory disease Granulomatous disease, including sarcoidosis, Wegener granulomatosis, and lethal midline granuloma, may also lead to NLD obstruction. When systemic disease is suspected, a biopsy of the lacrimal sac or the NLD should be performed at the time of DCR.

Lacrimal plugs Similar to the way they migrate and cause canalicular obstruction, dislodged punctal and canalicular plugs can migrate to and occlude the NLD. As with most forms of NLD obstruction, treatment consists of a DCR. Remaining segments of an improperly removed silicone stent have also been known to cause NLD obstruction.

Neoplasm Neoplasm should be considered in any patient presenting with NLD obstruction. In patients with an atypical presentation, including younger age and male gender, further workup is appropriate. Bloody punctal discharge or lacrimal sac distension above the medial canthal tendon is also highly suggestive of neoplasm. A history of malignancy, especially of sinus or nasopharyngeal origin, warrants further investigation. When malignancy is suspected, appropriate imaging studies (CT or MRI) should be obtained. Preoperative endoscopy is a quick and safe way to evaluate for intranasal neoplasm. Lastly, if an unexpected mass or other suggestive abnormality is encountered during surgery, a biopsy should be obtained.

When a neoplasm is encountered, treatment should focus primarily on the neoplasm. In patients with benign tumors, a DCR or CDCR can then be performed. In patients with malignant tumors, surgical correction of the nasolacrimal drainage system should be postponed until there is certainty of clear margins or freedom from recurrence, after which a DCR or CDCR may be undertaken.

Tumors of the lacrimal sac and NLD are discussed in further detail later in this chapter in the section specifically addressing neoplasms.

Management

Intubation and stenting Some clinicians believe that partial stenosis of the NLD with symptomatic epiphora sometimes responds to surgical intubation of the entire lacrimal drainage system. This procedure should be performed only if the tubes can be passed easily. In complete NLD obstruction, intubation alone is not effective, and a DCR should be considered. Most surgeons feel that stenting has no role in the management of acquired NLD obstruction, and they routinely proceed directly to DCR.

Dacryocystorhinostomy A DCR is the treatment of choice in most patients with acquired NLD obstruction. Surgical indications include recurrent dacryocystitis, chronic mucoid reflux, painful distension of the lacrimal sac, and simply bothersome epiphora.

Although there are many minor variations in surgical technique, all share the feature of creating an anastomosis between the lacrimal sac and the nasal cavity through a bony ostium (Fig 14-12). The most substantial distinction between techniques is whether one utilizes a more traditional external (transcutaneous) or an internal (intranasal) approach.

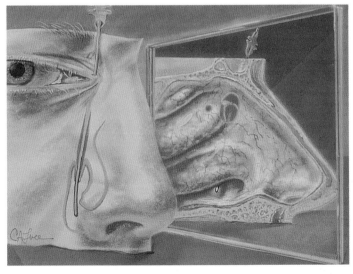

Figure 14-12 The origin of the middle turbinate corresponds well to the location of the lacrimal fossa *(green)*. *(Reproduced by permission from Zide BM, Jelks GW, eds.* Surgical Anatomy of the Orbit. *New York: Raven; 1985:39. Illustration by Craig A. Luce.)*

The advantages of an internal DCR include no visible scar, shorter recovery period, and less discomfort. Also, an internal DCR can be performed in slightly less time than an external DCR. However, the success rate of an external DCR is at least equal to and probably substantially higher than that of an internal DCR. Most series report a success rate of 90% or higher for an external DCR, whereas success rates for an internal DCR have been around 70%, according to reliable accounts. When selecting a surgical technique, the surgeon should also consider that second attempts following failed DCR—no matter which approach was used—have a significantly higher failure rate. Therefore, patients should be counseled that if an internal DCR fails, the likelihood of a successful external DCR is somewhat decreased. An external DCR is also superior for management of an unexpected neoplasm or an intraoperative complication.

Thus, *external DCR* remains the preferred procedure of most ophthalmic lacrimal surgeons (Fig 14-13). Traditionally, DCR has been performed with general anesthesia, but in most adults, local anesthetic infiltration combined with anesthetic and vasoconstrictive nasal packing can be used, with the patients under monitored anesthesia care. However, monitored sedation requires both a cooperative patient and relatively deep sedation, and even in ideal circumstances, some patients report substantial discomfort.

Whether DCR is performed under general anesthesia or monitored sedation, intraoperative hemostasis can be enhanced by preoperative injection of lidocaine with epinephrine into the medial canthal soft tissues and by internal nasal packing with vasoconstrictive agents (oxymetazoline hydrochloride or cocaine 4%). The skin incision should be made so as to avoid the angular blood vessels and prevent wound contractures leading to epicanthal folds. The osteotomy adjacent to the medial wall of the lacrimal sac can be created with a rongeur, trephine, or drill. A large osteotomy site facilitates the formation of posterior and anterior mucosal flaps from both the lacrimal sac and the nasal mucosa. Suturing of the corresponding posterior flaps and anterior flaps is common although not uniformly performed. Simultaneous stenting of the canalicular system may be needed, especially in patients who have common canalicular stenosis.

A biopsy with frozen-section examination should be considered if abnormal tissue is found. Some surgeons routinely perform a biopsy of the excised lacrimal sac. However, evidence suggests that in the absence of a grossly visible abnormality or indicative history, lacrimal sac biopsies are unlikely to reveal occult disease and should not be performed routinely.

Bernardini FP, Moin M, Kersten RC, Reeves D, Kulwin DR. Routine histopathologic evaluation of the lacrimal sac during dacryocystorhinostomy: how useful is it? *Ophthalmology.* 2002;109(7):1214–1217.

Tarbet KJ, Custer PL. External dacryocystorhinostomy: surgical success, patient satisfaction, and economic cost. *Ophthalmology.* 1995;102:1065–1070.

Internal DCR consists of removing a nasal mucosal flap over the area corresponding to the nasolacrimal sac and duct. An osteotomy is performed to remove the frontal process of the maxilla and the lacrimal bone covering the lacrimal sac. Often, the surgeon also has to remove the uncinate process to allow proper exposure of the superior aspect of the lacrimal passage. The lacrimal sac is then opened and the medial wall of the sac is removed, marsupializing the sac into the nose. Bicanalicular intubation is usually performed at the

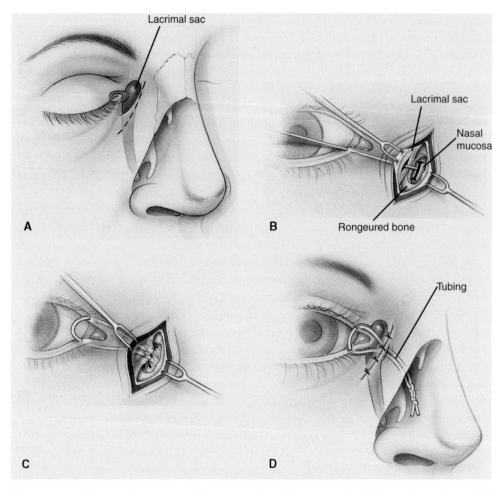

Figure 14-13 External dacryocystorhinostomy. **A,** Incision is marked 10 mm from the medial canthus, starting just above the medial canthal tendon and extending inferiorly. **B,** Bone from the lacrimal fossa and anterior lacrimal crest has been resected. Flaps have been fashioned in the nasal mucosa. A lacrimal probe extends through an incision in the lacrimal sac. **C,** Anterior lacrimal sac flap is sutured to the anterior nasal mucosal flap after a silicone tube is placed. **D,** Final position of the silicone tube following closure of the skin incision. *(Illustration by Christine Gralapp.)*

end of the procedure. Preserving the lacrimal and nasal mucosa may result in less scarring and a higher success rate, and techniques to preserve these structures have been proposed. Careful selection of patients with an adequate normal nasal cavity is crucial for success.

> Tsirbas A, Wormald PJ. Endonasal dacryocystorhinostomy with mucosal flaps. *Am J Ophthalmol.* 2003;135:76–83.

Several variations of internal DCR are available. Most surgeons use a fiber-optic probe passed through a canaliculus to transilluminate the lacrimal sac. This probe helps identify the thin lacrimal bone. Internal DCR can be performed endoscopically *(endoscopic DCR);* more recently, however, internal DCRs have been performed under direct visualization.

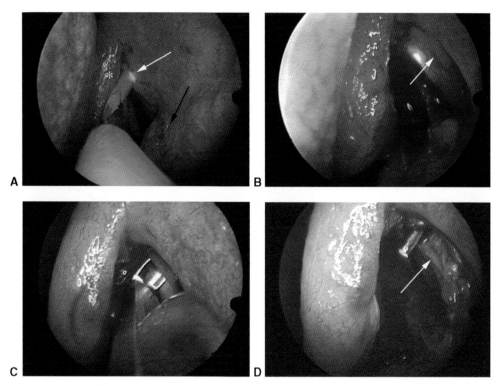

Figure 14-14 Transnasal laser dacryocystorhinostomy. **A,** Posterior incision behind the intra-canalicular transilluminator *(white arrow)*, above the inferior turbinate *(black arrow)*, and just anterior to the insertion of the middle turbinate *(*)*. **B,** Frontal process of the maxilla after nasal mucosal removal *(white arrow)*. **C,** Removal of frontal process of the maxilla with Kerrison rongeurs. **D,** Lacrimal sac has been opened *(white arrow)* and the transilluminator can be seen in the nose. *(Courtesy of François Codère, MD.)*

Transnasal laser DCR (Fig 14-14) has attracted much interest. *Endocanalicular laser DCR* has shown promise in some investigations, but long-term results have varied. *Balloon catheters* have also been used to enlarge osteotomy sites. Many of the above techniques require expensive equipment, and most surgeons find that no matter what variation is used, the results are not comparable to the higher success rate of an external DCR.

Bartley GB. The pros and cons of laser dacryocystorhinostomy. *Am J Ophthalmol.* 1994;117:103–106.

Gonnering RS, Lyon DB, Fisher JC. Endoscopic laser-assisted lacrimal surgery. *Am J Ophthalmol.* 1991;111:152–157.

Massaro BM, Gonnering RS, Harris GJ. Endonasal laser dacryocystorhinostomy. A new approach to NLD obstruction. *Arch Ophthalmol.* 1990;108:1172–1176.

Although DCRs are successful in most patients, failures do occur. Failures may be caused by fibrosis and occlusion of the osteotomy, common canalicular obstruction, or inappropriate placement or size of the bony ostium. The outcome of the DCR is also influenced by, among other factors, the following: which surgical approach is used; whether the patient has previous trauma or active dacryocystitis; whether postoperative infection develops; and whether the patient experiences hypersensitivity or foreign-body reactions to the stent. When an initial DCR fails, most surgeons attempt a second DCR before resorting to CDCR. Unfortunately, as stated previously, repeated DCR by any approach has a lower success rate. In an attempt to increase the likelihood of success, some surgeons will apply *mitomycin C,* a potent antiproliferative alkylating agent, to the surgical site. This is thought to prevent fibrosis at the osteotomy site. The appropriate role of mitomycin C in repeat and possibly primary DCR is still evolving.

Walland MJ, Rose GE. Factors affecting the success rate of open lacrimal surgery. *Br J Ophthalmol.* 1994;78:888–891.

Dacryocystitis

Dacryocystitis is an infection arising within the lacrimal sac. Most often it occurs because of stasis of fluid (tears and mucous secretions) that results from NLD obstruction. When possible, active infection is cleared before a DCR is performed. Dacryocystitis, including its management, is discussed further under the heading Infections.

Therapeutic Closure of the Lacrimal Drainage System

In cases of severe dry eye disease, occlusion of the lacrimal drainage system may be helpful. Dissolvable collagen plugs may be used on a trial basis. More commonly, permanent plugs, which are made of silicone, are used. The advantages of permanent plugs are that placement is fairly straightforward and that, in most cases, they are removable. There are several varieties, and they can be divided into 2 categories: those that seat within the puncta and those that are placed within the canaliculi. Although the permanent plugs are usually well tolerated, complications are occasionally encountered. Minor problems include ocular surface irritation and a foreign-body reaction. Pyogenic granulomas may develop, requiring removal of the plug. In most cases, the pyogenic granuloma regresses once the plug is removed, but occasionally surgical excision is needed. More serious complications usually relate to plug displacement.

Plug extrusion or *migration* is not uncommon. The ophthalmologist can best avoid these complications by using the appropriate size plug. There is an instrument that measures punctal diameter, and plugs are available in various sizes. When appropriately fitted, punctal plugs usually stay in place. When the plugs are improperly fitted, migration occurs. Most often, a disproportionately small plug will simply be extruded. However, if the plug migrates within the lacrimal drainage system, obstruction of either the canaliculus or the NLD may result. Most instances of canalicular obstruction have been the result of plugs that were designed to be placed within the canaliculus. *Canaliculitis* may also result from canalicular plugs or punctal plugs that have migrated to the canaliculus. Management of plug-related canalicular and NLD obstruction is discussed elsewhere in this chapter.

When occlusion with plugs is not successful, the clinician may consider surgical occlusion. Surgery should be reserved for severe cases and must be performed with caution. Surgical closure is almost always permanent. If a patient suffers from subsequent epiphora, no simple solution is available, with most cases requiring a CDCR. To avoid this complication, all patients should be given a trial of temporary closure before permanent closure.

Once the decision has been made to proceed with surgical occlusion, the puncta should be closed in a stepwise fashion, 1 punctum at a time. The upper and lower puncta of the same eye should never be closed simultaneously. Complete loss of lacrimal outflow can result in epiphora even in patients with fairly severe dry eye disease.

Numerous surgical techniques for occluding the lacrimal drainage system have been described. *Thermal obliteration* of the puncta and adjacent canaliculi can be performed with a handheld cautery unit. Although the argon laser can be used for thermal punctal occlusion, it offers no advantage over conventional techniques and is probably less effective. *Ampullectomy* can be performed with either direct closure or placement of an overlying conjunctival graft. Often, despite fairly aggressive attempts, the puncta may persist or reform. In these recalcitrant cases, complete excision of the punctal and adjacent canalicular epithelium can be performed.

Trauma

Canaliculus

Most traumatic injuries to the canaliculi occur in 1 of 2 ways: by direct laceration, such as a stab wound or dog bite; or by traction, which occurs when sudden lateral displacement of the eyelid tears the medial canthal tendon and associated canaliculus. Being without tarsal support, the canaliculus lies within the weakest part of the eyelid and is often the first to give. Whenever blunt trauma, such as from a fist or an air bag, results in a full-thickness eyelid laceration, the clinician should suspect and evaluate for an associated medial injury. The avulsion injury often appears trivial on superficial inspection, the full extent of injury revealed only with detailed examination of the area. When possible, diagnostic canalicular probing and irrigation may be helpful.

Because some patients who have only 1 functioning canaliculus may be asymptomatic, some clinicians consider the repair of an isolated single canalicular laceration to be optional. However, it is estimated that in patients with only 1 functioning canaliculus, 10% suffer from constant or nearly constant epiphora and 40% have symptomatic epiphora with ocular irritation, leaving only 50% fairly asymptomatic. Also, the success rate of a primary repair is much higher than that of a secondary reconstruction. Therefore, given the common occurrence of epiphora and the difficulties associated with delayed reconstruction, most surgeons recommend repair of all canalicular lacerations.

Repair of injured canaliculi should be performed as soon as possible, preferably within 48 hours of injury. The first step of the repair is locating the severed ends of the canalicular system. Often this can be frustrating, but the controlled conditions of an operating room, including the use of general anesthesia and magnification with optimal illumination, facilitate the search. A thorough understanding of the medial canthal anatomy guides the surgeon to the appropriate area to begin exploration for the medial end of the severed canaliculus. Laterally, the canaliculus is located near the eyelid margin, but for lacerations close to the lacrimal sac, the canaliculus is deep to the anterior limb of the medial canthal tendon. Irrigation using air, fluorescein, or yellow viscoelastic through an intact adjacent canaliculus may be helpful. Methylene blue should be avoided as it tends to stain the entire operative field. In difficult cases, the careful use of a smooth-tipped pigtail probe may be helpful for identification of the medial cut end. The probe is introduced through the opposite, uninvolved punctum, passed through the common canaliculus, and finally passed through the medial cut end.

Stenting of the injured canaliculus is usually performed to help prevent postoperative canalicular strictures. By placing the stent on traction, the surgeon draws together the severed canalicular ends and other soft tissue structures, placing them in their normal anatomical positions. Direct anastomosis of the cut canaliculus over the silicone tube can be accomplished with closure of the pericanalicular tissues. Direct suturing of the canalicular ends is probably not necessary. Lacrimal intubation also facilitates the soft tissue reconstruction of the medial canthal tendon and eyelid margin.

Traditionally, bicanalicular stents have been used, but monocanalicular stents are gaining popularity (see Fig 14-4). One type of monocanalicular stent is attached distally to a metal guiding probe. This probe is retrieved intranasally. Thus, the monocanalicular stent can be used in soft tissue approximation similar to the way a bicanalicular system is used. Other advantages of monocanalicular stents are the greatly reduced risk of punctal injury, or cheese-wiring, and their easier retrieval.

Stents are usually left in place for 3 months or longer. However, cheese-wiring, ocular irritation, infection, local inflammation, or pyogenic granuloma formation may necessitate early removal. Bicanalicular stents are usually cut at the medial canthus and retrieved from the nose. Monocanalicular stents are simply pulled through the punctum.

Kersten RC, Kulwin DR. "One-stitch" canalicular repair. A simplified approach for repair of canalicular laceration. *Ophthalmology*. 1996;103:785–789.

Loff HJ, Wobig JL, Dailey RA. The bubble test: an atraumatic method for canalicular laceration repair. *Opththal Plast Reconstr Surg*. 1996;12(1):61–64.

Wulc AE, Arterberry JR. The pathogenesis of canalicular laceration. *Ophthalmology*. 1991;98:1243–1249.

Lacrimal Sac and Nasolacrimal Duct

The lacrimal sac and NLD may be injured by direct laceration or by fracture of surrounding bones. Injuries of the lacrimal sac or NLD may also occur during rhinoplasty or endoscopic sinus surgery when the physiologic maxillary sinus ostium is being enlarged anteriorly. Early treatment of the lacrimal sac and NLD is appropriate and consists of fracture reduction and soft tissue repair, with silicone intubation of the entire lacrimal drainage system. Late treatment of persistent epiphora may require DCR.

Neuhaus RW. Orbital complications secondary to endoscopic sinus surgery. *Ophthalmology*. 1990;97:1512–1518.

Infection

Lacrimal Gland

Acute inflammation of the lacrimal gland *(dacryoadenitis)* is most often seen in sterile inflammatory disease and occasionally is the consequence of malignancy, such as lymphoproliferative disease. Noninfectious disease of the lacrimal gland is covered elsewhere. Dacryoadenitis is extremely rare, and occurrence of gross purulence and abscess formation are even more uncommon. Most cases are the result of bacterial infection, which may develop secondary to an adjacent infection or after trauma or hematogenously. Infections have also been reported to originate within a ductal cyst. Given the rare occurrence of these infections, large case series are lacking, as are a precise breakdown of causative organisms and suggestions on management. Moreover, many nonsuppurative cases are treated empirically without isolation of the alleged pathogen. Presumably, most cases are due to gram-positive bacteria, although cases due to gram-negative bacteria have been documented. There are numerous reports of dacryoadenitis related to tuberculosis, with the formation of discrete tuberculomas in several cases. *Epstein-Barr virus* is the most frequently reported viral pathogen. There have also been numerous isolated reports of uncommon pathogens, including *Brucella melitensis* and *Cysticercus cellulosae*.

Canaliculus

Canaliculitis, though usually of limited consequence, can be a challenge for patients and clinicians. Infection within the canaliculus is caused by a variety of bacteria, viruses, and mycotic organisms. The most common pathogen is a filamentous gram-positive rod, *Actinomyces israelii.*

The patient presents with persistent weeping, sometimes accompanied by a follicular conjunctivitis centered in the medial canthus. The punctum is often erythematous and dilated, or "pouting." A cotton tip applicator can be used to apply pressure to the canaliculus (ie, milking). The expression of purulent discharge confirms the diagnosis (Fig 14-15).

Canaliculitis can be somewhat difficult to eradicate, and the clinician should warn the patient that treatment may consist of several stages. A culture should be obtained when

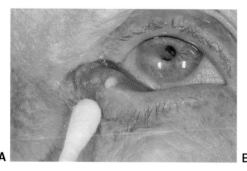 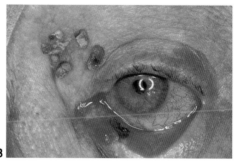

A **B**

Figure 14-15 Canaliculitis. **A,** Pouting punctum expressing purulent material. **B,** Several small stones curetted from canaliculitis. *(Courtesy of Jeffrey A. Nerad, MD.)*

the patient presents. Conservative management then consists of warm compresses, digital massage, and topical antibiotic therapy. Initially, a broad-spectrum antibiotic is selected and then refined when culture sensitivities become available. Many patients require more aggressive treatment, particularly those with *Actinomyces* infection, which has a tendency to form concretions, or "stones." Within these stones, organisms are protected from lethal antibiotic concentrations. Occasionally, curettage through the punctum is successful. However, in most cases a canaliculotomy is required to completely remove all particulate matter.

The canaliculotomy should be limited to the horizontal canaliculus and approached from the conjunctival surface. The incision is left open to heal by second intention and does not require stenting. Some surgeons irrigate or "paint" the canaliculus with povidone-iodine (Betadine) or use specially formulated penicillin-fortified drops perioperatively. If the infection is the consequence of an obstruction, such as iatrogenic plug placement, the surgeon may need to correct the obstruction in order to prevent recurrence.

Lacrimal Sac

Inflammation of the lacrimal sac *(acute dacryocystitis)* has various causes. However, in most cases the common factor is complete NLD obstruction that prevents normal drainage from the lacrimal sac into the nose. Chronic tear retention and stasis lead to secondary infection. Clinical findings include edema and erythema with distension of the lacrimal sac below the medial canthal tendon (Fig 14-16). The degree of soreness varies from no appreciable discomfort to quite severe pain. Complications include dacryocystocele formation, chronic conjunctivitis, and spread to adjacent structures (orbital or facial cellulitis).

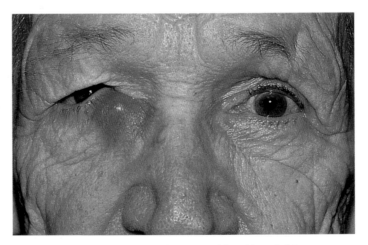

Figure 14-16 Acute dacryocystitis with cellulitis.

The following are guidelines for treating acute dacryocystitis:

- Avoid irrigation or probing of the canalicular system until the infection subsides. In most cases, irrigation is not needed to establish the diagnosis and is extremely painful in the setting of active infection.
- Similarly, diagnostic or therapeutic probing of the NLD is not indicated in adults with acute dacryocystitis.
- Topical antibiotics are of limited value. They do not reach the site of the infection because of stasis within the lacrimal drainage system. They also do not penetrate sufficiently within the adjacent soft tissue.
- Oral antibiotics are effective in most infections. Gram-positive bacteria are the most common cause of acute dacryocystitis. However, suspect gram-negative organisms in patients who are diabetic or immunocompromised or in those who have been exposed to atypical pathogens (eg, individuals residing in nursing homes).
- Parenteral antibiotics are necessary for the treatment of severe cases, especially if cellulitis or orbital extension is present.
- Aspiration of the lacrimal sac may be performed if a pyocele–mucocele is localized and approaching the skin. Information regarding appropriate systemic antibiotic therapy may be obtained from smears and cultures of the aspirate material.
- A localized abscess involving the lacrimal sac and adjacent soft tissues requires incision and drainage. The incised abscess is packed open and allowed to heal by second intention. This treatment should be reserved for severe cases and those that do not respond to more conservative measures, because a chronically draining epithelialized fistula that communicates with the lacrimal sac can form.

Dacryocystitis indicating total NLD obstruction requires a DCR in most cases because of inevitable persistent epiphora and recurrent infection. In general, such surgery is deferred until resolution of the acute inflammation. Some patients, however, continue to have a subacute infection until definitive drainage surgery is performed.

Chronic dacryocystitis, a smoldering low-grade infection, may develop in some individuals. This usually results in distension of the lacrimal sac. Massage may reflux mucoid material through the canalicular system onto the surface of the eye. Diagnostic probing and irrigation should be confined to the upper system in adults, because probing of the NLD does not achieve permanent patency in adults. If a tumor is not suspected, no further diagnostic evaluation is indicated to confirm the diagnosis of a total NLD obstruction. Chronic dacryocystitis needs to be surgically resolved before elective intraocular surgery.

Neoplasm

Lacrimal Gland

Neoplasms of the lacrimal gland are discussed elsewhere in this book.

Lacrimal Drainage System

Neoplastic causes of acquired obstruction of the lacrimal drainage system may be classified as (1) primary lacrimal drainage system tumors (most commonly papilloma and squamous cell carcinoma); (2) primary tumors of tissues surrounding the lacrimal drainage system that secondarily invade or compromise lacrimal system structures (most commonly eyelid skin basal and squamous cell carcinoma; also included are adenoid cystic carcinoma, capillary hemangioma, inverted papilloma, epidermoid carcinoma, osteoma, and lymphoma); and (3) tumors metastatic to the nasolacrimal region.

Primary lacrimal sac tumors are rare and may present clinically as a mass located above the medial canthal tendon. They are often associated with epiphora or chronic dacryocystitis. Dacryocystitis associated with tumor may differ from simple NLD obstruction in that the irrigation fluid may pass into the nose. Also, with irrigation, blood may reflux from the punctum, and more ominously some patients may report spontaneous bleeding. Tumors that invade the skin may produce ulceration with telangiectasia over the lacrimal sac. Metastasis to regional lymph nodes may also occur. Dacryocystography is useful to outline uneven, mottled densities in the dilated lacrimal sac. However, imaging with MR or CT is far superior in identifying neoplasms and determining disease extent. CT also has the advantage of clearly revealing bone erosion.

Histologically, approximately 45% of lacrimal sac tumors are benign and 55% are malignant. Squamous cell papillomas and carcinomas are the most common tumors of the sac. Many papillomas initially grow in an inverted pattern and into the lacrimal sac wall and, consequently, their excision is often incomplete. With recurrence, malignant degeneration may occur.

Treatment of benign lacrimal sac tumors commonly requires a *dacryocystectomy.* Malignancies may require a dacryocystectomy combined with a lateral rhinotomy, performed by an otolaryngologist. *Exenteration,* including bone removal in the medial canthal area, is necessary if a malignant epithelial tumor has involved bone and the soft tissues of the orbit. *Radiation* is useful in treating lymphomatous lesions or as a palliative measure in extensive epithelial lesions. The recurrence rate for invasive squamous and transitional cell carcinoma of the lacrimal sac is approximately 50%, with 50% of these being fatal.

Madreperla SA, Green WR, Daniel R, Shah KV. Human papillomavirus in primary epithelial tumors of the lacrimal sac. *Ophthalmology.* 1993;100:569–573.

Pe'er JJ, Stefanyszyn M, Hidayat AA. Nonepithelial tumors of the lacrimal sac. *Am J Ophthalmol.* 1994;118:650–658.

Developmental Abnormalities

Lacrimal Secretory System

Congenital abnormalities of the lacrimal gland are relatively uncommon. Abnormalities include hypoplasia and agenesis of the lacrimal gland. Either can occur in isolation or in some cases in conjunction with congenital abnormalities of the salivary glands. Though usually occurring sporadically, both aplasia and hypoplasia have been reported to occur with an apparent autosomal dominant pattern. Lacrimal gland prolapse has been reported in association with craniosynostosis syndromes. Ectopic lacrimal gland tissue has also been found within the orbit.

Occasionally, children are born with an aberrant ductule, previously referred to as a *lacrimal gland fistula,* which exits externally through the eyelid overlying the lacrimal gland. These aberrant ductules exit laterally several millimeters above the eyelash line and are usually accompanied by an adjacent cluster of eyelashes (Fig 14-17). Tears produced from the aberrant ductules can mimic epiphora. These ductules can be successfully managed with simple excision.

Lacrimal Drainage System

Most developmental abnormalities of the lacrimal drainage system relate to (1) failure of the epithelial core to completely separate from the surface ectoderm from which it originated (multiple puncta or lacrimal–cutaneous fistula) or (2) incomplete patency, either at the eyelid (punctal/canalicular hypoplasia or aplasia) or intranasally (NLD obstruction).

Duplication

Uncommonly, multiple puncta and additional canaliculi develop. When the extra opening is on the eyelid margin, it is usually inconsequential and requires no treatment. The term *lacrimal–cutaneous fistula* has been used to describe those fistulas exiting through the skin infranasal to the medial canthus; this abnormality is discussed next.

Congenital lacrimal–cutaneous fistulas

A congenital lacrimal–cutaneous fistula from an otherwise normal canalicular system or lacrimal sac is occasionally encountered infranasal to the medial canthal area (Fig 14-18). These fistulas are frequently asymptomatic or associated with a minimal amount of tears.

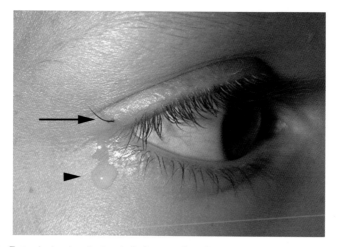

Figure 14-17 Ectopic lacrimal gland drainage site. A cutaneous ectopic lacrimal gland ductule *(arrow)* is occasionally encountered overlying the lacrimal gland. The ductule is usually accompanied by several lashes and produces tears *(arrowhead)* that mimic epiphora. *(Courtesy of Timothy J. McCulley, MD.)*

Figure 14-18 Congenital lacrimal–cutaneous fistula draining to the skin surface.

Approximately one third of patients have an underlying NLD obstruction, wherein chronic mucoid discharge from the affected nasolacrimal sac may be present.

In symptomatic patients, direct surgical excision of the epithelium-lined fistulous tract with direct suture closure is indicated. In patients with underlying NLD obstruction and chronic dacryocystitis, silicone intubation of the NLD may also be required.

Birchansky LD, Nerad JA, Kersten RC, Kulwin DR. Management of congenital lacrimal sac fistula. *Arch Ophthalmol.* 1990;108:388–390.

Aplasia and hypoplasia

Punctal hypoplasia or stenosis is encountered more frequently than true aplasia. Moreover, in many cases of presumed aplasia, close evaluation with magnification reveals an intact punctum with a thin overlying membrane. Management of punctal stenosis, membranes, and aplasia is covered in the section addressing lacrimal drainage obstruction.

Nasolacrimal duct obstruction

In most cases, congenital NLD obstruction is due to failure of the duct to fully canalize; however, associations with more severe abnormalities have been described. For example, major facial cleft deformities can pass through or be adjacent to the nasolacrimal drainage pathways and produce outflow disorders (Fig 14-19).

Sevel D. Development and congenital abnormalities of the nasolacrimal apparatus. *J Pediatr Ophthalmol Strabismus.* 1981;18(5):13–19.

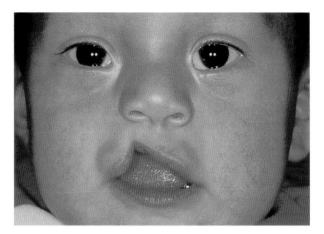

Figure 14-19 Cleft lip and palate with abnormal medial canthal angles and tearing as a result of hypoplasia of nasolacrimal ducts.

Basic Texts

Orbit, Eyelids, and Lacrimal System

Albert DM, Lucarelli MJ. *Clinical Atlas of Procedures in Ophthalmic Surgery*. Chicago: AMA Press; 2004.

Baker SR, Swanson NA. *Local Flaps in Facial Reconstruction*. St Louis: Mosby; 1995.

Bron AJ, Tripathi RC, Tripathi BJ. *Wolff's Anatomy of the Eye and Orbit*. 8th ed. Philadelphia: A Hodder Arnold Publication; 1997.

Chen WP. *Asian Blepharoplasty and the Eyelid Crease with DVD*. 2nd ed. Philadelphia: Butterworth-Heinemann/Elsevier; 2006.

Dutton JJ. *Atlas of Clinical and Surgical Orbital Anatomy*. Philadelphia: Saunders; 1994.

Dutton JJ, Byrne SF, Proia AD. *Diagnostic Atlas of Orbital Diseases*. Philadelphia: Saunders; 2000.

Hurwitz JJ, ed. *The Lacrimal System*. Philadelphia: Lippincott-Raven; 1996.

Lemke BN, Della Rocca RC, eds. *Surgery of the Eyelids and Orbit: An Anatomical Approach*. East Norwalk, CT: Appleton & Lange; 1992.

McCord CD, Tanenbaum M, Nunery WR, eds. *Oculoplastic Surgery*. 3rd ed. New York: Lippincott Williams & Wilkins; 1995.

Nerad JA. *The Requisites in Ophthalmology: Oculoplastic Surgery*. Philadelphia: Mosby; 2001.

Nesi FA, Lisman RD, Levine RM, eds. *Smith's Ophthalmic Plastic and Reconstructive Surgery*. 2nd ed. St Louis: Mosby; 1998.

Putterman AM. *Cosmetic Oculoplastic Surgery: Eyelid, Forehead, and Facial Techniques*. 3rd ed. Philadelphia: Saunders; 1999.

Rootman J, ed. *Diseases of the Orbit: A Multidisciplinary Approach*. 2nd ed. Philadelphia: Lippincott Williams & Wilkins; 2002.

Rootman J, Stewart B, Goldberg RA, eds. *Orbital Surgery: A Conceptual Approach*. Philadelphia: Lippincott-Raven; 1995.

Shields JA, Shields CL. *Atlas of Eyelid and Conjunctival Tumors*. Philadelphia: Lippincott Williams & Wilkins; 1999.

Shields JA, Shields CL. *Atlas of Orbital Tumors*. Philadelphia: Lippincott Williams & Wilkins; 1999.

Spencer WH, ed. *Ophthalmic Pathology: An Atlas and Textbook*. 4th ed. Philadelphia: Saunders; 1997.

Zide BM. *Surgical Anatomy Around the Orbit: The System of Zones*. Philadelphia: Lippincott Williams & Wilkins; 2005.

Related Academy Materials

Focal Points: Clinical Modules for Ophthalmologists

Alford MA. Management of trichiasis (Module 4, 2001).

Arpey CJ, de Imus CG. Periorbital skin cancers: the dermatologist's perspective (Module 1, 2006).

Biesman BS. Lasers in periorbital surgery (Module 7, 2000).

Cockerham KP, Kennerdel JS. Thyroid-associated orbitopathy (Module 1, 1997).

Dailey RA. Rejuvenation of the aging face (Module 2, 2004).

Dailey RA. Upper eyelid blepharoplasty (Module 8, 1995).

Dresner SC. Ophthalmic management of facial nerve paralysis (Module 4, 2000).

Dutton JJ, Fowler AM. Botulinum toxin in ophthalmology (Module 3, 2007).

Gossman MD. Management of eyelid trauma (Module 10, 1996).

Howard GR. Management of acquired ptosis (Module 8, 1999).

Laquis SJ, Haik BG. Orbital imaging (Module 12, 2004).

Lauer SA. Ectropion and entropion (Module 10, 1994).

Lucarelli JM, Kaltreider SA. Advances in evisceration and enucleation (Module 6, 2004).

Lyon DB. Evaluation of the tearing adult patient (Module 9, 2002).

Meyer DR. Congenital ptosis (Module 2, 2001).

Patel BCK, Anderson RL. Essential blepharospasm and related diseases (Module 5, 2000).

Rubin PAD, Bilyk JR, Shore JW. Management of orbital trauma: fractures, hemorrhage, and traumatic optic neuropathy (Module 7, 1994).

Spinelli HM, Riou J. Aesthetic surgery of the lower eyelid (Module 7, 1995).

Wiggs EO, Popham JK. Evaluation and surgery of the lacrimal drainage system in adults (Module 12, 1995).

Publications

Arnold AC, ed. *Basic Principles of Ophthalmic Surgery.* (2006).

Jordan DR, Anderson RA. *Surgical Anatomy of the Ocular Adnexa: A Clinical Approach* (Ophthalmology Monograph 9, 1996; reviewed for currency 2000).

Lane SS, Skuta GL, eds. *ProVision: Preferred Responses in Ophthalmology,* Series 3 (Self-Assessment Program, 1999; includes 2005 update).

Stewart WB, ed. *Surgery of the Eyelid, Orbit, and Lacrimal System* (Ophthalmology Monograph 8. Vol 1, 1993; reviewed for currency 2001. Vol 2, 1994; reviewed for currency 2003. Vol 3, 1995; reviewed for currency 2000).

Wilson FM II, ed. *Practical Ophthalmology: A Manual for Beginning Residents.* 5th ed. (2005).

Academy MOC Essentials

MOC Exam Study Guide: Comprehensive Ophthalmology and Practice Emphasis Areas (2005). *MOC Exam Self-Assessment: Core Ophthalmic Knowledge and Practice Emphasis Areas* (2005).

Preferred Practice Patterns

Preferred Practice Patterns Committee, Cornea/External Disease Panel. *Conjunctivitis* (2003).

Ophthalmic Technology Assessments

Ophthalmic Technology Assessment Committee. *Cosmetic Oculofacial Applications of Botulinum Toxin.* (2005).
Ophthalmic Technology Assessment Committee. *Endonasal Dacryocystorhinostomy* (2002).
Ophthalmic Technology Assessment Committee. *Functional Indications for Upper and Lower Eyelid Blepharoplasty* (1999; reviewed for currency 2003).
Ophthalmic Technology Assessment Committee. *Laser Blepharoplasty and Skin Resurfacing* (1998).
Ophthalmic Technology Assessment Committee. *Orbital Implants in Enucleation Surgery.* (2003).

Multimedia

Johns KJ, ed. *Eye Care Skills: Presentations for Physicians and Other Health Care Professionals.* (CD-ROM, 2005).
Nerad JA, Carter KD, Codère F, Kersten RC. *LEO Clinical Update Course on Orbit and Ophthalmic Plastic Surgery* (CD-ROM, 2003).

Continuing Ophthalmic Video Education

Wesley RE. *Ectropion and Entropion Repair of the Lower Lid* (1989; reviewed for currency 2004).
Wojno TH. *Cosmetic Blepharoplasty* (1996; reviewed for currency 2004).

To order any of these materials, please call the Academy's Customer Service number at (415) 561-8540, or order online at www.aao.org.

Credit Reporting Form

Basic and Clinical Science Course, 2010–2011
Section 7

The American Academy of Ophthalmology is accredited by the Accreditation Council for Continuing Medical Education to provide continuing medical education for physicians.

The American Academy of Ophthalmology designates this educational activity for a maximum of 10 *AMA PRA Category 1 Credits*™. Physicians should only claim credit commensurate with the extent of their participation in the activity.

If you wish to claim continuing medical education credit for your study of this Section, you may claim your credit online or fill in the required forms and mail or fax them to the Academy.

To use the forms:

1. Complete the study questions and mark your answers on the Section Completion Form.
2. Complete the Section Evaluation.
3. Fill in and sign the statement below.
4. Return this page and the required forms by mail or fax to the CME Registrar (see below).

To claim credit online:

1. Log on to the Academy website (www.aao.org/cme).
2. Select Review/Claim CME.
3. Follow the instructions.

Important: These completed forms or the online claim must be received at the Academy by June 2013.

I hereby certify that I have spent _____ (up to 10) hours of study on the curriculum of this Section and that I have completed the study questions.

Signature: _____

Date

Name: _____

Address: _____

City and State: _____ Zip: _____

Telephone: (_____) _____ Academy Member ID# _____
area code

Please return completed forms to: **Or you may fax them to:** 415-561-8575
American Academy of Ophthalmology
P.O. Box 7424
San Francisco, CA 94120-7424
Attn: CME Registrar, Customer Service

2010–2011
Section Completion Form

Basic and Clinical Science Course

Answer Sheet for Section 7

Question	Answer	Question	Answer
1	a b c d e	24	a b c d e
2	a b c d	25	a b c d e
3	a b c d	26	a b c d
4	a b c d	27	a b c d
5	a b c d	28	a b c d e
6	a b c d	29	a b c d e
7	a b c d e	30	a b c d e
8	a b c d e	31	a b c d e
9	a b c d e	32	a b c d e
10	a b c d	33	a b c d e
11	a b c d e	34	a b c d e
12	a b c d	35	a b c d e
13	a b c d	36	a b c d e
14	a b c d	37	a b c d e
15	a b c d e	38	a b c d e
16	a b c d e	39	a b c d e
17	a b c d	40	a b c d
18	a b c d e	41	a b c d
19	a b c d	42	a b c d
20	a b c d e	43	a b c d
21	a b c d e	44	a b c d
22	a b c d	45	a b c d
23	a b c d e		

Section Evaluation

Please complete this CME questionnaire.

1. To what degree will you use knowledge from BCSC Section 7 in your practice?

   ☐ Regularly

   ☐ Sometimes

   ☐ Rarely

2. Please review the stated objectives for BCSC Section 7. How effective was the material at meeting those objectives?

   ☐ All objectives were met.

   ☐ Most objectives were met.

   ☐ Some objectives were met.

   ☐ Few or no objectives were met.

3. To what degree is BCSC Section 7 likely to have a positive impact on health outcomes of your patients?

   ☐ Extremely likely

   ☐ Highly likely

   ☐ Somewhat likely

   ☐ Not at all likely

4. After you review the stated objectives for BCSC Section 7, please let us know of any additional knowledge, skills, or information useful to your practice that were acquired but were not included in the objectives.

5. Was BCSC Section 7 free of commercial bias?

   ☐ Yes

   ☐ No

6. If you selected "No" in the previous question, please comment.

7. Please tell us what might improve the applicability of BCSC to your practice.

Study Questions

Although a concerted effort has been made to avoid ambiguity and redundancy in these questions, the authors recognize that differences of opinion may occur regarding the "best" answer. The discussions are provided to demonstrate the rationale used to derive the answer. They may also be helpful in confirming that your approach to the problem was correct or, if necessary, in fixing the principle in your memory.

1. This nerve to an extraocular muscle does not pass through the muscle cone on entering the orbit.
   a. CN III
   b. CN IV
   c. CN V
   d. CN VI
   e. CN VII

2. Which of the following statements regarding orbital anatomy is *true*?
   a. The lacrimal gland fossa is located within the lateral orbital wall.
   b. The optic canal is located within the greater wing of the sphenoid bone.
   c. The medial wall of the optic canal is formed by the lateral wall of the sphenoid sinus.
   d. The nerve to the inferior rectus muscle travels anteriorly along the medial aspect of the muscle and innervates the muscle on its posterior surface.

3. The frontal, lacrimal, and nasociliary nerves are branches of the
   a. facial nerve
   b. oculomotor nerve
   c. ophthalmic division, trigeminal nerve
   d. maxillary division, trigeminal nerve

4. What structure is deep to the plane of the facial nerve branches in the lower face?
   a. masseter muscle
   b. parotidomasseteric fascia
   c. deep temporal fascia
   d. parotid gland

5. The superior transverse ligament is also referred to as
   a. Lockwood's ligament
   b. Soemmering's ligament
   c. the ROOF
   d. Whitnall's ligament

6. Compared with MRI scanning, CT scanning provides better
   a. views of bone and calcium
   b. views of the orbital apex and orbitocranial junction
   c. tissue contrast in disease processes
   d. definition of areas of demyelination

7. In patients with a facial nerve paralysis, all of the following characteristics may be present *except*
   a. eyebrow ptosis
   b. blepharoptosis
   c. lower eyelid ectropion
   d. epiphora
   e. ocular exposure symptoms

8. A 1-month-old infant presents with a purplish, spongy eyelid mass. The most likely diagnosis is
   a. rhabdomyosarcoma
   b. neurofibroma
   c. dermoid cyst
   d. capillary hemangioma
   e. metastatic Ewing sarcoma

9. A 65-year-old woman presents with a progressively enlarging mass in the right inferior orbit. Distraction of the lower eyelid reveals a "salmon patch" appearance to the fornix. The most likely diagnosis is
   a. reactive lymphoid hyperplasia
   b. lymphoma
   c. sebaceous carcinoma
   d. melanoma
   e. apocrine hidrocystoma

10. Which of the following signs is most likely to be present in a patient with thyroid-associated orbitopathy (TAO)?
    a. exophthalmos
    b. external ophthalmoplegia
    c. eyelid retraction
    d. optic neuropathy

11. Subperiosteal abscess of the orbit in children is more likely than in adults to
    a. require surgical drainage
    b. respond to single antibiotic therapy
    c. be polymicrobial
    d. arise from the frontal sinus
    e. arise from chronic sinusitis

12. The most important step in repair of a full-thickness eyelid laceration is
    a. placement of the gray line suture
    b. placement of a suture in the lash line to approximate the lashes
    c. sharp debridement of the wound edges to create squared tarsal edges
    d. careful approximation of the tarsus

13. Which of the following statements about the relationship of TAO and thyroid status is *true*?
    a. Ophthalmopathy resolves after hyperthyroidism is adequately treated.
    b. Ophthalmopathy generally develops prior to the diagnosis of thyroid dysfunction.
    c. Serum thyroid-stimulating hormone level is a good marker for the intensity of ophthalmopathy.
    d. Ophthalmopathy may develop even though a patient is euthyroid.

14. Congenital Horner syndrome is associated with miosis, ptosis, anhidrosis, and
    a. chemosis
    b. jaw-winking
    c. lagophthalmos
    d. iris hypopigmentation

15. The most common location for orbital lymphoma is
    a. the extraocular muscles
    b. retro-orbital fat
    c. lacrimal fossa
    d. orbital apex
    e. orbital floor

16. Biopsy of a conjunctival mass reveals low-grade B-cell lymphoma, MALT type. Management likely includes
    a. systemic steroids
    b. observation
    c. topical mitomycin
    d. radical surgical excision
    e. cryotherapy

17. All of the following are true regarding orbital varices *except*
    a. Enophthalmos is common on the involved side.
    b. A Valsalva maneuver during CT scan may be required for diagnosis.
    c. Surgery is essential for management in most cases.
    d. Phleboliths may be seen on plain-film radiographs.

18. A 20-year-old man is struck over the right eye, and radiography shows a fracture of the right orbital floor. Forced traction testing is equivocal because of poor patient cooperation. Four days after injury, 3 mm of right exophthalmos is present, and movements of the eye are restricted in upgaze, downgaze, and horizontal gaze. Treatment at that time should be

    a. conjunctival incision through the inferior fornix, with examination of the fracture
    b. Caldwell-Luc incision and packing of the maxillary sinus
    c. skin incision over the inferior orbital rim and covering of the fracture defect with a plastic plate
    d. skin incision beneath the eyelashes and covering of the fracture defect with a plastic plate
    e. none of the above

19. Which of the following features is most likely to be found on an orbital CT scan of a patient with TAO?

    a. an increased amount of orbital fat in the presence of normal-sized extraocular muscles
    b. diffuse, fusiform enlargement of the extraocular muscle belly and tendon
    c. pressure erosion of the lateral orbital rim from enlarged muscles
    d. chronic ethmoid and maxillary sinusitis

20. The most important determinant in selecting a corrective procedure for any type of ptosis is

    a. vertical height of the palpebral fissure
    b. age of the patient
    c. amount of levator function
    d. duration of the ptosis
    e. position of the upper eyelid margin relative to the corneal limbus

21. A 70-year-old woman has 4 mm of right upper eyelid ptosis and 1 mm of left upper eyelid retraction. She has a high eyelid crease in the right upper eyelid, with normal levator function of both upper eyelids. The treatment of choice is

    a. a moderate internal tarsoconjunctival resection (Fasanella-Servat operation) on the right upper eyelid
    b. a moderate levator recession of the left upper eyelid
    c. a levator aponeurosis advancement on the right upper eyelid
    d. a posterior-approach, standard müllerectomy on the right upper eyelid
    e. a frontalis muscle suspension on the right upper eyelid using a silicone rod to allow postoperative adjustment

22. All of the following tumors have a significant risk of metastasis *except*

    a. squamous cell carcinoma
    b. Merkel cell carcinoma
    c. basal cell carcinoma
    d. sebaceous cell carcinoma

23. In the evaluation of a child with unilateral exophthalmos, which assumption is *true*?
    a. Cavernous hemangiomas are among the most common benign orbital tumors in children.
    b. Thyroid ophthalmopathy is the most common cause of unilateral exophthalmos in children.
    c. Neurofibroma is the malignant tumor that most commonly produces exophthalmos in children.
    d. Optic nerve meningiomas are more common than gliomas in children.
    e. none of the above

24. Neurofibromatosis 1 is associated with all of the following *except*
    a. skin lesions known as adenoma sebaceum
    b. café-au-lait skin lesions
    c. plexiform neurofibromas in the eyelids
    d. optic nerve glioma
    e. cutaneous neurofibromas

25. Hemifacial spasm is usually characterized by all of the following *except*
    a. bilaterality
    b. age of onset usually over 50 years
    c. visual disturbance
    d. vascular etiology
    e. involuntary spasms of the orbicularis muscle

26. Surgical repair of lower eyelid involutional entropion generally uses which of the following techniques?
    a. lower eyelid retractor advancement
    b. levator recession
    c. boney orbital decompression
    d. transconjunctival fat redraping

27. All of the following are true regarding invasive aspergillus infections of the orbit *except*
    a. Bone destruction is not seen.
    b. Corticosteroids may produce an initial clinical improvement.
    c. An adjacent sinusitis is usually present.
    d. Septate branching hyphae of uniform width are seen histologically.

28. A 40-year-old woman presents with a rapidly enlarging mass below the eyelid margin. The lesion has a central crater with an elevated, rolled edge. The most likely diagnosis is
    a. epidermal inclusion cyst
    b. keratoacanthoma
    c. verruca vulgaris
    d. pilomatricoma
    e. basal cell carcinoma

29. A 3-year-old girl was bitten by her pet dog. A 6-mm-wide block of upper eyelid margin is hanging by a thread of tissue. This block of tissue left a defect in the upper eyelid approximately the same size as the tissue itself. The best treatment would be to
    a. send the block of tissue to pathology and repair the defect by approximating the 2 margins
    b. send the block of tissue to pathology and repair the defect by making a lateral canthotomy so that the skin edges can be approximated
    c. repair the eyelid by sewing the block of tissue into its normal anatomical position
    d. send the tissue to pathology and repair the defect by a transfer of tissue from the lower eyelid
    e. keep the tissue under refrigeration for later use if necessary and close the defect by approximation of the wound edges and lateral canthotomy

30. A 74-year-old woman presents with a 2-year history of a painless, progressively enlarging mass in the central aspect of the upper eyelid. This has resulted in distortion of the eyelid margin and loss of eyelashes. The most likely diagnosis is
    a. sebaceous gland carcinoma
    b. squamous cell carcinoma
    c. amelanotic melanoma
    d. basal cell carcinoma
    e. dermal nevus

31. The majority of orbital lymphomas
    a. are polyclonal proliferations
    b. are T-cell tumors
    c. are systemic at presentation
    d. are well differentiated
    e. involve both orbits

32. Which of the following statements about the levator palpebrae muscle and its aponeurosis is *true*?

    a. The levator muscle is normal in most cases of congenital ptosis.

    b. The orbital (deep) and palpebral (superficial) portions of the lacrimal gland are separated by the aponeurosis.

    c. The orbital septum fuses with the aponeurosis at the eyelid margin.

    d. Whitnall's ligament connects the levator aponeurosis to the lateral canthal tendon.

    e. Myasthenia gravis is the most common cause of adult acquired ptosis.

33. Six hours after a bilateral blepharoplasty, the patient complains of sudden pain near the right eye. The dressings are removed and the right eyelids are tense and ecchymotic. The first step would be to

    a. open the wound to release a possible retrobulbar hemorrhage

    b. consider the possibility of a cavernous sinus thrombosis and check corneal sensation

    c. measure visual acuity and check pupillary responses

    d. begin treatment with ice packs

    e. begin treatment with warm compresses

34. A 75-year-old woman complains of chronic tearing and discharge. Irrigation of the lower canaliculus produces mucopurulent reflux from the upper canaliculus. Which of the following statements is *true*?

    a. Jones testing will reveal dye in the nose.

    b. There is probably a common canalicular block.

    c. This condition usually resolves with a course of antibiotics.

    d. Some form of imaging is mandatory.

    e. External dacryocystorhinostomy is curative over 90% of the time.

35. A 5-month-old infant has had tearing and discharge from the right eye since shortly after birth. Which of the following statements is *true*?

    a. The dye disappearance test result is likely to be symmetric.

    b. This condition is likely to resolve spontaneously.

    c. The appropriate treatment is urgent nasolacrimal duct probing.

    d. Punctal abnormalities are the most common cause of tearing and discharge.

    e. Jones I and Jones II tests are necessary to make the diagnosis.

36. Blepharophimosis is generally associated with all of the following *except*

    a. ptosis

    b. epicanthus inversus

    c. distichiasis

    d. ectropion

    e. telecanthus

37. A 30-year-old man received a knife wound involving the right upper eyelid 1 hour before your examination. The patient is awake and alert. A 15-mm-long laceration is present 12 mm above the lash line. The patient has 7 mm of ptosis on the right side, and there is minimal swelling. After an appropriate evaluation of the globe, the best treatment is to

    a. repair the skin laceration and wait several months for the ptosis to resolve

    b. keep the wound clean and wait for the swelling to subside in 2–3 days before attempting repair

    c. repair the muscle layer and skin layer separately

    d. explore the wound to examine the levator aponeurosis and attempt to reattach the levator aponeurosis if it is severed from the tarsus, after which the skin and muscle should be repaired

    e. repair the skin laceration and tape the eyelid to the brow for several days to promote healing

38. The management of rhabdomyosarcoma of the orbit usually involves

    a. lumbar puncture to rule out central nervous system metastasis

    b. exenteration of the orbit

    c. enucleation and orbital radiation

    d. systemic chemotherapy and orbital radiation

    e. radical neck dissection if cervical lymph nodes are involved

39. Which of the following statements about canalicular trauma is *true*?

    a. It almost never results from blunt trauma.

    b. Stenting should be avoided.

    c. If not repaired, injury to the upper canaliculus may result in epiphora.

    d. It must be repaired within 6 hours of injury.

    e. Delayed repair (>6 months) would probably require a standard dacryocystorhinostomy (DCR).

40. Indications for repair of an orbital blowout fracture include

    a. 2 mm of enophthalmos

    b. fractures involving one third of the orbital floor

    c. inferior rectus entrapment

    d. inferior rectus weakness

41. The temporal pocket dissection for standard endoscopic brow lift is performed immediately below what layer?

    a. deep temporal fascia

    b. temporoparietal fascia

    c. frontalis muscle

    d. galea aponeurotica

42. In a subcutaneous rhytidectomy with SMAS, the tension of the lift is placed on
    a. skin
    b. osteocutaneous ligaments
    c. superficial musculoaponeurotic system
    d. periosteum

43. Cicatricial ectropion is generally associated with
    a. trichiasis
    b. anterior lamellar shortage
    c. blepharospasm
    d. symblepharon

44. All of the following are true regarding optic nerve tumors *except*
    a. Optic nerve gliomas in children are associated with neurofibromatosis 1.
    b. Optic nerve meningiomas in children are associated with neurofibromatosis 2.
    c. Radiation therapy is an accepted therapy for optic nerve sheath meningiomas.
    d. Optic nerve gliomas of childhood can be malignant.

45. When an enucleation is performed in a child,
    a. an implant should not be placed until the child is 7 years old
    b. a dermis-fat graft should be avoided because it does not grow along with the orbit
    c. the optic nerve should be cut flush with the posterior aspect of the sclera if retinoblastoma is present
    d. an adult-sized implant should be placed as soon as possible to promote orbital growth

Answers

1. **b.** CN IV is the only nerve that innervates an extraocular muscle and does not pass through the muscle cone on entering the orbit. CN IV passes over the levator muscle and enters the superior oblique muscle on its superior aspect at the junction of the posterior third and anterior two thirds.

2. **c.** The optic canal is located immediately superior and lateral to the sphenoid sinus wall.

3. **c.** These are the 3 main branches of the ophthalmic division of the trigeminal nerve.

4. **a.** The parotidomasseteric fascia is generally a thin, wispy structure that overlies the facial nerve branches, which overlie the masseter muscle, which is therefore the deepest of the structures listed.

5. **d.** Whitnall's ligament extends horizontally across the levator muscle several millimeters above its tendon. Lockwood's ligament is an analogous structure in the lower eyelid.

6. **a.** Bone and calcium are imaged well in CT scanning. Thus, CT allows superior evaluation of fractures, bone destruction, and tissue calcification.

7. **b.** Neurogenic blepharoptosis is due to a CN III palsy, not a CN VII (facial nerve) palsy. Patients with a total palsy of the facial nerve may have pseudoptosis secondary to an atonic, overhanging upper eyelid fold in the palpebral fissure.

8. **d.** A capillary hemangioma presents as a rapidly growing mass in the first month of life, enlarging until 6–12 months of age and subsequently involuting. Therapy is initially directed at ensuring that visual obstruction, anisometropia, or strabismus do not result in amblyopia.

9. **b.** The history and appearance of this mass are suggestive of a lymphoproliferative lesion. Approximately 90% of orbital lymphoproliferations prove monoclonal, suggesting a diagnosis of lymphoma; 10% are polyclonal, suggesting reactive lymphoid hyperplasia.

10. **c.** Eyelid retraction is the most common clinical feature of TAO (and TAO is the most common cause of eyelid retraction).

11. **b.** In patients younger than age 9, most of these infections are due to single organisms affecting the ethmoid sinuses, and they may drain spontaneously if vision is not threatened.

12. **d.** The tarsus is the backbone of the eyelid and must be appropriately approximated so that the repair is stable. The gray line suture is important in some methods of repair, mainly as an aid to lining up the eyelid structures.

13. **d.** Although TAO occurs most commonly in association with hyperthyroidism (and treatment of hyperthyroidism is important in the overall care of the TAO patient), the course of the ophthalmopathy does not necessarily parallel the activity of the thyroid gland or the treatment of thyroid abnormalities. In some patients, the characteristic eye findings occur in the absence of objective evidence of thyroid abnormalities (euthyroid Graves disease).

14. **d.** The lack of sympathetic innervation at birth in congenital Horner syndrome leads to a relative lack of pigmentation of the ipsilateral iris.

15. **c.** Up to 50% of orbital lymphoproliferative lesions arise in the lacrimal fossa.

16. **b.** Treatment recommendations vary for isolated MALT lesions. Simple excision may be diagnostic and therapeutic, with some authors recommending observation of isolated stable lesions.

17. **c.** Surgery should be avoided with orbital varices except when pain or visual loss necessitates treatment.

18. **e.** Additional observation is necessary to allow traumatic edema to subside. This subsidence may be enhanced by the administration of oral prednisone, 1 mg/kg per day for 1 week. Urgent exploration of orbital blowout fractures is necessary only if there is radiographic evidence of gross extraocular muscle entrapment beneath the fracture fragments. It is generally preferable to allow 10–14 days for swelling to resolve and motility to be reevaluated before proceeding with surgical repair.

19. **a.** See Figures 4-6 and 4-7. Although extraocular muscle enlargement is fusiform, it typically spares the tendons.

20. **c.** The amount of levator function is the most important determinant from both a diagnostic and therapeutic standpoint. In those cases in which levator function is good, innervation and strength of the muscle are usually normal, and the problem is usually one of mechanical disinsertion of the attachment of the muscle or loss of supporting sympathetic tone (Horner syndrome). In either situation, surgical correction would be directed toward strengthening the effective action of the levator muscle by shortening its insertion to the eyelid. Patients in whom levator function is reduced are more likely to have a problem with the innervation to the levator muscle (third nerve palsy), a problem at the myoneural junction (myasthenia gravis), or a problem within the levator muscle itself (congenital ptosis). If levator function is significantly reduced, procedures to strengthen the levator muscle will be ineffective in raising the eyelid and may also result in significant lagophthalmos. In these cases, the surgeon may consider slinging of the eyelid to the frontalis muscle so that the frontalis function can be used to elevate and depress the eyelid, bypassing the dysfunctional levator muscle.

21. **c.** This patient presents with typical clinical signs of levator aponeurosis dehiscence of the right upper eyelid. This may be idiopathic or may be related to previous ocular surgery with manipulation of the eyelids. The 1 mm of left upper eyelid retraction is secondary to a compensatory increased innervation of both levator muscles to clear the visual axis on the right side. Frequently, after levator muscle repair of the ptotic eyelid, the compensatory contralateral eyelid retraction will spontaneously resolve. The amount of ptosis (4 mm) cannot be easily corrected with either a moderate internal tarsoconjunctival resection or a standard müllerectomy. A frontalis muscle suspension is not needed in a patient with normal levator function.

22. **c.** Metastasis is very rare in basal cell carcinoma. Melanoma and sebaceous, squamous, and Merkel cell carcinoma all have a significant risk of metastasis.

23. **e.** Capillary hemangioma is the most common benign primary orbital tumor among children. Orbital cellulitis is the most common cause of unilateral exophthalmos in children. Metastatic neuroblastoma is the most common metastatic cancer of the orbit in children. Neurofibromas are rarely malignant and are uncommon orbital tumors in children. TAO is very rare in children.

24. **a.** Adenoma sebaceum is associated with tuberous sclerosis, another phakomatosis.

25. **a.** Hemifacial spasm is generally unilateral and typically begins in persons in their mid-50s with an intermittent high-frequency contracture of the orbicularis oculi. Bilaterality is very rare.

26. **a.** The levator is not present in the lower lid. Boney decompression or fat redraping would have no significant effect on involutional entropion.

27. **a.** In addition to acute fulminant fungal sinusitis with orbital invasion, aspergillosis can cause chronic indolent infection resulting in slow destruction of the sinuses and adjacent structures.

28. **b.** Keratoacanthomas appear to represent low-grade squamous cell carcinomas. They grow rapidly, with a central crater filled with keratin debris. Surgical excision is curative.

29. **c.** In general, traumatic eyelid margin flaps should always be saved and carefully reapproximated so that the eyelid margin architecture and the lashes can be preserved as much as possible and more involved closure techniques can be avoided.

30. **d.** Basal cell carcinoma occurs approximately 40 times more often than either sebaceous carcinoma or squamous cell carcinoma. Even though both sebaceous cell carcinoma and squamous cell carcinoma occur more often in the upper eyelid than they do in the lower and basal cell carcinoma occurs more often in the lower lid than in the upper, the far greater frequency of basal cell carcinoma results in its still being the most common malignant neoplasm of the upper eyelid.

31. **d.** Most histologically malignant lymphoid lesions of the orbit are relatively indolent or low-grade lymphomas.

32. **b.** The levator palpebrae muscle fibers are sparse and are usually replaced by fibrofatty tissue in congenital ptosis. The lacrimal gland is divided by the lateral expansion of the aponeurosis, and the orbital septum fuses with the aponeurosis just above the upper tarsal margin. Whitnall's ligament serves as a check ligament to the muscle to change its vector of force from anteroposterior to a more vertical direction to elevate the eyelid.

33. **c.** Sudden pain associated with tense, ecchymotic eyelids following blepharoplasty is indicative of a postoperative orbital hematoma. If there is no decreased vision, altered pupillary response, or other indication of decreased optic nerve function, the patient may be managed conservatively with close observation. If there is any evidence of optic nerve or ocular compromise, the wounds should be opened immediately and drains inserted to decompress a possible orbital hemorrhage. A lateral canthotomy and inferior cantholysis should be performed next if the above is not effective.

34. **e.** This is a typical presentation of primary acquired nasolacrimal duct obstruction. Mucopurulent discharge with compression of the sac or with irrigation is typical. If the common canaliculus were blocked, irrigation would not enter the lacrimal sac to cause a mucopurulent reflux. Medical management does not offer a long-term cure. Imaging is usually reserved for patients with an atypical presentation. The appropriate treatment is usually dacryocystorhinostomy, which enjoys a high success rate.

35. **b.** A child with congenital tearing is likely to have nasolacrimal duct obstruction. Other abnormalities, such as punctal agenesis, are rare but should be ruled out. The dye disappearance test result is usually markedly asymmetric. Jones testing is usually not feasible in young children and in most cases is not necessary to make the diagnosis. Spontaneous improvement is common; thus, initial treatment is usually conservative. If tearing is persistent at 12 months of age, nasolacrimal duct probing is the treatment of choice.

36. **c.** Blepharophimosis syndrome usually includes telecanthus, epicanthus inversus, and ptosis with poor levator function. Ectropion occurs less often. Distichiasis is not associated with the syndrome.

37. **d.** If ptosis is present, the wound should be explored. If orbital fat (preaponeurotic fat pad) is visible, the deeper orbital structures should be explored. Repair of the levator aponeurosis is indicated as a primary procedure.

38. **d.** Rhabdomyosarcoma is not treated by surgery but rather by systemic multiagent chemotherapy and by orbital radiation therapy (4500–6000 cGy) that begins approximately 2 weeks after the initiation of chemotherapy.

39. **c.** Canalicular trauma often results from tangential (lateral) forceful traction on the eyelid causing an avulsion type of injury at the weakest point, medially, where tarsal support is lacking. Repair usually involves reconstruction over a stent and can be delayed up to 48 hours. Delayed lacrimal repair (>6 months) usually requires a conjunctivodacryocystorhinostomy. Loss of the superior canaliculus may also cause epiphora and should be repaired when possible.

40. **c.** In blowout fractures, entrapment of the inferior rectus muscle, pain, and the oculocardiac reflex on upgaze; fractures involving greater than half of the orbital floor; and cosmetically unacceptable enophthalmos are indications for surgical repair.

41. **b.** The temporal dissection occurs in the potential space between the temporoparietal fascia superficially and the deep temporal fascia. The frontalis muscle and surrounding galea are superficial to the central subperiosteal dissection.

42. **c.** The superficial musculoaponeurotic system (SMAS) is a fibromuscular layer that provides excellent long-term support for the face. Face-lifts that rely on the skin for tension fail early and can cause a "surgical" appearance; they also tend to be associated with more obvious scarring and earlobe deformities.

43. **b.** Cicatricial shortening of the anterior lamella (skin and muscle) relative to the posterior lamella (tarsus and conjunctiva) of the eyelid produces an outward rotation of the lid margin and retraction of the lid away from the globe, leading to exposure keratopathy.

44. **d.** Optic nerve gliomas are uncommon, usually benign, tumors that occur predominantly in children in the first decade of life. Malignant optic nerve gliomas (glioblastomas) are very rare and most often occur in middle-aged males. Approximately 25%–50% of optic nerve gliomas are associated with neurofibromatosis.

45. **d.** An orbital implant has some effect on inducing orbital growth. Dermis-fat grafts in children tend to grow, expanding the socket. When performing an enucleation in a patient with retinoblastoma, the surgeon should remove a long segment of nerve to attempt complete excision of the tumor.

Index

(*f* = figure; *t* = table)

DDT. *See* Dye disappearance test
Decompression
    optic canal, for traumatic visual loss, 108
    orbital, 118–120, 119*f*
        complications of, 121
        for lymphangioma, 67
        for thyroid-associated orbitopathy, 52–53, 118
        for traumatic visual loss, 108
Deep mimetic muscles, 139
Deep plane rhytidectomy, 252–253, 253*f*
Deep superior sulcus deformity, anophthalmic socket
    and, 128, 128*f*
Deep temporalis fascia, 137, 140
Depression of eye (downgaze)
    disorders of, in blowout fractures, 102–103
        surgery and, 104–105
    ptosis exacerbation in, 215
    ptotic eyelid position in, 218, 223*t*
Dermal melanocytosis (nevus of Ota), 178, 178*f*
Dermal nevus, 176
Dermatochalasis, 235, 235*f*
    brow ptosis and, 241
    pseudoptosis and, 226, 226*f*
Dermis, 137
Dermis-fat grafts
    after enucleation in children, 125
    for exposure and extrusion of orbital implant, 129
    for superior sulcus deformity, 128
Dermoids (dermoid cysts/tumors), orbital, 61–62, 62*f*
Dermolipomas (lipodermoids), of orbit, 62, 63*f*
Dermopathy (pretibial myxedema), in hyperthyroidism/
    thyroid-associated orbitopathy, 51
Dexamethasone, for nonspecific orbital inflammation,
    56
Diazepam, perioperative, for facial and eyelid surgery,
    154
Diffuse soft-tissue histiocytosis. *See* Histiocytosis
Digital eversion test, for cicatricial entropion, 211
Diplopia
    after blepharoplasty, 240
    in blowout fractures, 102–103
        surgery and, 104–105
    in thyroid-associated orbitopathy, 51, 53
Distichiasis
    acquired, 148
    congenital, 148, 162, 163*f*
Dog bites, eyelid injuries caused by, 194
Dog tapeworm (*Echinococcus granulosus*), orbital
    infection caused by, 46
Doppler imaging, in orbital evaluation, 32
Double convexity deformity, 243
Double elevator palsy/paresis (monocular elevation
    deficiency), 220
Downgaze. *See* Depression of eye
Drugs, canalicular obstruction caused by, 282
Dry eye syndrome
    in blepharospasm, 232, 234
    lacrimal plugs for, 290
        canalicular obstruction and, 282, 290
        nasolacrimal duct obstruction and, 285, 290
    lymphocytic lacrimal infiltrates and, 91
Duane syndrome, synkinesis in, 217, 224, 224*f*
Dural cavernous fistula, 68

Dye disappearance test, 275, 276*f*
Dysthyroid ophthalmopathy. *See* Thyroid-associated
    orbitopathy
Dystonia, facial, 232–234

Ecchymosis, periorbital, in blowout fractures, 102, 103*f*
Eccrine sweat glands, of eyelid, 172–173
    tumors arising in, 173, 174*f*
ECD. *See* Erdheim-Chester disease
Echinacea (*Echinacea purpurea*), cessation of before
    surgery, 152*t*
Echinococcus granulosus (echinococcosis), orbital
    infection caused by, 46
Ectropion, 201–207, 202*f*
    anophthalmic, 130
    cicatricial, 202*f*, 207
        after blepharoplasty, 240
    congenital, 158, 159*f*
    involutional, 201–204, 202*f*, 203*f*
    mechanical, 202*f*, 207
    paralytic, 202*f*, 205–206, 206*f*
    tarsal, 204
Edema, eyelid, 166
    in blowout fractures, 102
Edrophonium, in myasthenia gravis diagnosis, 219
Eicosapentaenoic acid (fish oil), cessation of before
    surgery, 152*t*
Electrolysis, for trichiasis, 213–214
Elevated intraocular pressure, in traumatic optic
    neuropathy, 107–108
Elevation of eye (upgaze)
    disorders of, in blowout fractures, 102–103
        surgery and, 104–105
    monocular deficiency of (double elevator palsy),
        220
Embryonal rhabdomyosarcoma, 79
Emphysema (ocular), of orbit and eyelids, in blowout
    fractures, 102, 104
Encephaloceles, 37
Endocanalicular laser dacryocystorhinostomy, 289
Endophthalmitis, evisceration for, 127
Endoscopic brow and forehead lift, 246–248, 247*f*
Endoscopic brow lift, 248
Endoscopic dacryocystorhinostomy, 288
Endoscopic midface lift, subperiosteal, 250, 251*f*
Endoscopy, nasal, for acquired tearing evaluation, 279
Enophthalmos, 22, 23
    in blowout fractures, 102, 103–104
        surgery and, 105
    orbital varices and, 70
Entropion, 161–162, 162*f*, 207–213
    acute spastic, 207–208, 208*f*
    cicatricial, 211–213, 211*f*
    congenital, 161–162, 162*f*
    involutional, 208–211, 209*f*, 210*f*
    lash margin, in anophthalmic socket, 131
Enucleation, 123–127
    in childhood, 125
    complications of, 127
    definition of, 123
    guidelines for, 125
    ocular prostheses after, 126
    orbital implants after, 125–126

Iodine, radioactive, for thyroid (Graves) disease, 51–52
Irrigation, of lacrimal drainage system
  for acquired tearing evaluation, 277, 278f, 279f
  for canalicular obstruction, 277, 278f, 279f, 281–282
  for congenital tearing management, 267–268, 269f

Jaw-winking ptosis/syndrome, Marcus Gunn, 217, 224, 224f
Jones I and Jones II tests, 276–277, 276t
Jones tubes, 200, 283–284
Junctional nevus, 176

Kaposi sarcoma, of eyelid, 190, 190f
Kasabach-Merritt syndrome, 64
Kava kava (Piper methysticum), cessation of before surgery, 152t
Keratoacanthoma, 180, 180f
Keratosis
  actinic (solar), 178–179, 179f
  seborrheic, 169, 170f
Klonopin. See Clonazepam
Krause, glands of, 142f, 147, 261

Lacerations
  canalicular, 193, 291–292
  eyelid
    lid margin involved in, 192–193, 192f
    lid margin not involved in, 191
    ptosis caused by, 225–226
    repair of, 191–194, 192f. See also Eyelids, surgery/reconstruction of
      secondary, 194
Lacrimal bone, 6f, 7f, 8f
Lacrimal canaliculi. See Canaliculi
Lacrimal–cutaneous fistula, congenital, 297–298, 298f
Lacrimal drainage system, 261–264, 262f. See also Nasolacrimal duct
  anatomy of, 261–264, 262f
  development of, 259, 260f
    abnormalities of, 297–298, 298f, 299f
  diagnostic tests for evaluation of, 275–280, 276f, 276t, 278f, 279f, 280f
  disorders of, 265–290. See also Tearing
    infectious, 293–295, 293f, 294f
    neoplastic, 296
    traumatic, 291–292
  duplications in, 297
  irrigation of
    for acquired tearing evaluation, 277, 278f, 279f
    for canalicular obstruction, 277, 278f, 279f, 281–282
    for congenital tearing management, 267–268, 269f
  obstruction of
    acquired, 272–290
      evaluation of, 272–280
      neoplastic causes of, 296
    congenital, 265–272
      evaluation of, 265
  reconstruction of, 200
  therapeutic closure of, 290–291
Lacrimal ducts, 17, 260–261

Lacrimal gland fistulas, 297, 297f
Lacrimal glands, 17, 259–261, 260f. See also Lacrimal system
  accessory, 142f, 147, 261
  anatomy of, 259–261, 260f
  development of, 259
    abnormalities of, 296–297, 297f
  infection of. See Dacryoadenitis
  sarcoidosis involving, 57–58
  tumors of, 88–91
    epithelial, 88–90
    exenteration for, 90, 132
    nonepithelial, 90–91
Lacrimal nerve, 12f, 13, 261
  eyelid innervation and, 149
Lacrimal outflow evaluation, 275
Lacrimal plugs
  canalicular obstruction and, 282, 290
  for dry eye, 290
  extrusion/migration of, 290
  nasolacrimal duct obstruction and, 285, 290
Lacrimal probing
  for acquired nasolacrimal duct/canalicular obstruction, 277
  for congenital nasolacrimal duct obstruction, 266–267, 267–268, 268f
Lacrimal pump, 263f, 264
Lacrimal sac (tear sac), 262–263, 262f
  cast formation in (dacryoliths), 285
  distension of, 272, 273f
    in dacryocystitis, 294
  evaluation of, 275
  inflammation of, 294–295, 294f. See also Dacryocystitis
  trauma to, 292
  tumors of, 296
Lacrimal scintigraphy, for acquired tearing evaluation, 279–280, 280f
Lacrimal system. See also specific structure
  anatomy of, 259–264, 260f, 262f
  development of, 259, 260f
    abnormalities of, 296–298, 297f, 298f, 299f
  disorders of, 265–299. See also Tearing
    acquired, 272–290
    congenital, 265–272
    developmental abnormalities, 296–298, 297f, 298f, 299f
    infection, 293–295, 293f, 294f
    neoplastic, 295–296
    therapeutic closure of drainage system for, 290–291
    traumatic, 291–292
  excretory apparatus of, 259, 260f, 261–264, 262f. See also Lacrimal drainage system
  physiology of, 263f, 264
  secretory apparatus/function of, 259, 259–261, 260f. See also Lacrimal glands
  silicone intubation of
    for acquired nasolacrimal duct obstruction, 286
    for canalicular trauma, 292
    for congenital lacrimal duct obstruction/tearing, 268–269, 270f
  tumors of, 295–296